W9-BAB-519

Three Essential Shutoffs

In case of emergency, know the location of these shut-offs:

Main Water Valve

The main water valve is located near the water meter, usually near an outside wall near the front of the house or in the basement, if you have one (see Chapter 31, "Either It Leaks ... [Plumbing, Part I]"). Use this valve to shut off water: a) When a pipe is leaking; b) whenever you leave home for long; and c) while making repairs without a shut-off. Use the outside shut-off, found under a steel plate toward the street, if your main shut-off does not work, or if there's trouble on the street side of the shut-off.

For a private water system, shut off the circuit breaker or switch feeding the pump. Shut the valve on the output side of the pressure tank, and open valves at low spots on the house.

Main Electric Switch

On the circuit-breaker or fuse box (see Chapter 27, "Breaker, Breaker on the Wall: Electric Fundamentals"), the main electric switch is the breaker marked "100," "150," or "200." In a fuse box, it's the big black fuse-holder marked "Main," "60," or "100." The main switch may be a big lever handle on the outside of a switch box.

Fuel Line Shut-Off

A gas shut-off should be on the gas meter. Turn the big lug 90° (it looks like a giant screwdriver blade). Other gas shut-offs, with smaller steel lugs or brass handles, may be on gas pipes inside the house. Turn them 90°, across the pipeline. On propane systems, look for a valve on top of the tank.

An oil shut-off is usually a small valve at the bottom of an oil tank or (if the tank is outside) on the oil line where it enters your house.

Your Essential Tool Kit

- ⅜-inch variable-speed reversing drill with drill bits and a Phillips bit
- Locking plier
- Adjustable wrench
- 16-inch pipe wrench
- Hammer
- Wrecking bar
- Screwdrivers (slotted and Phillips)
- 12-foot tape measure
- Aluminum square
- Hand rip saw
- Block plane
- Utility knife
- Wood chisel
- Nail set
- Hacksaw
- Wire stripper
- Circuit tester
- Paint scraper
- Paint roller and pan
- 2½-inch trim brush
- Drywall knife or margin trowel
- Caulking gun
- Two saw horses or plastic milk crates

Your Essential Supply Cabinet

- Wood primer
- Drywall primer
- Wood hole filler
- Carpenter's glue
- Drywall compound or another hole filler
- Sandpaper (various grades)
- Steel wool
- Screw-on wire connectors
- Spare outlets and two-way switches
- Spare fuses (if you have a fuse box)
- Drywall screws (1¼-inch, 1½-inch, 2¼-inch, 3-inch)
- Finishing nails (4d "penny," 6d, 8d, 10d)
- Cement-coated sinker nails (6d, 8d, 10d, 16d)
- Roofing nails (1½-inch, 2-inch)
- Assorted drywall anchors or molly

alpha
books

Your Essential Safety Kit

Goggles
Rubber and leather gloves
Dust mask

Respirator with cartridges for organic solvents, if you work with them
Ear plugs or ear protectors

The Essential Home Inspection

The roof: From outside, look for broken, missing, or torn shingles, and loose flashing. Check for a sag in the ridge. From the attic, look for stains, fungus, and soft spots indicating leakage.

Foundation: Look for sagging, bulging, cracking, and decay of masonry; perennial damp spots; and mold build-up on wood.

Interior: Look for soft spots on floors, out-of-square or jammed windows and doors, major drywall or plaster cracking or decay.

Electrical and mechanical: Inspect the general condition and age of pipes, wiring, and heating system. Is everything orderly or a mess? Are cables hanging from the ceiling, or are they well-mounted?

How to Tell If a Circuit Is Hot

Try to turn off the circuit with the most logical fuse or circuit breaker.

Put one prong of the electrical tester in each slot of the receptacle. Test each slot against the ground hole. If the tester lights, the circuit is hot.

For a two-way switch, unscrew the outlet cover with a plastic-handled screwdriver. Plug a grounded extension cord into a working grounded outlet. (See Chapter 28, "Getting Wired Without Getting Zapped," for details on this important procedure.) With your circuit tester, touch one lead to the ground hole and the other to the screw terminals on the switch. If the tester lights, the switch is hot.

Home Maintenance and Repairs You Should Never Have to Hire Again After Using This Book

Window glass replacement
Stuck window or door
Sticky lock mechanism
Interior painting
Minor foundation or concrete repair

Leaky faucet
Replacing light switches and electric outlets
Simple drain cleanout
Replacing toilet mechanism

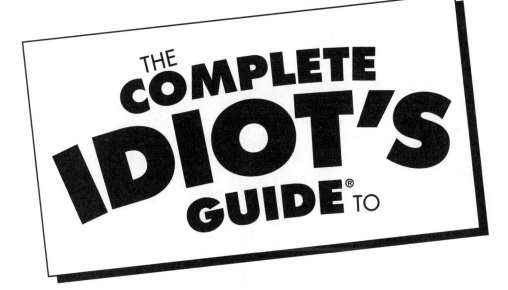

THE COMPLETE IDIOT'S GUIDE® TO

Trouble-Free Home Repair

Second Edition

by David J. Tenenbaum

alpha books

Macmillan USA, Inc.
201 West 103rd Street
Indianapolis, IN 46290

A Pearson Education Company

THE COMPLETE IDIOT'S GUIDE TO & Design is a registered trademark of Macmillan USA, Inc.

International Standard Book Number: 0-02-863262-1
Library of Congress Catalog Card Number: 99-64465

01   00   8   7   6   5   4   3   2

Interpretation of the printing code: the rightmost number of the first series of numbers is the year of the book's printing; the rightmost number of the second series of numbers is the number of the book's printing. For example, a printing code of 99-1 shows that the first printing occurred in 1999.

Printed in the United States of America

Alpha Development Team

Publisher
Kathy Nebenhaus

Editorial Director
Gary M. Krebs

Managing Editor
Bob Shuman

Marketing Brand Manager
Felice Primeau

Acquisitions Editors
Jessica Faust
Michelle Reed

Development Editors
Phil Kitchel
Amy Zavatto

Assistant Editor
Georgette Blau

Production Team

Development Editor
Doris Cross

Production Editors
Jenaffer Brandt
Christy Wagner

Copy Editor
Krista Hansing

Cover Designer
Mike Freeland

Photo Editor
Richard H. Fox

Illustrator
Jody P. Schaeffer

Book Designers
Scott Cook and Amy Adams of DesignLab

Indexer
Riofrancos and Company Indexes

Layout/Proofreading
Juli Cook

Contents at a Glance

Contents

xiii

Foreword

Facing floods? Excited about electrical ailments? Dumbfounded by drywall damage?

Fact is, millions of homeowners are afraid to repair their most valuable possession. They want to fix it themselves, and they may even know which end of a hammer to hold. But they don't know which nail to select or how to pound it home. They have the ambition; they just lack the knowledge.

There's good reason for this confusion: Home repair has gotten so complicated that even the pros must specialize. To homeowners, this strategy looks like the old divide and conquer: First they divide up the skills, then they charge an arm and a leg for the privilege of working on your house.

If you're a homeowner wanting escape from the astronomical cost of home repair, there's good news. This revised and expanded edition of *The Complete Idiot's Guide to Trouble-Free Home Repair* gives you simple practical advice on everything from how to prevent small problems from mushrooming into large ones, to how to negotiate for the best repair—from the best repairer. David Tenenbaum helped demystify the field three years ago by writing the first edition of this book. He took a common-sense approach, breaking complex tasks into easy-to-follow steps, and leavening the whole thing with a sense of humor.

Dave's ability to explain things clearly and logically is one reason we repeatedly feature him on *Home Matters*, the series I host on The Discovery Channel. At *Home Matters*, we talk with lots of guests who know about fixing houses, yet none has Dave's combination of authoritative information and sense of humor. We prize him for his ability to translate obscure jargon into everyday language and transform complex repairs into plain procedures that almost anyone can follow.

This book was written for homeowners like you—people who have the desire, but not the information, to start repairing the home front. As Dave walks us through dozens of repairs, he guides us away from safety hazards and toward the tools and materials best suited to each repair. You'll save money, learn some new skills, and even enjoy yourself in the process. Who could ask for a better deal?

Susan Powell, host, *Home Matters* on The Discovery Channel

Introduction

I don't know how you got interested in home repair. Perhaps it was after buying a house that needed—well, let's just say a bit more attention than you bargained for. Perhaps it was after an anxiety attack sparked by paying psychiatrists' wages to a plumber who repaired a drippy faucet—after which you realized that the task was actually pretty straightforward. Perhaps it was when you realized that you could convert your free time into money.

I do know how I started a lifetime involvement in home repair. It was courtesy of my father, an electronic engineer possessed of the strange notion that he could do almost anything. Wiring? No problem. Television repair? All in a day's work for a guy who designed radar and computers. Carpentry? Well, anything was simpler than TV repair. A new phone line to the study? Sure—even if it wasn't quite legal at the time. A new darkroom in the basement? Sounds like a great winter project (even if we had to drill a ridiculous number of holes in concrete that was hard as—well, concrete).

One of the many lessons my father taught me was that there's a tool for anything—a hammer for pounding nails, a crowbar for pulling them. Sanders, drills, jigsaws, levels—the list never ends, unfortunately. But he also taught me to improvise: to use a screwdriver (within reason) as a pry bar, a hammer as a mallet, a locking pliers for almost anything at all.

I'm not sure exactly what's in your toolbox. But I do know that every toolbox needs a tool to make you confident, skilled, and prepared for the predictably surprising problems you'll meet as you become your home's physician.

Guess what? You're holding that tool. At this point, I'm proud to say that it has been tested by so many readers that we've decided to issue a second edition. While this edition is revised, expanded, and better illustrated, it retains the attitude that made the first edition so successful: Home repair is within your grasp, if we make it simple, plain, and possible.

Where to Find What You Need in This Book

In Part 1, "It's Handy to Be Handy," you'll find that effective home repair is partly a state of mind. To use a hackneyed maxim, you should be prepared—in skills, materials, and tools. Most important is the fixer's mindset: When something goes wrong, you will "phone yourself" before reaching for the Yellow Pages. In Part 1, I'll talk about planning, and about fitting your home repair work into the rest of your life. Then we'll take a close look at the home place, starting with two critical elements: the foundation and the roof. I'll ask you to think a bit about whether, in your heart of hearts, you want to tackle certain projects. If you decide that the project requires more skills, tools, or time than you can supply, we'll meet the people who are ready to work for you.

In Part 2, "Safety, Tools, and Materials: The Building Blocks of Success," I explain that while the first rule of intelligent tinkering is to save all the parts, the second is not to end a weekend project in the emergency room. Thus, we'll examine some basic safety rules and ponder the all-important stupidity factor. Although hand tools seem pathetically antiquated in this hyper-electrified era, you'll be doing most of your repairs with them. We'll sketch out a basic array of hand tools, emphasizing those that are versatile enough to help in many repairs. Then we'll rev up the motor and look at some nearly essential electric tools. Because fasteners—nails, screws, and hardware—can literally make or break a project, we'll take a brief tour of the hardware store, concentrating on some clever inventions that can make your life a good deal easier. Then we'll talk about your workshop, the place where you store all this junk. Finally, we'll talk about wood, still the basic construction material for the average home.

Part 3, "Strictly for Outsiders: The Exterior View," is devoted to essential stuff: the foundation, siding, roofing, masonry, and concrete. Talk about important—these are your home's only protection against the elements! We'll start easy—with caulking, weather-stripping, and insulating—and talk about the decay you've noted on your deck and those pimples on your siding. Then we'll get serious and climb up on the roof to discuss safe, dry repairs. Finally, we'll devote two chapters to masonry and concrete, two ageless materials that should not be visibly aging in your house.

In Part 4, "An Inside Job," we'll take a walk around your interior. We'll examine windows and doors, two notorious troublemakers. If your floor squawks like a frightened hen, or your drywall and wallpaper still show the slings and arrows of the previous owner's riotous children, you've come to the right place. Fortunately, curing these woes is easier than you think—if you know some professional tricks. If you have the urge to paint or wallpaper and start fresh, we'll discuss what materials you should be using and how you should put them on the wall. We'll even stray into tiles and moldings, two projects that scare homeowners far more than they should.

In Part 5, "Mechanicals for Non-Mechanics," we'll talk about the tough stuff: wires, pipes, and heating systems. Remember the old threat from energy crisis days: Let them freeze in the dark. Without your mechanical system, that's what would happen (when you weren't poaching in the humidity). We'll start with the electrical system, where a determined homeowner can save plenty of bucks. We'll stop by the more-intimidating heating system and then go up to the chimney, intent on curing this regular cause of roof leaks. Finally, we'll get our feet wet (heh, heh!) in plumbing, where everything seems to leak—unless it's not draining.

In Appendix A, "Nuts and Bolts Glossary," we'll answer some vital questions: Where does a soffit meet a rake edge? What's a light? (Hint: It's not a kind of beer.) Why is glazing never galvanized? Why does this guy keep asking stupid questions? The glossary will prepare you for builder's jeopardy so you'll never again feel baffled at the building-supply house.

Extras

This book is dedicated to the proposition that the human species is defined by the ability to use tools and the ability to read an instruction book. To help you make the most of this instruction book, I've salted it with helpful signposts. Here's how they work:

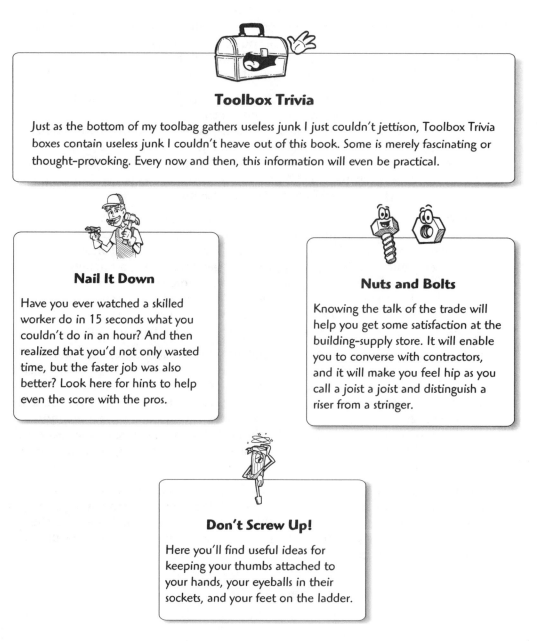

Toolbox Trivia

Just as the bottom of my toolbag gathers useless junk I just couldn't jettison, Toolbox Trivia boxes contain useless junk I couldn't heave out of this book. Some is merely fascinating or thought-provoking. Every now and then, this information will even be practical.

Nail It Down

Have you ever watched a skilled worker do in 15 seconds what you couldn't do in an hour? And then realized that you'd not only wasted time, but the faster job was also better? Look here for hints to help even the score with the pros.

Nuts and Bolts

Knowing the talk of the trade will help you get some satisfaction at the building-supply store. It will enable you to converse with contractors, and it will make you feel hip as you call a joist a joist and distinguish a riser from a stringer.

Don't Screw Up!

Here you'll find useful ideas for keeping your thumbs attached to your hands, your eyeballs in their sockets, and your feet on the ladder.

Acknowledgments

Lots of people have contributed to my handy-guy education: Albin Myher, a kind-hearted auto worker who paid me to build an addition to his house 30 years ago; David Ahlers, a recalcitrant, opinionated, and wickedly judgmental perfectionist of a mason and plasterer who hired me as his assistant 24 years ago; Ron Gedrim, my fiercely intellectual partner in the Wisconsin Barn Board and Beam Company; former Moscow correspondent Henry Shapiro, whose astonishment at finding a journalist capable of manual work did not prevent him from hiring me to fix his house; Orlando Kjosa, a talented carpenter and true friend, who paddled his last canoe entirely too young. Finally, I'd like to thank electrical whiz Fred Brown; Ken Schuster, roofer extraordinaire; and Carl Lorentz, a gifted plumber who gets it right the first time—each contributed immensely to the relevant chapters. Robert Alexander, a scribbler's guru and a veteran wordsurgeon, rose to the challenge of splicing a strand of humor into the tangled thread of home repair.

First among unequals is my wife, Meg Wise, a pillar of support who always assumed I could write books, but who is everlastingly impressed that I can replace a garbage disposal!

Special Thanks from the Publisher to the Technical Reviewers

The Complete Idiot's Guide to Trouble-Free Home Repair was reviewed by experts who checked the technical accuracy of what you'll learn here, to help us ensure that this book gives you everything you need to know to begin your transformation into a handy person. We extend special thanks to the following:

Mark Genovese is a licensed marine engineer and an industrial waste water treatment plant operator for an environmental engineering firm. He actively pursues a woodworking hobby and is an assistant SYSOP for CompuServe's Family Handyman Forum. In the forum, he answers home-repair questions based on his experience as a "super" of several family owned rental properties.

Don Linstroth has been a campus administrator and Chairman of Apprenticeship in the Wisconsin Technical College System since 1980. He spent 13 years in the construction trades and six years as an instructor in the Painting and Decorating Apprenticeship Program. He served a Painting and Decorating apprenticeship and has a three-year diploma in building and estimating, an associate degree in civil-structural technology, and a B.S. degree in vocational education. He is a master's degree candidate at the University of Wisconsin-Madison.

Fred Brown is a veteran electrical inspector and electrical apprentice instructor at Madison [Wisconsin] Area Technical College. He has taught code, inspection, and installation at regional and national workshops.

Illustration Credits

Computer illustrations by David Tenenbaum and Scott Dougald.

Photography by David Tenenbaum and Meg Wise.

The author wishes to thank the following for their kind permission to reprint artwork: W.H. Maze Company; National Manufacturing Company; Macklanburg-Duncan; Klauer Manufacturing Company, Dubuque, IA; The Glidden Company, a member of ICI Paints; The Kohler Company; Moen Incorporated; Delta Faucet Co.; and Fluidmaster.

Trademarks

All terms mentioned in this book that are known to be or are suspected of being trademarks or service marks have been appropriately capitalized. Alpha Books and Macmillan USA, Inc. cannot attest to the accuracy of this information. Use of a term in this book should not be regarded as affecting the validity of any trademark or service mark.

Part 1
It's Handy to Be Handy

I'm always baffled when a brain surgeon, who thinks nothing of cutting open the skull of a breathing human, is befuddled by the thought of replacing a burned-out light switch, or when a teacher who can control, entertain, and even educate two dozen young people blanches at the prospect of fixing a leaky roof.

Many homeowners think home repair is some form of rocket science and instinctively dial 1-555-4REPAIR when they hear the complaints of an ailing house. My friend Kathy, for example, was ready to summon a plumber to replace a leaking sink trap. Instead, I lent her a pipe wrench, and she bought a replacement trap and screwed it into place. She not only saved upwards of $50, but she had the uniquely satisfying experience of being paid to learn something useful.

I think most houses are relatively simple creatures, and you, like Kathy, can do many of the repairs that you've been paying for. In Part 1, "It's Handy to Be Handy," I'll explain how to start declaring your independence from the home-repair professionals. I'll suggest that you examine your home—from the foundation to the wallpaper—as seen through the steel-rimmed spectacles of a hard-boiled building inspector. I'll talk about professional help—how to find the right specialist, how to compare bids, and how to get a contract that works for you. I'll even try the impossible: insulating you from the universal tendency to believe you can get something for nothing.

Chapter 1

Is Your Home Looking Homely?

In This Chapter

➤ A realistic attitude toward home repairs

➤ The pros aren't perfect either

➤ When to fix it, and when to leave it alone

This chapter is about Murphy's Law, carpenters' adages, perfectionism, and the "hero-or-wimp" conundrum. It's about why busy homeowners should happily accept some challenges—say, caulking windows or replacing their panes—and duck others—such as replacing plumbing fixtures or repairing a steep, leaky roof. It's about the decisions you'll face as you ponder an upcoming home project, and about the satisfactions you'll get from tackling it.

I'll begin by demystifying the professionals and their supposedly cold, calculating approach. I know your morale will be boosted by realizing that even the seasoned pros can screw up. Then we'll work on the "who-when-how" decision issues that must precede your first trip to the hardware store—or your call to a pro.

Dr. Murphy's Home-Repair Service

Carpenters have the best adages—easy to comprehend, steeped in dry humor, and freighted with the wisdom of the ages. My favorite is this absurdism: "I cut it off three times, and it's still too short." Much more helpful is, "Measure twice, cut once." But because houses hide more pitfalls than a Tom Clancy novel, I'll expand on that: "Think thrice, measure twice, cut once."

Doubtful? Then listen to a story about the late Orlando Kjosa, the classic "careful carpenter." For years, to save money on renovations or major repairs and to get expert carpentry tutelage, I used to hire this skillful, experienced, and patient friend to work with me. One broiling August day, Orlando spent five hours nailing in roof rafters to support a new skylight. Then he marked the opening for the skylight and sawed deliberately, precisely, and idiotically through those same rafters.

It was not, I imagine, a day when any builder would want the customer working alongside, yet Orlando was unruffled. He had been in the home building and repair business long enough to know that *anything* can go wrong and that *everything* will go wrong—on bad days.

I took away this lesson: If you've never felt like an idiot, you've never worked on a home. By liberating me from the fear of feeling stupid, that experience helped me approach subsequent projects with a certain black humor. Things will go wrong, undeniably, but in the last analysis, things will also get done.

The Golden Mean: A Sensible Attitude Toward Home Repair

As I've mentioned, my attitude toward home repair was shaped by my father, who believed he could do just about anything. I can think of a lot of reasons why *you* might want to repair your home, but for me, it's in my blood—I am constitutionally unable to call somebody to repair a faucet or a roof.

Did that sound convincing? Perhaps, but it's not entirely accurate: My policy is to try a repair and then, if it resists too much, to call in the heavy artillery. In 12 years at my present address, I'm proud to say that I've not had to call an electrician. I did, however, hire a drain cleaner to ream out a nasty clog in an underground sewer, a problem that would have taken me far deeper than I wanted to go into that noxious business.

I've also hired Carl Lorentz, a plumber friend, for four jobs over those years. One time came after I wasted an hour trying to disassemble a pigheaded faucet. Carl wrestled with the same ornery hunk of metal for a sweaty half-hour and then muttered that dreadful phrase: "I need a special tool." (Special tools are fetish objects that separate mortals like you and me from home-repair superheroes like Carl.) Even with the special tool, Carl spent a good two hours fixing that faucet.

I'm trying to explain that home repair is a matter of degree. Particularly when you are getting started, the smartest course is to skim the creamy jobs and hire out the gritty ones. When my roof finally gave out, I paid a top-flight roofer to replace it even though I have nailed my share of shingles (I also nailed *your* share while reroofing a giant barn near Waterloo, Wisconsin, during a stifling heat wave). I'm willing to patch a roof that's not too steep, but I have neither the time nor the back for a whole-house job.

But just as there's no shame in acknowledging your limits, there's no shame in going for what turns you on. If you develop into an eager-beaver roofer, or if you look forward to augering out drain pipes, I'll stand back and cheer. Likewise, if you're interested only in replacing the occasional light switch or staining the backyard deck, I'm equally enthusiastic. In either case, you'll save some money, learn about your house, gather more tools, and gain confidence for your next task.

One final word on attitude: Neither a wimp nor a hero be. Even if you think the world is short on heroes, don't be a stupid hero. Don't hurt yourself making a repair (see Chapter 6, "Health, Safety, and Common Sense"). Even a complete idiot should know when to say "when."

Sorting out the Tasks

Although I won't presume to judge your skills in home repair, I do have some suggestions for jobs that are suitable to various levels of homeowner expertise. (As you read this, keep in mind that the list is not inclusive and that some building codes require that you hire a licensed plumber or electrician for certain projects.)

Jobs for Beginners

➤ Weather-stripping doors and windows (see Chapter 12, "Skin-Tight: Caulking, Weather-Stripping, Insulation, and Ventilation")

➤ Replacing window panes (see Chapter 18, "A Paneless Guide to Windows")

➤ Lubricating door hinges and locks (see Chapter 19, "An Entry-Level Treatise on Doors")

➤ Resurfacing an asphalt driveway (see Chapter 13, "In the Yard: No Rest for the Weary")

➤ Minor-league drywall or plaster repairs (see Chapter 22, "Cosmetology 101: Drywall and Plaster Repair")

➤ Painting, staining, and varnishing (see Chapter 25, "Putting a Good Face on: Choosing Paint and Painting Tools," and Chapter 26, "Lay It on—but Not Too Thick")

➤ Replacing outlets and switches (see Chapter 27, "Breaker, Breaker on the Wall: Electric Fundamentals," and Chapter 28, "Getting Wired Without Getting Zapped")

➤ Unclogging drains (see Chapter 31, "Either It Leaks … [Plumbing, Part I]," and Chapter 32, "… Or It Doesn't Drain [Plumbing, Part II]")

Jobs for the More Confident

➤ Repair on a relatively flat and low roof (see Chapter 15, "Gimme Shelter—and Other Advice on Repairing Roofs")

➤ Masonry and concrete repairs (see Chapter 16, "Bricks and Stones: Doing Masonry and Concrete Without Getting Stoned," and Chapter 17, "Bricks and Stones: Masonry and Concrete [the Sequel]")

➤ Fixing large holes in plaster or drywall (see Chapter 22)

➤ Installing new outlets or switches (see Chapters 27 and 28)

➤ Installing small amounts of copper or plastic pipe (see Chapters 31 and 32)

Jobs for a Pro

➤ Replacing windows or doors (but see Chapter 19)

➤ Serious drain cleaning

➤ Installing galvanized pipe

➤ Working on high or steep roofs

➤ Repairing the fuse box or circuit-breaker box

➤ Fixing an air conditioner

Is It "Perfect Enough"?

Are you a perfectionist? Does your blood congeal at the idea of leaving a job before it's flawless? I'm sorry to hear that. Perfectionism may not be a diagnosable personality disorder—at least to psychologists—but it is a serious obstacle to learning home repair. Nit-pickers can find flaws in any repair—particularly the ones they've made. (And when they hire repair folks, they can dramatically increase costs by demanding that the workers spend extra time satisfying extravagant demands.)

If you're not sure whether I'm talking about you, repeat "perfect enough" aloud three times. If your teeth are already gnashing, cut yourself some slack. You're just learning to do home repairs, so you'll probably have to leave some jobs "perfect enough." Consider making a training run on something that isn't obvious; for example, adjust a closet door before tackling the front door.

As time passes, you'll learn what you're doing. You'll gather a better selection of tools and will learn to distinguish possible projects from preposterous ones. Then, when you're ready to play in the major leagues, remember that I knew you when you were just learning to hit.

Earning While Learning

For many people, the prime motivation for doing home repairs is saving money. I wish I could tell you from experience how much you can expect to save, but I don't hire out enough work to know. I do know that my annual maintenance bill (on a 1,700-square-foot Cape Cod with a garage and a basement) usually runs less than $500.

Your checkbook should give you an idea of what you're spending. In my area, the cost of replacing a couple of faucet washers (which sell for less than $1 in the hardware store) starts at about $70—the plumbing contractor's hourly minimum. A roofing contractor quotes $50 per hour, plus materials, to repair a few leaks in the roof—a job you can usually handle for about $4, including materials. Electricians here charge $45 per hour and up, plus materials.

Granted, you won't be able to make these repairs as quickly as a pro, but even if you take three times as long, you're going to save big money. That's particularly true if you would have to pay for a whole hour for a quick repair, or if you must pay "port to port" for travel to and from the contractor's shop.

Yet the economic imperative is not the only reason to fix your house. Equally important is the primitive gratification of swinging a hammer and the fulfillment you feel as you stand up, sweaty and grimy, and look at a repair you've accomplished for the first time. In some cases, you'll feel the intellectual thrill of figuring out why the bathtub always ran cold or why the paint on the porch railing loved peeling.

And don't forget another advantage: getting the job done in the first place. If the building business is busy, there's a good chance that you will have trouble finding any qualified person to take on a small job.

Finally, home repair offers you a chance to experience the most sublime form of education: being paid to learn. Whether I was farming, salvaging lumber from old barns, or working as a mason and plasterer, I've always believed in learning while earning. And while opportunities to gain wealth and wisdom simultaneously are never as common as they should be, I'll bet your house has them by the roomful.

But It Ain't Broke ...

Have you ever stirred up a hornets' nest of home-repair trouble and then, while mulling over your options (all of them grim), been advised, "If it wasn't broke, why did you fix it?" This kind of brain-dead "wisdom" sounds reasonable enough, but it ignores the fact that most people don't deliberately stir up hornets' nests—they stumble across them.

Sometimes you have no choice—you can't impersonate an innocent bystander when a leaky pipe is irrigating your basement or when the outlet behind your refrigerator is fusing into a glob of molten plastic.

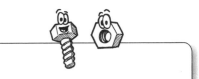

Nuts and Bolts

While this book focuses on repairs, it also talks about maintenance. Generally, **maintenance** tasks—things such as cleaning, painting, and caulking—are intended to keep the home in good condition, while **repairs** are designed to heal injuries. It's something like the relationship between daily exercise and heart surgery: Ideally—but not always—the one can prevent the other.

I don't find the "ain't broke" rule very useful in home repair, and two disasters explain why. A few years ago, I tried to fix a faucet that was just starting to leak, and I ended up wrecking something that really wasn't broken (but when I finished, at least I had a brand-new kitchen faucet with some modern features). More recently, I put off painting a rusting shower stall. When I finally took a closer look, I saw that it had rusted through, and I got an unwanted lesson in installing shower stalls. The experience also taught me why some people are motivated to maintain their homes: so they don't have to learn time-consuming lessons in shower installation.

And even if it ain't broke, it may not be factory-fresh. Here you'll face shades of gray: A faucet that's dripping ever so slowly may still stain the sink or simply drive you berserk. An electrical outlet that has not yet begun sparking may still have an ominous wobble. In cases like these, you'll have to exercise judgment about whether to haul out the toolbag.

In Chapter 2, "Assessing Your Home," I'll describe a quick home inspection that may unveil a few repair and maintenance projects. For now, though, just remember this: Even if it ain't broke, it might still be half-shot.

The Least You Need to Know

➤ In home repair, the perfect is the enemy of the good. Don't be afraid of making a "perfect enough" repair. Remember, rookies seldom start in the major leagues.

➤ Size up your projects: Some are easy and some are hard. Hire professionals for the ones that are plain impossible. Your morale and your home will both benefit.

➤ If it ain't broke, it may still need fixing.

Chapter 2

Assessing Your Home

In This Chapter

➤ Seeing home sweet home through an expert's eyes

➤ Inspecting the roof, foundation, walls, and floors—the bones and sinews of your home

➤ Setting priorities for maintenance and repairs

Have you taken a critical look at the home place recently? Have you ever looked dispassionately at the various components—the roof, the furnace, the foundation, the walls, doors, and windows—of your dwelling? Have you crawled through the shrubbery to look at the foundation, gotten your pants dirty in that miserable crawl space under the kitchen, or eyed the attic from the cramped hatchway in the ceiling?

Maybe not—who likes hunting for trouble? And chances are, you don't consider yourself qualified for the arcane task of inspecting a home. But while "out of sight, out of mind" may be a smart attitude about some possessions, it's not reasonable regarding something as temperamental, weatherworn, and expensive as a house. That's why I suggest taking a level-headed look at your house, with special emphasis on the all-important foundation and roof. If you're lucky, the problems you find will be the kind covered in this book. Even if you're unlucky enough to find more serious trouble, though, an inspection will probably save you money in the long run because you will catch the deterioration before it gets too grim. And, if you have to hire the work out, we'll give you an idea of what to say on the phone. Chapter 4, "Dial a Home Fixer: Building Rescue," has a rundown of who to call for various repairs.

On the Virtues of a Hyperactive Home Inspector

My friend Josh Martin was calling for advice. He was about to close a deal on a nice-looking house when his home inspector delivered a 75-page report bursting with ominous phrases like "serious flaw," "needs immediate repair," and "potential liability." For example, the stones on the front path should be replaced—yesterday!—lest a senior-citizen tour group trip, fall, and maul his homeowner's policy with a class-action lawsuit.

I read the inspector's report and tried to persuade my friend to heave this hazardous hovel. Nevertheless, Josh and his wife, Rita, ignored me, bought the place, and haven't found any major problems. In fact, they have yet to be sued. (Although I'll bet their daughter, Julia, has tripped on that walk. How long, in today's litigious climate, before she sues her parents?)

This story of a zealous inspector obsessed by trivialities is not as absurd as it sounds. In a backward way, it demonstrates what a good inspection can do: If even this paranoid fellow could not find problems with the critical systems—the foundation, structure, and roof—then the house was indeed a solid buy.

I am not advocating that you hire a home inspector, but I do suggest that you look at your place as an inspector might. Sentiment aside, how do the siding and foundation really look? If you were looking for a place with many unused miles, would you be impressed?

Nuts and Bolts

A **home inspector** is somebody who's in the business of assessing the physical integrity and code compliance of existing homes. These experts are usually hired by buyers during a home purchase, but they can also supply an outsider's impartial view of the need for repairs. Because they will not be making the repair, home inspectors do not stand to gain by suggesting unnecessary work.

Should a sane person who already owns a home go searching for trouble? Don't most do-it-yourselfers already have the refrigerator covered with the spouse's repair orders? An inspection will take you to new and exotic places (not the Amazon basin or the Paris Opera, unfortunately, but to a crawl space, that barely accessible attic, and up on the roof). These seldom-traveled locations can harbor festering problems that will eventually burst into your consciousness—and your checking account.

An inspection can save money if you find drafts to plug or peeling paint caused by a buildup of moisture, but its preventive value is most important on the roof. It's one thing to repair a few leaking shingles; it's quite another to replace roof boards, drywall, and rafters that were all rotted by an unnoticed leak. Look at it this way: Whether you inspect or not, you'll wind up making a repair. It's just a matter of how much you'll have to fix—and how much you'll pay.

So even if you already have a list of home to-dos, let's take a quick tour of the major parts of your house. Along the way, I'll discuss problems that a home-repair novice can cure and problems that indicate the need for professional help.

A Worm's-Eye View: Foundation, Basement, and Crawl Space

The foundation—the walls that rest on the ground and support the structure—may look homely (it's usually concrete), but this is the most important part of your house. That's why your inspection should start at the bottom.

From inside and outside, look for crumbling concrete or mortar, as well as loose blocks, bricks, or stones. A bit of spalling (surface deterioration) is usually acceptable in older homes and is usually the result of poorly formulated concrete. Likewise, don't obsess about small cracks—they're common and usually harmless. But cracks that are moving or that are wider than about a quarter-inch can indicate serious settling. Examine the building above the crack: Are the windows and doors jammed or out-of-square? Do the floors seem level? Will a marble start rolling across the floor? Do cracks on the interior walls indicate major movement? (I've heard of drawing a line or gluing a piece of glass across a crack to see if it's moving, but not having done it myself, I'll just pass the tips along without endorsement.) If you have a moving crack, you may be looking at a structural problem that's beyond idiot territory; first, though, see Chapter 16, "Bricks and Stones: Doing Masonry and Concrete Without Getting Stoned," and Chapter 17, "Bricks and Stones: Masonry and Concrete (the Sequel)," for a discussion of foundation and basement repair.

Do you see evidence of carpenter ants—small holes and piles of sawdust—or termite damage—primarily tunnels from the soil to the wood? Keep an eye out for the discoloration and softening that signals wood decay, particularly in damp parts of basements and crawl spaces (mini-basements where the ceiling is usually only no more than 4 feet high). (Chapter 11, "Wood: Still Champ After All These Years," contains details on wood preservation and decay.)

Shingle Talk

Most roof shingles are designed to last about 25 years, but you should still check regularly for problems. Why? Maybe you have cut-rate shingles that are deteriorating ahead of schedule, or maybe the roofer flubbed the installation. Put a ladder to the edge of the roof, or use binoculars from the ground, and search for torn, missing, or curled shingles. Inspect the sheet metal flashing around skylights, vents, pipes, and chimneys. Is it nailed solidly and tarred as necessary, or is it loose or rusty? Do you see goopy black tar or silicone caulking on the flashing, indicating a leak that has resisted repair? Chapter 30, "Champion Chimneys," has lots of information on flashing installation and repair.

Examine the eaves troughs at the bottom of the roof for rust, plugging, and leaks. Also known as gutters, eaves troughs catch water from the roof and route it to the ground, protecting siding and windows from runoff. If you're using binoculars, you may be able to see a build-up of leaves plugging the gutter. But binocs won't help you see if the gutters are full of mineral granules from the shingles, a sign that the roof is nearing retirement (see Chapter 15, "Gimme Shelter—and Other Advice on Repairing Roofs"). Look inside the house or attic (particularly near the chimney) for discoloration that indicates leakage. Don't ignore leaks—no matter how many reasons you can invent to make them go away, they won't. They'll just get worse.

Siding, Windows, and Doors

It may not be obvious until you think about it, but unmaintained siding, windows, and doors can become big repair items. There's another financial incentive for keeping these items in good condition as well: lower energy bills. Look for large sections of peeling paint (indicating moisture migrating from the interior); fungus (a speckled discoloration that washes off in a diluted bleach solution); loose siding; delaminating plywood; and poor caulking between the siding and windows, doors, trim, and vents (see Chapter 14, "Beauty's Only Skin Deep: Care and Healing for Your Siding"). Also look for eaves troughs overflowing onto the siding, a situation that can cause leaks, staining, and decay.

Nail It Down

Here's the one good use for cigarettes. Wait for a cold day, light up a coffin nail, and hold it near a closed window or door. The smoke will help you pinpoint drafts.

Check for smooth operation and tight, draft-proof fit of doors and windows. Storm windows should be fairly tight and should move easily (see Chapter 18, "A Paneless Guide to Windows," and Chapter 19, "An Entry-Level Treatise on Doors").

Slide on Inside

Even if the exterior passes inspection, it's a good idea to take a close look inside. Before you worry about surface defects—peeling wallpaper and butchered drywall—look for the structural problems that signal the need for major repairs. Look for cracks in ceilings or walls (particularly above doors or windows) that indicate weakening of posts, sagging of beams, or settling of the foundation. Stamp around on floors to feel for weak spots. If you find these sorts of problems, see Chapter 20, "Getting a Solid Footing on Floors," or call a carpenter before more damage occurs.

Other interior problems are unlikely to cause collateral damage, but they can make a good house look dilapidated. Examine floors for stains, gouges, degraded finish, and carpet problems (described in Chapter 20). Examine the drywall or plaster for cracks, decay, and discoloration (see Chapter 22, "Cosmetology 101: Drywall and Plaster Repair"). Check the condition of wallpaper (see Chapter 23, "The Will to Wallpaper") and paint (see Chapter 25, "Putting a Good Face on: Choosing Paint and Painting Tools," and Chapter 26, "Lay It on—but Not Too Thick").

Meet the Mechanicals

Broadly speaking, "mechanicals" are the systems that require wires, ducts, or pipes—things like the plumbing, heating, and wiring systems. And while there's no disguising the fact that mechanical problems can be complicated, expensive, and frustrating, it's usually pretty easy to check the operation of these systems and figure out what action is needed.

Take a look at exposed parts of the electrical system (see Chapter 27, "Breaker, Breaker on the Wall: Electric Fundamentals," and Chapter 28, "Getting Wired Without Getting Zapped"), particularly in the basement. Is the wiring shipshape or a spider's web of sagging cables and exposed wires? Do you see a rat's nest of boxes, switches, and cables around the fuse box or circuit-breaker box? (Incidentally, breaker boxes are preferable to fuse boxes because blown circuit breakers can be reset rather than replaced.) Look at the rating on the biggest fuse or the main circuit breaker to determine if the overall electrical system is rated at less than 100 amps. Any of these signs may indicate an inadequate electrical system and may call for a professional evaluation.

Are the outlets the three-hole, grounded type required by many modern electrical gizmos? If not, you may need to update them if the boxes have a grounding conductor. Using a circuit tester, check the operation and grounding of all outlets. Test all switches for correct operation—these are problems you can generally tackle.

Check that the heating and/or cooling system responds to the thermostat. Examine the condition of ducts, vents, and registers. Do the furnace and air conditioning units look solid, with sound wiring, or do you see electrician's tape, dangling wires, and a generally disheveled appearance? These signs may mean nothing—or might indicate that it's time for a checkup from the heating and cooling doctor (which is usually advisable every few years anyway). Heating systems are taken up in Chapter 29, "A Welcome Blast of Hot Air: Heating System Tips."

Finally, ask your utility company about a free home energy audit. These evaluations, which were popular during the energy crisis in the 1970s, will tell you how to save your heating and cooling money.

First Things First

Now that you've gone through the gruesome inspection process, it's time to assess the results. Some problems, including leaking roofs, drafty windows in cold climates, electrical hazards, and plumbing leaks, require immediate attention. Others, such as paint and wallpaper glitches, can be deferred.

In general, builders and remodelers start with major problems and work toward the minor ones. If you found structural problems, those come first. For larger projects, it helps to organize your repairs by area of the house or type of task. In other words, do the dining room first and then move to the living room. Or, do all the electrical work, then move to the plumbing, and finally do the drywall and painting. If you've got only minor flaws, approach them in any reasonable sequence.

Don't be tempted to ignore those boring maintenance tasks—the chores that can keep you out of big trouble down the road—in favor of the more sexy repair work. Is a railing getting rusty? Then your choices are to paint it now or replace it later. Is the gutter getting clogged with leaves? Then you can either clean it in the fall (and think about putting on some screens to keep leaves out in the future) or have water pouring down your siding when the gutters plug up, and still have to face the disgusting cleaning task in the spring.

Some maintenance tasks—cleaning gutters, affixing storm windows, and checking caulking and weather-stripping—must be done every year. Depending on your inclination, you might want to make a list of things that need annual attention. Even if you don't, it's not a bad idea to take a gander at the major home systems occasionally, just to make sure that decay is not sneaking up on you.

The Least You Need to Know

➤ Building problems generally leave evidence on the surface; in general, the sooner you find and correct a problem, the less it will cost.

➤ Horrors! There are good reasons to go looking for trouble.

➤ Foundation, roof, and structural problems can reverberate through a building and cause multiple disasters. If you have time to meet only a few parts of your house, start with the bones: the bottom and the top.

➤ Maintenance—the recurring problem of protecting your home from decay and the elements—may not be glamorous, but it will save you money in the long run. (Don't believe me? Then tell my neighbor, Doug Mitchell, who just called to ask for advice about replacing the studs in a wall. Why does he need this? Because an uncaulked window leaked for years, and now the wood around it is totally rotten.)

Chapter 3

Get a Plan, Stan (Can You Do It?)

In This Chapter

➤ The role of family, job, time, and money in home care

➤ Time-saving ideas for your home fix-up strategy

➤ What you must *always* bring to the hardware store (aside from your wallet)

➤ Building permits and your friendly neighborhood inspector

So the results of your home inspection were a bit, ah, disappointing? Instead of buried treasure, you found a closet full of skeletons? A sagging beam? A crumbling foundation? Extensive water damage? Now it's time to decide what to do about these discoveries and to assess your tools, time, and skills. Is it possible to undertake the repair yourself? Is it wise? Do you need help or advice? In other words, should you sit on the sidelines or jump into the game?

I approached my first significant home project in an absolutely gung-ho manner, with a dangerous blend of naiveté and foolish overconfidence. I was trying to undo the efforts of a farmer who, long before, had glued linoleum to the floor *and walls* of my kitchen. Fortunately, he didn't use waterproof paste, but I didn't anticipate how many buckets of steaming water I'd need to slosh on those walls, and how long it would be before the reek of linoleum paste would vanish from the old farmhouse. If I'd known, I'd have thought twice about the job.

Yet as the refinished maple floor in that kitchen proves, there's a lot to be said for a "damn the torpedoes" attitude. Still, I don't advocate closing your eyes before jumping off a cliff—or starting a home repair (acts that can be almost indistinguishable). The first step in any large home project is to examine your skills, so I'll start by looking at that issue. Then I'll talk about some relevant social, economic, and legal factors.

Your Skills and Your Project

To decide whether you have the skills for the task, you'll need a better idea of what the task entails. Start by reading the pertinent sections of this book. If you need more information, consult library books that focus on topics I don't cover in detail, or talk with knowledgeable friends.

When you have a better notion of what the job will require, these pointers will help you decide whether it's for you:

➤ Are you good at solving problems in this field? If you are an ace roofer but a complete zero at plumbing, take this into account.

➤ Do you own—or know where to borrow or rent—the tools you'll need?

➤ Can you get professional advice suggested for a major project if you need it?

➤ Can you do the work alone? If you'll need help, is it available?

➤ How soon must the project be finished, and will bad weather hold you up?

➤ How long will it take?

➤ How much of your house will be out of commission (due to shutting off the electricity or water, or because of floors covered by tools or dropcloths)? Some rooms are expendable, but bathrooms and kitchens should not be out of commission for long.

Your Family and Your Project

You imagine that your project won't disrupt your family because you're not ripping old linoleum out of the kitchen—you're just replacing a "now-you-see-light-and-now-you-don't" switch. That's great—even if it won't rival the Magna Carta as a contribution to civilization. So you make the ritual trip to the hardware store, assemble your tools, and start randomly shutting off circuits. Then you hear a shriek from your spouse, whose blacked-out computer just devoured three hours' worth of unsaved work.

That problem could have been avoided if you had heeded the home-repairer's cardinal maxim: Communicate, communicate, and communicate. At least make sure that your family knows—and, if necessary, approves of—your plans. In my case, for example, even though I wash the dishes, I would still ask my wife to advise on the purchase of a new kitchen faucet. The best bet is to schedule your repair and maintenance projects when there will be a minimum of disruption. (However, keep in mind that if you hurt yourself, you'll be happy to have somebody around for assistance.)

Your Job and Your Project

The impact of home projects can extend to your workplace. How will your boss respond when you blame a late arrival at work on an emergency trip to the plumbing supplier for an essential "bezel-to-bezerk" fitting? Will your boss care that you were trying to save your family another day without running water?

As somebody who has scarcely had a boss over the past 20 years, I'd be the last to advise you on handling this peculiar species. But it does make sense to work around job strictures, to maximize the use of weekends and vacations, and to set realistic expectations, particularly at first. Be sensible.

Nail It Down

If you list the rooms and appliances served by each circuit or fuse (see the section "Making a Circuit Map" in Chapter 27, "Breaker, Breaker on the Wall: Electric Fundamentals"), you can easily shut off only the right circuit. Still, just to play it safe, use your circuit tester to double-check that the outlet is cold before sticking your fingers in it. Always.

Your Money and Your Project

How much will it cost? Here we meet a good reason to hire a good contractor who will give you a firm cost estimate. With do-it-yourself home repair, you could end up wasting money—buying the wrong supplies or tools—or mangling innocent bystanders—like the drywall near a fried electric outlet.

Having said this, I really don't have a good solution to figuring out what it will cost. I'd suggest pricing the major materials and estimating the incidentals, then multiplying your total by at least two. That may seem excessive, and you may occasionally come in under cost. But if you end up spending triple your original estimate (as often happens), you'll still be close to that final (doubled) number.

What about tools, which can cost a lot more than materials? It's helpful to estimate what they will cost, although you may find yourself needing another tool midway through a job. Even though tools may be expensive, they will reduce the cost of a future repair. To anyone wanting to save money on home repair, tools are a good investment.

Your Time and Your Project

If Murphy (the lawgiver) wasn't a fixer-upper, he must have been in the remodeling business. "If anything can go wrong," the wise Murphy told us, "it will go wrong, and at the worst possible moment." That's putting it mildly.

In my experience, a predictable memory lapse in the building-supply store is guaranteed to require a second trip so that you can buy the *right* reducer to hook up the three-quarter-inch elbow to the half-inch outlet on your water heater. A slight error in measuring the thickness of a roof board inevitably causes a second trip to the lumber yard. And saws don't slip—until the last cut on a complicated, one-of-a-kind replacement board.

If you feel obligated to estimate how long a job will take, think hard about how many hours it should require, and then multiply that figure by two or three. (For better accuracy, throw some dice. Making estimates is the toughest part of repairing—just ask anyone who does it for a living.)

Tips for Saving Time

There are some ways to reduce your burden under Murphy's Law and also save some time on home repairs. I'll admit that most of the suggestions on the following pages sound pretty pedestrian, but I'll lay them out and let you ignore any or all of them. Generally, I suggest systems that you set up in your spare time; in the midst of a repair, who can be bothered labeling nails or organizing tools?

1. Store your tools intelligently. In Chapter 7, "The Bare Essentials: Hand Tools," I've made suggestions for a ready-to-go toolkit. Keep other tools in their places (a pegboard, with its customized hooks, makes excellent organized, visible storage). If you don't need to search for tools, you can get right to work. Chapter 10, "A Workable Workshop," has hints on a productive workshop.

2. Use labels. I keep a stack of adhesive mailing labels and a marker in the workshop, along with a bunch of empty containers. With labels on the cans, I don't have to grope for $1^1/_2$-inch drywall screws or 16-penny nails.

3. Store containers with the label facing out. This may sound anal-compulsive, but it saves time.

4. To avoid extra trips to the hardware or building-supply store, keep a supply of extra, broken, and didn't-fit parts on hand (see Chapter 9, "Fast Guide to Fasteners"). While you're in the store, why not buy some extra nails or screws? After all, you needed them once, so you're likely to need them again. The price of these spare parts is less than the price of another trip to the store.

5. Don't lose stuff. This sounds breathtakingly obvious until you squander a quarter-hour searching for a screw that was "here just a minute ago." Remember the advice of conservationist Aldo Leopold: "The first rule of intelligent tinkering is to save all the parts." (Leopold was talking about preventing species extinctions, but his advice derived from the fix-up trade.) Keep tin cans and plastic containers around to hold small parts, and use them, even for a 5-minute repair. (Tiny parts can enter the Twilight Zone in 30 seconds flat.)

6. Know what you're doing—by reading this and other books and by talking with people who have been in your shoes. Got a drain that's getting slow? Mention this casually at the next ice-cream social. Maybe Nelson will stop blathering about his golf score for a millisecond and talk about something useful, like how he fixed a similar problem. Who knows? He might even offer to lend you a pipe wrench.

7. Always bring the carcass of whatever you're replacing to the store (unless it's a refrigerator!). You may be amazed at how many sizes, features, threads, and materials the store stocks for any particular part; only with the old one in hand can you choose correctly.

8. Bring a list to the store so you don't return half-shopped.

9. Rent those fun, heavy-duty tools, "just like the pros abuse." These macho monsters can shave hours from many miserable tasks, including heavy-duty sawing, drilling into concrete, or tackling tedious nailing jobs (see Chapter 8, "The Bare Essentials with Oomph! Power Tools").

10. Don't start an optional plumbing or electrical fix when your relatives are arriving. Ditto for weekends—you'll be lucky if specialty stores are open at all on Saturday, and they are sure to close at noon just before you drive up with your busted parts.

11. Number and sequence all parts as you take things apart.

12. Do stuff in logical sequence: all the demolition, all the framing, all the electrical, all the drywall, and all the painting. This reduces the need to haul out tools and helps you concentrate on the task.

Building Codes and Your Project

Before starting to build a porch on my farmhouse, I called the township building inspector to ask about a building permit. He wasn't home, so I started putting in posts. A week later, he delicately asked whether I was thinking of getting a permit. As I muttered some half-truths about my heroic efforts to reach him, he cut me off: "I'll be out that way tomorrow, and we'll write one up." He did, and we did; I paid my $5 fee, and that was that.

I wouldn't count on such understanding treatment from building inspectors nowadays. These folks are generally zealots who have memorized codes containing uncountable paragraphs on the size, safety, structure, materials, and use of a living space. Codes or local laws may also govern who can do the work; in some localities, for example, only licensed contractors can do certain electrical and plumbing tasks.

It's tough to generalize about building codes, since there are at least three in the United States, not to

Nuts and Bolts

A **building code** is a rulebook your municipality uses to govern building construction and repair. A **building permit** is a document issued to a contractor or building owner that allows a project to be started, as long as it adheres to plans on file with the building inspector. When you're done (and perhaps even in mid-project as well), the inspector will come to check that you've followed your plans—and the code.

mention codes covering natural gas, electricity, plumbing, heating, ventilating, air conditioning, and indoor kite-flying, for all I know. In many cases, you can replace stuff without a permit, but you would need a permit to make a significant change. You are not likely to need a permit to replace a window (a project that novices are not advised to tackle anyway) because that's replacing an existing feature. But you might need a permit to cut in a new window, because that's a structural alteration. In some municipalities, re-roofing requires a permit, particularly if the existing roof must be stripped off. In other cases, a permit may be required if the price of the project exceeds a certain dollar value.

Building inspectors won't give out information from the code, even to the taxpayers who pay their salaries. If you plan to span a certain opening with a 2-by-12 beam, the building inspector will tell you whether that is acceptable. But if you inquire what the code requires to span that opening, they'll stay mum. It's maddening, but they do have a rationale: The former question certifies that your plans meet code—an inspector's function—while the latter relates to designing buildings—an architect's or engineer's function.

After repeated dealings with building inspectors, I've concluded that they ask tough questions not just to learn about your *plans*, but also to learn about your *skills*. After you convince them that you can distinguish a finial from a fascia board, they will be more inclined to sign off on your project.

Trouble, with a capital "T," occurs when an improvement triggers a requirement that the whole room, system, or building be brought up to code. That's unlikely to affect your efforts to replace a storm window or realign a door, though. If in doubt, ask your inspectors, but don't go out of your way to make the job sound bigger than it is. Warding off trouble is one thing; begging for it is quite another.

One final note on building inspectors and permits: After your project is finished, the building assessor might want to visit to see whether the project has increased the value of your house.

Friends and Pros: Vital Sources of Help and Information

Chances are, some of your friends do home repair for fun, which makes them potential sources of information or assistance. I have an informal work-trading arrangement with my friend Doug Swaine, who's a recovering general contractor (to which I attribute his relaxed manner). When I needed help installing new kitchen counters, I found that he had actually done it before. (I was confident I could bluff my way through, but his expertise made everything faster and smoother. I later repaid him by helping nail vinyl siding to a giant garage that was immediately dubbed "the Taj m'Garage." That's how our deal works.)

When it comes to learning from professionals, working alongside them is probably the best option, but there are others as well. Pay attention next time you hire somebody to work on the house. Which part of the job does the repairer do first? What tools are important enough to "live" in the toolbox? What special power tools would you rent to do this job? How does a plumber thread a pipe? All these observations—let alone what you can learn from a talkative fixer—will come in handy down the line.

The Least You Need to Know

➤ If you value your family life, keep the lines of communication open before and during your project.

➤ A little planning, a little luck, and a stockpile of tools and parts will save time on any repair.

➤ Most repairs require no building permit, but it pays to check in advance for bigger projects.

Chapter 4

Dial a Home Fixer: Building Rescue

Which single invention sabotaged the average person's building skills? It wasn't the plumber's van or the forget-about-fixing-it membrane roofs. No, it was the brainchild of the humble tinkerer Alexander Graham Bell. Since his telephone, we've had the option of dialing someone else instead of doing the hammering ourselves.

Bell made it easier to decide that your skills, ambitions, and time don't permit you to tackle a problem. Perhaps it's an electrical project calling for the special tools needed to bend conduit (the thin-wall pipe that carries wires). Perhaps that little roof leak actually signaled the need for an entire reroofing job, and you simply don't have the time. Perhaps it's a carpentry job that calls for the physical strength of an ox. Perhaps it's a plumbing disaster that's clearly beyond your grasp.

Next question: Who will do the work? Although I'll devote the rest of this book to helping you handle your own repair projects, I don't intend to abandon you as you reach for the phone book and try to divine which advertisements are credible and which are hokum.

So let's spend a couple of chapters talking about finding the right someone else. In other words, we'll talk about how to find, evaluate, hire, and live with a good contractor.

Get a Good One

Even though the people in the home-repair business may have been created equal, some have turned out better than others. When I was in the masonry business, I never left an unsatisfied customer. I returned every phone call promptly and never treated anybody rudely. And despite my affordable prices, my work was flawless.

Just kidding. But I never pulled the kind of monkey business uncovered a couple of years back by the New York State Department of Consumer Affairs. In response to a litany of complaints from homeowners, these consumer cops rented a house, mounted some concealed video cameras, summoned 65 contractors for various repairs, and wound up charging 23 of them with fraud. Some were overeager: An appliance repairer who found a towel jammed in a water pump replaced the entire pump, even though it worked perfectly once the rag was fished out. Others were under-eager: A chimney sweep, for example, who climbed the roof and returned to the ground without ever touching the chimney (see the section "Scams" in Chapter 5, "Talk Contract—and Live to Tell About It!").

As a homeowner, you have legal protections, even if you don't have electronic spy equipment. Many states require licenses for some tradespeople, particularly general contractors, electricians, and plumbers. What this actually means varies from state to state, but it may give you some leverage in a dispute. If the license number is not on the contract, ask to see a copy of the license. It's best to avoid problems in the first place by "qualifying" your repairer. Start by gathering information from friends and neighbors; make a point of asking who nailed on that beautiful new roof or who gouged that oak floor. You can also contact the standard sources: the Better Business Bureau and the local department of consumer affairs.

What Kind of Help Do You Need?

Once, builders were carpenters or they were masons. Nowadays, the trades have subdivided until you might need a doctorate in construction management to puzzle out the Yellow Pages. As you read the following descriptions of who does what, re-member that when the building business is busy, everybody gets picky. Carpenters won't do roofing, and painters won't do gutters. When the business slacks off, repairers suddenly remember forgotten skills.

In cold regions, winter is the slow season for people who work outside—particularly roofers, masons, and painters (although painters may have inside work, and some masonry jobs are enclosed). These trades will welcome inside work and then put it off until bad weather forces them off an outside project. Electricians, plumbers, and drywallers are less affected by weather because most of their work is inside. Much of this is common sense: Heating technicians are busiest in fall, and air conditioning folks are busiest in the spring or early summer.

If you find that your repair project is too picayune to interest a builder, try letting a few repairs build up until your list is attractive to somebody who's trying to make a living. Or, call a handyperson.

Handymen and -Women

If you've made a dozen calls looking for someone to repair a defective light switch, you probably need an old-fashioned handyperson. These are the people who fill the gap between your skills and those of the big contractors. Generalizing about these folks is not going to help much; about all they have in common is a van, home-repair skills, and experience. To find a handyperson, ask a friend or look on the bulletin board at the hardware store. For a small project, there's no point going through an FBI-style background investigation. Many of these folks will try to make a repair on the first visit, to save the hassle of returning.

Carpenters

Carpenters do wood work, everything from repairing wood siding to installing new windows and making doors close smoothly. Carpenters can also help with structural problems, such as sagging beams or rotten posts. Carpenters generally shy away from other specialties, but some may fix a gutter or a roof leak, especially as part of a larger project.

General Contractors

"Generals" are builders—often carpenters or former carpenters—who direct subcontractors, or "subs." In return for dealing with the inevitable hassles, conflicts, and screw-ups of a big building project, generals receive a percentage of each sub's pay.

It sounds like a hustle—after all, you can tell an electrician where to install an outlet just as easily—but it's not. Generals work only on big jobs, when somebody must anticipate and solve conflicts between the subs. Is the plumber planning to run a hefty drain line where the carpenter wants to put a beam? If so, the general can make a snap decision that keeps the subs working. Generals also have more leverage than you because the subs may be working for them on another job next week.

Having said all that, you probably won't be meeting any general contractors in the course of home repairs, which usually involve only one or, at most, two trades. Never-theless, it's worth understanding their role, in case you ever contemplate remodeling (in which case, I'd advise taking two Prozac and thinking it over carefully in morning's harsh light—but that's another book).

Drywallers and Plasterers

Either of these trades (see Chapter 22, "Cosmetology 101: Drywall and Plaster Repair") may be willing to take on repair work, particularly when new jobs are scarce. But don't expect to get help for a small nick in the wall—that's more likely to interest a handyperson. Also remember the wild card in wall repair: If the framing is rotten or damaged, the repair cannot begin until the wall is torn apart and repaired.

If a drywaller suggests putting a new layer of drywall over a damaged wall, remember to add the cost of altering moldings and door and window jambs to the cost of drywalling. Tearing out and replacing the old drywall may actually be cheaper.

Sparky the Electrician

Electricians deal with most parts of home wiring, from the electric meter to the last outlet. They install conduit, connect the electric meter to the breaker box, and install outdoor and underground wiring. However, electricians may or may not work on the following:

➤ The "drop," which connects the utility lines or a buried supply cable to your electric meter. (It may be maintained by the utility company.)

➤ Cable television and alarm systems—both specialty jobs.

➤ Phone wiring, which can be repaired by you or a phone installer.

➤ HVAC wiring, which is the province of heating and cooling specialists.

Hot Shots in the Heating, Ventilating, and Air Conditioning (HVAC) Business

HVAC folks work on the heating and cooling plant (the furnace, air conditioner, or heat pump), the controls that tell these machines when to work, and the ducts or pipes that distribute the heat or cold. Some companies may specialize in oil burners or gas furnaces, or in hot water or steam heat-distribution systems. In certain areas, these trades are licensed. HVAC companies also will perform routine maintenance on your heating/cooling equipment, such as an annual tune-up.

Plumbers, Drain Cleaners, and Other Snake Charmers

Plumbers are the gold miners of the contracting world: They earn lucrative sums in return for installing and maintaining the pipes that handle fresh and waste water, drain vents, and natural gas. Partly, that's because their trucks must be rolling warehouses of steel, plastic, and copper pipe, together with reducers and elbows of all descriptions. And let's face it: It's partly because they spend their days doing plumbing.

Septic-Tank Cleaners: A Flush Beats a Full House

Think I invented that one? I wish I were that creative. That's the slogan of a real, live septic-tank cleaner who used to advertise around here.

The idea behind toilets is simple: "Flush and forget." But that's not always possible if you have a septic tank, a home sewage system that decomposes that-which-you-flush and makes water and sludge. When the sludge builds up, it must be pumped out or the system will malfunction—an aromatic and polluting prospect. To protect the groundwater, a periodic pump-out by a septic-tank cleaner is suggested for all septic systems. Some states require pump-outs.

The Original Rockers: Masons and Concrete Workers

Masons build chimneys, fireplaces, and foundations from concrete block, brick, and stone (see Chapter 16, "Bricks and Stones: Doing Masonry and Concrete Without Getting Stoned," and Chapter 17, "Bricks and Stones: Masonry and Concrete [the Sequel]"). Some will also do concrete work (or at least concrete repair), but don't assume—ask. Some concrete workers specialize in flat work—driveways, floors, and steps. Others specialize in form work, meaning foundations and other walls. Mud-jackers or slab-jackers can raise sunken slabs of concrete in driveways and sidewalks, saving the cost of replacement.

A Primer on Painters

Painting is about the cheapest trade to enter, and simple paint jobs are not exactly rocket science, so painters range from college students to lifers. Some painters make minor repairs to trim or gutters, but all should do as much preparation as the job requires (see Chapter 25, "Putting a Good Face on: Choosing Paint and Painting Tools," and Chapter 26, "Lay It on—but Not Too Thick"). Cleaning, protecting shrubbery, scraping paint, and repairing siding and trim can take as much work as the painting itself.

The Top Trade: Roofers

Roofers have one thing in common: They love heights. Some do only shingling; others specialize in tar-and-gravel or membrane flat roofs. A roofer will usually detach and reinstall gutters, but whether they will take on a new gutter job might depend on the current demand for their trade.

Exterminators: They Shouldn't Bug You

Bugs! Most insects play valuable ecological roles in assisting plant pollination, controlling other insects, and decaying organic matter. But your home is not ecology—in fact, you probably want to remove it from the food chain altogether. Some insect problems can be controlled by changing the conditions in your house so that it's less attractive to insects (see the section "The Enemies of Wood" in Chapter 11, "Wood: Still Champ After All These Years").

If your insect-control measures don't work, call an exterminator. I suspect exterminators are a mite overzealous when it comes to bugs, but then so are many homeowners. If you're queasy about the chemicals they're using, get information from a library or from state or federal environmental or health regulators. The exterminator should supply a Material Safety Data Sheet (MSDS), detailing the health effects of the pesticides used.

Other Specialists

You thought we were finished? Not in this hyper-specialized era:

➤ Flooring experts usually specialize in tile, carpet, or wood. Tile folks will also do walls, counters, and tub enclosures.

➤ Refinishers sand and treat wood floors.

➤ Basement waterproofers do what the name implies. Caution: They tend to jump to the most expensive solution first. See the section "May We Talk About Your Soggy Basement?" in Chapter 17 first.

➤ Door and window installers replace doors and windows and also install storm windows and skylights.

➤ Garage-door repairers—guess what they do?

➤ Landscape contractors plant trees and shrubs. Some also build decks, fences, and gazeboes.

➤ Phone installers add new lines or repair existing ones.

➤ Siding installers may specialize in aluminum or vinyl siding.

➤ Gutter installers may install a seamless gutter, which is formed from a roll of flat aluminum. With fewer joints, seamless gutters should have fewer leaks.

The Least You Need to Know

➤ If you don't want to tackle a problem, plenty of specialists are willing to do it for you, particularly if the project is large enough or if you can group several repairs.

➤ Make sure your job falls within the expertise of your contractor.

➤ The best source of information on repairers is friends and neighbors.

Talk Contract— and Live to Tell About It!

In This Chapter

➤ Qualifying contractors

➤ The difference between an estimate, a bid, and a contract

➤ How the contract specifies the job

➤ How to protect yourself from building scams

If you are lucky, you've identified reliable contractors who will arrive promptly, do the job right the first time, and charge reasonable prices. With these repairers, you may feel no need for a contract. And for a job costing less than a couple of hundred dollars, the contract may be unwritten (although you should certainly understand the terms in advance).

Larger jobs and those done by unfamiliar contractors should be backed by a contract whose size and complexity should reflect the scope of the job. For a simple re-shingling, one page is sufficient. But a bathroom or kitchen renovation calls for a comprehensive contract with drawings describing in detail the carpentry, drywalling, electrical, cabinets, and plumbing work.

In this chapter, I'll describe how to evaluate a contractor, how to negotiate the terms of the job, and how to arrive at a contract. I will also describe how to protect yourself from rip-off artists who prey on homeowners.

Contacting Contractors

After you've identified the type of contractor you'll need, use references from friends or the Yellow Pages, and call a few. In general, unless the job is tiny or is an emergency, phone three contractors to compare their prices and approaches to the job.

On the phone, don't just describe your job and ask about prices. Inquire about the contractor's expertise and experience:

➤ How long have you been in business?

➤ Are you a member of a trade association?

➤ Are you insured?

➤ Are you state-licensed? (If so, the estimate form should carry the license number.)

➤ Do you charge for an estimate? (They shouldn't.)

When the repairer arrives to inspect your job, you'll get a chance to inspect him or her. Do they take a serious look at the project, or do they breeze through and rattle off a price? Do they explain things so that you understand them, or do they rely on baffling jargon? Are they in a hurry, insisting that you sign for the job right now? That can be a bad sign—unless you're also in a hurry.

Time and Materials, Estimates, Bids, and Contracts

Home repairers use a variety of systems for charging: time and materials, a flat price, or something in between. No matter what the method, you should not have to pay for time spent looking the job over or writing an estimate.

Many repairers bill small jobs by time and materials—the hours they work, plus the materials they use. If the contractor is honest, you can benefit because the contractor won't have to pad a fixed price to account for unexpected problems.

Appliance repairers and phone installers commonly levy a job charge for the first hour or fraction thereof, and charge a lower rate for subsequent periods. If they cannot finish the job on the first visit, you should not have to pay a second job charge. Many building repairers charge a minimum rate for the first hour, and some charge from the moment they leave their shop.

Larger repairs and remodeling projects should be preceded by some negotiation over price. Amateurs—and some builders—talk about "estimates," "bids," and "contract prices" as if they're the same thing. Before we clarify what they mean, remember that local terminology can differ—be sure you understand what the terms mean in your case.

➤ An *estimate* is a rough guess as to what the job will cost. It may have little relation to actual cost, depending on your choice of materials, what the builder finds when the project begins, and how often you change your mind.

➤ A *bid* is a closer approximation of the cost, after you have selected materials and narrowed your options. It may still be lower than the final price, depending on your changes, the project's surprises, and the contractor's honesty and skill.

➤ A *contract price* is a binding agreement between you and the contractor. It should specify all tasks and materials, the job schedule, the payment schedule, and what will happen when the predictable surprises arise.

Is the Lowest Price the Best Price?

So you followed instructions (see the previous section, "Contacting Contractors") and got three prices. Will you automatically accept the lowest price? After all, isn't that the point of getting three bids? Not exactly. The bidding process is also a chance for you to size up the bidders. Ask questions. Call references and look at previous jobs, if you're unsure who would do the best work.

Now that the contractors are no longer just voices on the phone, are you confident that the lowest bidder will do a good job? Does this person have the best grasp of what's involved? Did the price include all the costs listed in the other prices? Does it specify the same quality materials and brands?

If so, you've saved money and aggravation, and you can start finalizing a contract with the low-price contractor. But if you have a queasy feeling at this point, take a closer look at the other bidders. Do whatever it takes to convince yourself that you've chosen the cream of the crop. Remember, when the job is finished, you don't want to feel like taking out a contract on your contractor.

The Contract

Building contracts are largely boilerplate—standard text written by lawyers who work for contractors. Because contracts are written from the builder's perspective, you may want to seek legal advice before signing a contract for an expensive or complex project. Even if you don't hire a lawyer, remember that you can discuss problematic areas of the contract and attempt to change them to suit your needs.

These contracts typically contain six sections: names and addresses of both parties; the scope of the project; the completion date; the payment schedule; a signature and date; and general conditions of the work. Although most of the contract is self-explanatory, let's take a look at a couple of sections.

The completion date may not be as early as you'd prefer, particularly when the building business is booming. Even if you don't want to wait several months for completion, you may have to wait a while. Maybe that's not so terrible—would you rather have a contractor who's in demand, or one who can't keep busy?

In the payment schedule, it's best to reserve at least 20 percent—and preferably much more—for a final payment that is due when you are satisfied. If the final payment is too small, it will not give you enough leverage to ensure that the finishing touches are completed. Keep in mind your hidden costs of delay, including interest costs or the price of take-out pizza while a kitchen is being remodeled. You might also consider setting a deadline for completion, with specified penalties for non-performance.

Probably the most important section of the contract is its description of the project. This section should specify exactly what will be done, in terms you can understand (or that the contractor can explain). It's not enough to say, "Replace the roof with new shingles." Instead, the contract should detail the steps:

> "Remove shingles down to bare wood. Replace tar paper and re-roof in 240-lb. per square 'mortuary black' fiberglass shingles made by Tar Pit Shingle Conglomerate. Install new edging and valley flashing. Inspect all flashing. Remove and reinstall existing gutters. Remove trash when done. Any replacement of rotten boards, and flashing (aside from valley flashing), will be done at extra charge of $_____ per hour."

The conditions section typically specifies that the work will be done "in a workmanlike manner." While this may sound as concrete as a jellyfish, a court can interpret this phrase simply by asking somebody in the same trade if the work is acceptable. Finally, contracts can specify that disputes be settled by mediation or arbitration (legal negotiation processes that help avoid a lawsuit), which may save time and money over going to court.

Time to Autograph the Check

After a job is completed, and before you write a check, make a detailed inspection with the contractor. If anything is puzzling, now's the time to ask about it. If anything is unsatisfactory, now's the time to complain about it. Write up a "punch list" detailing the changes you expect before paying the bill. The ground rule is this: Don't pay until you're satisfied. For jobs that take some time to set, such as masonry or painting, don't pay until it's really done.

If your job is big enough to require a building permit, don't pay until the inspector signs off that the job meets code standards. The building code is a minimum standard, and a job that's only medium-quality will still pass the code. Furthermore, while there's no guarantee that the inspector will notice every flaw, he or she does provide an expert, outside evaluation of the work, which is not something you can afford to ignore. Finally, builders tend to listen to building inspectors, who can make their lives miserable by nit-picking in future inspections.

A Word on How Contractors Really Work

Now that you've signed a contract, you sit back and wait for the crew to arrive. And, sometimes, you wait. Even after the work gets started, you may find strange absences— say, at the opening of trout fishing season, or for no discernible reason. The job is poised for completion, and nobody shows up.

The explanation for this pattern may damage your self-image as the most important customer in the world. The fact is, the builder must start looking for new jobs—visiting prospects, making bids, and drawing up plans—before your project is completed. There's no other way to stay in business.

It's entirely possible that your contractor is working several jobs at once because the competition will not take over a half-finished job. Is that kosher? I guess it depends on your perspective, but it's a fact of life in the building business, and one you should be prepared for.

Scams

Trust me: No single book could possibly vaccinate you against the human capacity for concocting convincing scams—or the human eagerness to fall for them. The old rule is still the most reliable: If something seems too good to be true, it probably is. Trust your instincts.

Be ready to recognize these standard symptoms of home repair hustlers:

➤ They pressure you to sign right now, and they want large amounts of money up front.

➤ They cruise the neighborhood, looking for immediate work "to use up the supplies from my last job."

➤ They are reluctant to give references.

➤ They have a quick answer for everything.

➤ Their explanations raise more questions than they answer.

Many states allow you to renege on door-to-door contracts (including those for repairs) for a few days after signing. If you have that queasy feeling that you've fallen for a fast-buck artist, take advantage of this cooling-off period.

The Least You Need to Know

➤ You should be able to understand your repairer's explanations. If not, trouble may be on the way.

➤ If you recognize that builders must think about other jobs, you'll be in a better position to work together.

➤ Trust your instincts when it comes to building scams—if an offer seems too good to be true, it probably is.

Part 2

Safety, Tools, and Materials: The Building Blocks of Success

Home repair is like hockey: It's a sport that requires equipment. (I hope you didn't expect to get away without buying, begging, or borrowing some tools.) But because my object is to help you get on with your life, not to make your wallet feel like it got zapped by a hockey puck, I'll emphasize versatility, improvisation, and economy rather than buying tools just for the sake of having them.

That said, however, there's still an argument for buying special tools on occasion: they can pay for themselves in just one use. When you ponder the universal tool problem—where can I get my hands on the right ones without bankrupting my family?—don't forget that a friendly neighbor may own just what you need.

Materials are the other thing you'll be buying, so I'll talk about nails, screws, other hardware, and wood, the organic heart of most housing. And because your body is your most important tool, I'll start with safety.

Q: What's worse than an accident?

A: An accident that could have been prevented by following safety practices.

Accidents, it turns out, are almost all avoidable—if you use common sense and don't set yourself up by acting stupid.

Chapter 6

Health, Safety, and Common Sense

In This Chapter

➤ Danger spots—and how to avoid them

➤ Most accidents are stupid accidents

➤ Good preparation will protect your home from your project

➤ Keeping away from nasty chemicals

Safety is everywhere these days. Those warning labels on automatic doors make them sound as dangerous as a guillotine. According to some paranoids, frying an egg would expose you to shock hazards from the electric stove, burning hazards from the pan, intestinal hazards from egg-borne bugs, and arteriosclerotic hazards from butter-borne fat. And that's not to mention the danger of slipping on the way to the table or goring yourself with the fork or biting your tongue while eating ....

That's not my attitude. I'll stress the major safety hazards—the areas you really need to watch. And I'll talk about some attitude problems—primarily the stupidity factor—and work practices that grease the skids for accidents. I'll talk about health hazards you might encounter in your home-repair battles, and I'll discuss a limited but highly effective safety kit that should protect you from most of the hazards. Finally, I'll talk about safe use of ladders, which account for the lion's share of home-repair accidents.

The Stupidity Factor

A few years ago, while trying to rig up a hoist to lift my canoe, I confidently leaned my 14-foot ladder against the black locust tree along the driveway and climbed up. Having written a book for painters, I knew I wasn't supposed to do this, but I did it anyway. When I reached the top, the ladder suddenly flipped, and both it and I squashed some shrubbery.

Dazed but fortunately intact, I realized with embarrassment that I had learned a simple lesson: Don't do stupid stuff. If you really must lean a ladder against a tree, find a football lineman to anchor the ladder. Or buy those straps made to secure ladders to trees. Best of all, forget the whole idea. Trees are round, and ladders are made to lean against flat stuff.

And the canoe hoist? It didn't work any better than my ladder technique. Serves me right.

Because the stupidity factor is behind so many accidents, I offer some suggestions for working safely and controlling the universal human urge to act like a complete bozo:

➤ Don't work when you are exhausted, distracted, or angry. Any of these conditions can cause you to rush, ignore hazards, or just plain act half-witted.

➤ Keep the place neat. Coil electric cords so you don't trip on them; stack lumber neatly so it's not strewn all over the place; don't leave boards with nails sticking up, ready to impale you; and store and use sharp tools with caution so they cut only what they're supposed to.

➤ Don't try to do things without first understanding what needs to be done and how to do it.

➤ Get help with big tasks: holding something while you fasten it into place, hauling heavy objects, or anchoring ladders that may be unstable.

➤ Work with adequate lighting so that you can spot and avoid hazards.

➤ Use appropriate health and safety equipment.

For suggestions on electrical safety, see Chapter 27, "Breaker, Breaker on the Wall: Electric Fundamentals," and Chapter 28, "Getting Wired Without Getting Zapped."

The Best Protection Is Self-Protection

Do you adore arsenic or crave chromium? Well, neither does wood fungus, a lower life form that gobbles up wood posts, decks, and almost any wood that is constantly wet. That's why pressure-treated lumber often contains the toxic chemical CCA (chromated copper arsenate). If you don't protect yourself while sawing or sanding treated lumber, you'll breathe a good dose of arsenic and chromium (yum, yum!).

CCA is one of many ways in which repair work can expose you to dust, grit, and toxic chemicals. But because you are not facing a day-after-day, industrial exposure, it's usually pretty easy to shield yourself with prevention, common sense, and protection.

To prevent toxic exposure, use products that contain no toxic materials. For example, if you use latex or other water-based coatings, you will not need protection against the nasty ingredients in solvent-based paints (but check the label to be sure—some still contain toxic solvents). If I were building a new deck, I'd buy the new pressure-treated lumber that contains no CCA, which would reduce, if not entirely eliminate, the toxic exposure.

Nail It Down

If you're concerned about the toxicity of materials you are using, ask the store or manufacturer to supply a Material Safety Data Sheet (MSDS), which must, by law, be available to users of the product.

Another way to prevent exposure is to let George do it. Instead of using a toxic paint stripper, take furniture to a commercial stripper (who strips finishes in tanks). That way, you can forget about protecting yourself against the toxic crud found in most paint strippers.

Common sense tells you to read the label and follow exposure precautions. Use toxic chemicals outside, or at least with the windows open. Common sense also says that because things will go wrong, you should anticipate as many problems as you can and take steps to minimize their impact.

After you have exercised prevention and common sense, you'll want to keep some protective measures available (see the following illustration of health and safety equipment you should consider).

Health and safety equipment.

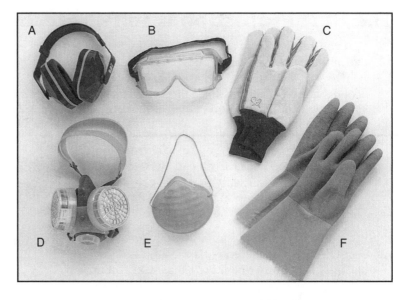

A. Ear protectors (the kind worn by people who guide jets on airport runways) will dampen the shriek of a circular saw or router. Use them if you like your hearing, or if you are working indoors, where echoes amplify the noise. You also can use ear plugs, which are cheaper and equally effective.

B. Goggles are helpful for nailing, hammering, sawing, demolishing, drilling, sanding, or any other home-repair sport that makes dust, chips, or other flying crud. These are *great* for working overhead.

C. A pair of leather work gloves is useful for handling rough lumber, working with concrete, and wrecking stuff.

D. A snugly fitting respirator will protect you against various organic solvents and dusts (buy the cartridge according to the specific hazard you face).

E. A dust mask—even this cheapo pollen mask—is used while sanding, wrecking, sawing, and sweeping.

F. Rubber or neoprene gloves are excellent for painting, working with paint stripper, and performing other toxic tasks. Remember that many solvents can pass right through your skin.

Another good safety item is a pair of stiff work boots. For real abuse, steel-toed boots have a steel liner to protect your toes from dropped tools.

Nervous About Leaded Paint?

If your home is at least 20 years old, chances are good that it contains some paint containing lead. (Lead, a good pigment, was used in many types of paint, particularly for trim, enamel, and exteriors.) Lead is toxic to the adult nervous system and is much more harmful to children, who can be injured by tiny exposures. To find out if lead is in various painted surfaces in your home, you can take samples to a public health or toxicology laboratory.

You can get leaded paint professionally removed, if you have the money (but check local regulations on lead removal first). A better option may be to keep the paint in good condition and to use caution any time you might raise dust, such as by sawing or sanding.

Basic Steps to Ladder Safety

So that leaking thing-a-ma-jubber up near the eaves has put you in the mood for some second-story work? So your roof needs an inspection (and, you pray, nothing more)? What should you do? You burrow into the garage, bring out that old wooden ladder, bet your life that some kind of rot hasn't eaten its way through anything important, like a rung, and then slap it against the wall and start climbing.

Wrong.

You look at the job, clear away any obstacles, and then go into your storage area and look over your ladders. You pick out the right one, inspect it for damage, and bring it to the job. You look overhead for electrical wires, and you safely raise the ladder. Then you check that the ladder is soundly erected. Finally, you begin climbing.

Remember: One fall from a ladder is one too many. From the endless menu of ladder safety rules, these seem most important:

1. Inspect the ladder before using it, to make sure it hasn't deteriorated since its last use.

2. Make sure the footing under the ladder is solid so that the ladder cannot slip away from the wall.

3. The feet of the ladder should be one-fourth of the height away from the wall. This gives the best stability, the best combination of staying upright without tipping over backward or slipping out from under you.

4. Check that your shoes are dry so that you don't slip on the rungs.

5. When climbing, hold your hands on the rails (the long side beams), not the rungs. Then, if you start to fall, your hands will always be in position to grip the ladder.

6. Don't climb above the third rung from the top; you will be unstable and likely to fall.

7. Don't carry more than one hand's worth of stuff, or you won't be able to grasp the ladder securely. If you need more tools or materials, get a nail apron, use bigger pockets, make another trip, or rig up a rope hoist.

8. As my father used to tell me, "One hand for yourself, and one for your work." In other words, hold on with one hand. If you absolutely must work with both hands, slip one arm through the rungs to hold yourself in case of a slip.

9. Keep your center of gravity inside the rails so that you don't tip the ladder sideways. Don't lean too far back so that you don't tip over backward.

10. Take the time to move the ladder so that you can reach the work easily. Leaning sideways is asking for a fall.

Ladders are an excellent place for neighbors to pool resources because ladders are used rarely. Or, you might discuss a barter with a neighbor who's long on ladders.

In some cases, the ladder you need won't be a ladder at all, but a rented scaffold. Scaffolding is particularly handy for large siding repairs, big tuckpointing (brick-joint repair) jobs, painting, and window replacement. When renting a scaffold, remember to ask about renting planks (the boards you walk on). They cost extra, but they are worth it. Why bother renting a real scaffold and then standing on those old 2-by-10s you've stored behind the compost heap? (Hint: Consider renting aluminum planks, which are lighter and easier to handle than wooden planks.)

A Ladder Made in Heaven

Ladders come in four basic flavors: stepladders, straight ladders, extension ladders, and folding ladders. In all cases, because ladders lean in use, they will not take you quite as high as their length. For example, a 16-foot ladder will touch a wall at about 15 feet above the ground. And because you will be standing three rungs below the top, your highest reach will be slightly over 15 feet. Remember, when you put a ladder up to an eave (the bottom edge of a roof), it should extend about 3 feet above the eave to give you handholds for climbing on the roof.

➤ Stepladders can range in height from about 3 feet—which is ultra-handy for repairing and painting rooms—all the way to the 10-foot monster I share with some friends for replacing light bulbs on cathedral ceilings.

➤ The straight ladder has a self-explanatory name for an inexpensive ladder that's not very versatile.

➤ An extension ladder has two straight sections joined together, giving excellent adjustability in height. Because the sections must overlap when extended, an extension ladder made of two 10-foot pieces extends only to about 16 feet. You can use an extension ladder at its shortest setting—half the advertised length. Some extension ladders may be disassembled so that you can use the lower section as a straight ladder. (Don't use the upper section as a straight ladder because one rung is missing to allow for the extension mechanism.)

Don't Screw Up!

Always check for electric lines above and near the repair before erecting a ladder. Touching an electric wire with an aluminum or wood ladder could ruin your whole week.

➤ A folding ladder can be used as a straight ladder, a stepladder, or a small scaffold. Folding ladders are convenient but expensive; you can buy an extension ladder and a stepladder for the same price.

In fact, my advice to the average homeowner is just that: Get a stepladder and a short extension ladder. (Depending on your house, 16 feet to 28 feet should be long enough. Longer ladders are expensive, awkward to handle, and hard to store.) Fiberglass ladders are the safest because they don't conduct electricity, but they are expensive. I would buy aluminum—it's cheap, light, and strong, and although it does conduct electricity, you won't be using your ladder near power lines, *right*?

Raising a Ladder

To raise a stepladder, simply stand it up, straighten the dividers between the sections, and position it so that you can reach your work safely. Check the footing by rocking the ladder slightly—all four legs should be on the ground. Then climb, staying two steps below the top, and observe the usual don't-lean-too-far rules. A folded-up stepladder can be quite stable leaning against a wall; that's handy for cleaning or repairing ground-floor windows.

Straight or Extension Ladder

I've seen too many people trying to wrestle long ladders into position with a technique that ignores the laws of physics. Let's look at an easier and safer technique for raising a ladder.

Nail It Down

If you really must work near electric lines, ask your electric utility to install rubber insulating sheaths over the wires. Utilities hate to have customers electrocuted (who's going to pay the bill?), so they may offer the same service to you that they do to professional builders.

1. Place the base of your ladder against something solid, such as your house, the base of a tree, or the foot of a willing slave. (Direct the slave to push *down* on the bottom rung with the foot.)

2. Lift the top of the ladder, and stand underneath it. Walk toward the base, lifting the ladder one rung at a time (see the following illustrations for raising a straight or extension ladder).

3. When the ladder is vertical and near the building, move its bottom into position. Gently lean it against the building.

4. Now check your work. Is the base about one-fourth of the ladder's height from the building? Are both feet solidly planted? Are both rails firmly against the building? Give the ladder a slight shake: If it gyrates, something needs fixing. Don't climb until two ends are solidly against the ground and two are against the building.

5. Lower the ladder by reversing this procedure.

Somebody's foot can serve if a house is not available.

Ladders are easy to move once they are vertical—as long as you keep them near a building and watch for power lines.

Nail It Down

Aluminum siding is easy to dent and scrape. To prevent damaging it with a ladder, pull old gloves over the rail tops.

Once an extension ladder is standing, you may be able to adjust its height with its miserable and barely workable rope-and-pulley system. Because the rope is much better for lowering the extension than for raising it, I prefer to extend the ladder a bit more than necessary before I raise the ladder. Then, once the ladder is leaning against the wall, I can easily lower it into position.

Protecting the House While You Work

When I was in the masonry business, I literally measured my progress by how fast our crew messed up somebody's premises. Only when we had a dismaying array of tools, scaffolds, ladders, and materials strewn about the yard could we really go to work. The fact is, messes are part of home repair, so it pays to ignore the natural inclination to throw up your hands and delay protecting the premises until you get halfway through the repair.

To a pro, failure to protect the premises is a sure-fire antidote to the problem of having too many customers. To an amateur, this failure could mean—well, let's just call it familial strife. Yet even with long experience at this game, I still underestimate the need to protect the premises before I start. (By the way, it's much smarter to do this work beforehand. Once the house is clouded with drywall dust, what's the point of hanging tarps?)

In general, plastic tarps, used carpet (often found on the curb), duct tape, and plywood are the key resources for protecting the house. Most of this is just common sense. If you're walking outside a lot to get tools or materials, think about laying out a plastic or carpet walkway from the door to the work area to absorb dirt and grit. Some types of work are predictably nasty, so here are some standard suggestions for containing the mess:

Job Type	Protection Suggestions
Dusty jobs: Repairing drywall, plaster, tile, or masonry, or sanding. Any job using a power sander, grinder, or wire brush.	To prevent dust from escaping the scene of the crime, cover doorways and heat ducts with plastic. Your best friend is thick, 4-mil plastic. Don't skimp and buy those 1-mil dry-cleaner bags posing as "plastic dropcloths"—they are fragile and hard to tape down. You can reuse heavier plastic several times, so it ends up being cheap. Secure the plastic with 2-inch masking tape. For covering doorways, use duct tape: It's much more secure.
Filthy jobs: Plumbing, masonry, and painting.	Use plastic or cloth dropcloths in the work area. Keep your hands clean to avoid spreading dirt, particularly with plumbing. Keep a broom and dustpan around, and sweep occasionally to contain the filth. For more on painting, see the section "Preparing for an Inside Job" in Chapter 26, "Lay It on—but Not Too Thick."
Dangerous to floor: Carpentry, masonry, and plumbing.	Protect floor with old carpet or scrap plywood.

The Least You Need to Know

➤ A small kit of safety equipment will take you safely through virtually every procedure in this book.

➤ The stupidity factor is probably the biggest cause of accidents. It causes you to do idiotic things you would never do, idiotic things you didn't consider doing, and idiotic things you're embarrassed to admit you actually did.

➤ The best antidote to the stupidity factor is to think ahead and work systematically.

➤ Working safely on a ladder is a great way to improve your odds of surviving a home repair.

➤ For improved domestic sanity, protect your home from your project.

➤ If safety is boring, keep your life boring.

Chapter 7

The Bare Essentials: Hand Tools

In This Chapter

➤ The fundamental hand tools for home repair

➤ Seven versatile tools—your secret weapons for fast, smooth home repairs

➤ Money-saving strategies for buying and using tools

If the use of hand tools distinguishes human beings from other primates, then some humans are more distinct than others. I'm trying, as delicately as I know how, to say that some people fear tools. My wife, Meg Wise, was once one of them; she probably thought "vise grips" was slang for a police squad targeting gambling and prostitution. Yet her story shows there's hope for tool-phobes: Early in our courtship, as she helped me nail some flooring, I whined at her, "Bend your wrist!" With a wicked backhand, she flung the hammer across the room and told me where to get off.

Several years later, while wrestling with a pipe fitting, I gave her an arc-joint plier to hold the pipe, and after a brief struggle, she demanded a locking plier (AKA "vise grip"), which, I shamefacedly admitted, was ideal for the job.

If Meg can overcome her fear of tools, so can you. One of the best ways to do this is to actually get some tools and learn to use them. And while I have what some people would consider a surplus of tools (I think I'm just scraping by), I've tried in this chapter to imagine starting with an empty toolkit. Which would be the most important and versatile tools, the ones I would buy first? How would I save money on those tools? Could I devise a way to convert normal holidays into occasions for receiving tools?

The Basic Tools

You can build up a basic toolkit over the years as you take on new projects. Chances are, it will contain many of the tools in the following illustrations (basic pliers, wrenches, and screwdrivers; drilling, cutting, measuring, and construction tools). In the appropriate chapters, we'll cover specialty tools for repairing roofing, masonry, drywall and plaster, wallpaper, painting, electrical work, and plumbing. See Chapter 10, "A Workable Workshop," for suggestions on tools for your basic toolbag or toolbox.

Basic pliers and wrenches for home repair.

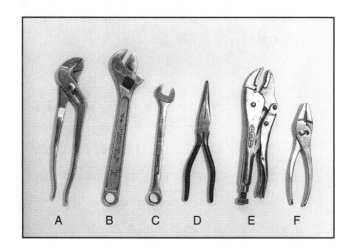

A. The grip of an arc-joint (or groove joint; also known by the brand name Channel Lock) plier expands to 1¹/₂ inch and up. It's useful for plumbing and mechanical work.

B. An adjustable (crescent) wrench turns hexagonal and square nuts and bolts. The 12-inch size is best for all-around use.

C. A combination wrench has an open end and a box end; it holds nuts and bolts better than an adjustable wrench. You're better off buying a set. For the strongest grip, use the box end, which is less likely to slip off a nut or bolt.

D. Long-nose (needle-nose) pliers are useful for almost everything; in electrical work, they are great for looping wire to connect to a screw terminal.

E. Locking pliers are often called by the brand name Vise Grip. They can be used for turning nuts (admittedly with some scarring), grabbing other tools, and pulling nails. They also make an emergency vise, clamp, and handle. Get a 10-inch model for general use.

F. A slip-joint plier holds small stuff, such as a screwdriver or chisel.

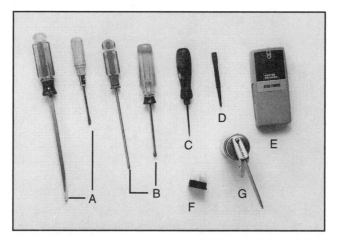

Screwdrivers and so on.

A. You'll need at least two or three slotted screwdrivers for innumerable tasks. Save money and buy an assortment.

B. A couple of sizes of Phillips screwdrivers are essential, but you'll probably use a power screwdriver or a variable-speed drill for driving most Phillips screws.

C. An awl marks wood and metal. It can punch holes for starting small wood screws or prevent a drill bit from wandering as it starts.

D. A nail set is used to punch finishing nails below the surface, preventing hammer dents in wood. I'd start with an all-purpose $3/32$-inch model.

E. An electronic stud finder helps you find support for a shelf, picture, or bracket. They're a bit tricky to use, and I never assume they are correct (see Chapter 22, "Cosmetology 101: Drywall and Plaster Repair," for more ways to find a stud).

F. A magnetic stud finder works more slowly, but it's cheaper. When the magnet nears a nail, it shifts position to let you know that you've found the stud.

G. An oil can is used to lubricate tools, hinges, or almost any squeaky metal. (Penetrating oil, such as WD-40, is good for loosening rusted parts, but to prevent further rust, you need a heavier, less-volatile motor oil such as SAE 10 or SAE 10W30.)

Drilling, cutting, and measuring tools.

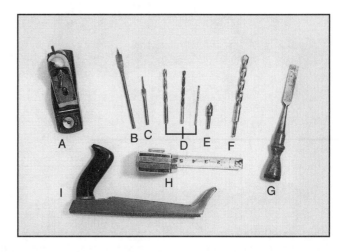

A. A plane is used for general wood removal, such as smoothing the edges of doors, windows, and drawers. A block plane works on the end grain found on door bottoms. Planes are great for removing saw marks after rip sawing. Hint: Start with a shallow cut, and increase the depth if the plane cuts smoothly. Hold the plane at a slight angle to the direction of travel to help it cut smoothly.

B. Spade drill bits come in various sizes. Usually sold in sets, they are used for drilling large holes in wood. Caution: If you hit a nail, the bit will be wrecked.

C. A contoured bit matches the taper on wood screws and countersinks the head in one operation. Sold in sets, they greatly simplify the chore of hand-driving old-fashioned tapered wood screws.

Nail It Down

To quickly bring most of what you need to the site of a repair, store your essential tools in one bag. I let screws and nails accumulate in the bottom of my toolbag, and there's still room for special tools and hardware: the screws and brackets for installing a bookshelf, or the shims and drill for shoring up the basement stairs.

D. Combination wood or metal drill bits make holes for rivets, sheet-metal screws, and bolts. Use them to drill wood if you're likely to hit nails or screws. At the very least, buy a kit ranging in size from $1/16$-inch to $1/4$-inch, and plan to buy the $3/8$-inch and $1/2$-inch sizes soon.

E. A countersink removes wood so that a flat-head screw can rest flush with the surface.

F. Masonry drill bits are sold in various sizes for drilling into masonry or concrete. Buy only the size you need, as each anchor requires a specific size.

G. A wood chisel ($1/2$- to 1-inch wide) removes wood to make mortises (cutouts) for locks and hinges, and other purposes. Don't bother buying the most expensive one—medium quality is fine. I've owned this wood-handled beauty for 40 years!

H. A tape measure, sized from 8 feet to 25 feet, is essential for almost any repair job. A 12-foot or 16-foot model is a good compromise length—small and affordable, but large enough to lay out carpet or bookshelves. A locking button holds the tape in position while you make a measurement.

I. A Surform brand wood rasp will remove wood across or with the grain. It leaves a rough finish but is good for fitting doors, windows, and drawers, particularly on end grain. Use a plane to smooth the surface afterward. The flat-bladed variety is great for trimming drywall.

The Role of Price

How much *can* you spend for tools? Ferrari prices, particularly if you're looking in a specialty woodworker's catalog. But how much *should* you pay for tools? Probably more like Chevy truck prices. Remember, a good tool may make your job easier—and it *will* last longer—but don't let anybody convince you that it will make you a lot more skilled than a decent tool.

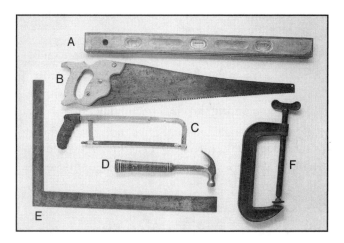

Construction tools for home repair.

A. A 16- to 24-inch level helps in marking electrical box openings, installing appliances and shelving, and repairing doors. Or, substitute a 9-inch torpedo level, shown in the "seven cool tools" photo.

B. A rip saw is useful for fast cutting with the grain and for rough cutting across the grain.

C. A hacksaw cuts steel, copper, aluminum, or plastic. Eighteen teeth per inch is a good blade for general purposes; buy a blade with coarser teeth for thick metal (¼-inch and up). To eliminate vibration and speed the work, place the cut no more than ¼ inch from a vise, locking pliers, or C-clamp.

D. A 16-ounce claw hammer is an all-around tool for hammering and pulling nails. (Polish the hammer face with sandpaper or an emery cloth to grip nails better.) Framing hammers are excellent for pounding big nails; these extra-long, 24-ounce whammers may have a waffle pattern to grab the nail. But that pattern makes a mess if it hits the wood—don't use them for finish work!

E. A carpenter's square is used to measure and mark straight or square (90°) lines. It's helpful for layout work, picture framing, and door straightening. Often the aluminum square shown in the figure of seven cool tools is handier.

F. A C-clamp is one of the handiest tools you can own. It will clamp wood for gluing, make a substitute vise, and hold two pieces of wood together as you nail them tight.

Nuts and Bolts

Rip sawing is cutting with (or parallel to) the grain, and **crosscutting** is cutting across the grain. **Rip saws** have coarser teeth than **crosscut saws**, but either will work for occasional work. If I had to choose one hand saw for all-around rough sawing, I'd choose a rip saw. Why? It cuts faster.

That said, I must add that many cheapo imported tools have nothing going for them except a bargain-basement price. The screwdrivers twist, the drills break, the files dull, and the saws don't even start out sharp—this kind of economy can get expensive after a while! The best bet is to buy a good grade of tool from an established manufacturer (meaning one you've heard of).

Suggestions for saving money on tools without buying garbage are listed here:

➤ Hunt around at rummage and estate sales.

➤ Make a detailed list for friends and family, just in case they want to know what you want for an upcoming birthday or holiday.

➤ Buy tools in sets, which sell for about half the total price of the individual tools. Although a set may have more variety than you need right now, eventually—when you lose some tools—you'll thank yourself for having bought the set.

Marking from a Tape—Accurately

Accuracy is something that distinguishes real builders from the rest of us. Have you ever marked from a tape measure and made a line that wandered off toward, say, Nebraska, and then forgotten which part of the line was accurate? Then you'll have to check out the figure that follows. Notice that the mark is darkest and most accurate where it starts, near the tape. If you mark this way, just use the dark part of the mark as your measurement. (Some carpenters make a V-shaped mark, placing the angle of the V exactly at the measurement.)

Marking from a tape.

Place the pencil next to the dimension on the rule, then quickly pull it away as you ease up on the pressure. Even if your mark runs crooked, the dark part will be accurate.

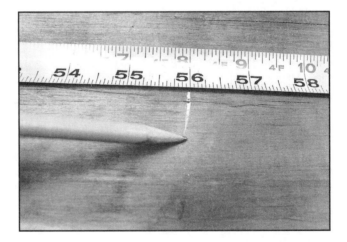

Seven Cool Tools You Must Meet

Every handy person has a set of favorite tools: the overlooked, under-appreciated gems in the toolbox. I've put mine on the table in this illustration of seven cool tools.

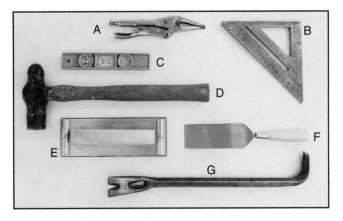

Seven cool tools.

A. A *needle-nose locking plier* is versatile enough to replace three tools: wire cutters, plier, and needle-nose pliers. Unfortunately, it's weaker than a regular locking plier for big-time gripping jobs.

B. An aluminum or plastic square (sold under the brand *Speed Square*) guides a circular saw for a perfect a 90° cut. You can even slide the saw along the square to trim 1/8-inch from a board (a job that could befuddle a pro). It's also handy for marking square lines and angles and for making small measurements (see the section "Cutting Remarks on Slick Sawing Technique" in Chapter 11, "Wood: Still Champ After All These Years").

C. A *torpedo level* substitutes for those clumsy wood or aluminum models for quick leveling of electric boxes, shelves, pictures, and cabinets. Light and compact, it will make a believer of you. With a level, there's no need to stand back and eye that marvelous Elton John poster. If it's level, it will *look* level—unless your house is seriously out of whack.

D. A *3-pound hammer* is the primordial blunt object. Use it to clean masonry before repairs, to drive posts in the garden, to pound stakes for concrete forms, and for big-league metal chiseling.

E. A *sanding block* looks so dumb that many people (including your author) have been tempted to use a hunk of scrap wood instead. But the block has a big advantage: It grabs the sandpaper. The result? Less sandpaper wastage, less work expended, and a smoother surface. Just about any sanding block will deal with wood. Buy the open-framed variety for drywall sanding, and use the drywall sanding screens, which, unlike sandpaper, don't get clogged with drywall dust.

F. A *margin trowel* is designed to patch masonry, but it's also perfect for working with drywall and plaster. Use it to scrape paint, glaze windows, and ease things apart. It's particularly good for removing molding, or you can slip it beneath the head of a claw hammer to protect the wood while you pull nails.

G. This *wrecking bar* disassembles stuff much more neatly than others because the flat tongue slips under things. Note: Avoid flat steel bars, which have so much spring that they jump back at you when you hammer them. This bar has a rigid hexagonal cross-section. To lift furniture, place a scrap of wood under the fulcrum, slide the tongue under the furniture, and step on the end. Then insert a scrap of carpet—pile side down—under each leg, and slide the furniture across the floor. Bye-bye, lumbago.

The Least You Need to Know

➤ Many tools are far more versatile than most people realize, giving you one more reason to buy them.

➤ Your most frequently used tools should be your best-quality tools.

➤ Save time and frustration by keeping your basic tools in one place, ready to go to work.

Chapter 8

The Bare Essentials with Oomph! Power Tools

In This Chapter

➤ Drills, saws, and sanders—the first members of your electric toolkit

➤ Tips for using power tools safely and effectively

➤ Rentals—the key to part-time (tool) love affairs

If you were so inclined, you could squander a bundle on power tools before you even started a repair. Creative designers seem to invent a new electric- or gasoline-powered "labor-saving device" about every week or so. But because our goal is to minimize the time and financial cost of owning a home, and to give you a little satisfaction in the process, I'll take a different tack. I'll be concentrating on the tools you'll really need and helping you plan a way to rationally accumulate power tools without breaking the bank.

As we talk about each basic electric tool for home repair, I'll discuss whether you really need it, suggest the size most suitable for home repairs, and offer tips for use. I'll also talk about how much quality you need and whether you should buy a cordless model.

Cord or Cordless?

An increasing number of power tools are sold in cordless models, which is a polite way of saying you'll have to mess with batteries instead of electric cords. I used to think battery-operated tools were toys, until I bought a cordless 3/8-inch reversible drill, and it quickly became my mainstay for screwdriving and light drilling. Then the batteries burned out, and I returned to my old standby, a drill with a cord. I think I'd be even less enthusiastic about a cordless circular saw; I can't imagine that its batteries would last very long.

Contractors, for whom time is money, swear by battery-operated tools. The key advantage of cordless tools, shockingly enough, is that you won't have to bother with a cord or an extension cord. That translates into less to shlep, less to trip on, and one more outlet available for another tool or a light.

Don't Screw Up!

"Contractor quality" means almost nothing—except a guaranteed high price. Homeowners should not waste money buying tools designed for day-in, day-out work. Consult *Consumer Reports* or another rating service for advice on tool quality for the service you expect.

But cordless tools have a couple of disadvantages: First, they run out of power. It may be breathtakingly obvious to point out that this tends to happen while you're using the tool, not when it's on the shelf, but it's true. Then you'll have to wait for a recharge or you'll have to borrow a tool. Tools with replaceable batteries avoid this problem, but the extra expense might take us beyond idiot territory.

Cordless tools are not for sustained use (unless you have those replaceable batteries). I would not consider a cordless drill to screw up a roomful of drywall unless I had a bunch of spare batteries. But if you're interested in driving a few screws for a new bookshelf, or drilling a few holes to fix flashing on the roof, that's exactly what cordless drills are designed for.

Variable-Speed, Reversing Drill (Doubles as Power Screwdriver)

The drill has always been the first power tool to buy, simply for drilling holes in wood and metal and for wire-brushing paint and rust. A variable-speed, reversible drill (see the figure that follows) will drive screws. A giant improvement that has come along in recent years is the keyless chuck. They are quick and handy, and you'll never lose another chuck key. Why, oh why, did it take so long to invent this brilliant timesaver?

Nuts and Bolts

A **keyless chuck** is tightened by hand instead of a key. The **shank** is the part of the drill that the chuck grips.

Electric drills are sized by the maximum opening of the chuck (the rotating clamp that holds the bit). Power, weight, and price all increase along with chuck size. The common sizes are $1/4$-inch, $3/8$-inch, and $1/2$-inch; for home use, I'd buy a $3/8$-inch model first. If you need to drill a hole larger than the chuck diameter, buy a bit with a reduced-diameter shank.

Can You Get by Without This Tool?

No. If I had no power tools, a variable-speed, reversible ³/₈-inch drill would be my first buy. You can use a hand drill for a few small holes in wood, or a brace and bit (which is expensive) for larger holes. But you need a power drill to drill metal, or to drill many holes, or to do wire-brushing. And to drive all those incredibly handy screws, you'll need a variable-speed, reversing drill.

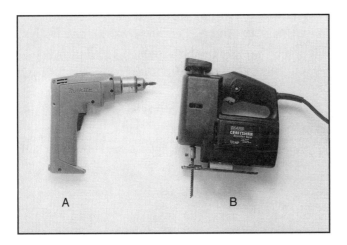

Electric drill and saber saw.

A. The ³/₈-inch variable-speed, reversing drill is the all-around hero of home repair, used for drilling, screwing, polishing, and rust removal. Get a cordless model for occasional use and a plug-in type for sustained use.

B. A saber saw makes curvy cuts a breeze. It even cuts a straight line once in a while.

The Power of Screwdriving

Screws have revolutionized the home-repair business. They work in places too tight to swing a hammer, and they're easy to remove if you (like me) assemble something backwards. Unlike nails, screws won't crack plaster or drywall. Strong and non-violent, they would resemble a great son-in-law if it weren't for the fact that they are so easy to drive home ….

The power-driven screws craze began with drywall screws, but when carpenters began using these handy items for securing framing and hardware as well as for repairing wood and fastening trim, manufacturers responded with an expanded line of specialty screws. For a description of what's available, see the section "Screwing Up Again?" in Chapter 9, "Fast Guide to Fasteners."

You can buy a power screwdriver to drive screws, but a variable-speed, reversible drill is much more powerful. For fast action, get one of the quick-change devices shown in the following figure. They allow you to drill pilot holes and drive screws without loosening your drill chuck.

Almost all power-screwdriver bits have a ¹/₄-inch hexagonal shank, making a driver assembly able to accommodate most of your screwdriver bits. If there's plenty of room around the screw, you can put most bits directly in the drill chuck. For fastening hardware, a bit extender is generally necessary.

These are my suggestions for using a drill as a power screwdriver:

➤ Avoid slotted screws; the bit will slip. Phillips drives are good if you're strong enough to put a lot of pressure on the drill, or if you're smart enough to drill a pilot hole first. If you're doing a lot of screwing, check out the square drive screws. The bits really grab these screws, saving wear and tear on your arms.

➤ For rough work, there's no need for a pilot hole if you can press hard enough.

➤ Use a pilot hole for finer work, wood that's prone to splitting, or big jobs. The result will be more accurate, and your arms will appreciate the reduced stress.

➤ Don't let the bit slip; it will ruin the screw head. If the bit starts slipping, reverse the drill and try again.

➤ When screwdriver bits wear out, replace them. They're cheap.

➤ Keep your fingers away from the action end of a power screwdriver.

Nail It Down

If the bit slips repeatedly, drill a pilot hole or use a square-slotted screw.

The power of screwdriving.

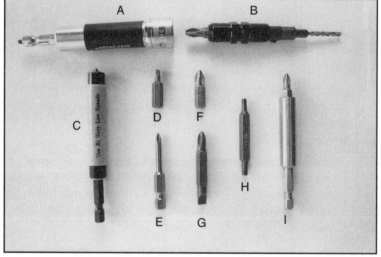

A. This quick-change screwdriver-drill holder allows you to switch between drill and screwdriver without loosening the drill chuck.

B. This is the removable driver-drill unit for A. above. The drill and the screwdriver bit can both be changed. This model adjusts easily and is better than most.

C. This screwdriver-bit holder is designed for use with drywall; run it slowly, and it sets the screw to the correct depth.

D. A square bit is needed for the handy, easy-to-drive square-headed screws.

E. A fine Phillips bit is great for precision work.

F. A standard Phillips bit is the power screwdriver that revolutionized the home-repair business.

G. This combination Phillips-straight bit fits directly into the drill chuck.

H. This bit has two sizes of square bits.

I. A magnetized screwdriver bit holder grabs screws for easy driving.

Thrilling Drilling Tips

Drilling may seem utterly straightforward—and, for the most part, it is. But if you're new to the sport, take advantage of my hard-won experience with these suggestions for getting the most from your drill.

➤ If your drill is slightly too small to make a pilot hole for a wood screw, carefully wobble the drill while it's running. Don't get too aggressive, or you'll break the bit.

➤ Breaking too many of those little ($1/8$-inch or smaller) wood bits? Then do what the pros do: Use a finishing nail instead. They're cheap, so you can replace them when lost or bent. Just cut off the head with a wire cutter and slip it into the chuck. Although finishing nails are not very accurate, that's seldom necessary for pilot holes (which allow a wood screw to penetrate wood). This trick works best on softwood; use it on hardwood only if you're desperate.

➤ A power drill with a wire brush is the best tool for removing rust from tools, railings, and so on. Run it at top speed, and grab the drill with both hands. Hold small pieces in a vise or locking pliers.

Always wear safety glasses when using a power drill.

Test Your Mettle: Drilling Metal

When you first start drilling metal, you'll long for the days when your opponent was mere wood. Metal—particularly steel—hates being drilled. To get action in steel you'll need more force, more technique, and sharper bits. (Fortunately, brass, copper, aluminum, and other soft metals are distinctly less challenging.)

1. Make a small dimple to prevent the bit from wandering as it starts. In soft, thin metal, tapping a nail will work. In iron and steel, use a center punch, a pointed tool that looks like a small chisel and that's designed to make these dents.

2. Clamp the bit in the chuck using two tightening holes. This tightens better because the gears are aligned when you move to the second tightening hole. A tighter chuck prevents the bit from slipping.

3. Use a faster rotation speed for smaller holes, and use a slower speed for large holes.

4. To make holes $3/16$ inch and larger in iron and steel, first drill a pilot hole with a smaller bit, and then enlarge the hole with a second bit.

5. Cool the bit with motor oil to prevent the heat from damaging it.

6. Keep bits sharp, or buy new ones.

Don't try to drill hardened steel, found in tools and some hardware. If a sharp drill won't cut the metal, back off—it's probably hardened.

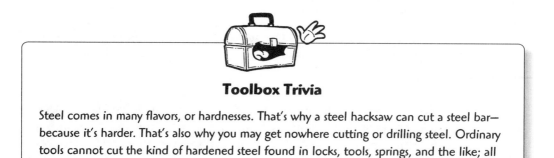

Toolbox Trivia

Steel comes in many flavors, or hardnesses. That's why a steel hacksaw can cut a steel bar—because it's harder. That's also why you may get nowhere cutting or drilling steel. Ordinary tools cannot cut the kind of hardened steel found in locks, tools, springs, and the like; all you will do is waste your time and dull the tool.

En Garde—and Other Tricks with the Saber Saw

A saber saw is a portable jig saw; it drives a small, straight blade back and forth to make straight or curved cuts. Always push down while cutting to prevent vibration, and press forward lightly at first. Once the saw is fully in the cut, you can press harder. For a straight cut, run the saw along an aluminum square (see the section "Seven Cool Tools You Must Meet" in Chapter 7, "The Bare Essentials: Hand Tools") or another type of square. A saber saw is shown in an earlier figure.

This economical saw may come with many features, none essential:

➤ Variable speed: Helpful for cutting plastic (or even cellulose ceiling tile) and for starting cuts.

➤ Adjustable angle: The blade can be angled to about 45° from the base. Use a square (see Chapter 7) to set the blade back 90°; it may be difficult to do this accurately.

➤ Pivoting blade: A handle on top allows the blade to pivot 360° while cutting so that you can cut your way into a corner. This feature helps you orient the tool so you can see the blade while cutting, but make sure the blade can lock into position for straight cuts.

Can You Get by Without This Tool?

This is an optional but handy tool, best for occasional cutting, intricate work (such as repair of "gingerbread" trim on a Victorian house), or installing electrical outlets in drywall or plaster.

Belt Sander

Belt sanders move a 3- or 4-inch-wide sanding belt in bulldozer-tread fashion. They are great for removing a lot of material, heavy-duty refinishing, or smoothing the edge of a door. Don't use for removing paint as paint will clog the belts, which are expensive. Belt sanders are great for smoothing dried hole-filling material in wood.

Some sanders need a drop of motor oil on the front roller with each use. A model with a 3-by-24-inch belt should be plenty for home work (see the following figure). Make sure to install the belt in the direction indicated by the arrow inside the belt, or the belt will tear. Always keep moving, and sand with the grain, not across it. If you're more interested in final finishing than in rough wood removal, see the orbital sander, described later in this chapter.

Don't Screw Up!

Some new sanding belts work in either direction, but be sure to read the package before you install one. If you run a one-way belt the wrong way, bye-bye belt.

Can You Get by Without This Tool?

Definitely. But if you ever need to smooth some gouged wood or straighten the edge of a door, then you're a prospect for a belt sander. (However, a rented power planer is the ideal tool for trimming a door edge.)

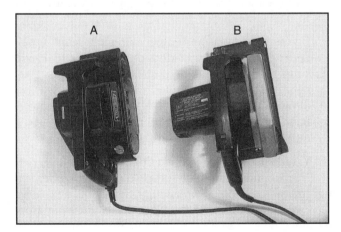

Big-time sanding and sawing.

A. A belt sander is a heavy-duty answer for flattening and smoothing wood. Use it with care, as it removes wood quickly.

B. A circular saw is essential for cutting plywood and particle board and is handy for general sawing. It will even cut brick, but don't be a dufus—get a blade designed to cut brick!

Circular Saw

A circular saw, often called by the trade name Skil-saw, is a standard tool at construction sites. You can adjust the depth of the blade and angle it cuts. Some saws stop instantly when you release the trigger; that's a nice safety feature, although the blade guard is supposed to snap down and cover the blade pretty effectively (see the previous figure).

In general, adjust the blade so it reaches through the wood by about a $1/2$-inch; a deeper setting will just strain the motor and make the job more dangerous. For some great hints about sawing wood, see Chapter 11, "Wood: Still Champ After All These Years."

Special blades can cut some bricks and concrete blocks (although it's a dusty, noisy job, at the bottom of the recreational scale; see the section "Busting Blocks and Breaking Bricks," in Chapter 17, "Bricks and Stones: Masonry and Concrete [the Sequel]").

A circular saw is probably the most dangerous tool in a home workshop. Read and follow the instructions, particularly regarding eye protection and setting up the cut. Don't work in cluttered areas, or in low light, or when you're tired. Use two hands to guide the saw, and know what's on the bottom side of the board. In short, if you've got to act stupid, *don't* do it while holding a circular saw.

Some Sharp Words on the Blade

You can buy dozens of blades for a circular saw, but you can get by with one or two. For cutting 1- and 2-inch lumber, the primary blade (once you've dulled the cheapo blade that came with the saw) is a $20 to $40, 18-tooth, carbide-tipped blade. Carbide teeth stay sharp much longer than steel teeth, particularly if they hit a nail. Money really buys quality when it comes to blades; an expensive blade will make faster, smoother cuts.

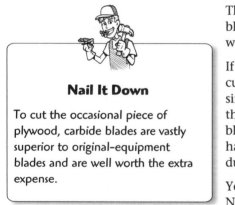

Nail It Down

To cut the occasional piece of plywood, carbide blades are vastly superior to original-equipment blades and are well worth the extra expense.

The second blade to buy is a fine-toothed plywood blade, which also cuts paneling, particle board, and wooden siding.

If your saw starts smoking, making a hideous shriek, and cutting crooked, the blade is dull. Dull blades can also singe the wood, making it difficult to finish or glue. And they can damage the motor and draw enough current to blow a fuse. Dull blades are also unsafe because you have to push so hard. Have I convinced you to avoid dull blades? Good. But how? Avoid nails.

Yet normal cutting will eventually dull a blade, too. Non-carbide blades are surprisingly easy to sharpen with a good, fine-toothed triangular metal file. Hold the blade tightly against a table and sharpen the cutting side (not the circumference) of the teeth that angle away from you. Cut downward, toward the table. When half the teeth are done, flip the blade, reclamp, and sharpen the other set of teeth. Good carbide blades can be professionally sharpened; cheap carbide blades can be replaced.

Can You Get by Without This Tool?

A hand saw will work fine for cross-cutting a few 2-by-4s. But to cut many boards, rip saw a long plank, or cut plywood or particle board, get a circular saw. Most have a $7^1/_4$-inch blade diameter, which is adequate for virtually everything you'll attempt. If the blade is not quite big enough, set it to cut slightly more than halfway through the wood, and flip the wood over and complete the cut.

Orbital Sander

Orbital sanders rotate a disk of sandpaper, often $4^1/_2$ inches in diameter, up to 25,000 revolutions per minute. Orbital sanders (also called "random orbital sanders") are great for refinishing. They won't flatten a surface as nicely as a belt sander (see the previous section) because they won't remove as much wood, but orbitals are perfect for dressing up furniture, especially after stripping paint.

Practice on a scrap of wood, and follow these tips for using an orbital sander:

1. Wear safety goggles.
2. Position the sanding disk as close as you can to the center of the tool's spinning disk.
3. Grab the sander with both hands and allow it to reach full speed. Holding the disk parallel to the wood, slowly bring it into contact and immediately start moving across the surface, with the grain.
4. The major hazard is holding the sander at an angle, which will cause skipping and gouging. Make sure the whole disk touches the wood.
5. To cut damaged spots deeper, move the sander back and forth across them.
6. You may be able to skip coarse grit and start with medium or fine paper. Always work one step at a time toward fine or extra-fine sandpaper.

Be sure to let the sander stop spinning before you put it down.

Can You Get by Without This Tool?

You bet. The hand sanding block described in Chapter 7 can take care of minor sanding problems. Power sanders are not for drywall repair, as they will cut too deeply and cause a dust storm. An orbital sander is handy for refinishing furniture, or for flat parts of molding and doors. If you need to flatten very rough wood, a belt sander (discussed previously) will work much faster. If you do much furniture refinishing, though, the orbital sander is relatively cheap, and it will start to seem mighty handy, mighty fast.

The orbital sander is cheap, effective, and a bit hard to use—until you get the hang of it. Hold the sander without pressing down, and allow the disk to run at nearly full speed.

Power Miter Box

A power miter box is a circular saw hinged to a small mounting table. The price has come down, and you may be able to pick one up for $175, making it suitable for serious do-it-yourselfers. The advantage of this saw is simple: straight, true cuts, each time, every time (so long as the saw is adjusted correctly).

All power miter boxes will cut miters (cuts at up to 45° to square, as seen in the following figure). The blade remains vertical as it swings from side to side. The more expensive "compound miter" saw will also cut miters when seen from the side (the blade pivots to the side and descends at an angle).

Power miter boxes are great for cutting molding and 2-by-4s. You can clamp a block to the fence and get repeated cuts of short lengths with only one measurement.

Don't Screw Up!

The "extended" version of the power miter box has rails, allowing the saw to move toward you and cut a much wider board. That's handy, but watch out; this tool is expensive and weighty.

Can You Get by Without This Tool?

Definitely. An aluminum square, described in Chapter 7, and a circular saw combined give reasonably good cuts for less than half the price. But a lot of frustrated home-repair types now swear by power miter boxes, particularly for cutting molding, as described in Chapter 24, "A Scolding on Molding." Get a basic or compound model; the extended variety is way beyond idiot territory.

The power miter box is no longer a contractor's specialty. Fairly cheap, highly accurate, and nearly foolproof, it is the ultimate solution to crosscutting and mitering for careful carpenters. Make sure the saw is adjusted before you start it, or you'll get consistently inaccurate cuts.

Power-by-the-Hour—Renting Big-Time Tools

Howard Tate, an unjustly forgotten rhythm 'n' blues singer, sang this plaintive blues line: "Got to find me a part-time love." That's how I see renting tools—as an opportunity for part-time love, the kind of love you don't have to maintain, repair, or store (not to mention buy in the first place).

Even though I have a decent collection of tools, over the years, I've rented floor sanders, chain saws, wood splitters, post-hole diggers, concrete mixers, and an electric jackhammer. (I even rented a hefty hammer drill to drill through a brick wall. The drilling went fine, until I hit a backing wall of 8-inch solid concrete. From there on it was strictly Alcatraz work.)

Tool rental yards should have most of the goodies listed in the following table. Many of these tools are designed for large jobs, but that's the point: This is where you get pro equipment. Even if you don't exploit these tools to their limit, you've still lightened your load. Tool rental outfits may also rent ladders, scaffolding, and extension cords.

Nail It Down

If you rent a tool on Saturday morning, chances are that a one-day fee will take you through to the rental yard's opening time on Monday—you'll get almost two days for the price of one.

Rental Tools and Uses

Tool	Uses
Nail or staple gun	Repeated nailing, as of siding or roofing (most require an air compressor)
Hammer drill (AKA rotary hammer)	Drilling holes in concrete, concrete block, and brick
Electric hammer	Small jackhammer for demolishing concrete, brick, block, and pavement
Half-inch drill	Drilling metal, concrete, or large holes in wood
Right-angle drill	Drilling large holes, and in confined spaces (as between studs or joists)
Screw gun	For large-scale screwing, as in drywall or decks
Reciprocating saw (AKA "Sawz-All")	Cutting flush to a surface; cutting into walls, ceilings, roofs; and cutting steel pipe, angle-iron, and flat stock; ideal for remodeling work
Table saw	Accurate rip sawing of material up to 24 inches or wider
Hand power planer	Smoothing edges or end grain of doors so that they swing freely
Radial arm saw	Fast, accurate crosscut sawing of material up to 24 inches wide
Diamond-bladed tile saw	Cutting tile and brick
Pipe wrenches and threader	Cutting, threading, and assembling steel pipe
Pipe auger (snake)	Cleaning clogs from drain pipes
Power grinder or wire brush	Polishing metal, removing paint or rust from metal, and cleaning brick joints for tuckpointing
Paint sprayer (air or airless)	Spray-painting large areas, indoors or out
Portable generator	Supplying 120-volt electricity in remote locations
Floor nailer	Invisible (blind) nailing of hardwood flooring
Masonry nailer	Shooting hardened nails into masonry and concrete (uses a powder charge)
Compactor	Compressing earth while building patios or foundations

Tool	Uses
Air compressor	Driving air tools, such as nailers, staplers, and air-powered paint sprayers
Power washer	Washing the house, especially before painting or staining
Power wheelbarrow	Moving heavy loads of sand, soil, and concrete
Concrete mixer	Mixing (gasp!) concrete (get one with a trailer hitch if you have a way to pull it)
Power trowel	Finishing large, flat concrete work
Post-hole digger	Digging holes for fence posts, basketball posts, signs, and lights
Pumps	Drying out basements and other low areas

A Friend in Deed Is a Friend You Need— or How to Borrow Tools Without Losing Friends

Rental outfits are not the only source of tools—friends can be equally valuable, and much more affordable. But before you ask Joe to loan you his pipe cutter, consider the parable of Doug and Arnold. Arnold used to borrow drills, hacksaws, and even the occasional sledgehammer. I didn't mind—after all, there was no point in him wasting money on something he'd need only once in his lifetime. But that's how long it seemed to take for Arnold to return my tools—a lifetime. I've quit offering, and he's quit asking.

At the other extreme, when my friend Doug borrows my reciprocating saw, he does it in high style: He asks ahead of time, so I can make plans. Then he borrows it for the minimum time, and sometimes he even checks back to see if I've found a sudden need for it. When he does return the saw, I usually find a couple of new blades in the case.

More tool-borrowing etiquette follows:

➤ Don't ask to borrow a tool you can't control. For example, I'm happy to lend out a miter box or an electric drill, but I don't lend out my chain saw.

➤ Return the tool—quickly, and in good condition.

➤ Offer to repay the favor by working alongside your benefactor.

As time goes on and you amass your own set of tools, lend them in return. But keep track of them by marking them with your name or a bright color to be sure you get them back.

The Least You Need to Know

➤ When it comes to electric tools, choose carefully and buy the most versatile ones first.

➤ Just because you'll need a tool once in a while does not mean that you should buy it. Try borrowing from a friend or renting.

➤ A variable-speed, reversible $3/8$-inch drill is the obvious first choice for an electric tool, but it's important to understand your needs. Cordless is popular, but it's not for everybody.

Chapter 9

Fast Guide to Fasteners

In This Chapter

➤ How to select and use nails, screws, and anchors

➤ Identifying and choosing hardware for repair projects

➤ Time-saving hints for using fasteners

Fasteners—the generic term for nails, screws, hardware, and anchors—are like the joints in your body. They aren't exactly the structure, but structure is impossible without them. Almost every home repair project—replacing a bookshelf, patching a roof, or hanging a lava lamp—calls for fasteners at some point, which means that you need to know what the hardware mavens are selling.

In this chapter, you'll learn that nails have ... well ... come a long way in the past few years, as manufacturers finally figured out that one size does not fit all applications and that a nail's main job is not to split the wood but to hold it. At the same time, screws have taken their rightful place as the fastener of choice: versatile, strong, and non-destructive. Not to be outdone, manufacturers of other hardware have put on their creative hats and come up with some novel answers to the age-old problem of keeping it together. After you've met the fasteners, we'll finish by discussing a some-what unorthodox approach to buying materials—one that gives you a fighting chance of having the right item in stock when you need it. Information on materials for specific repairs appears in the chapters on wood, caulking and weather-stripping, masonry, drywall, wallpaper, painting, electrical work, and plumbing.

A Nail for What Ails You

Nails are the oldest wood fastener around, unless you count bark and vines that once were used to bind branches together. But old needn't mean old-fashioned: A glut of new nails has reached the market in recent years—and for good reason. Common nails, long the industry standard, had a nasty habit of splitting lumber. Today's nails are less likely to split and more likely to grab. Some are almost as strong as screws but are faster to drive (see the following illustration). Here are the most common kinds of nails you'll use in your home-repair projects:

Toolbox Trivia

Nails are sized by an archaic and baffling system of "pennys." Basically, 4d (4 penny), is $1^1/_2$ inches long, 16d is $3^1/_2$ inches long, and the other sizes are in between. Fortunately, most nail manufacturers recognize that the penny system is gibberish to the average homeowner and list nail length in inches.

Pole barn: Tough and springy, up to 6 inches long; rings on the shank prevent pulling out (meaning that you should never put one in the wrong place!).

Roofing: A galvanized, big-headed nail for asphalt shingles and securing fibrous materials. The nails are available up to 3 inches long, and should sink at least a half-inch into the roof decking.

Sinker ("coated"): A lighter version of the common nail that causes less splitting; a cement coating makes it easier to drive and improves the grip.

Box: A light-duty nail for assembling thin and/or brittle wood; it's almost split-proof.

Siding: A galvanized (rust-resistant) version of the box nail, available up to $3^1/2$ inches long, for fastening wood siding.

Ring shank: A medium-duty nail that has rings on the shank for a better grip, often used for plywood.

Spiral: A heavy flooring nail that obtains a kind of screw grip that resists pull-out and reduces squeaking; a galvanized version is sold for outdoor use.

Drywall: A thin, big-headed nail for fastening drywall and plaster lath.

Paneling: A skinny, hardened nail for wood paneling; buy a color that matches the paneling.

Finishing: A thin, inconspicuous nail for window, door, or baseboard trim.

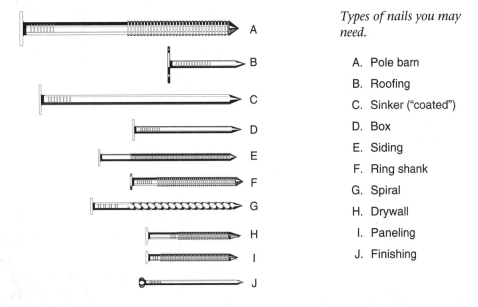

Types of nails you may need.

A. Pole barn

B. Roofing

C. Sinker ("coated")

D. Box

E. Siding

F. Ring shank

G. Spiral

H. Drywall

I. Paneling

J. Finishing

Screwing Up Again?

When it comes to fastening, screws have four advantages: They're strong, they're gentle, they're secure, and they're removable. Most screws must be driven into a pilot hole, but drywall screws don't have to be—at least when used in drywall. (Pilot holes, incidentally, are preliminary holes drilled to guide a screw and prevent wood from splitting.) For small wood screws, you can drill the pilot hole with a finishing nail.

Don't Screw Up!

If you've ever wrestled a box of Phillips-drive drywall screws into the wall, you know that they exact a toll on the hands and forearms. Square-drive screws are remarkably easier to drive, and the only cost of changing over is the $2 cost of square driver bits for your power screwdriver.

Wood, drywall, and sheet metal screws have a thread tailored to their particular material. Machine screws and machine bolts must be screwed into a nut with the correct thread. Compared to wood screws, machine screws and bolts are stronger, less likely to pull out (particularly if you use flat washers with them), and more homely.

Wood and sheet-metal screws are made with straight (slotted), square-drive, or Phillips heads. Many are available in galvanized (rust-resistant) steel. For a price, you can buy solid brass, which is much more attractive but weaker than steel (see the photo of screws you may need). Here's a brief description of each of the more useful kinds of screws:

Round-head: For attaching hardware to wood.

Oval-head: A decorative version of the round-head.

Flat-head: The top of the head sits flush to the surface; ideal for mounting hinges.

Drywall: For attaching drywall, and dozens of other uses. Sold with Phillips or square drive heads, from $7/8$ inch to 4 inches long. The screw has no taper and drives easily with a power screwdriver. The square-drive version is much easier to drive.

Nail It Down

Smear dry hand soap on wood and drywall screws before driving. This will reduce friction and save your palm—or the batteries in your drill. For hand screwdriving, remember this rule: Right makes tight. Turn the top of the screwdriver to the right to tighten a screw.

Construction: A beefier version of the drywall screw; lengths range from $1 1/4$ inch to 3 inches.

Trim: For securing railings, moldings, and other indoor uses. Stronger than drywall screws, but with a smaller shank and head; sold in $1 5/8$-inch, $2 1/4$-inch, and 3-inch lengths.

Deck: For securing decks, railings, and other outdoor uses. Available in steel with ceramic coating, or stainless steel. Available in 1-inch to 3-inch lengths. Stronger than drywall screws, but otherwise similar.

Lag: For heavy-duty fastening; comes with a square or hexagonal head; from 1 inch to about 6 inches long.

Cement board: Made specifically to fasten cement board (which is an under-layment for tile). The head automatically countersinks the screw, which is treated to resist corrosion. Sold in $1 1/4$-inch, $1 5/8$-inch, and $2 1/4$-inch lengths.

Tapcon: For fastening metal or wood to concrete, brick, or block. Faster and simpler than using lag shields and lag screws because you need a smaller hole and won't need to disassemble the project to place the anchor after drilling (see the "Anchors" section, which follows). These super-hard screws actually cut a thread in concrete, concrete block, mortar, and some bricks.

Sheet metal: For joining sheet metal; doubles as an emergency wood screw.

Machine screw and nut: Fastens all the way through a joint. Note: The nut and screw must be the same diameter and have the same number of threads per inch.

Machine bolt and nut: A heavy-duty version of the machine screw; usually sold with a hexagonal head. Sold with "coarse" or "fine" threads. Fine threads are smaller, so there are more of them per inch. For most purposes, use coarse threads.

Nail It Down

Brass screws are pretty but soft. If you're having trouble driving one into a hole, drive a steel screw first. After it cuts the threads, the brass screw should go right in.

Flat washer: For reinforcing wood and sheet metal before fastening with machine screws or bolts. Flat washers are handy: They strengthen a joint, prevent leakage, reduce friction, serve as emergency shims, and let you use a small bolt in a large hole. In other words, keep extras around—they're that handy.

Lock washer: To prevent machine nuts from loosening; used mainly where vibration occurs, as on autos and appliances.

Crown nuts: Has a polymer to grab the bolt and eliminate the need for a lock washer. (Alternatively, use "Lock-Tite," a commercial goop that holds nuts tight but allows the nut to be loosened.)

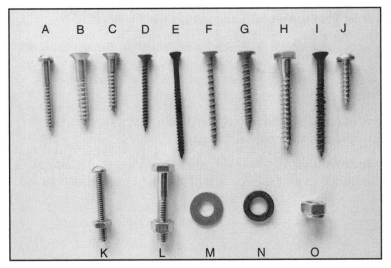

Screws you may need.

A. Round-head
B. Oval-head
C. Flat-head
D. Drywall
E. Trim
F. Deck
G. Cement board
H. Lag
I. Tapcon
J. Sheet metal
K. Machine screw and nut
L. Machine bolt and nut
M. Flat washer
N. Lock washer
O. Crown nut

Anchors

So you're trying to hang that gilt-framed black-velvet Elvis portrait on plaster or drywall, and you can't find any studs to support the art? You could consult the section in Chapter 22, "Cosmetology 101: Drywall and Plaster Repair," called "Seven Ways to Find a Stud." Or you could get a strong picture hook. For hanging other stuff, many anchor varieties are available. The general routine for fastening anchors is the same: Drill a hole, insert the anchor, drive the screw into the anchor (if it's a separate piece), and tighten. To fasten to concrete, use a lag shield on a lag screw (it's a nuisance, but it really holds), or try the newer Tapcon screws, which require a smaller hole and are easier to install. Here's when and how to use anchors:

Nail It Down

For mounting heavy mirrors or pictures on drywall or plaster, it's best to nail a pair of heavy picture hooks in adjacent studs. If the studs are in the wrong place, drive two expansion anchors about 12 inches apart. Place a flat washer under each screw head, insert the anchor in the hole, and tighten to secure the bolt to the back of the wall. Back the screws out slightly and hang the mirror with the picture wire under the washers.

Light plastic anchor: A quick, cheap anchor; good for light jobs.

Hollow plastic anchor: Sold in various diameters; stronger than the simple nylon anchor.

Winged plastic anchor: A more expensive, heavier-duty version of the plastic anchor.

Molly-screw (expansion) anchor: Requires a large drill hole and is cumbersome to fasten, but it's the strongest way to fasten to drywall or plaster. Drill a hole, insert the anchor, and tighten the screw. Then remove the screw (the anchor will remain in the wall), stick the screw through whatever you are mounting, and screw it back into the anchor. Best driven with a power screwdriver or drill.

Spring toggle: Drill a hole, insert the screw through the object to be mounted, thread it into the anchor, slip the anchor into the hole, and tighten. The wings automatically expand to grab the wall.

Picture hook: Nailed at an angle into plaster or drywall. Vastly superior to a simple nail because it pulls along the whole length of the nail.

Lag shield (concrete anchor): Drill a hole in concrete with a special masonry bit, insert the anchor, insert a lag screw through the object and into the anchor, and tighten.

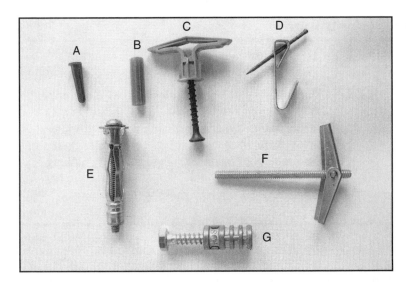

Anchors and their uses.

A. Light plastic anchor

B. Hollow plastic anchor

C. Winged nylon anchor

D. Picture hook

E. Molly-screw (expansion) anchor

F. Spring toggle

G. Lag shield (concrete anchor)

Hardware Basics: Types and Identifications

Choosing hardware can be simple: You take the busted part to the store and replace it. But if you don't know what you need, or if the store doesn't have a replacement, consult the following illustrations of door hardware and other hardware for suggestions. Remember: *Always* take the broken piece to the store if you have it; you may confront an unimaginable mix of sizes, finishes, and styles.

Door Hardware

Item	Description
	Butt hinge: For standard doors, sized up to 4 inches long. These hinges must be installed in a recess, or mortise.
	Strap hinge: Doors and gates in yards, basements, and garages. Can only be used where the door and trim are flush with each other.
	Tee hinge: Similar uses to strap hinge.
	Semi-concealed hinge: Mainly for kitchen cabinets; the hinge is screwed to the back of the door.
	Doorstops: To prevent a door from damaging walls and woodwork, a doorstop may be screwed to the baseboard, or slipped over the hinge pin.

continues

Door Hardware (continued)

Item	Description
	Door straightener: Prevents sag in a wooden screen door. Screw diagonally into place, with the upper end toward the hinge side.
	Storm door closer: Closes a door slowly without slamming.
	Hook and eye: For quick, easy, light-duty locking of a door.
	Barrel bolt: For slightly more secure locking of door.

Other Hardware

Item	Description
	Corner iron: Reinforcing furniture or installing shelves.
	Joiner (strap, L, and tee): Reinforcing furniture and shelving.
	Shelf bracket: Installing shelves.
	Continuous (piano) hinge: Strong attachment of folding shelves or box lids.
	Pull: Replacing or updating drawers and cabinet doors.
	Chair and corner brace: Strengthening leg attachment on chairs and tables.
	Sash catch: Locking sash in double-hung windows.

Gorgeous Glues

Over the past decades, industrial chemists have invented a shelf-load of glues and cements, but you can probably get by with the ones listed in the following table.

Glues and Their Uses

Name	Uses
Yellow carpenter's	For porous materials in dry situations: wood, cloth, and paper. This basic workshop item is perfect for fixing split wood, building or repairing furniture, and so on. Working time is 15 minutes. The joint must fit well and be nailed, screwed, weighted, or clamped for $1/2$ hour, while the glue sets. Save white glue for paper—it's not as strong or as water-resistant and is harder to sand. Yellow glue cleans up with water, has no odor, and is as strong as the wood itself in a good-fitting joint. Also sold in a water-resistant variety.
Resorcinol	Two-part glue excellent for high-moisture gluing in kitchen, bath, and outdoors.
Contact	For gluing countertops and other flat materials to plywood or particle board. This cement grabs instantly, so you've got to align the parts perfectly in advance.
Construction	Sold in tubes for caulking guns. When combined with nails or screws, this stuff makes an extremely strong joint.
Foam panel	Sold in caulking-gun tubes. Used to fasten foam panels to concrete or wood.
Panel	Sold in tubes for caulking guns. Used to fasten wood paneling to studs (or substitute construction glue).
"Super" or "Krazy" glue	Fast-setting glue that makes strong joints in metal, ceramics, and some plastics. Use with care—it can bond to your skin. Although nail-polish remover may be able to remove it from your skin, it's smarter to use gloves in the first place.
Hot glue (glue gun)	Heated plastic that grabs most materials when it cools. Handy, fast-setting, versatile, but weak. Good for dissimilar materials: plastics, carpets, weather-stripping.
Epoxy	A heavy-duty, two-part cement for metal, glass, ceramic, wood, and concrete. Expensive and extremely strong; may fill gaps.

Sandpaper

Sandpaper is abrasive paper used for removing paint, smoothing wood, and roughening surfaces before painting.

Try these sanding hints:

➤ Tear a sandpaper sheet into three strips by ripping along the edge of a table. Then fold each sheet in three, making a sanding pad. As the sandpaper clogs, refold the sheet to expose a fresh surface.

➤ For sanding drywall compound, special screens prevent clogging. These are best used on sanding blocks built especially for them.

➤ The sanding block shown in Chapter 7 (see the section "Seven Cool Tools You Must Meet") is extremely handy for sanding a flat surface.

➤ Use the correct grit: Fine paper will not remove enough material for flattening a surface, and coarse paper will leave a rough surface. You'll save a lot of time by starting at medium or coarse and working toward fine or extra fine paper. See the following table for advice on the use of sandpaper. If you don't want to buy a raft of sandpaper, get a selection of medium and fine sandpaper; that should take care of most needs.

Selecting Sandpaper

Name and Grit	Purpose
Extra coarse (40-grit)	Stripping paint and extra-heavy sanding of uneven or painted surfaces.
Coarse (60-grit)	Stripping paint and heavy sanding; surface flattening.
Medium (100-grit)	First sanding of unpainted wood, drywall repairs, and wood repairs.
Fine (150-grit)	Final sanding of drywall, between coats of paint and varnish.
Extra fine (200+-grit)	Further sanding of varnish, fine furniture and molding.

A Word on Acquiring Materials

Your mother—or whoever indoctrinated you with the myth that cleanliness was next to godliness—will hate me for this, but I'll say it anyway: Don't throw stuff away. When you rip apart a wall, save good wood and any electrical boxes and receptacles that are modern and in good shape. When you take apart old plumbing, save the good fittings. These odds and ends can save time and money: An electrical box can cost $3, and a trip to the building supplier can devour 90 minutes (if you count driving, parking, and wandering around gape-mouthed in search of a size-7 snarf hinge in antique brass finish).

Another way to save time is to buy extra nails and screws. About $15 worth of sorted and labeled fasteners can eliminate countless supply trips. See Chapter 10, "A Workable Workshop," for storage hints on keeping all this junk straight.

Toolbox Trivia

Good hardware stores (not those cut-rate chain stores) have much more than nails and nuts. Many stores keep a huge set of drawers containing fasteners in every conceivable size, shape, and material, along with curiosities such as bizarre brackets for folding furniture. Hardware stores may also cut glass, repair screens, cut and thread steel pipe, and sharpen knives, scissors, and saws.

Finally, there's the prospect of shopping on the curb. Are you too proud to poke around in the trash, looking for a good 2-by-4 and a sheet of plywood for a basement shelf? Not me. I consider the curb a public utility—kind of like clean water. On garbage nights, I drive slowly, scanning for large piles of goodies. I don't think of it as trash-picking, but as a 24-hour store where every item carries a money-back guarantee.

The Least You Need to Know

➤ Always bring the broken part to the store when you buy a replacement.

➤ Hardware is available in a bewildering variety of types, sizes, and finishes, for virtually any task.

➤ Buy some extra screws and nails for each project; eventually your collection will save you trips to the store.

➤ In many cases, used is as good as new. A collection of used hardware and fasteners will save time and money.

Chapter 10

A Workable Workshop

In This Chapter

➤ The essentials of the home workshop: storage, lighting, and workspace

➤ How to store more stuff in less space

➤ Time-saving hints for putting tools away—and finding them again

---

If the term "workshop" conjures up the elves from the Brothers Grimm, where age-weathered artisans patiently paint handmade dollhouses—relax. We're not interested in recreating the workshops of days gone by. In this liberated era, a workshop can be as plain or as picturesque as you want, as long as it meets three basic functions. First, it's got to store the junk you need and make it accessible when you want it. Second, it's got to give you a place to get things done fast. And third, it's got to have enough light so that you won't need a headlamp to find a $1^1/_4$-inch screw.

Storage, a work surface, and lighting: Meet the holy trinity of home workshops. Fancier is fine if you have the time and money, but the main point is providing the essentials.

Here's the key question: Where to put the workshop? A basement, if you have one, is warm and accessible. But it's got too little air circulation for dusty work or toxic chemicals, and you probably can't haul large projects to it. The garage, the other obvious choice, is hot in summer, cold in winter, and may be crammed with cars. Still, it's a better place for painting, sanding, and noisy work, and it's better suited to large projects.

The choice is yours. My choice is to have a primitive workshop in the garage and a more extensive one in the basement. That gives me the best of both worlds (except that the tool I need is always in the other workshop).

Wherever it is, the true test of a home workshop is convenience. The need for fast-in, fast-out access dictates the iron rule of organization: Everything gets a place. Because most home repairs won't occur in the workshop (you simply can't drag a wall, window, or roof into the shop), its main function is as handy storage. We'll take up that first.

The Storage

I never understood the rationale for good storage until I asked Ron Gedrim, my partner in Wisconsin Barn Board and Beam Co., why he was so compulsively neat about storing his stuff. I had asked offhandedly, but he answered in a dead-serious tone: "I hate looking for stuff."

Not only could I relate to his answer, but I quickly became a firm believer in the virtue of good storage. Not because my mother told me (how many times???) to be neat, and not because I care what you, dear reader, think—but because it's faster and less frustrating.

I've listed my best storage ideas here.

Don't You Need These Kinds of Storage?

Tool or Hardware	Suggestions
Power tools	Cases (if you have them), open shelves, hooks (for drills and other tools with appropriate handles), or plastic milk crates placed sideways.
Hand tools	Pegboard (see the next section), tool bag (for the most common tools), drawers, nails or hooks for squares, levels, and so on.

Tool or Hardware	Suggestions
Clamps	On pegboard or hanging on lag screws.
Health and safety equipment	One box or crate holding everything. Keep dust masks and respirators clean by storing in plastic bags.
Extension cords and trouble lights	Nails or hooks. Coil the cord into a long hank. When about 4 feet of cord remains, wrap the cord tightly around the middle of the hank, then tuck the end through the loops. That's fine for quick storage yet easy to untie.
Fasteners: nails, screws, and bolts	Cans, plastic containers, and original boxes, if convenient. All containers should be labeled and stored with the label facing out. Small shelves (4 inches high and 3 inches deep) are ideal for storing many fasteners.
Hardware	Boxes on shelves, sorted into categories and labeled.
Wood	Boards, standing upright, as close to vertical as possible, standing on scrap wood. Or, attach horizontal 16-inch 2-by-4s to every other stud. Use a string to lay out the shelves straight so the wood won't warp.
Plywood and other panels	Store on edge, as upright as possible. The key point: keep wood dry. If there's any chance of moisture, put scrap wood underneath.

If storage is starting to sound like a lot of work and expense, many storage units can be had secondhand or off the curb.

Toolbox Trivia

My storage devices are nothing to be proud of: Some shelves came with the house; others I built from scrap lumber. Some drawer units I've had since childhood; others I inherited. But none cost me a dime.

All Hung Up: Pegboard

Right out in the open—that's where pegboard hangs your tools. It's a good thing, too, because opening drawers can get kind of boring, especially when you're continually opening the wrong ones. Although pegboard is handy, cheap, and straightforward, I'll still offer some suggestions for using it sensibly (see the figure that follows).

Gimme space: Pegboard needs a half-inch of space behind it, or else those handy hangers can't engage the holes. Mount the board on furring strips ($^3/_4$-inch-by-$1^1/_2$-inch wooden strips) fastened to the wall.

Be smart: Buy a bunch of pegboard hangers so you can really get organized.

Be logical: Store similar tools together.

Quit singing the "I can't remember where it goes" blues: Store all your slot screwdrivers in one pegboard rack, and then label it. For larger tools, trace their outlines on the board with a crayon or marker.

Cure that tool population explosion: Store tools close to allow room for growth.

VIPs only: The pegboard is for commonly used tools. Keep the micrometer you bought at a rummage sale in a drawer labeled "Measuring tools," "Small tools" or something similar.

The Pegboard Solution: The pegboard takes away every excuse for being disorganized. Try to house similar tools in the same neighborhood, but don't waste space by being compulsive about it.

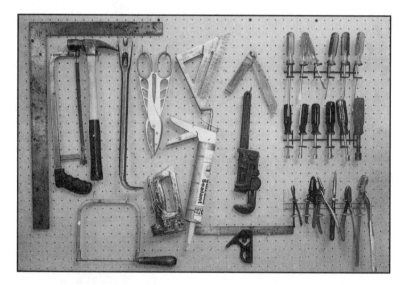

In the Bag

I said the pegboard is for important tools. Now I must backtrack to stress that the really important tools don't get hung—they get stashed in the toolbag or toolbox. (I use a toolbag, so that's what I'll call this essential item.)

Ideally, the toolbag should carry enough tools to give you a shot at completing a task without endless fetch-it trips to the workshop. Here's what lives in mine:

➤ 16-oz. claw hammer

➤ Electric drill (³/₈-inch reversible, variable speed, with cord)

➤ Assortment of drill bits and power screwdriver bits, in a small bag

➤ Locking, arc-joint and needle-nose pliers

➤ Assorted screwdrivers

➤ Nail set and awl

➤ Pencils and scriber (divider)

➤ Torpedo level

➤ Utility knife

➤ Hand plane

➤ Wood chisel

➤ Pointing trowel

➤ Magnetic stud finder

➤ Tape measure

➤ Aluminum square

➤ A few screws and nails

➤ Wire stripper-cutter, twist-on wire connectors, and electrical staples

➤ Circuit tester

➤ Soldering iron, solder, and electrical tape

➤ And whatever small tools and supplies remain from my last repair

You'll notice that this short list leaves room for the special tools and hardware needed for any particular job. It also makes the bag light enough to carry to jobs that don't seem to call for many tools. I've found that all fixes (short of, say, tightening a single screw) require five times as many tools as I expect. This kit carries most of them.

One last point: Now that you've gone to the trouble of assembling this handy kit, store it in a convenient place, such as smack in the middle of the workbench. For more information on hand and power tools for home repair, see Chapter 7, "The Bare Essentials: Hand Tools," and Chapter 8, "The Bare Essentials with Oomph! Power Tools."

The Workbench

Because the workshop will not be the scene of most home repairs, the workbench is less important than storage. Nevertheless, you still need a workbench—where else will you put all that clutter? (This is no idle question: You do need a receiving area to

Nail It Down

There's no real reason to buy a workbench; they're easy to build from 2-by-4s and ³/₄-inch plywood. If you're feeling really cheap and lazy, locate an old sink cabinet on the curb and top it with plywood.

dump tools and supplies while you're caught up in a project. Ideally, you'll move the detritus to its legitimate storage place ASAP....)

The workbench should have a surface at least 2 feet deep, and ideally about 8 feet wide. Install diagonal bracing, or fasten the workbench to the wall to prevent sway. This is about home repair, not offshore sailing.

One essential on a workbench is a decent vise. I don't care if it's designed for woodworking or metalworking, just so long as it's firmly attached to the workbench and is available instantly. Use the vise for holding tools while you sharpen them, for clamping, and for holding objects while you drill or saw them. When sawing, keep the wood (and particularly metal) as close as possible to the vise. There's no way around it: In the workshop, vice may be nice, but a good vise is nicer.

The Lighting and Electric Receptacles (AKA "Plug-Ins")

I can't find it anywhere! If you have kids, you know that refrain. But if you don't have enough lighting in your workshop, you've sung it, and too recently.

Don't curse the everlasting darkness: Bring on the lights and banish the shadows. The last requirement, unfortunately, means that you'll be needing fluorescent lights. I know, I hate their glare, too, but for cheap, no-shadow illumination, nothing else comes close. To save time starting and stopping, wire several lights to one switch.

Almost as important as lighting is good access to electric receptacles. In too many basements, the wiring ranges from lamentable to downright dangerous. It pays, in safety and convenience, to devote some time to upgrading this kind of junk, using the suggestions in Chapter 27, "Breaker, Breaker on the Wall: Electric Fundamentals," and Chapter 28, "Getting Wired Without Getting Zapped." A good rule is to place a receptacle every 4 feet in the back of a workbench. Locate the receptacles at an easy height, cover them with steel plates for protection, and double-check the grounding system.

Other Stuff Your Workshop Needs

Think you're off the hook yet? Not quite. No home workshop is complete without some incidentals, such as places for painting supplies, stepladders, and sawhorses.

I used to swear by milk crates: They're stable, cheap, and foolproof. But I've been converted by sawhorses, which hold the work at a comfortable height for my back and can support a couple of planks for sawing plywood. I find that working more comfortably translates into better accuracy, too. Use the bracket style shown in the following figure if you can find them; they're the best.

Like most sawhorse brackets, these handy items make collapsible sawhorses. Unlike most brackets, they make sturdy horses. Simply loosen the nut to remove the legs. For convenience, I replaced the original wing nut with a hex nut and tightened it with a ratchet wrench.

The Least You Need to Know

➤ A home workshop should be built for speed. Plenty of lights, lots of storage, and handy electric receptacles all help you work faster.

➤ Forget about trusting your memory: Use labels promiscuously. Draw the tool's outline on pegboard.

➤ Sawhorses bring the work up to your level, saving your back and increasing accuracy.

Chapter 11

Wood: Still Champ After All These Years

In This Chapter

➤ Understanding lumber lingo

➤ Wood's strengths and weaknesses

➤ Sawing, gluing, and nailing techniques

Let's face it: Wood is so good that if nature hadn't evolved trees, we'd probably be trying to invent them. That's difficult. Despite enormous effort, nobody has perfected a substitute, and wood—whether in boards or as some chopped, sliced, and glued derivative—remains the material of choice for building houses.

But while we see wood as a strong, beautiful material, fungi and insects see it as food or a place to call home. Nails, for their part, see it as something to split. In this chapter, you'll learn to exploit wood's strengths and overcome its weaknesses. You will also learn to speak the misleading language of lumber, and you'll be introduced to manufactured wood products, which no longer means just plywood.

Nominal Size, Actual Size, and Other Misleading Lumber Lingo

Walking into a lumberyard is like dropping through the looking glass, where nothing is what it seems. Once upon a time, a 2-by-4 measured 2 inches by 4 inches, but this simple, straightforward approach is hopelessly antiquated. These days, lumber is named with a bald-faced swindle called "nominal size." The ubiquitous 2-by-4, for example, has shrunken to $1\frac{1}{2}$ inch by $3\frac{1}{2}$ inches. Why? Because it's cheaper for the manufacturer—but not necessarily better for you. That new 2-by-4, for example, contains two-thirds the wood of its nominal-size namesake.

Like three-card monte or a shell game, the swindle has rules:

➤ Lumber is identified by thickness × width × length, so if you wanted an 8-foot 2-by-4, you'd ask for a 2-by-4-by-8.

➤ For framing (or "dimension") lumber (with a nominal thickness of 2 inches), subtract a half-inch from each nominal dimension to find the actual size. Thus, a 2-by-6 is actually $1\frac{1}{2}$-by-$5\frac{1}{2}$.

➤ The actual thickness wide of nominal 1-inch lumber is $\frac{3}{4}$ inch.

➤ The actual width of nominal 1-inch lumber is $\frac{3}{4}$ inch less than the nominal width (a 1-by-10 actually measures $\frac{3}{4}$ inch by $9\frac{1}{4}$ inches).

➤ You can find boards that are actually 1-inch thick. Just ask for "five-quarters." (Did I claim this would make sense?)

➤ Believe it or not, Ripley, but the length of lumber is stated accurately: A 10-foot board will be 10 feet long!

➤ Just to keep you guessing, plywood, paneling, and drywall are sold in full dimension: A 4-by-8 sheet measures 4 feet by 8 feet, and its thickness is also true.

The properties of natural wood (leaving aside plywood for a moment) are determined by the fibers that make it up. These fibers, which run more or less vertically in a growing tree, are strong as individuals, but the bonds between them are much weaker. That's why wood can split between the fibers (along the grain), but the fibers themselves will essentially never break.

Toolbox Trivia

Lumber is graded by a confusing system that's mostly irrelevant for our purposes. The best stuff, with no knots, is called "clear," "select," or "No. 1." Straight-grained, comely, and costly, it's used mostly for molding and other places where appearance is more important than cost. "No. 2" lumber (AKA "common"), is cheaper and suitable for most uses where the Queen of England is not expected to tea. "No. 3" is questionable, at best.

This Is a Sheet Goods Cheat Sheet

In the brave new world of lumber, you will meet these "manufactured wood products." All are made in 4-by-8-foot sheets, unless noted otherwise.

➤ *Plywood*, a sandwich of thin sheets glued at right angles, is a stable, strong, and versatile flat material used for shelving, sheathing, and furniture. The best grade is "A," and the worst is "D." Plywood with an "X" in the rating is suitable for exterior use. If the plywood will be painted, ask for AC grade, or "good one side"—the knots will be plugged for a smoother surface. Also pay attention to the number of plies—three, the minimum, is much weaker (and cheaper) than five or seven plies. Plywood is sold in $3/8$-inch, $1/2$-inch, $5/8$-inch, and $3/4$-inch thicknesses.

➤ *Hardwood-veneered plywood* is used to make furniture and built-in accessories. It's much cheaper and more stable than whole boards, but you'll need to cut it carefully and to glue bands to hide the ugly edges. You can find this stuff in $1/4$-inch, $1/2$-inch, and $3/4$-inch thicknesses.

➤ *Oriented strand board* (OSB) is a replacement for plywood, made of wood fragments glued together. It's cheap, homely, and stinky, and is used for roofs and other sheathing purposes. OSB is sold in $1/4$-inch, $3/8$-inch, $7/16$-inch, $1/2$-inch, and $5/8$-inch thicknesses. The thinner versions are generally for reinforcing existing sheathing.

Nail It Down

When buying lumber, pass up the first few pieces in the stack and look for the good boards below them. How to distinguish good lumber? It's straight when you eyeball it from the end. It's neither twisted nor knotty. Generally, once you reach the good wood in a pile, you'll find what you need pretty quickly, but you may have to wade through a lot of junk. Don't be sheepish—sorting is a sign of lumberyard sophistication.

➤ *Particle board* is a strong, dense pile of glued sawdust that's used for shelving, furniture, and countertops. It's generally used inside, although some siding is made of particle board. This stuff rapidly dulls a saw and produces sharp, obnoxious grit while sawing; it's available in $1/2$-inch, $5/8$-inch, and $3/4$-inch thicknesses.

➤ *Medium-density fiberboard* (MDF) is essentially sawdust glued together into a heavy, stable, and relatively cheap backing board. MDF can be used for countertops and furniture. A $3/4$-inch MDF board may be surfaced with oak or birch veneer; it's a cheaper replacement for veneered plywood.

➤ *Hardboard* (or *Masonite*) is a thin, flexible material that can be used for concrete forms (hence the name) and other light-duty purposes. When Masonite is drilled with holes in a square pattern, it becomes the tool-mounting board called pegboard. Both materials are sold in $1/8$-inch and $1/4$-inch thicknesses.

The Enemies of Wood

For such a lovely material, wood has an outsize share of enemies: sunlight, water, fungus, and insects. To defeat these enemies, you've got to know their *modus operandi*, you've got to stay vigilant—and you've got to keep the wood dry.

Outdoors, unprotected wood starts degrading almost as soon as it's exposed to the elements. Ultraviolet light from the sun strips off the surface, causing the wood to turn gray. Rain causes swelling, dryness causes contraction, and cracks develop, giving water and mold access deeper into the wood. The wood starts to dry more slowly, making it yet more hospitable to decay organisms (see the following table).

The Six Plagues of Wood and What to Do About Them

Plague	Nature and Signs	Geographic Location	Location in Home	Cures
Dry rot	A fungus that consumes the cellulose in wood, leaving a soft skeleton that reduces to powder. Look for wet, powdery, flaky, or discolored wood.	Humid climates.	Under roof leaks, in damp basement, near cold-water pipes with condensation. May soften wood for attack by insects. Important: eats only damp wood.	Figure out where moisture originates and cure that problem.

Plague	Nature and Signs	Geographic Location	Location in Home	Cures
Carpenter ants	Large black ants that tunnel through wet wood and rigid foam insulation. Look for piles of sawdust beneath the tunnel openings.	Widespread	Under roof leaks, in damp basements or crawl spaces, in wall cavities, etc.	Dry out the damp areas; call exterminator if problem persists.
Termites— subterranean	Look for tunnels running up the foundation— these termites can't stand sunlight (except while swarming through the air to mate).	Widespread	Starting from the bottom up.	Keep wood out of contact with soil; look for tunnels on foundation; call exterminator if problem persists.
Termites— dry wood	Do not require contact with ground; can enter through gaps in siding and attic vents; leave droppings that resemble tiny seeds.	Southern states	Near doors and windows.	Call exterminator.
Termites— damp wood	Usually attack wet wood, but may spread further.	Pacific Northwest	Damp wood	Call exterminator.
Wood-boring beetles	Often called "worms"; look for wormholes wood.	Widespread, especially in older basement beams.	May enter in a load of firewood or from a nearby tree.	Call exterminator if problem is widespread and active (as shown by new sawdust on floor).

Dry rot, which attacks damp or wet wood, earned its misleading name because the rotten wood looks dry. Dry rot is easier to prevent—by keeping the wood dry—than to cure, so see the section "Home Ventilation: Why and How," in Chapter 12, "Skin-Tight: Caulking, Weather-Stripping, Insulation, and Ventilation," and the section "May We Talk About Your Soggy Basement?" in Chapter 17, "Bricks and Stones: Masonry and Concrete (the Sequel)."

Carpenter ants and termites are colonial beasts; you get one, and you may soon have a million. If you stay alert for signs of these silent villains, you can deal with invasions before they get too bad. Termites can be prevented by construction that puts no wood in contact with soil and uses pressure-treated wood and metal termite shields.

Although exterminators will happily spray poison on insects, calling the bug-killers should be a last resort. Start by changing conditions to make the house less hospitable to insects. Carpenter ants, for example, burrow only in wet wood; you can send them packing by closing whatever leak is soaking the wood. Extermination also raises health concerns: Chlordane, used for termite control until 1988, is a persistent, carcinogenic pesticide, and although newer pesticides are less hazardous, who's to say they are perfectly safe? If you're forced to choose between extermination and watching your house being gnawed to death, that's an easy choice. But remember that many pesticides are nerve toxins, so err on the side of caution in protecting yourself and your family.

Treated Lumber

Industrial chemists have responded to the threat fungi and insects pose to wood by inventing pressure-treated lumber, which is universally used for decks, steps, and other outdoor or below-grade work. The most common pressure-treated wood is a greenish variety treated with chromated copper arsenate, called CCA. CCA is relatively safe, unlike two earlier preservatives, pentachlorophenol and creosote, which are now tightly restricted due to health and environmental concerns. Nevertheless, CCA contains the toxic chemicals chromium and arsenic, so you should cut it with care. Work outside, and wear a dust mask to avoid breathing sawdust. A long-sleeve shirt can also help, as some people report skin irritation from working with this stuff. Think of it this way: "If it's green, it's mean." Don't even try to burn green wood, as that could release arsenic-laden vapors. If this discussion is giving you the heebie-jeebies, look for the new varieties of treated wood that contain neither arsenic nor chromium.

Nuts and Bolts

To a builder, **grade** is not something on a report card; it's ground level (not to be confused with "ground zero"). Something that is **below-grade** is below ground level, whether it's actually in contact with the earth or not.

Even though treated wood is not appetizing to bugs, it does require attention, as I learned when sunlight and rain began darkening and splitting the pressure-treated deck in my backyard (see the section "Treating Decks," in Chapter 13, "In the Yard: No Rest for the Weary"). For advice on applying water repellent and other wood treatments, see Chapter 26, "Lay It on—but Not Too Thick."

Cutting Remarks on Slick Sawing Techniques

Cutting wood accurately sounds easy—until you try it. Then you notice that the saw binds in the board, or wanders from the line, or doesn't cut in the first place. That's when you realize that you need a sharp saw and savvy technique.

Sawhorses are the traditional way to support wood while sawing, and they are helpful for keeping the work at a comfortable height. Still, plastic milk crates are cheaper, easier to store, and helpful for supporting other stuff you may need to repair, from cabinets to lawn mowers.

Arrange the supports so that the cut-off piece can fall free. If you saw between supports, the board will sag, the saw will bind vise-like, and you'll get a crooked cut, at best, and an injury, at worst.

Basic Sawing Technique

1. Keep the cut reasonably close (within 4 inches) of the support, and use enough support to hold the work securely.

2. Push the raised edge of the square against the board, and then mark your cut (see the following figure). Select either hand- or power-sawing technique.

Don't Screw Up!

When you cut plywood or paneling with a circular saw—even with a fine-toothed plywood blade—the top side will splinter. If the plywood must look good, you'll have to cut with the good side down. Imagine the piece backwards, and then mark and cut from the back. Don't bother doing this unless you care about appearance; splintering does not weaken the wood.

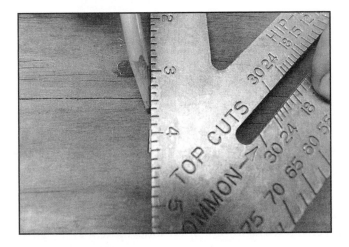

When marking your cuts, the pencil, not the edge of the square, should be on the cutting line.

Hand saw fundamentals.

Hand Sawing

3. Hand sawing is best done with clamps or a vise, although the knee or foot is a time-tested and usually workable alternative.

4. Start the cut by drawing the saw backwards against your thumb, keeping your skin away from the teeth. Stroke smoothly, hewing to the line.

5. Finish with a good hard push, to prevent splitting at the end.

Circular Sawing

3. Slide the square aside and move your circular saw into position. Be sure to guide your saw with an aluminum square (see the section "Seven Cool Tools You Must Meet" in Chapter 7, "The Bare Essentials: Hand Tools"). Fast, facile, and fiendishly accurate, it's a carpenter's best friend.

4. When the blade is where you want it, slide the square against the saw's baseplate.

5. Pull the trigger and slide the saw along the square (see the next photo). Once you get the hang of it, you won't need to watch the blade—just hold the square in position.

6. For a wide board, stop cutting halfway, move the square to the other side of the board, and finish (or, if you're feeling rich, buy a 12-inch square). For material that's too thick to cut in one pass, adjust the saw to cut a quarter-inch past halfway. Make the first cut, flip the board over, and saw the other side.

If you're cutting a long piece from a board, it will split when it falls—unless someone holds it. If a servant is not available, use a third support about as high as the other supports. The support can be slightly shorter, but if it's too tall, it will push the wood up and bind the saw.

Safe circular saw technique.

A. Firm support close to one side of the cut, with foot pressing the wood down.

B. No obstructions or snarled extension cords.

C. Saw glides firmly along the square.

To saw large pieces of plywood, paneling, or particle board, use a wooden guide or a drywall square. Support the panel well with long 2-by-4s placed along the cut. Start the cut by guiding the saw along an aluminum square, then shut off the saw and place the long square next to the cut (see the photo of sawing a large panel). Use a clamp to secure the far end of the square, and push against the square with your body to keep the closer end in position. Then simply slide the saw along the square for a perfect cut. Alternatively, secure a straight board into position with two C-clamps. (Hint: Place the good side of a panel down to prevent splintering. If both sides must be good, slice through the veneer at the exact cut line with a utility knife, using a square for guidance.)

For cutting small pieces, such as molding, use a miter box. You can buy or rent a power miter box (see Chapter 8, "The Bare Essentials with Oomph! Power Tools"), or use a simple wooden model with a back saw. Using a hand miter box, and other aspects of cutting and nailing molding, are described in Chapter 24, "A Scolding on Molding."

Sawing a large panel.

Hammering for the Ham-Handed

When I was a kid, the county fair offered a prize to anybody who could whump a big nail into a knotty 2-by-4 with three whacks. I never came close to winning, but I did learn that while hammering may look neolithic in its simplicity, it's a tricky knack. In case you didn't get to the county fair, heed these suggestions:

➤ Use a natural swing, and flex your wrist.

➤ Try to hammer downward. Nailing overhead is tiring and clumsy; if you must, drill a pilot (preparatory) hole for the nail. Much better: Use a power-driven screw.

➤ Nail the thinner board to the thicker one; nail the siding to the stud, for example, and the plywood to the floor framing.

➤ Use a nail set (see Chapter 7) to prevent hammer dents in finish work. Sets are also helpful if you can't quite reach the nail with the hammer.

➤ For a better grip on the nail head, clean corrosion from the hammer face with sandpaper.

➤ Get good support behind the work. If you must nail into something that springs back, use a screw, secure the boards with a C-clamp, or see the figure that follows.

Nailing to a moving target.

A. My friend John Christenson showed me this amazingly effective trick for nailing to a wobbly post. Hold something about as heavy as your hammer—like another hammer or a pipe wrench—behind the nail. As long as the backup tool bounces back when you hit the nail, it will absorb the blow, and you'll have a tight joint.

Why Wood Splits—and How You Can Prevent It

One of the biggest drawbacks of wood that comes directly from a tree (I'm not talking about plywood and similar products) is that nailing tends to split it. Wood splits between the grain (the fibers that are vertical in a living tree) because the "glue" bonding the fibers is weaker than the fibers themselves. Splitting is a real problem in old, dry wood.

To minimize splitting:

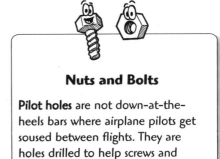

➤ Drill a pilot hole through the top board; this is almost a requirement for hardwoods like oak and hard maple (unless you use an air or floor nailer).

➤ Use a small nail. Use box or sinker nails instead of common nails; they are much easier to drive and end up being stronger because they cause less splitting.

➤ Dull the nail by hammering the point so that it cuts through the grain instead of splitting it.

> **Nuts and Bolts**
>
> **Pilot holes** are not down-at-the-heels bars where airplane pilots get soused between flights. They are holes drilled to help screws and (sometimes) nails get where they are going.

➤ Use plywood or oriented strand board instead of regular lumber. This stuff may be ugly, but it won't split.

➤ Stagger your nails; don't put them all into the same grain fiber.

➤ Avoid nailing near the end of a board, or drill a pilot hole.

Instead of overnailing to make a superstrong wood joint, use one of these tricks:

➤ Apply glue to the joint before nailing, then use fewer nails.

➤ Bolt the joint and use flat washers on both sides.

➤ Use a sheet-metal or strap-iron mending plate (sold at lumber yards and hardware stores).

➤ Glue and nail or screw a triangular reinforcer (called a gusset; made from scrap 2-by-4s or plywood) to the joint.

Toe Nailing

Toe nailing—nailing diagonally through one board into another—is your only choice if you can't get behind a joint to nail straight through. Toe nailing is usually used for construction, not repairs, but it's a handy trick to know. Make sure you have a tight joint. You may have to hold the upper piece still by placing your boot or nailing a temporary block of wood behind it. If you have trouble toe nailing, substitute a drywall screw in an angled pilot hole.

1. Punch a starting dent in the upper board, about $1^1/_2$ inches from the end. Hold the nail perpendicular to the wood, as shown in the following figure.

2. Hold the point in the hole you just made, but angle it steeply toward the bottom piece and hammer it tight (see the following figure). If you're smashing the wood with the hammer, use a $^1/_8$-inch nail set to finish nailing.

Starting to toe nail.

A. To start toe nailing, aim the nail directly at the wood and tap with the hammer. As soon as the nail is started, hammer it downward.

B. Toe nailing is almost impossible if the pieces don't meet tightly. Cut the pieces correctly, or use a shim to get good contact.

C. Make sure the nail is angled steeply toward the second board, or you'll just push the top piece to the side.

The Glue Doctor Will See You Now

Done right, gluing is the perfect—that is, strong and invisible—repair. Done wrong, however, it's a botched job that will prevent anybody from ever making a good repair. How handy is wood glue? A bottle of yellow carpenter's glue should be part of any elementary toolkit, because it's a one-stop cure for many wood ailments. For help on picking glues, see the section "Gorgeous Glues" in Chapter 9, "Fast Guide to Fasteners."

Good gluing calls for good clamps, which are the best way to hold the wood into the intimate relationship needed while the glue sets. To me, that usually means buying a lot of clamps. Bar-type clamps (costing $10 to $15 apiece) are easy to adjust, strong and versatile, and are best used in pairs. You may be able to avoid buying clamps by holding the pieces together with locking pliers, heavy weights, rope, or wire. One good solution is to loosely tie rope around the repair and then tighten the rope by inserting a nail between two strands to twist them.

If a piece of wood starts to split, avoid disaster by gluing it back before it breaks entirely. Ease glue into the crack with a finishing nail, or with a piece of string or paper (or blow the glue into place using a can of compressed air). Then clamp securely.

Nail It Down

Lumber yards sell wood shims—essentially long wooden wedges—which are great for filling gaps before nailing. Place one shim atop another, and slide them together until they're the right thickness. Nail through the shims, then cut them off if you want.

Here are more prescriptions for great gluing:

1. Save the chips that split off moldings and furniture. With a little glue and smart clamping, they will make a great repair.

2. Before gluing, hold the parts together and make sure they mate evenly. Clean off old glue or splinters that prevent mating. Use a plane, saw, or sandpaper to get a clean, flat surface.

3. Apply glue to the entire mating surface—enough that some oozes out when you tighten the clamps. Scraps of wood or cardboard make good glue spreaders.

4. End grain makes a very weak joint. If you must glue to end grain, use a double dose of glue, and screw a wooden glue block beside the joint as a reinforcement.

5. Work quickly: Observe the glue's working time. Don't start gluing a complicated joint that you won't be able to finish.

6. Mop up spills with a wet rag before the glue sets. If you must remove a bead of dried glue from the joint, use a sharp chisel or utility knife.

Filling Holes in Wood

Like people, wood can show its age. Unlike people, you won't need a plastic surgeon to repair the occasional hole, scratch, or dent in wood. Instead, you need a can of wood filler and a couple of tricks. If you're planning to stain the wood, choose a filler that will absorb stain. We'll show you how to test the stain so you're sure to get the color you want.

Filling holes. To prevent a big sandpapering chore afterward, scrape off all filler from the surface of the wood.

Note: Don't bother using filler on nicks and scratches. Just rub some wood stain onto the blemish and forget it. If the surface is varnished, revarnish when the stain is dry.

1. Clean the surface with a putty knife, utility knife, small trowel, or sandpaper. *Make sure nothing remains above the final surface level.* Otherwise, the patching material will bulge out and you'll need to do too much sandpapering.

Nail It Down

I buy wood filler in powder form and mix it with water when I need it. Powder seems less convenient than ready-mixed filler, but that stuff dries out in the can while powder lasts forever on the shelf. When mixing, add water slowly—a little goes a long way.

2. Mix up some wood filler, and push it firmly into the hole. If you'll stain the patch, smear a thin coat on scrap wood for color-testing purposes.

3. Scrape the patching flush with the knife almost perpendicular to the surface (see the previous figure), and allow it to set a while. Scrape with the grain of the wood.

4. If needed, press another coat into place.

5. Wait until the patch is partly hardened. To reduce sandpapering, dampen a rag with water for a water-based filler, and solvent for other fillers. Wipe away excess filler. Repeat a half-hour later to remove any haze on the surface.

6. Lightly sandpaper the patch when it's dry to level it. Do the same on your test scrap.

7. Use the test piece to check that the stain will achieve the color you want. Then stain or prime and paint the real thing.

The Least You Need to Know

➤ Moisture, insects, and fungi are wood's No. 1 enemies.

➤ Wood is easy to saw—if you use a sharp blade and good support.

➤ The right nail and the right technique can simplify nailing and prevent splitting.

➤ Manufactured wood can solve lots of problems, if you know how to select and handle it.

➤ Glue, screws, and reinforcing plates are helpful alternatives to nails.

➤ If you're trying to restore beat-up wood surfaces, wood filler is your best friend.

Part 3
Strictly for Outsiders: The Exterior View

The exterior of your home—the foundation, siding, caulking, and roof—is the first part your friends see. It's also the only part the weather sees. The exterior is supposed to keep everything and everybody inside warm, cozy, and dry (or cool, cozy, and dry, depending upon where you happen to live). But if your house is past toddlerhood, I'll bet its skin has developed problems, including wrinkles, sags, leaks, and even blemishes.

Hollywood stars buy facelifts all the time—and why should your home get any less pampering? In this chapter, we'll talk about giving the old place a minor facelift. Even if you're not planning a Hollywood audition, its appearance and durability will only benefit from a little touch-up.

Chapter 12

Skin-Tight: Caulking, Weather-Stripping, Insulation, and Ventilation

---

In This Chapter

➤ Your caulking and weather-stripping—are they up to the job?

➤ Where, how, and when to caulk and weather-strip

➤ What it takes to stay warm in winter and cool in summer

➤ How to protect your home from moisture build-up

In college, I rented an old brick farmhouse in the upper Midwest with a little problem: winter. The big chill was particularly severe in the kitchen, where six dilapidated doors and four wobbly windows failed to keep the weather at bay. I cut my teeth on caulking and weather-stripping in a house where you could fly a kite—inside—on a blustery January evening.

Log cabins were once chinked with straw, mud, and clay—low-tech materials that kept some weather out. Nowadays, these organic materials have been replaced by caulking (the gooey stuff that squeezes into cracks) and by weather-stripping (the flexible seals for doors and windows). Caulking and weather-stripping don't just keep out annoying things like rain, wind, cold, heat, insects, and noise. They also offer a quick return on your investment in the form of lower utility bills; they often pay for themselves in less than a year. Insulation has a somewhat longer payback, but you can't stay warm without it in northern climates.

Unfortunately, modern caulk, weather-stripping, and insulation may be too effective, causing a problem that would have been inconceivable to log-cabin dwellers: a buildup of moisture inside the home. We'll conclude this chapter with some tips on home ventilation.

Where and When to Caulk

You'll need to caulk almost anywhere dissimilar building materials meet. That's because when the temperature changes, different materials expand and contract at different rates, creating cracks that can be sealed only by a flexible sealer, such as caulk.

A good way to learn about controlling heat and moisture, and where better caulking is needed, is to obtain a home energy audit, courtesy of your local utility (see Chapter 29, "A Welcome Blast of Hot Air: Heating System Tips"). Or, spend an hour on a particularly hot or cold day looking for drafts.

Outdoors, caulk these areas:

➤ At the joint between the foundation and siding (if you can reach it).

➤ At cracks in the foundation (see the section "A Word on Foundation Repair," in Chapter 17, "Bricks and Stones: Masonry and Concrete [the Sequel]").

➤ Around windows, doors, faucets, vents, and other openings in siding.

➤ Around chimneys, vent pipes, and vents in the roof.

➤ Note: In brick houses, don't caulk the small, regularly spaced holes just above the foundation, doors, and windows. These "weepholes," designed to allow moisture to escape the wall, must be left open.

Indoors, caulk these areas:

➤ At cracks around exterior door and window frames.

➤ Where pipes or wires enter, as under a sink or tub.

➤ At floor joints near a tub or toilet (to prevent spills or condensation from damaging floors and walls).

Spring and fall are ideal caulking seasons because it's warm enough to meet the minimum temperature requirement of caulking, because surfaces are dry, and because you won't get broiled (caulking in the heat of summer is 100 percent slavery). Sadly, most caulking won't flow or adhere well in cold or damp weather, even though winter is when you are most likely to feel motivated to cure drafts.

Caulking Materials

So what are you going to use in that caulking gun? The short answer is the best stuff you can afford. The lifetime of caulking rises quickly along with its price, so unless you actually enjoy caulking (you know who you are!), buy stuff that will last 10 years or more. A huge variety of reasonably priced silicone caulks are now on the market with promises of longevity just short of the Sphinx (see the following table).

Use the Right Caulk for the Right Job

Type	Lifetime	Notes
Acrylic latex base	5–25 years	Use on wood siding and windows, indoors or out. Water cleanup, low odor, easy to apply, fast curing, sold in various colors; some are paintable. Not very flexible; don't use on joints that are moving, as indicated by large gaps in the old caulking. Avoid non-porous surfaces, such as metal.
Siliconized acrylic	25–50 years	Use on wood, metal, glass, tile, masonry. Flexible. Use indoors and out; cures quickly, sold in colors, and may be painted. Water cleanup and excellent resistance to weather, but slow to cure and subject to some shrinkage.
Silicone	20–50 years	Best for smooth surfaces (tile, metal, glass) exterior or interior. Very flexible and durable. Some can be painted. Sold in transparent or white, black, brown, or gray. Pungent odor during application, but can be applied at hot or cold temperatures. Not suitable for masonry. Requires solvent cleanup.
Butyl	5–10 years	Exterior use, especially on concrete, metal, or masonry. Water-resistant, and good for places where water may collect. Cures slowly.
Polyurethane or urea foam		Excellent for filling deep, irregular wounds in the exterior. Sold in pressurized cans. Caution: expands rapidly and can be hard to cut off afterward; rather homely once installed.

Caulking Cracks

Caulking is real idiot-proof work. First, you clean the crack. Then you pump the caulk into place. Finally, if you're feeling ferociously fastidious, you smear it flat. While many tasks *sound* easy, this one truly *is* easy. About the only complication is deciding that caulking is more important today than paddling a canoe or reading a book.

You'll need a paint scraper, screwdriver, trowel or other cleaning tool, brush, caulking gun, caulk, utility knife, ladder, and rag. Buy your caulk before starting; each variety has limitations on temperature and how big a crack it can fill. To do the job, follow these steps:

1. Clean the crack with a tool and/or stiff plastic brush. Remember that any surface irregularities will show up in the caulking. If you want the caulking really smooth, you'll have to remove any bumps at the edge of the joint and drive in any raised nailheads.

2. Remove all the dust. If the crack is very deep, see the section "Are You Extremely Cracked?" later in this chapter.

3. Put the tube in the gun, cut the tip at an angle, and pierce the seal with a long nail. Make a wider opening for wide cracks.

4. Start caulking, holding the gun at an angle, and pressing the tip against the crack.

Keep steady pressure on the caulking gun, and try not to let bulges form when the gun snags on obstacles. Remember: It's much easier to make a smooth application than to fix it afterwards.

5. Move the gun steadily along the entire crack, gradually squeezing the trigger. Release pressure just before the end of the crack, because the caulking will ooze out for another few seconds. If your gun has a pressure release, push it just before the end of the crack.

6. Optional: Smooth the caulk and press it into place with a moistened finger, the handle of an old toothbrush, or a rag dampened with whatever solvent the manufacturer specifies.

Are You Extremely Cracked?

In my house, some cracks are more like glacial crevasses: They seem to extend down toward the center of the earth, and they could suck up entire tubes of caulking without accomplishing much except wasting money. To fill these cracks, I've got to stuff a backing material in with a trowel or a putty knife to give the caulk something to press against. You can buy fiberglass made for filling cracks, or you can just rip some material off a roll of fiberglass insulation—just make sure no packing sticks out when you're done. Spray cans of urethane foam insulation are excellent for sealing and backing up caulking, but be careful: The foam expands so much that it tends to rise above the surface, and it's very difficult to cut back.

If the crack is only slightly too wide for your caulking, try this trick: On the first pass, aim the gun at one side of the crack, giving the caulk a good grip on that side. Let the caulk harden a bit, and then caulk the narrower crack that remains.

Weather for Stripping

What's the best weather for stripping? A summer thunderstorm, when the cool rain relieves the muggy heat, and when housebound neighbors won't notice you splashing, bare-bunned, in the cloudburst.

But the best weather for weather-stripping is a midwinter storm. Only then can you appreciate how much frigid air can move through cracks in doors and windows. But since it's a trifle difficult to weather-strip a door when it's 20° below, you've got to keep on the lookout for cracks during warmer weather.

Weather-stripping has improved immeasurably over the years. Old windows and doors didn't even have the stuff, while their modern counterparts have an array of impregnable plastic and magnetic barriers. (The improvement in weather-stripping alone may justify the expense of replacing drafty windows, but that's not our province here.)

Nuts and Bolts

Jambs are not something you want to get out of—they're the 1-inch wood members that encase doors and windows.

Many varieties of weather-stripping are being sold these days; do yourself a favor and avoid the ineffective foam tape and felt. This stuff looks ugly, works worse, and croaks in a couple of years—some economy! In some cases, you'll have to contact the window or door manufacturer to replace an intricate weather stripping.

Weather-Strip Varieties

Item	Description
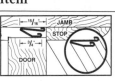	*Compression weather strip:* Nails to the jamb; the vinyl gasket folds up slightly when the door closes to make the seal.
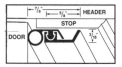	*Tubular gasket:* A plastic tube with a strip that's nailed or screwed to the stops; slots allow easy adjustment to the door. The vinyl gasket should be replaced when it gets stiff.
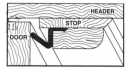	*Vinyl-wood stop:* A wood strip with vinyl weather-stripping that is nailed to the jambs. The door folds the vinyl slightly to make the seal. This style can be nailed to the existing stop, or it can replace the stop.
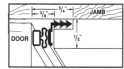	*Magnetic weather strip:* For steel-clad doors only. The weather-strip slides into a notch in the jamb, and the strip magnet pulls the weather-strip to the door, for a very tight seal. You may have to contact the manufacturer or distributor for an unusual variety.

One of the most versatile weather strips is a V-shaped strip of flexible plastic that's glued on one side. Use this so-called "Vee-strip" in door and window jambs or stops; it adheres tightly to clean surfaces, even in cold weather. The only tool you need is a utility knife or scissors.

Various sweeps, shoes, and thresholds are sold to prevent wind and rain from gusting below your door. See the following table, and read the section "Diagnosing and Curing Poor-Fitting Doors" in Chapter 19, "An Entry-Level Treatise on Doors." Note that while sweeps allow you to avoid sawing the door bottom, they are visible from the inside, and they may have trouble riding over a carpet or a very unlevel floor.

Don't Screw Up!

When choosing weather-stripping for a door bottom, do not underestimate the challenge of cutting the door accurately enough to make a gasket threshold work. Measure several times before you remove the door from its hinges; mark with a knife, not a pencil; and use a straight edge to guide the saw.

Door Bottom Solutions

Item	Description
	Gasket threshold: This basic door-bottom sealer makes a good seal, but you may have to remove the existing threshold and/or saw the door to exact length. After a few years, plan on pulling out the vinyl gasket and replacing it.
	Adjustable-height threshold: This threshold has set screws to fill an uneven gap at the bottom of the door. It's good for an inaccurate gap, and a lot easier than sawing the door bottom!
	*Aluminum and pile door sweep:* This sweep is easier to install, but it will not seal as effectively as a gasket threshold. Note that the sweep must contact a relatively flat portion of the threshold. Sweeps are also available in a glue-on variety (which I wouldn't trust), and with plastic frames instead of metal.
	Oak and vinyl sweep: This sweep can be stained or painted to match the door trim.
	Drip cap: This comes in aluminum, vinyl, or brass, and keeps the rain out.
	Combination: A combination drip cap, threshold, and door sweep is a comprehensive solution to door woes.

Insulation

Want to stay warm? Need to stay cool? Then you'll need insulation: Keeping out drafts with weather-stripping is not enough. The biggest variable in insulation is access: Installing insulation in walls is generally a professional job because somebody's got to bore holes in the walls and spray the insulation into place. But foundations, crawl spaces, and accessible attics are all places where you can save money by insulating yourself. And if you happen to be undertaking major repairs, always check that the insulation in exposed walls is up to par.

113

The effectiveness of insulation is rated by "R-factor": The higher the R-factor, the more insulating power you get. Usually, the R-factor applies to the thickness of a whole insulation product. If you see an R per inch rating, that describes a type of material. In other words, a 2-inch foam panel, rated at R-8, has an R per inch value of R-4.

Insulation is sold in roll or batt form (typically made of fiberglass), foam panels, and various materials that can be blown into place. (See the following table for more information on insulation varieties.) Inch for inch, isocyanurate foam has the best insulating value, but it's expensive, so if thickness is not a problem, buy thicker but cheaper material.

When applying insulation in older homes, be sure to follow your building codes—don't just throw the stuff anywhere. Avoid:

➤ Covering old knob-and-tube electrical wiring or recessed lighting fixtures (see Chapter 28, "Getting Wired Without Getting Zapped").

➤ Covering vents in the soffit (the lower edge of a roof), which allows moisture to escape from the roof.

➤ Installing insulation without a vapor barrier, which prevents air-borne moisture in the warm house from condensing upon reaching a cool area. This condensed moisture can wreak havoc on wood, drywall, and paint. Many insulation materials lose insulating power when wet, and cellulose can even rot. Wet foam won't rot or stop insulating, but it will retain humidity in the building and contribute to destructive moisture buildup.

➤ Plugging the air channel under the roof sheathing, between soffit vents and ridge vents. This channel allows air to pass above the insulation, removing moisture in the winter. It should be at least 1 inch deep. (See the section "Home Ventilation: Why and How," which follows.)

Fiberglass is probably the most common do-it-yourselfer insulation. This is the best material for stuffing into irregular spaces to seal gaps; I've always preferred fiberglass for filling gaps between the foundation and the framing above it, and for filling the tiny gaps that appear around window framing when I remove molding. It's also good in hot areas because it's fireproof. (I've used it to insulate near stove pipes, for example.) Fiberglass is often bonded to water-resistant paper that serves as a vapor barrier when stapled to the studs or joists. Use $5/16$-inch staples in a staple gun.

Cut fiberglass with a giant shears or a big kitchen knife. To use a knife, place a scrap board on the floor, lay down the fiberglass with the paper side up, and step on another scrap board next to the cut. Slice the insulation next to the upper board.

Use caution with fiberglass: Protect your lungs with a dust mask, and wear long sleeves—this stuff is ferociously itchy and not helpful to your breathing apparatus. For a big job, I'd pay extra for the "encapsulated" variety. This fiberglass is wrapped in plastic to contain the dusty fibers.

Cement foam insulation to concrete by squirting foam board adhesive from a caulking gun. Attach the foam to wood with special insulation nails, which have a 1-inch plastic washer to hold the insulation. Foam is flammable and must be covered with drywall or another fire-resistant material.

Insulation Varieties

Form	Material and R Per Inch	Uses	How Installed	Comments
Rolls or batts (shorter pieces), sized to fit framing spaced 16 inches or 24 inches on center	Fiberglass: 3.3	Walls, floors, ceilings, attics, and roofs	Stapled to studs, rafters, or floor joists, laid into cavity between ceiling joists.	Best for do-it-yourselfers but requires access to the insulated area. Awkward to apply if the gap between framing is irregular.
Fill (loose or blown)	Fiberglass: 3.3 Cellulose: 3.8 Vermiculite: 2.4	Walls, ceilings, inaccessible and finished areas	Pour between joists or blow into walls. Vermiculite is great for sealing gaps left in fiberglass batts.	Best for irregular or inaccessible areas; easy to pour between exposed ceiling joists; otherwise installation is a pro job. Make sure cavities are completely full. Cellulose can rot.
Panels	Molded or extruded polystyrene: 5	Walls, masonry surfaces, and exteriors	Nailed or glued into position; foam must be covered with drywall or other fire-resistant material.	May be available with reflective finish, which bounces radiative heat back into room. Best insulation value per inch, but highly flammable (except for fiberglass board).

Home Ventilation: Why and How

Caulking, weather-stripping, and insulation keep the weather out, and they hold moisture in. This moisture from breathing, cooking, washing, and bathing causes problems in winter, when it migrates through your walls toward the colder, drier conditions outside. Moisture that condenses inside the walls can peel paint and rot wood, plaster, and drywall. Condensation on windows can block your winter view, ruin paint, and rot your sash.

In Southern Florida and other places where humidity and fungus are constant problems, the best solution to humidity may be whole-house air conditioning. But in most other climates, simpler measures can reduce the moisture problem. Start by operating exhaust fans in the kitchen and bathroom. Run a dehumidifier in the basement in the summer. For suggestions on dampness below stairs, see the section "May We Talk About Your Soggy Basement?" in Chapter 17. Aside from roof vents (see the following section), most long-term solutions to moisture build-up, such as installing vapor barriers in walls, are virtually impossible without remodeling.

Roof Vents

One of the best ways to allow moisture to escape is through roof vents, which have the fringe benefit of cooling the house by allowing hot air to escape the attic. The system relies on vents at the soffits and peak, as show in the following figure on attic and roof ventilation. Notice that when roof rafters are insulated, you must leave a 1-inch gap above the insulation to allow air to circulate between the soffits and the peak.

Any do-it-yourselfer can vent a shingle roof that's not too steep. To ensure good circulation, put vents in the soffit (beneath the eave) and near the ridge (peak of the roof). Use a string to line up soffit vents. The ventilator package should explain how many ventilators your house needs, based on square footage.

Aluminum soffit is usually vented with narrow slits. You can install round ventilators into a wood soffit with a hole saw or a right-angle drill. Drill between each rafter, and push the vent into the hole. You'll need good ladders and goggles to shield your eyes from flying crud.

To insert a roof ventilator under the shingles near the ridge, you'll need chalk or a pencil, a hammer, a saber saw or a keyhole saw, a drill and bits, a trowel, the ventilator, roof cement, and roofing nails.

Nail It Down

Here's a quickie fix for a kitchen vent fan that's spinning slowly due to a grease build-up. Cut off the electricity, remove the filter, and remove the screws securing the fan. Squirt WD-40 on the fan shaft near the motor, spin the blade by hand, reinstall everything, and turn on the circuit. WD-40 will soften the grease dragging on the fan shaft, and you'll have a like-new fan.

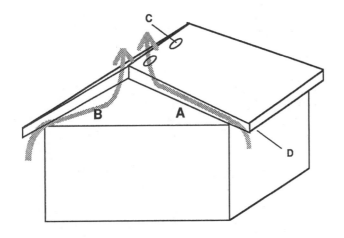

The attic or roof above any heated room in a cold climate must be ventilated. Air enters at soffit vents and leaves at ridge or roof vents. Roof vents are shown. Ridge vents run along the ridge of the roof.

A. When the attic is inhabited, the air flows above the insulation and between the rafters.

B. If the attic is unused, air can flow through the attic itself.

C. Roof vent

D. Soffit vent

1A. If you can enter the attic: Locate the ventilator from below by punching a nail through the midpoint between the rafters about 18 inches below the ridge. Use this nail as a center point for the hole. Go to step 2.

1B. If you must work from above: Locate the rafters by pounding on the roof, and mark the center of the ventilator at a place with maximum bounce.

When you cut the opening for a roof ventilator, hold the saber saw firmly against the roof to prevent vibration.

117

Work slowly with the trowel to minimize damage as you separate the shingles.

Theoretically, you don't need any roof goop on the bottom of the ventilator, but it's better to overdo things than have to return to fix a leak.

2. Place the ventilator on the roof—centered on the nail from step 1A or the mark from step 1B—and mark the opening (*not* the outer dimension) on the shingles with chalk. (Some ventilators come with a template for this hole.)

3. Start the hole with a $^3/_8$-inch drill for a saber saw or a $^1/_2$-inch for a keyhole saw. Cut through the entire roof thickness and remove the hole.

4. Slip the trowel under the shingles above the hole to loosen the cement bonding them to each other. Clear away the debris.

5. Coat the bottom of the ventilator base with roof cement and slip it under the shingles.

6. Nail the ventilator in place, and coat visible nail heads with cement. Squirt a line of cement under the shingles you loosened in step 4, and press them into the cement.

The Least You Need to Know

➤ Caulking and weather-stripping offer about the fastest payback of any home repairs.

➤ Most of the expense of caulking is the labor of installing it, so you might as well buy material that will last for many years.

➤ Insulation can save money and make the house more comfortable at the same time. Like everything else, though, it's got to be chosen and installed correctly.

➤ Moisture accumulations can damage paint, wood, drywall, and plaster. To improve the ventilation in your home, operate whatever vents you already have, and consider installing vents in the roof.

Chapter 13

In the Yard: No Rest for the Weary

In This Chapter

➤ The best way to paint railings, mailboxes, and other outdoor metal

➤ Repairing, cleaning, and preserving decks and other outdoor wood

➤ Asphalt maintenance: a money-saver in the long run

If you think you can shirk your home repair obligations just by lounging in the backyard, I've got news for you: Sunlight, snow, rain, and fungus exact their heaviest toll outdoors, and the yard is ideal territory for rot, decay, and rust (did I hear anyone mention moral decrepitude?). But it's also a place to save money in tomorrow's repair bills and in next year's replacement bills.

Even if you'd rather be napping in the hammock or just plain asleep at the switch, the forces of decay are happily rotting, rusting, and ruining your outdoor possessions. So slurp down that beer and let's get down to some yard work. (For more advice on painting and staining, see Chapter 25, "Putting a Good Face on: Choosing Paint and Painting Tools," and Chapter 26, "Lay It on—but Not Too Thick.")

"All Hands on Deck—Prepare to Be Boarded!" (Replacing Rotten Deck Boards)

Ah, wooden decks—the delightful replacement for front porches, the staging ground for innumerable barbecues, the whining ground for mosquitoes, and the battleground of your home's struggle with the elements.

Nuts and Bolts

A **joist** is a piece of framing—2-by-6 or larger—that supports a floor, a ceiling, or both.

Deck boards can go bad for any number of reasons, from poor original quality to subsequent abuse and neglect. If the deck is *screwed* down, you're in luck: Simply unscrew the damaged board, cut a replacement to the same length, and screw it down. You'll need rustproof deck screws, a power screwdriver, and a pilot drill bit.

Deck boards that are *nailed* down are more difficult to remove and replace. You may need a saber or keyhole saw, an aluminum square, a pencil, a hammer, a pry bar, a chisel, replacement board, scraps of treated 2-by-4 or 2-by-6, and galvanized deck nails or deck screws. It will be very handy to have a circular saw and a C-clamp as well.

Start by sizing up the problem. It's easier to remove whole boards, but if the damage is small, you can replace only a portion of a board (for stability, it's best to make boards span at least three joists). Since taking out a part of a board is more complicated, we'll cover it here. Follow these steps:

1. At the end of the section to be replaced, mark a square cutting line on the board, to the near side of the joist. Sight down from above, and make the line directly above the *edge* of a joist. Sawing at the edge of the joist gives room for the saw blade while leaving the good piece of decking nailed to the joist.

2. Cut along the line, preferably with the saber saw. Use the aluminum square to make a straight, square cut (see the photo for this step, which follows).

3. Pull as many nails as possible. If you have a small wrecking bar called a "cat's paw," hammer it under the nails and pull them. If not, gouge around the nail head with a wood chisel (without hitting the nail), then pull the nail with a hammer or wrecking bar (as shown in the photo).

4. Once most of the nails are out, pry the board loose with the wrecking bar, using shims to protect nearby boards.

5. Cut a section of pressure-treated 2-by-4 or 2-by-6 about three times as long as the *width* of your decking. (If the board you removed was sound 2-inch lumber, use a piece of it). Place this nailer against the joist where you sawed out the old board. If you have a C-clamp, clamp the nailer into place as you nail it. Drill pilot holes, or start the nails before putting the nailer into place, or use screws. Fasten the nailer to the framing, with the top tight to the bottom of the deck (see the accompanying figure).

6. Cut the new board to length, and nail it into place. Drill holes for the end nails to prevent splitting (see the accompanying figure). Finish per suggestions in the section "Treating a Deck or Stairway," later in this chapter.

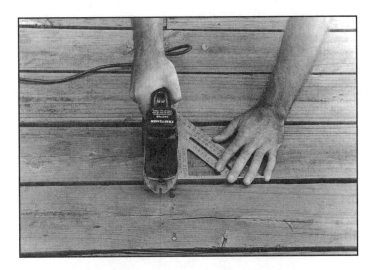

Cut straight and square along the line. Don't let the square slip.

Gouge around the nail head with a wood chisel until your hammer can grab the nail head. Then pull it.

Start the nails into the nailer, then C-clamp it tight to the bottom of the surrounding decking while you finish nailing.

At the ends of boards, a pilot hole will prevent splitting.

Treating a Deck or Stairway

Chances are, your outdoor deck or stairway is made of treated lumber—the faintly green stuff that's so full of poison that even bugs and fungi won't sink their teeth (or the fungal equivalent) into it. Treated lumber is great stuff. It lasts forever. It never needs painting. It's like, permanent.

Wrong. Treated lumber may be repellent to insects and fungi, but it won't last forever unless you paint, stain, or otherwise adorn it. Sadly, if you want it to last a long time in good condition, you'll have to do this every year or two.

Why? Because when water seeps into wood, it causes expansion and cracking, and eventually splitting. And while sunlight helps keep wood dry, it contains ultraviolet rays that degrade wood. Just as you need sunscreen at the beach, your deck (and other outdoor wood) needs sunscreen, too.

Swab the Decks!

If you're like me, you've shirked your duty to protect your backyard deck (or any other outdoor wood). Now you've got a funky deck, a dirty deck. So you've got to do what I just did: Use deck cleaner to brighten and clean the wood before staining. (Although deck cleaner may sound like a backyard version of Love Canal, the stuff I used was pretty non-toxic once it was mixed with water. Still, it's expensive, and if I am more diligent about protecting the deck, I won't need to use brightener again.)

To clean a dirty deck, use a pressure washer, a bucket, and a brush with stiff bristles, or a garage broom. (Must I remind you to read the instructions on the deck cleaner you buy? Then do it!)

1. Sweep the deck with a broom.

2. Mix the cleaner per instructions, and apply to a small area at a time.

3. Work the cleaner back and forth with a brush (I used a garage broom, which worked faster and was much easier on my back than a hand brush).

4. If you've got stains, try removing them with a diluted solution of household bleach.

5. Hose off and allow the wood to dry for at least 24 hours before staining.

Treating Decks

Now that you've repaired and cleaned the deck, it's time to protect it. Don't be tempted to use paint; it's not flexible enough to expand and contract when the wood responds to changes in humidity and temperature. Instead, use a water-repellent treatment to protect against water absorption and ultraviolet light and to forestall warping, swelling, and cracking. Many of these products will stain the wood in the same operation.

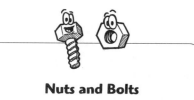

Nuts and Bolts

Cutting in is not being aggressive at a dance. It means painting around the edges in places where a roller can't reach.

I'd suggest using a product with a low percentage of volatile organic compounds (VOCs), which cause ozone smog. Low-VOC coatings are not just good for the environment, but they're also good for you. You won't endure that refinery stench as you use the stuff, and you will be able to clean your tools in water instead of paint thinner.

Outdoor wood needs a new protective coating as soon as raindrops start to sink in. Choose a warm day when leaves are not falling and when rain, dogs, and children are not in the forecast. You'll need a 2-inch paintbrush, a roller with roller pan, and a garage broom (or the short-bristled broom sold for coating asphalt driveways). To save your back, think seriously about using a roller extension handle or a sprayer. The wood should be fairly dry (although some products do not require absolute dryness). Here are the steps for treating your deck:

1. Clean the deck; use a brightener (described earlier in this chapter) if necessary.

2. Using the 2-inch brush, cut in near the house, cracks, and other non-rollable areas. Do not get too far ahead of the roller.

3. Apply the coating as indicated on the can. I used a roller (as shown in the photo) because buying a sprayer for this one purpose seemed too extravagant.

4. After 2 to 5 minutes, brush away puddles and drips.

5. Roll the end grain again, as it absorbs lots of water repellent.

6. Clean up tools and keep traffic off the deck. Do not re-recoat unless the label directs.

Apply deck coating with a roller, but don't lard it on—this stuff is supposed to penetrate, not puddle on the surface. Brush out the coating after a few minutes with a clean garage broom or a stiff-bristled brush.

With a long handle on a wide brush, you can smooth out a deck coating in short order.

In the Tar Pits: The How and Why of Asphalt First–Aid

There's no getting around it: Asphalt is handy stuff. Asphalt, a mix of gravel and asphalt binder, would last forever in the ideal world. In the real world, of course, it gets damaged by water and frost. Although asphalt is high on most "I'll-do-it-next-year" lists, the stuff needs occasional treatment. This nasty task is a surprisingly simple way to help your asphalt reach a ripe old age. (For information on concrete repairs, see Chapter 16, "Bricks and Stones: Doing Masonry and Concrete Without Getting Stoned," and Chapter 17, "Bricks and Stones: Masonry and Concrete [the Sequel].")

But asphalt is not perfect. It gets holes, and its surface deteriorates. To fix a small *hole* in asphalt, remove all loose crud. If the hole is more than 3 inches deep, fill it with coarse gravel or sand up to 3 inches below the surface. Tamp firmly with a 4-by-4. Then pour in some cold-patching asphalt, available at building suppliers. Fill it to within 1 inch of the surface, and stir with a trowel to eliminate air pockets. Tamp firmly. Refill to make a mound slightly above the surface. Tamp again, and then drive your car over the patch to compress it. Dust sand on the surface to prevent you from tracking the fresh asphalt into the house.

When I first decided to coat my asphalt driveway, I knew I'd arrived in the suburbs. Asphalt coating is cheap and easy to apply—and hardly as grubby as it might seem. Again, a low-VOC product will minimize the environmental toll of maintaining your driveway. The first step is to clean off weeds, and fix and fill cracks. Finish by putting on the black goop. You'll need a garage broom, square shovel, trowel or hooked tool, hose with spray nozzle, wide brush, plastic milk container, gloves, knife, crack-filling compound, and surfacing compound (which covers about 100 square feet per gallon). Once you've gathered what you need, follow these steps:

Spread the asphalt coating from one end to the other, using a homemade extension to the brush sold for applying asphalt goop. Don't stretch the coating too thin, or you will leave gaps that become surprisingly obvious later.

1. Cut around the perimeter of the driveway with the shovel to remove dirt and vegetation.

2. Clean out the cracks with a trowel or a hooked tool.

3. Sweep the driveway thoroughly, then flush the cracks with the hose at full pressure.

4. If the surface is oily, clean it with household cleaner. Flush the driveway clean with a hose.

5. Fill deep cracks with sand to about a half-inch from the surface, and then drench the sand to settle it.

6. Apply crack-filling compound per directions on the container, then trowel it flat for better adhesion. Let the filler dry. Put on a second coat if the cracks reappear. (Guess what? They will!) Give the filler 24 hours to dry.

7. For the actual coating, choose a moderately warm day—preferably not a stifling one, with no rain forecast. Cut the plastic jug to make a ladle, and use it to pour the surfacing goop onto the driveway. Brush the goop out, but not too thin (see the previous photo).

8. Protect the driveway from traffic for 24 hours.

The Least You Need to Know

➤ Treated lumber needs protection from rain and ultraviolet light; use a water-repellent, ultraviolet-resistant coating.

➤ If water soaks into the surface of outdoor wood, it's time to renew the water-repellent treatment.

➤ If your deck is old and dirty, clean it with a brightener before coating.

➤ Filling cracks and resurfacing asphalt driveways is no-brainer, big-payback work for homeowners.

Chapter 14

Beauty's Only Skin Deep: Care and Healing for Your Siding

Siding may seem dull, but it can conceal nasty surprises. Shortly after I moved into a house with new aluminum siding, a board blew loose. Then, a few days later, I received further proof (was any needed?) that Murphy's Law also applies to siding: The stuff started peeling off the whole side of the house. It turned out that the contractor had saved time and money by using nails that didn't quite reach the studs—a brilliant bit of false economy that forced my wife and me to waste a beautiful evening renailing siding.

Still, not much goes wrong with siding that's properly installed and maintained. But if you fail your house-painting auditions, or if you let moisture build up behind the siding, you can expect trouble. With siding, as elsewhere, it's smarter to prevent problems than be forced to solve them.

Wood Shingles

Wood shingles—they're usually made of cedar—are a traditional siding material in the East. Shingles are sometimes left unpainted; near the ocean, they weather to a beautiful gray. If you want longevity, though, it's probably better to give shingles occasional treatment with a water-repellent, ultraviolet-light inhibitor (see the section "Wood

Shingles and Shakes" in Chapter 15, "Gimme Shelter—and Other Advice on Repairing Roofs," for information on these treatments). To replace wood shingles in siding, adapt the technique for replacing asphalt roof shingles (see "Presto-Chango Shingle Replacement," also in Chapter 15).

Wood Lap Siding

Wood lap siding, also called clapboard, comes in various styles and is often made of cedar or redwood. Like all wood, lap siding needs paint, stain, or a water-repellent treatment every few years. Good eaves and functional gutters will definitely reduce damage and peeling paint caused by water dripping down the siding.

Hardboard lap siding is a form of particle board, formed to resemble wood siding, and primed at the factory. Paint new hardboard as soon as possible, because the primer degrades in sunlight.

Damage to lap siding is commonly due to water. After you've isolated and cured that problem, it's time to repair lap siding. You'll need a keyhole saw and/or a backsaw, prybar, hammer, nail set, wood wedges or wood scraps, replacement siding, and galvanized screws (preferably) or galvanized siding nails.

To repair lap siding, follow these steps:

Don't Screw Up!

Peeling paint, mold, and carpenter ants in your siding all indicate one thing: moisture. Excess humidity, whether it comes from outside or inside, is probably the biggest danger to your siding (and the structure beneath it). Moisture is a lurking disaster that must be fixed before you repaint or re-side (see the section "Home Ventilation: Why and How" in Chapter 12, "Skin-Tight: Caulking, Weather-Stripping, Insulation, and Ventilation").

1. Find the nails at both edges of the damaged area, and punch them through the siding with a nail set. (If you cannot punch the nails through, carefully reach under the siding and saw the nails with a hacksaw blade.)

2. Mark vertical cuts through the nail holes, which mark the center of the studs.

3. Pry the damaged siding away from the wall, and prop it in position with a block of wood. Using the keyhole saw, carefully saw out the damaged piece from behind. Try not to gouge the good siding. As the concealed nails come into view, punch them through.

4. Saw the replacement piece $1/8$-inch shorter than the gap (for clearance) and insert it. Nail or screw it in place, and caulk any obvious gaps. Screws will fill the existing nail holes and provide a stronger grip, but they're kind of homely.

Plywood Siding Repair

Plywood siding comes in several textures and thicknesses. About the only way to wreck this strong stuff is to neglect your obligation to paint or stain it. Once water gets inside plywood, delamination and destruction are sure to follow. Pay special attention to joints between the sheets, as the end grain absorbs an outsize share of water.

To repair plywood siding, you'll need a circular saw with a plywood blade, a carpenter's square, a level, a pencil, a nail set, a hammer and chisel, tin snips, galvanized siding screws or nails, aluminum "Z-bar" flashing, and replacement siding. If you can't locate the Z-bar flashing, bend some flat aluminum flashing over two scraps of 2-by-4s.

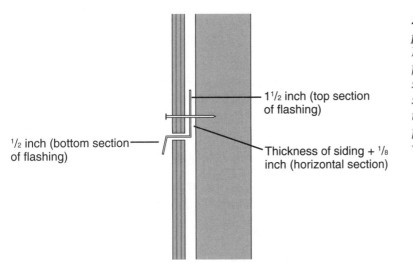

1½ inch (top section of flashing)

½ inch (bottom section of flashing)

Thickness of siding + ⅛ inch (horizontal section)

Z-bar flashing between pieces of plywood siding. Nail the top section of the flashing into two or more studs. Note the bottom section is slightly above the siding. Paint the flashing to match the wall.

1. Mark out a rectangular cutout around the damaged area. Vertical cuts should run down the center of studs (nail holes reveal the stud locations). Use a level to mark all lines so that the cutout is rectangular.

2. Punch nails on the cutting lines beneath the siding with a heavy nail punch so they don't wreck the saw blade. (If you have a cat's paw—a small, nail-pulling crowbar—you can try to pull the nails, but this could damage the siding.)

3. Fit a circular saw with a plywood blade. With the saw adjusted just deep enough to penetrate the siding, saw along the lines. Finish the end of the cuts with the wood chisel.

4. Pull any nails holding the damaged piece and remove it.

5. Cut a piece of new siding about ⅛ inch smaller in each direction, matching the grain and pattern.

6. Buy Z-bar flashing to prevent rainwater from seeping into the plywood through the horizontal joints. Or, make a strip of aluminum flashing for the top, taking the dimensions from the drawing. Mount a 2-by-4 in a vise. Hold the sheet metal over the 2-by-4 and bend it with a second block of a 2-by-4.

7. Slip the flashing under the existing siding above the repair, and nail it into place through at least two studs (see the accompanying figure).

8. Slip the new plywood under the flashing, and fasten it with galvanized screws or siding nails.

9. Caulk the seams, allow the caulk to dry, and stain or paint the siding and flashing.

Popped Nails

You will see nails in wood siding. And if they pop above the surface, you'll see them all too clearly. What to do?

If only a couple of nails have popped, pound them back in place with a hammer and nail set, fill the holes with exterior putty, prime, paint, and forget. If the nails don't grab, pull them out and drive in a siding or a deck screw, slightly larger and longer than the nail.

But if a whole section of nails has popped, you may have a structural problem, such as warped studs or a shifting structure, and renailing probably won't help. It's best to find and cure the root problem. At the least, replace the nails with screws, which will knit the structure together more soundly and may prevent things from getting worse.

Aluminum and Vinyl Siding

Vinyl and aluminum are cheap but durable replacements for wood. Aluminum, which tends to dent easily, is factory-painted. The ubiquitous vinyl siding comes in many styles and textures. Because it is dyed rather than painted, it can't chip (although it can fade).

If aluminum siding needs repainting, find primer and paint made for aluminum. Consult the paint can for cleaning instructions. To clean a house sided with either aluminum or vinyl, I'd rent a power washer (see Chapter 26, "Lay It on—but Not Too Thick"). Large repairs in aluminum and vinyl may be professional jobs because large pieces are hard to cut without special tools. Small repairs, however, are not a big deal.

For small dents in aluminum, drill a hole and insert a sheet metal screw. Grab the head of the screw with locking pliers, and pull outward. (To repair larger dents, use several screws.) Then fill the damaged area remaining with plastic aluminum or auto body filler. Smooth the filler before it dries, then prime and paint to match the surroundings.

For larger damages in aluminum, find a scrap of matching material in the garage, basement, or attic, and follow these directions:

1. Mark out the damaged area with two vertical lines along the edge of the damage, as shown in the accompanying figure, and a horizontal line 1 inch below the upper course of siding.

2. Drill holes at the corners of this cutout, and remove it with tin snips.

3. Cut the patch piece 3 inches longer than the repair area. Cut across the top so that the patch will slip under the upper course of siding.

4. Test that the patch will engage the bottom lip of the siding, and snap into place. Once it works, apply silicone caulking to the back of the patch (near the top and sides). Engage the bottom and snap into place. Paint to match, if needed.

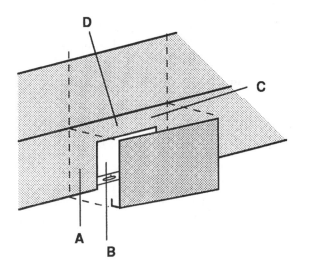

Fix gouges in aluminum siding by removing the damaged area and cutting a replacement. Caulking behind the scenes helps keep everything watertight.

A. 1½-inch overlap

B. Remove damaged area

C. Caulk beneath patch

D. 1-inch overlap (slip patch under upper course)

Vinyl siding repair takes a slightly different approach. The material expands and contracts considerably with temperature variations, so nails should be slightly loose. That allows the siding to shift as the temperature changes. Fasten with galvanized roofing nails that penetrate ¾ inch into solid wood. Center nails in the nailing slot so that the material can shift to either side. Make sure to work when the temperature is above about 50°—vinyl siding gets brittle and cracks in colder weather.

To cut vinyl siding, follow one of these steps:

➤ Score with a utility knife and bend it back and forth.

➤ Use aviation snips (a tin snip with compound leverage).

➤ Or saw with a fine-toothed circular saw. Reverse the saw blade for the smoothest cut.

Repairs will be simplified with a "zip" tool (available from siding suppliers and some hardware stores) that unlocks the joint between the two courses. Look around your house for spare siding left by a benevolent previous owner. If you do find some, follow these instructions:

1. Decide how much vinyl to remove. If the damage is near the end of a piece, cut from the damage to the end. If it's in the middle of a long piece, cut out only the

damaged area. In either case, make sure to span past a couple of studs for nailing purposes.

2. Cut the ends of the repair area with a utility knife alongside an aluminum square held tight to the siding. Cut as far to the top of the siding as possible.

3. Slip the zip tool into the lower joint and, holding it firmly down, slide the tool the length of the piece you're removing. When the bottom siding is loose, pry out the nails holding it into place.

4. If your patch will end at one end of the old siding, cut the replacement piece $1^1/_2$ inches longer than the removed piece. If you cut twice through the siding, cut the new piece 3 inches longer than the repair.

5. Lock the replacement piece into the lower course of siding, and nail through the top into a stud. The patch overlaps at one or both ends.

6. Lock the upper course into place by pressing firmly against the replacement piece, or use the zip tool to lock the joint.

If the vinyl is cracked, or if you can find only off-color siding, repair the vinyl from the back. Remove the entire damaged piece in one piece with the zip tool. Flip the piece over, clean the back with PVC (polyvinyl chloride) cleaner, and attach a patch to the back with PVC cement. Replace the piece when the cement dries, and touch up the paint as best you can (little of the patch should be visible, so an exact color match is not crucial).

The Least You Need to Know

➤ Siding is pretty durable stuff, and siding damage is often a side-effect of other problems, such as structural movement or moisture build-up.

➤ Small repairs in most kinds of siding are easy, assuming you can reach the damage and find repair material.

➤ Plywood and hardboard siding desperately need protection against the weather. Don't skimp on paint or stain.

Chapter 15

Gimme Shelter—and Other Advice on Repairing Roofs

In This Chapter

➤ Detecting, isolating, and repairing roof leaks

➤ A fascination with flashing

➤ Replacing rotten roof boards

➤ Gutter maintenance and repair

We've reached the chapter I've been awaiting. Now that we're talking roof, I won't have to convince you about the value of preventive maintenance—even a complete idiot understands why a house needs a working roof. Roof leaks can be sneaky; by the time you recognize one problem (a leak) you may have a bigger problem, such as damaged drywall and framing caused by a silent but deadly drip, drip, drip. Call it the homeowner's water torture.

Until this point, I haven't asked you to look for trouble; if you live in a house, trouble knows where to find you. Now, however, I will suggest that you look for trouble because the best way to avoid the water torture is to look around once in a while and to follow the roofers' advice: Think like a raindrop. But before we start doing that, we'll get our feet wet by learning the anatomy of roofs. For information on chimney flashing, see Chapter 30, "Champion Chimneys."

Roofing Lingo

Like everybody else, roofers are entitled to a private dialect. The following illustration will clarify the key terms you must know to handle the roofing jobs in your future.

Parts of a roof.

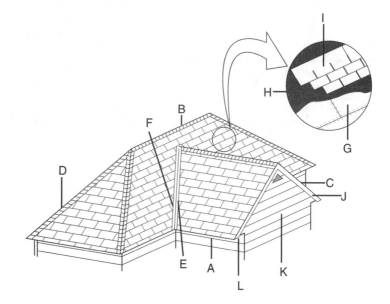

A. Eave: The lower, horizontal edge.

B. Ridge: The horizontal line along the peak.

C. Rake edge: The slanting edge.

D. Hip: Where two roof planes meet in a convex angle.

E. Valley: Where two roof planes meet in a concave angle. (Valleys can be "open," meaning the shingles are cut off to expose the flashing material, or "closed," in which case the shingles cover the flashing.)

F. Valley flashing: Metal used to seal the valley. (Should be present in open and closed valleys.)

G. Sheathing (decking): The plywood or boards nailed to rafters.

H. Roofing felt (underlayment): Gives a final seal in case the shingles leak.

I. Shingle: Usually 12-by-36 inches total size, with 6 inches showing.

J. Fascia: Vertical face of rake edges and eaves.

K. Gable: Area under a peaked roof.

L. Soffit: Horizontal section under an eave or rake edge.

The Basic Principle of Roofing ...

... is that water runs downhill, so upper pieces of roofing overlap lower ones. Pitched (sloping) roofs are really that simple (except where they intersect a chimney or another roof).

Because shingles, flashing, and everything else on a roof expands and contracts in response to changes in temperature, a repair that looks solid today may turn flimsy in a year or so—particularly when wind blows the rain almost horizontal. Thus, a bit of overkill is acceptable—even wise—in a roof repair.

Most roofing shingles are made of a fiberglass mat that is soaked in asphalt and covered with colored, sunlight-resistant mineral granules. These shingles last 15 to 25 years, depending on their quality and the environment on your roof. When you start seeing lots of mineral granules in the gutters, your roof is showing its age and will soon need replacement.

Roofers don't talk about the slope of a roof in degrees or percentages. Instead, they talk about "roof pitch" (this is *not* what happens when a roofer tries to sell you a shingling job you don't need). Pitch is measured in "rise over run," the number of inches in height gained every time you move 12 inches horizontally. Knowing the pitch can help you decide whether you want to walk on the roof. (The 4–12 pitch found on ranch houses and many new homes is pretty flat. A tolerable pitch is 6–12, but if the roof is much steeper, you need a pro.) Roofing contractors and suppliers also can use pitch to calculate roof area from the floor plan dimensions of a house.

To measure your roof pitch, you'll need a ladder, a level, and a carpenter's square. Stand on a ladder leaning against the rake (slanting) edge of the roof. Move the 12-inch marker on one leg of the square to the edge of the roof. Use the level to make this leg horizontal. Read the rise where the vertical leg meets the roof (see the following illustration). To estimate pitch on the ground, hold a board against the siding, and ask somebody to tell you when it's parallel with the rake edge. Then use the above technique to measure the rise.

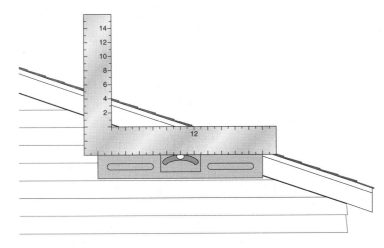

Measuring roof pitch. Pitch is simply the number of inches a roof rises per foot of horizontal "run." Use a level and a square to measure pitch, with the horizontal leg held at 12 inches; the pitch shown is 4–12.

Special Tools and Materials

Roofing doesn't call for much in the way of tools. You could get fancy and rent a nail gun to put on a new layer of shingles, but for repairs a hammer will do just fine (see the illustration for roofing tools and materials).

Roofing tools and materials.

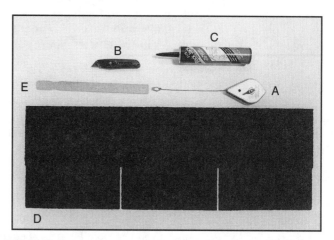

A. Chalk line: Used to draw long, straight lines for starting or finishing shingling. Pull the line out, stretch it tight above where you want the line, pull it up, and snap.

B. Utility knife: Cuts shingles (from the back, if possible).

C. Roof cement (AKA "tar"): Seals gaps and nailheads, and holds old shingles down. Also sold in cans.

D. Asphalt shingles: The primary roofing material. (Nails go just above the slot between the tabs, so the nail heads will be covered by the next course of shingles.)

E. Paint stirrer (for applying tar): Trowels work great, but you'll have to clean them afterward.

Not Looking for Trouble? Then You Won't Find the Leak

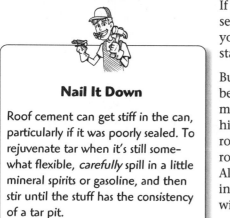

Nail It Down

Roof cement can get stiff in the can, particularly if it was poorly sealed. To rejuvenate tar when it's still some-what flexible, *carefully* spill in a little mineral spirits or gasoline, and then stir until the stuff has the consistency of a tar pit.

If you're lucky, a roof leak will announce itself. Maybe a section of drywall will fall into your living room when your boss is just starting dessert, or some black crud will start oozing down the chimney on Christmas Eve.

But as my friend Steve Sinderson learned, roof leaks can be far more subtle. Steve is a former carpenter who asked me to help him find an inscrutable, occasional leak in his living room. We spent half a befuddled day on his roof and grew desperate enough to saw out a strip of roof decking, which taught us absolutely nothing. Although the chimney flashing seemed tight, in the interest of thoroughness we did re-tar and refasten it with screws. To our surprise, that fixed the roof.

Steve figures that the culprit was windblown rain entering under the loose flashing. Windy rain is nasty because it negates the basic principle of roofing by blowing water sideways, even uphill. As we learned, wind causes nightmare leaks because roofs that work fine when water obeys the basic principle of roofing can fail when water disobeys it.

Scanning Your Roof from Inside

In the final analysis, you don't have much choice about roof leaks. Like sponging relatives, they won't disappear; they will only get worse. So, you've got to find them and fix them.

Even if your attic is accessible only through a hatchway, I'd suggest that you occasionally visit the dust and cobwebs living up there, preferably after a downpour. Pay special attention to brick chimneys, which are a big source of leaks (see the section "Chimney Flashing Loves Leaking," in Chapter 30). If the chimney is connected to a wood-burning stove or fireplace, it may bleed a disgusting, evil-smelling, flammable form of liquefied creosote. This may indicate a water leak, a serious chimney hazard, or both (see the section "Santa Don't Like Your Chimney, and Other Ruminations on Chimney Fires," in Chapter 30).

Nail It Down

You can check for leaks around flashing, if you don't mind making them temporarily worse. Spray a hose thoroughly around the base of the chimney from all conceivable directions while a lackey looks inside the house (in the attic, if possible) to check for leaks. There's always the chance that you'll "detect" a leak that really doesn't exist, but spraying with a hose is a good diagnostic trick.

Leaks in the roof may not be directly above the wet spots in your ceiling, so it pays to poke around uphill from the wet spot. Look for dampness, mold, or discoloration, which indicate that the wood is starting to rot, and soft spots, which are actual rot. Poke around with a flashlight to identify the precise leak. If you're going to fix the leak right away, pound a 16-penny nail up through the leak, and find the nail from the outside. Otherwise, measure diagonally down from the peak and horizontally across from a wall, chimney, ridge, or other landmark.

Scanning Your Roof from Outside

Now head up to the roof and try to identify the flaw that's causing your woe. If your roof is shallow (say 4–12 to 6–12 pitch), get a ladder and haul yourself up. If it's steeper, use binoculars from the ground, or climb a ladder to the eave. Look for broken, buckled, or missing shingles, and rusted or detached flashing. Pay special attention to any place the roof meets something else—a dormer, chimney, vent, skylight, or another section of roof. Trouble loves these junctions.

If none of this works, wait for a dry spell. Ask a lackey to spray water on the roof while you scan from the attic. Your helper should start spraying the bottom of the suspect area and then gradually work uphill until the leak shows its miserable self.

139

Quickie Shingle Fixes

When you think about it, the blights that afflict old shingles sound suspiciously like the diseases of aging humans: buckles, bald spots, blisters, and premature curling. Let's diagnose and treat these ills, recalling that a bit of attention now can save serious woes later.

Nail It Down

Dry roof tar is murder to remove from tools. (You can rub off fresh tar with a gasoline-soaked rag, but that's a poisonous and explosive solution.) For your next roof repair, use a paint stirrer (or a split piece of wood) as a tar paddle. Then just pitch it out when you're finished.

➤ If a corner of a shingle curls up, wait for a warm day and smear roof cement under the curled portion. Nail it flat with a couple of roofing nails, and tar the nail heads.

➤ If a shingle is cracked, smear roof cement under and on top of the crack. Better yet, slip a rectangular piece of aluminum flashing as far as possible up under the shingle, nail it into place, and tar the nail head. Or, best, replace the shingle, as shown next.

➤ If a shingle is torn, treat it as a crack, but nail down the loose parts and goop the nail heads.

Presto-Chango Shingle Replacement

If a few shingles on your roof have lost their mineral coating, are curled beyond repair, or are split, missing, or otherwise AWOL, you'll have to replace them with fresh recruits (but see the section "A Total Loss?" later in this chapter before doing so). When you buy shingles, note that one bundle usually covers $33^1/_3$ square feet.

Mind these roof repair cautions as you go:

➤ Bend old shingles carefully, particularly in cold weather, when they're especially brittle.

➤ Use care on the roof: Wear non-slip shoes and rig up a safety line, if needed.

➤ In hot weather, put a lawn sprinkler on the roof for an hour or so to cool the shingles so that you won't damage them (you'll also be more comfortable).

➤ Use common sense. If you're not happy and secure on the roof, get down and get help.

Old shingles cut easily, even with a dull utility knife. The step flashing, shown along the right edge, is commonly used to flash walls, skylights, chimneys, and other structures that project past a roof.

To fix shingles, you'll need a ladder, a hammer, a prybar, a trowel, a utility knife, roofing nails, new shingles, and roof tar. A nail apron or tool belt will be extremely handy to prevent tools from rolling down the roof. Follow these steps to make your repair:

1. Examine the area and figure out how many shingles need replacement. Seriously curled, bare, or broken shingles are all candidates.

2. Separate the uppermost damaged shingles from the good shingles above them with a trowel (preferably a brick trowel). Slide the trowel back and forth to break the seal. Don't be in a hurry, or you'll tear good shingles.

3. Work downward, releasing shingles as you go. Use a trowel, hammer, or prybar to pull nails.

4. Remove all bad shingles down to the bottom of the repair area. To remove part of a shingle, cut from the top (see the accompanying figure).

5. Clean out loose nails and scrap shingles.

6. Starting from the bottom, nail in the replacement shingles, matching the old pattern. Score new shingles from the back, and then fold to separate them. Use the side of the hammer to nail under old shingles so that you don't curl them too much (see photo).

7. Continue nailing shingles all the way up. Don't allow seams between shingles to line up with those of lower courses; stagger them 6 inches.

8. Smear roof tar on exposed nail heads, under broken or split shingles, and under the first course of new shingles. Don't worry if the new shingles take a while to lie flat: The sun will soften them and bond them together.

Treat old shingles with respect; nail the last replacement shingle with the side of the hammer so that you needn't curl the old shingle too much.

Follow the old pattern when nailing the new shingles. Never allow the vertical joints between shingles to line up.

Flat Roofs and Other Sob Stories

I'm always sorry to hear that someone has a flat, or "built-up," roof. To a homeowner, these tar-and-gravel roofs play a typical Dennis Hopper role: trouble with a real snarl. You can repair blisters and other small problems on a flat roof, but big repairs are a pro job (unless you know how to handle large amounts of gravel and molten tar, which means that you are already a professional roofer).

The relatively new plastic membranes have solved many flat-roof woes, but they must be applied by roofers. To make the limited number of repairs possible on a built-up roof, sweep away the gravel from the injury and use techniques in the next section on roll roofing.

The Three R's of Repairing Roll Roofing

Roll roofing is a cut-rate stand-in for shingles. It's generally 36 inches wide and laid in horizontal courses, or strips, with at least a 3-inch overlap at the top and bottom seams.

To repair a *blister* in roll roofing, cut the blister with a utility knife, smear roof tar under the edges (make good contact between the roofing and the substrate), and go to step 2.

To patch a *hole* in roll roofing (up to about 12 inches by 12 inches), you'll need a utility knife, a hammer, roof cement, a paint-stirring stick, new roll roofing, and roofing nails. Chalk would be handy, too. Follow these steps:

1. Cut out a rectangular piece of roofing around the hole with the utility knife.
2. Cut a piece of new roofing 6 inches larger in each dimension than the cut-out section. Center it over the hole and mark its perimeter, preferably with chalk.
3. Remove the patch and smear the entire hole with roof tar, out to the marks from step 2. Sneak some tar under the edges of the good roofing.
4. Replace the patch, and fasten it securely with a nail about every 3 inches. Tar the nail heads.

Wood Shingles and Shakes

Wood shingles and shakes are high-class roofing, usually made of rot-resistant cedar. They are more attractive, more durable, and more expensive than the common asphalt-fiberglass shingles. Wood shingles are sawn smooth and are about 16 inches long; shakes are usually split and about 24 inches long. Because wood swells when it gets damp and shrinks when it dries, in dry weather you may actually see sunlight through a working wood roof in a shed or barn; the decking boards under wood shingles may be spaced a couple inches apart.

The principle for replacing shingles and shakes is the same as for asphalt shingles (see the section "Presto-Chango Shingle Replacement," earlier in this chapter), except that you will need roofing nails designed for wood and you don't need to cement the shingles together.

Wood roofs need protection from water, fungi, and ultraviolet light, particularly in damp climates. A build-up of leaves, pine needles, or moss will prevent water from running off, keep the wood wet, and promote wood-destroying fungi. Clean the roof with a hose or broom. If necessary, prune nearby trees to reduce organic buildup and allow sunlight to dry the roof. If it's still rotting, keep reading.

143

Treating a Wood Roof

If you've cleaned the roof and still see signs of dirt or decay (furry fungi, for example), a cleaning solution will kill the little rotters and remove stains. (Use appropriate hand and eye protection with all the following treatments.)

Cleaning solution for wood shingles:

> 3 ounces trisodium phosphate (TSP or a non-phosphate equivalent, sold at paint stores)
>
> 1 ounce laundry detergent
>
> 1 quart 5 percent liquid laundry bleach
>
> 3 quarts warm water

Brush the solution onto the roof with a garage broom, and then rinse it off. Rinse nearby plants if you spill any solution on them.

If stains persist, pour a stronger bleach solution directly onto the stain, and wash it off within half an hour.

To control moss, use moss-killing chemicals sold at building material, roofing, or paint stores.

If, after all these measures, fungus is still alive on an otherwise solid roof, you'll need penetrating preservatives sold at the same stores. Use a sprayer on a calm day. To get maximum retention of the preservative, use several light treatments, and let the end grain soak up as much as it wants.

Rotten Board Replacement

Let's say you've neglected your fiduciary duties to your roof, and you discover that a venerable leak has rotted the roof boards or decking. My most intimate experience with a rotten roof occurred when Joe Lynch, a pure gentleman and an old-time Wisconsin farmer, asked me to look over his roof while I was rebuilding his chimney. I promptly fell through and wound up hip-deep in decay. When I stopped falling, I started laughing. Joe, a master of understatement, allowed that he hadn't used that wing of the house for a while. From the look of it, he meant a decade or three.

It's not smart to let your roof take such a lengthy bath. If you find a persistent leak or notice that a section of roof is feeling, well, spongy, you'll need to replace the decking and roofing. It's a dirty job, but on a shallow roof, not a difficult one. You'll need a pencil, a level, a prybar, a circular saw, a hammer, a utility knife, a trowel, a tape measure, roof nails, replacement decking, shingles, roofing paper, and roof tar. A cat's paw, a small pry bar designed to pull nails, would be extremely handy as well. Follow these steps:

1. Pull off all shingles from the rotten spot slightly past the rafters (the framing that supports the decking) at each end of the repair area.

2. With a level, mark a rectangular area of decking to be replaced, along the center of the rafters. With a cat's paw or prybar, remove any nails along the marks.

3. With the circular saw set to cut the thickness of the roof decking (to avoid cutting the rafters), saw out the bad spot. Remove all debris.

4. Saw the replacement board to fit, leaving it $1/8$ inch short to allow for expansion. It may be better to use the same type of wood, but the most important thing is to be sure it's as thick as the decking (commonly $3/4$ inch in older homes and $1/2$ inch in newer ones). Nail the patch with cement-coated 8d (8-penny) nails about 6 inches apart. Renail existing roof boards around the edges.

5. Tack or staple roofing felt on the new section. If the house has several layers of shingles, lay new shingles flat to shim the patch up so that the roof is flat. Finish according to suggestions in the "Presto-Chango Shingle Replacement" section, earlier in this chapter.

A Total Loss?

As I've said, there's not much point in fixing a roof that's basically shot. How do you know when a shingle roof is a total loss? Maybe you're seeing lots of mineral granules in your gutters. Maybe you're seeing lots of tired, bald, cracked, or curled shingles. Maybe you, like me, are starting to see multiple leaks inside the house. (Remember, drywall does not get dark and damp all by its lonesome.)

But whatever the reason, at a certain point you just plain need a new roof. Small, simple, and shallow-pitched roofs are easy to replace. That's beyond the scope of this book, but if you are motivated, plenty of how-to books cover the subject. My advice is not to spend too much time repairing something that basically needs replacement.

Building codes—and common sense—both limit the build-up of shingles on a roof to two or three layers. Roofing material is heavy, and if it's too thick it can collapse the framing. Furthermore, thick stacks of shingles wrinkle and collect water instead of shedding it. When a roof gets that thick, the best solution is to tear off the shingles and start over on the decking. But that's a lot of sweaty work.

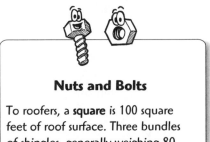

Nuts and Bolts

To roofers, a **square** is 100 square feet of roof surface. Three bundles of shingles, generally weighing 80 pounds apiece, usually cover one square. A **course** is one horizontal row of shingles.

You may be able to count layers from the rake edge, or you can estimate based on the age of the house, using 20 years as the average lifetime for asphalt shingles. (If the first layer contains wood shingles, figure that it lasted 30 to 40 years.) Thus, a 40-year-old house that's approaching a reroofing job probably has two layers of asphalt shingles and may need a tear-off. Unless you're a real masochist or have lots of energetic friends, that's a pro job.

If you contemplate tearing off roofing, you should be aware that a small percentage of old shingles contain asbestos, a known cause of cancer. If you suspect that your shingles do contain asbestos, a firm that recycles roofing material may be able to test them for you.

Flashy Flashing Fixes

Many roof leaks reflect a flashing problem, not a shingle problem. Flashing is the rust-resistant, flexible metal (galvanized steel, aluminum, or copper) that joins roofs to other roofs and to chimneys, vents, skylights, and walls. Flashing keeps the roof tight even when the various parts move due to expansion or contraction from changes in temperature.

Oops! If this fairy tale were always true, you wouldn't be reading about flashing. The truth is that flashing can get sick—through rust, perforation, or simply separating from whatever it once joined.

Don't Screw Up!

If you're like my boys, Alex and Josh, you'll get a kick out of walking on a shallow roof. But keep your roof-hiking to a minimum, particularly in cold weather (when shingles are brittle) or in hot weather (when they're gooey).

Generally, the nails that secure flashing are covered by shingles, but some (such as those at the lower end of chimney base flashing) are visible. If you see flashing nails coming loose, don't just hammer them down and smear them with roof tar—they'll inevitably loosen again in a year or so because they've lost their grip (does this sound familiar?). Replace the nails with galvanized screws, and then coat the heads with roof tar. (If you've got copper flashing, use copper nails; galvanized fasteners will cause rapid corrosion.)

Valley flashing is the V-shaped metal that joins two roof planes in a concave joint, called a valley. You may be able to repair a small hole with gutter repair compound: Wire-brush the surface clean, apply the compound, and smooth it off. Then keep an eye on the patch. Valleys carry a lot of water, and as soon as the leak recurs you'll need to take action. Large flaws in valley flashing really demand a tear-off and roof replacement because the flashing must be laid under the shingles.

Step flashing, made of a series of folded rectangles, is used to seal vertical projections that extend through roofs, such as walls, chimneys, and skylights. Why use multiple pieces of flashing instead of a continuous strip? Because any water that gets under a long strip would be trapped. With step flashing, the water drops to the next step of flashing and is safely routed onto the top of the shingles. Step flashing is illustrated in the chimney flashing diagrams in the section "Chimney Flashing Loves Leaking," in Chapter 30.

Damn Ice Dams

In colder regions, one of a roof's worst enemies is an ice build-up, or ice dam. The problem usually occurs near the eaves, where snow that has melted from higher on the roof tends to freeze. Water trapped by the dam can build up and enter the roof, severely damaging the shingles and sheathing.

Try these solutions to ice dams:

➤ Insulate the attic or roof to prevent heat from escaping and melting the snow.

➤ Increase ventilation through the attic and roof (see the section "Roof Vents" in Chapter 12, "Skin-Tight: Caulking, Weather-Stripping, Insulation, and Ventilation").

➤ Install de-icing tapes (sold at building suppliers or hardware stores) near the roof edge.

➤ Install roll roofing or a special ice-dam membrane under shingles at the eaves. This requires a reshingling job because you'll need to rip out several courses of shingles. But you can insist that the roofer take this step.

Down in the Gutter: Repairing Eaves Troughs

Gutters, or eaves troughs, always look so—well, optional. All they do is collect water that has already run off your roof and dump it on the ground. The water would end up there anyway, so why bother with eaves troughs? Because they save your siding from the stress of shedding all that water. They also route water away from the foundation (see the section "May We Talk About Your Soggy Basement?" in Chapter 17, "Bricks and Stones: Masonry and Concrete [the Sequel]"). And most important, they give you one more thing to fix!

Let's start with some gutter talk. The following table illustrates the different parts of a gutter system.

Gutter Parts

Item	Description
	Gutter section: Sold in 10-foot and 20-foot lengths
	Downspout: Sold in 10-foot lengths
	Inside corner: Requires slip connector at each end
	Outside corner: Requires slip connector at each end
	Slip connector: Used to join gutter sections
	End cap: Has different left and right versions
	Downspout elbow: Comes in two styles: curving front to back, or side to side
	Downspout connector, or drop outlet: Connects gutter to the downspout
	Gutter mounting strap: Is nailed to eaves under shingles
	Gutter mounting bracket: Is nailed to fascia board
	Spike and ferrule (nail and spacer): Mounts gutter to the fascia board
	Downspout guard: Keeps debris out of downspout

The best thing you can do for your gutters is, alas, to clean them regularly (use rubber gloves if you're squeamish about rotting crud). If you do this once or twice a year, organic litter won't have time to ferment, so the task will be far less disgusting than if you wait until Bonsai trees have sprouted along the eaves. Clean gutters are also less prone to overflowing, icing up, and falling off, and they carry water away from the house much more effectively.

Follow these hints for a healthier relationship with your gutters.

➤ Keep leaves out of gutters by installing protective screens. You can buy screens—some even have hinges allowing you to clean out crud that filters through them. Or, use this cheaper suggestion from my friend Hugh Iltis, botanist and preservationist: Clip aluminum screen sold for protecting trees from rabbits to the gutters with steel binder clips. Remove the clips when you need to clean out the gutter. If you dislike the thought of the clips rusting (they will) attach the screens with aluminum rivets or screws.

➤ If the gutter is not draining, check for plugging at the downspout connector. Then check the slope by holding a level against the gutter at several places. The gutter should slope consistently toward the downspout, about 1 inch per 20 feet of run. Then remove and reattach gutter nails, straps, or connectors to get the right slope.

➤ If gutter straps are broken, repair them with sheet metal screws or rivets.

➤ If the gutter is leaking at connectors or through rusted holes, use gutter repair goop in a caulking gun.

➤ To refasten or repair gutters, use sheet-metal screws or a hand riveter. Use aluminum rivets on aluminum gutters.

➤ To saw a gutter or downspout section, mark square lines for an accurate cut. Turn the gutter upside-down with a 2-by-4 or a 2-by-6 inside, and cut with a fine-toothed hacksaw.

➤ Before making slip connections, fill the connector with gutter repair cement.

The Least You Need to Know

➤ Keeping an eye on your roof is one of the most effective and remunerative forms of preventive maintenance.

➤ Most roof leaks occur where something such as a chimney, vent, skylight, or another roof meets a roof.

➤ Wood shingles and shakes need protection from sunlight, dampness, fungus, and moss.

➤ Many roof problems are repairable, but don't bother fixing a roof if it really needs replacement.

➤ Gutters are an essential part of your home's protection from the elements; gutter problems can damage the roofing, interiors, foundation, and basement.

Chapter 16

Bricks and Stones: Doing Masonry and Concrete Without Getting Stoned

---

In This Chapter

➤ How masonry and concrete differ from all other building materials

➤ To work with mortar and concrete, you've got to know their timing

➤ What the other do-it-yourself books won't tell you about masonry

➤ Sage suggestions for satisfying stonework

Let's face it: Masonry scares do-it-yourselfers—even gung-ho types who would routinely tackle a nasty roof leak or a rotten floorboard. That's too bad, because stones are the most ancient form of construction, and masonry can be a satisfying—and economical—knack that's not hard to learn. (If you're really lucky, you may even have a pleasant flashback to idle sandbox days with childhood chums.)

How did masonry earn its fearsome reputation? Partly because the material sets the pace in a way that's true of no other building material except plaster. And partly it's because every tool and material seems to have three obscure names. (This may be intentional: When I wrote my masonry book, a friend who is a mason and an architect explained: "We masons are an old guild, and we don't like to give away secrets.")

But you don't have to join the mason's guild (or the Freemasons, either) to learn to repair brick, block, stone, and concrete. As an ex-mason, I'm happy to reveal trade secrets, starting with the ABCs of masonry:

A. The materials are gritty, caustic, and heavy (this is the "nasty, brutish, and short" principle of masonry).

B. Mortar and concrete don't hold stuff together; they hold it apart.

C. Mortar and concrete harden according to an internal clock. You can't rush them, but you can't fall behind, either.

Principle A being self-explanatory, we'll dwell on B and C. When we're done, you'll never again feel marooned at the thought of a simple masonry repair. Instead, you'll feel an itch to grab your trowel and start mixing mud. (I admit this might seem a bit peculiar, but keep things in perspective—some people actually look forward to *plumbing* repairs.)

The Foundation Principle of Masonry and Concrete

Mortar and concrete (masons call them both "mud," for obvious reasons) are roughly 10 times as effective at holding things apart (this is called *compressive strength*) as at holding things together (*tensile strength*). Thus, mortar is perfect for separating things that would otherwise fall in on each other, such as the stones, blocks, and bricks in a foundation or chimney.

When concrete is pulled apart, as it is in bridge beams, the tensile strength is supplied by hidden steel reinforcing rods. If you must use mortar to glue things together, you'll need special materials and techniques, which we'll discuss later. (Mortar will adhere to stone and brick if you set up the right conditions—I'll explain how—but don't expect too much from the bond.)

Nuts and Bolts

Mortar is a mixture of portland cement, lime, mason's sand, and water. (Lacking portland cement, old mortar is weaker and whiter than modern mortar.) **Concrete**, a mixture of portland cement, gravel, sand, and water, is used to build bridges, beams, roads, and driveways. Concrete is often called "cement," but that's too confusing—I call it concrete, or 'crete.

Mortar and concrete don't "dry"; they "set." Setting results when water and portland cement undergo a chemical reaction and the cement expands and hardens. You don't want mud to dry before it sets because it will be weak when there's too little water for complete hardening. That's why you see sprinklers or tarps on fresh concrete in summer: to help it set completely.

Concrete will not set while it's being mixed. The slower concrete sets, the stronger it eventually becomes. And the less mixing water you use (within reason), the stronger it sets. Finally, mortar and concrete are likely to shrink slightly when they set, which accounts for those hairline cracks around the edge of repairs.

Bricks come in essentially two flavors, depending on how hot they were fired during manufacture.

Low-temperature bricks—including most antique bricks—are porous (as are concrete blocks). High-temperature bricks are smoother, glassier, and nonporous. Why should you care? Because you must dampen porous bricks before repairing them; otherwise they will dry out the mortar and weaken it. If you moisten high-fired brick, however, the mortar will drip from the joint like an ice-cream cone in the desert. To find the porosity of your bricks, simply splash water on a section (not near the repair). If the brick quickly absorbs the water, it's porous. If water stays on the surface for half a minute or so, it's nonporous.

Toolbox Trivia

Portland cement—the cement in concrete and mortar—was named for its resemblance to portland stone, a rock in Britain. Portland cement was patented by British bricklayer Joseph Aspin in 1824. It's made by cooking and pulverizing lime in a giant kiln at 2,800° F, making an extremely fine powder. Why should you care how cement is made? For no reason, except that cement products are quite dusty, and you should use a dust mask when dry-mixing them. While you're at it, be sure to use leather or rubber gloves while handling portland cement, concrete, and mortar; they will parch your hands.

Keeping Time

Unlike virtually every other building material, masonry and concrete have their own rhythm. Because the material changes as it sets, you'll need to change tools and techniques as hardening occurs. So even though mortar and concrete are (literally) as dead as a stone, they may seem alive in their response to temperature, humidity, and the condition of the bricks and stones (and, seemingly, your frustration level). In carpentry, you can nail boards at your own pace. In masonry, however, sometimes you'll have to rush, and sometimes you'll twiddle your thumbs. If you tool (smooth) a mortar joint before the mud has set, the mud will squish out. But if you wait too long, the mortar will be as hard as rock.

It may sound complicated, but working with these materials is mostly a matter of mind-set. If you are aware of the changes as the mortar or concrete sets, the battle is half won. I'll help you win the other half in Chapter 17, "Bricks and Stones: Masonry and Concrete (the Sequel)," where we jump from the preparation to the actual repairs. Then I'll explain in each procedure how the material changes as it sets and when to perform each step of the repair.

Armed with the principles of masonry, there's only one reason to defer a project: if the temperature is likely to fall below about 40° F. Mortar and concrete must set before they freeze, and masonry is wretched winter work—take it from someone who's done it.

Special Tools

Most mason's tools—at least, the trowels, chisels, and hammers a homeowner might need—look heavy, strong, and impossibly clumsy until you watch a mason deftly build a wall with them. Masonry starts with trowels, and while catalogs list them in infinite variety, you will need only two or three. Incidentally, many masonry tools have multiple uses, which reduces the sting of their price. As usual, there's no need to buy everything at once; buy what you need, and let your tools accumulate along with your skills. Just don't buy the worst ones you can find. Quality matters in trowels.

The first stage in a masonry repair is usually to destroy something (such as old mortar or concrete). To do this, you'll need a 2- or 3-pound *hammer* (for this kind of walloping, nail hammers are flyweights). Don't spring for a fancy new hammer unless you are in a mood for squandering; I bought a real Neanderthal at a rummage sale for a buck.

Tools of the masonry trade.

A. 2-lb. hammer

B. Brick chisel (brick set)

C. Mason's hammer (with pointed and wedge-shaped ends)

D. Brush

E. Brick jointer

F. Tuckpointing trowel

G. Margin trowel

H. Concrete float

I. Homemade joint raker

J. Brick trowel

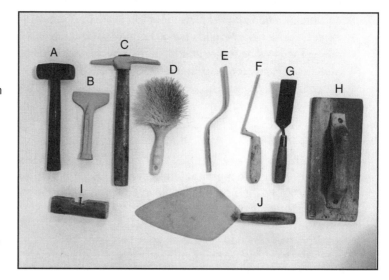

A hammer needs something to smash (aside from your wrist, that is). Use a 2- to 4-inch-wide *brick chisel* for breaking bricks, removing mortar for stone repairs, beating up on rotten concrete, and generally expressing yourself Neolithically.

A *mason's hammer*, available in various sizes and styles, is essentially two flying chisels mounted on a handle. It's excellent for cleaning old stonemasonry before a repair; I'd get one that weighs about 24 ounces, but only if I had a lot of stone to fix.

Masonry is a grungy pursuit, so you probably figured there'd be a *brush* here somewhere. The one I use is sold for cleaning dairy equipment (did I mention that I'm from Wisconsin, America's Dairyland?). I use this cheap, durable, and effective plastic brush for cleaning dust and crud after chipping out loose mortar. I use it for removing extra mortar around the edge of a repair, for repairing stucco, for cleaning wheelbarrows and tools, and even for cleaning up before painting.

The *tuckpointing trowel* is a single-purpose item that will pay its freight in the first hours of tuckpointing. Push mortar from a brick trowel with a tuckpointing trowel into brick or block joints, or substitute a pointing or margin trowel. This long, skinny trowel comes in various widths; buy one that fits easily into the joint you're fixing.

After you have replaced the mortar, you've got to press it into place, and then (and only then) you will need a *jointer*. Round and V-shape jointers come in several sizes, to match the kind of joint you are repairing (see the accompanying figure illustrating joint varieties).

Nuts and Bolts

When masons say **pointing**, they're not talking about hunting dogs, but about replacing the mortar in a degraded joint. **Tuckpointing** is replacing mortar between bricks, because you must "tuck" the mortar into the joint.

For pure versatility, my favorite tool is the *margin trowel*, the duck-billed platypus of masonry. This small rectangular trowel is first-rate for patching masonry and drywall, great for stirring and applying wood filler, and ideal for scouring the bottom of a goopy paint can, prying molding, scraping paint, and even glazing windows. How many $10 tools have such a repertoire?

A *concrete float* settles the gravel and brings the sand-cement paste to the surface of a concrete repair. It's easy to make: Simply nail a 1-by-3-by-8-inch handle to the center of a 1-by-6-by-14-inch piece of scrap wood. If the larger piece is slightly warped, so much the better: Nail the handle to the concave side.

A homemade joint raker will remove mortar to make the recessed joints called "raked joints" (see the next section, "Four Flavors of Masonry Joints"). You can buy a raker, but they're kind of expensive for occasional use, and this works just as well. Saw a rectangular notch from the center of a block of 1-by-2 or ³/₄-inch plywood. Drive a drywall screw into the center of the notch, and adjust its depth so that it protrudes enough to rake out mud from the joint, matching the existing joint.

The *brick trowel* may look awkward, but a good one (I'm not talking $3.95!) is anything but. First of all, it can stir and deliver mortar quickly. Second, the corner, or heel, makes a great one-hand chisel for chipping mortar off old bricks or nubbins off over-size stones, and breaking the occasional brick. Finally, it's perfect for separating shingles during a roof repair, and it even makes a tolerable paint scraper.

Four Flavors of Masonry Joints

Look closely, and you'll notice that the mortar joints between bricks and stones are not created equal. Each of the common joint styles requires a different tool, which you must obtain before starting the repair.

Masonry joints.

A. Concave joint, made with jointer (try to buy the correct size). To save money, substitute an 8-inch length of old garden hose.

B. Vee joint, made with vee jointer. You may be able to make this joint with a piece of wood having a sharply sawn corner.

C. Raked joint, made with an adjustable joint raker. For a handmade raker, see the previous figure of tools of the masonry trade.

D. Struck joint, made by moving the edge of a brick or pointing trowel quickly along the joint.

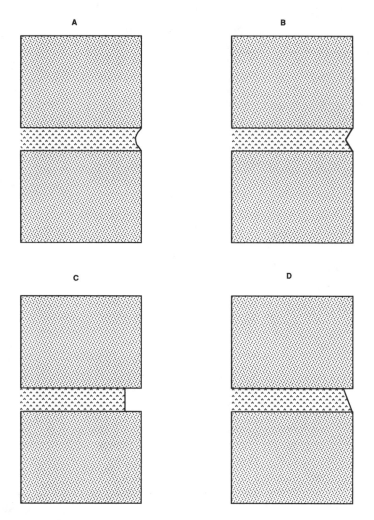

Mixing Mortar and Other Fun in the Mud

Now that we've met the tools and materials, it's time to get our hands dirty and actually mix some mud. One thing most handy-andy books ignore—if they even bother with masonry—is how to actually work with mortar. I won't fall into that trap; instead, I'll discuss the care, feeding, and mixing of mortar.

Most people use premixed mortar, which is a blend of cement and sand but it's hard to work with. I much prefer mason's cement, mixed with clean (and very cheap) mason's sand. Most brickyards sell several colors of cement.

Speaking of color, do you want your repair to stand out or blend in? To blend in, you must study the color of the existing mortar. In many cases, that gray premixed mortar is the wrong stuff to use. In the old days, many stones and bricks were laid with white lime mortar. More recently, red, brown, and black have all been popular. If you buy sand and cement rather than premixed mortar, buy a colored cement that approaches the mortar you're matching, Pigments sold by masonry suppliers will tint premixed or sand-and-cement mortar.

In any case, mortar changes color as it dries, so take this tip from the pros: Mix a bit of mortar, let it dry on a trowel blade in the sun, and use that color for comparison; it will be much closer to the final color of the dried mortar.

Aside from color, the key rule of mortar is not to mix up too much, particularly in hot weather. If the mud hardens too quickly, you'll either have to dump the stuff or rush your work. In summer, prepare only as much as you can use in half an hour. In cooler weather, it's probably okay to mix up an hour's worth. (You can safely add a little water to soften stiff mud once, but be careful: A lot of water weakens the batch. It's better to mix small batches in the first place.)

Start mixing after all your preparations are complete:

1. Add dry material to a wheelbarrow. For a small repair, mix in a clean plastic bucket.

2. If you're using sand and cement, dry-mix $2^1/2$ to 3 parts of sand with 1 part cement, until they are thoroughly blended.

3. Push the dry stuff to the front of the wheelbarrow. Add water and layer the dry mix over the water, using the trowel, shovel, or hoe.

4. After you've created sandwiches of dry and wet (yum-yum!), start stirring. Remember, you're not making soup du jour; mortar must be fairly stiff to stay where you put it. If it gets soupy, add a bit of dry mix. Mix for 3 minutes.

5. Dump the mix onto a metal sheet or scrap of plywood, roughly 2 feet square.

6. As you use the mortar, occasionally lift it with the trowel and throw it against the mud on the board. Watch masons at work: They do this reflexively because it keeps the mortar flexible and able to flow.

Nail It Down

Before you begin a visible repair, check the mortar color. Gray is the standard in both premixed mortar and cement, but most brickyards also sell white and brown cement and possibly pigments for custom-tinting mortar (and concrete). Even if you don't hit the perfect shade, any effort to match the color will be repaid with a repair that's less noticeable.

And Then There Were Stones

I get a kick when homeowners brag that their old stone house was built of stones from the quarry just down the road. I love meeting somebody who's turned on by the most earthy and beautiful of building materials. And it's also true that, until recently, all stone was local because stones tend to be heavy and hard to transport. Nevertheless, there's a lesson here: The appearance, hardness, density, and handling of stones are all influenced by their origin. So, it's tougher to generalize about stonework than most building substances. Some stone is soft, some is hard, some splits easily (usually in just one plane), while some is hard to saw with a diamond blade. Some ages nicely, and some doesn't.

Furthermore, stone repair calls for more artistry than brick or block repair. First, if any stones are loose, they are more difficult to replace. Second, the joints are usually wider, which means that you must apply the mortar more slowly, allowing the first layer to set before you add more mud. (In fact, stonework requires too much patience for people who like to finish jobs in a linear sequence.) Third, it's more difficult to match the joint style in stonework than in brick and block work. Nevertheless, stonework is my favorite kind of masonry because the rewards of a deftly repaired stone wall greatly exceed the effort.

Hints for Working Stone

To make stonework more rewarding and less laborious, follow these suggestions:

➤ If you must pull out loose stones before replacing them, mark the location and top side on each with a light pencil.

➤ For a large repair, don't allow vertical joints to line up; this weakens the wall.

➤ To build up thick joints, use chips of concrete block to dry and stiffen the mortar (just make sure they won't show when you're done). Or, use wooden wedges to prop up the stones for a few minutes while the mortar sets.

➤ Take your time—large mortar joints set slowly, and rushing will just squeeze mortar from the joint.

➤ If possible, find extra stones that match the original wall.

➤ To enliven old, moldy, discolored limestone, give it a light wash of muriatic acid. Make a mild mixture, don your goggles and rubber gloves, and sprinkle it on the wall. Then flush with clean water.

The Least You Need to Know

➤ Mortar holds things apart; it doesn't hold them together.

➤ Because mortar grips rather weakly, many surfaces need a careful cleaning before repair.

➤ To do masonry, invest in a few simple tools.

➤ Pay careful attention to mortar color; you won't get a second chance to choose the right one.

➤ Stir mortar repeatedly after you mix it; stiff, crumbly mortar is worthless.

➤ Stonework is the most difficult—and most rewarding—part of masonry.

Chapter 17

Bricks and Stones: Masonry and Concrete (the Sequel)

In This Chapter

➤ The fundamentals of masonry and concrete repair

➤ Tuckpointing for amateurs

➤ Repairing sidewalks and steps

➤ Curing water damage before you get in over your head

Having read Chapter 16, "Bricks and Stones: Doing Masonry and Concrete Without Getting Stoned," you know the principles underlying the ancient sport of masonry and its modern cousin, concrete. Now that you're itching to grab a trowel, let's describe the general procedure for repairing masonry and then tailor it to common repairs.

But first grant me the opportunity to quote myself. In masonry, remember, the mud calls the shots, and you've got to go with the flow. Mortar and concrete harden at their own rates, depending on surface porosity, temperature, and chemistry, and you can't finish the job until the mud has set to the right consistency. Be prepared to leave one part of a repair alone for a few minutes while the mud sets up, and then return for further work.

Repairing Masonry and Concrete for Keeps: The General Procedure

Have you gathered your tools? Then let's dive into the general recipe for repairing masonry and concrete:

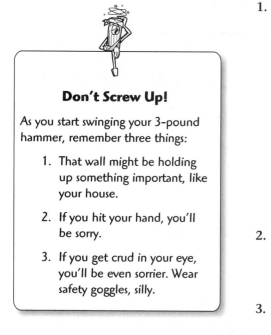

1. Masonry repairs are like dental repairs—although usually cheaper and less painful. Why? Because you can't build on decay. The first step in most repairs is to remove decayed mortar with a mason's hammer, or a 2- to 3-pound hammer and a brick chisel. Although cleaner is usually better, use some judgment. Loose pieces of brick or stone must be removed and replaced, but a big hunk that shifts only slightly can probably remain in place because the new mortar will firm it up. If you try to remove every bit of old mortar and barely loose brick, you may end up with more work than you bargained for.

2. When you've removed the rot, clean out the hole with a stiff brush (and a vacuum, if you're the fastidious type, which I doubt—few fussy folks fiddle with masonry).

3. Test bricks and concrete blocks for porosity by splashing water on them. If the water seeps into the surface within a half-minute or so, they will absorb water from the mortar and must be moistened—particularly where the mud will be thin—before mortaring. Dip a 3- or 4-inch paintbrush in water, and flick it at the repair, particularly where the mortar will be shallow. Get the surface wet, but not saturated. Dip porous bricks and blocks for 30 seconds—no more—in a bucket of water, and allow them to dry for 15 minutes or so.

4. Ladies and gentlemen! Start your—er, mix your mortar! (See the section "Mixing Mortar and Other Fun in the Mud" in Chapter 16.)

5. On a wall repair, start by filling the deepest holes (this is not necessary for a pavement patch). Often the best way to do this, believe it or not, is to throw the mortar into place with a trowel. (Overhand and sidearm are both acceptable.) Thrown mortar gets good contact and better adhesion with the surface. A more delicate approach is to use a small trowel to push mortar off a larger trowel.

6. Avoid the temptation to fill large holes at once: Work several parts of the repair simultaneously. Insert chips of block, stone, or brick in the mortar to stiffen up heavy areas. After the first coat has stiffened, add more mud.

7. As you finish the patch, let it set. Tool it to match the surrounding masonry, using a trowel, a length of hose, or a jointer to match the joint varieties (illustrated in Chapter 16). To use a jointer, simply rub it along the joint a couple of times until the joint takes the proper shape and the mud is pressed firmly into place. If you're working near a corner, start the jointer at the corner and move toward the center of the work. (To smooth concrete, see the section "Finishing Concrete—From Stone Soup to Smooth as Glass," later in this chapter.)

8. Finally, when the mortar is hard enough and bristle marks won't show, brush the area diagonally with a stiff, plastic brush (a steel brush could leave rust stains). Brushing removes trowel marks and smeared mortar from the stones, blocks, or bricks.

Tuckpointing

Tuckpointing—repairing mortar in bricks or blocks—is a simple, tedious, glamorless, and necessary (to owners of masonry homes, anyway) skill that almost anyone can master. Doing your own tuckpointing has two advantages: It can save you money, and you can subdivide a large job, repairing smaller sections as time (or boredom) permits. Here are the steps of tuckpointing:

1. Clean out the old mortar to at least ¹/₂ inch deep (³/₄ inch is better) with a chisel or a rented grinder with a diamond blade. Wear goggles. Take care not to damage the brick, and don't get too aggressive. It may be better to leave some soft mortar in place rather than chisel out the whole mortar joint.

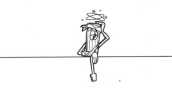

Don't Screw Up!

Masons leave small holes in brickwork, called **weep holes**, to allow water that gathers behind the wall to exit without causing damage. You'll find weep holes above windows, doors, and foundations. If these are plugged with debris, they may need cleaning, but don't be tempted to fill them with mortar—they have a job to do.

2. Brush or vacuum debris from the joint. Don't use a water hose unless the repair can dry for a day before continuing.

3. Test the brick for porosity (see step 3 in the general procedure detailed previously).

4. Mix a small amount of mortar, and push it into the deepest joints, using a two-trowel technique to minimize spillage. Hold the mortar on a brick trowel, and push it in with a tuckpointing trowel (a margin or pointing trowel will also work). Fill deep cracks in two or three steps.

5. When joints will still show your thumbprint, tool them by running a jointer back and forth a couple of times. Press hard to compress the mud and make the joint stronger, cleaner-looking, and more watertight.

6. Let the mud set for a while, and then brush diagonally to remove extra mortar and smooth irregularities.

Busting Blocks and Breaking Bricks—Not Just for Lifers

If you have a few bricks or concrete blocks to shape (say, you need an odd length), you should be able to cut them with hammer and chisel. Lay the brick or block on sand or something else that will support it uniformly (good support is crucial to this technique). Then gradually start tapping at the line where you want the break. Continue tapping on the line, and turn the brick to hit all four sides, gradually increasing your force. When the noise turns hollow, indicating that the brick or block is about to fracture, hit it harder. Although you may need practice, this technique is far more effective than it sounds. The big mistakes are not obtaining enough support, and striking too hard at first.

You also can saw most bricks with a circular saw and a fiberglass masonry blade—a noisy, dusty, but usually workable solution. Use several passes rather than trying to cut the whole depth in one shot.

A more sophisticated approach is to rent a diamond-blade tile saw (if the rental company permits you to saw brick with it). These saws are more accurate, quieter, and, because they are water-cooled, virtually dust-free. However, some bricks are too hard for these saws, so use them gingerly until you get the hang of it—and wear goggles.

A Word on Foundation Repair

Can you fix a crack in a concrete, concrete block, or stone foundation?

Yes.

Will it stay fixed?

That depends. Is the crack still moving?

Enough Socratic dialog—home-repair manuals should be light on philosophical blather. What I'm trying to say is this: Don't expect a little line of mortar to hold a foundation together if the foundation's got traveling on its mind.

Some new foundations crack a bit when the soil settles and then stay put. Look closely at the crack: If you see dirt, insect cocoons, or other crud inside, you may be lucky enough to have an old, inactive crack. Then go ahead and fix it, using the general repair procedure outlined earlier in this chapter.

If the crack is fresh and clean inside, then it's probably new and may still be shifting due to unstable soil or frost heaving. If you think water is running under the foundation and freezing, see the section "May We Talk About Your Soggy Basement?" later in this chapter. If that doesn't work and you're worried that the shifting will damage plaster, doors, or windows upstairs, you're in pro territory—consult a mason or a foundation repairer.

Stucco Repair: The Jackson Pollock Solution

Stucco is a decorative, irregular mortar coating surface that can be finished in various ways. Although the repair procedure is simple, few homeowners know it—and judging by the average stucco repair, few masons do, either. All you need are the instructions in this section; the usual tools; a big, coarse-fibered brush; and a bit of patience. Why patience? Because you'll need to let the mortar set a while between operations. Here are the steps:

1. Clean out all the loose, crumbly stuff from the hole with a hammer, chisel, and brush. For a small repair, go directly to step 3.

   For a deep repair, you've got to adhere a base coat. Choose 2A or 2B.

2A. *If the hole is backed up by masonry or concrete*: Clean the back-up wall by brushing with diluted muriatic acid (it's sold at brickyards; be sure to protect your eyes and hands). When the acid stops foaming, wash it off with water, and then allow the surface to partially dry.

2B. *If the damaged area is backed by anything else*: Buy some wire lath from a plaster or masonry supplier to anchor the new stucco (some people use chicken wire or $1/4$-inch screening, but wire lath is stronger). Cut the lath to fit inside the damaged area, and nail it to the studs with roofing nails. Cut it with tin snips, and wear gloves—cut wire lath is sharp and nasty. Make sure the lath stays tight, or it will protrude from the wall.

3. Moisten the edges of intact stucco so that it won't dry out the new mortar. (If you washed the backing with muriatic acid, you can probably skip this step.)

4. Mix a batch of mortar and trowel it into the deepest areas first. Press the mortar into the wire lath. Gradually work up to the surface level. If the mortar sags, you're adding it too quickly. If it dries out, you're adding too slowly.

   For a *swirled stucco* finish, go to step 11. For the common, *nubbly stucco finish*, continue here.

5. When the whole repair is almost up to the level of the existing stucco, stop and allow the mortar to set up for a while—maybe 20 minutes in warm weather.

6. Soften the mortar still in your wheelbarrow with water. It should be medium-soupy, about the consistency of half-melted soft-serve ice cream.

7. Now start the Jackson Pollock routine. (Remember the paint-throwing abstract expressionist from the 1950s?) When the mortar on the wall is stiff but you can still press your thumb into it, begin throwing mortar. Take your stiff cleaning brush, smoosh it directly into the softened mud in the wheelbarrow, and throw this mud at the mud already on the wall.

8. If the thrown mud penetrates too deeply, wait a few minutes so the wall can harden a bit. Then resume throwing the soft mud, blending the patch to match the original.

9. If the original stucco was flattened on top, wait a few minutes longer, and then trowel the high points flat to match that texture.

10. Cover and moisten the patch repeatedly during the first week so that it can cure properly, and you're done.

    For a *swirled finish*, continue here from step 4. You will also need a 4-inch paint brush and a soft rubber float (see the photo of plaster and drywall tools in Chapter 22, "Cosmetology 101: Drywall and Plaster Repair").

11. Bring the mortar up to the surface level, and allow it to set for a while.

12. When the mortar is fairly stiff, moisten the float and flick some water on the surface. Then start swirling the stucco with the float, attempting to match the surroundings. If the float digs in too much, wait a while. If it does not dig in enough, add more water to the surface. Cure, as in step 10.

Taking the Bloom off Bloom

What do masonry walls have in common with angel food cakes? Not much—unless they have a disease called "bloom," an ailment that shows up as a white "frosting" on the exterior. Bloom—AKA efflorescence—is a deposit of white salts that is carried to the surface by water from the mortar, bricks, blocks, or stones. The problem requires moisture, which can come from the outside (rain or groundwater) or from the inside (condensation).

Efflorescence is not a pretty picture, and it's easier to prevent than cure. (Aren't warnings like this wonderfully helpful? Why would anyone bother preventing bloom unless they already had it? And by then, it's too late. Still, you may be able to prevent the bloom from getting worse.) If the moisture is coming from outside, see the section "May We Talk About Your Soggy Basement?" later in this chapter. If the water is coming from inside, see the section "Home Ventilation: Why and How," In Chapter 12, "Skin-Tight: Caulking, Weather-Stripping, Insulation, and Ventilation."

To remove bloom, try a stiff brushing with water. If that doesn't work, brush on 1 part muriatic acid to 12 parts water (using caution, goggles, and rubber gloves). Then rinse with water—sparingly: Water can cause more bloom.

Some people suggest waterproofing the outside of a wall to prevent water from entering and causing bloom. But the Brick Institute of America, which presumably knows something about the subject, warns that a waterproof treatment can trap moisture inside the building and cause even worse deterioration.

Concretely Speaking?

So much for masonry. What about its big gray sister, concrete? Chances are, you have some of this handy, homely stuff around the house—in the driveway, the foundation, or the basement floor. What to do if concrete takes sick? First, you figure out a plan of action; second, you carry it out. We'll take things in that order.

Like all good doctors, a concrete doctor starts with a diagnosis. If the stuff is heavily cracked or broken—usually as a result of poor ingredients or a dumb pouring technique—the only solution may be to replace it. Unless you love jack-hammering or it's a tiny job, that's best left to the pros. Fortunately, usually the problem is more localized—a crack, chip, or break amidst an expanse of good 'crete.

Toolbox Trivia

Concrete walks and driveways that have settled can be jacked back into position in one piece by specialists called **mudjackers** or **slabjackers**. Mudjackers drill holes in each slab, pump in soupy concrete to raise it, and allow the mud to set. Although it's not cheap, it beats replacing a slab.

As usual, the first step in repair is to "pound the pavement" and remove the damaged stuff with a hammer, chisel, and brush. No matter what the shape, try to avoid thin, weak edges in the repair, which will crack immediately. If possible, cut the edges at a sharp angle (see the accompanying illustration).

Preparing to patch concrete.

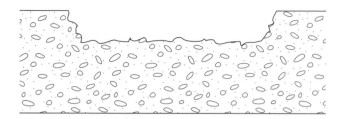

Cut the edges as square as possible, but don't get obsessive and try to make them perfect—it's impossible unless you rent a diamond saw made for cutting concrete. Strongly suggested: For better adhesion, clean the area, moisten it, and brush on a bonding agent or a paste of portland cement and water. Also see the section "Thin Concrete Surfacing," later in this chapter.

Unless you're patching a hole on something flat, you'll have to set up temporary bracing, called *forms*, to hold the fresh concrete in place as it sets. If you're like me, you'll try to get away with the sleaziest, most entry-level form imaginable. And if your luck is like mine, you'll be repaid by a form that bulges, slips, or otherwise fails just when you need it most—when the 'crete is half-poured.

So do something slightly more impressive. Make a stake by sharpening the point of a 2-by-4 with an ax or a handsaw. Then drive it into the ground with a sledgehammer, a 3-pound hammer, or the back of an ax. Cut diagonal braces to fit, wedge them tight against the form, and nail into place. If there's no soil for stakes, anchor the braces with concrete blocks or other weighty objects.

Remember, your vertical repair will never be better than your form. Go ahead—overdo it when nailing the diagonal bracing to the stakes.

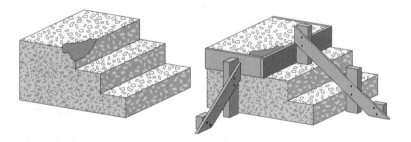

Finishing Concrete—From Stone Soup to Smooth as Glass

Before I explain a concrete repair, you must understand how to finish concrete—how to convert fresh concrete into a smooth concrete driveway. In other words, you must learn how to smooth stone soup. Most people don't seem to think about finishing until they are midway through a concrete job—at least, that's my style. Unfortunately, that's a bit late. Without finishing, you'll wind up with a lumpy surface, a gunmetal-gray version of kidney-bean stew.

As I learned after one disastrous encounter with stone soup, the trick in finishing is to repeatedly work the surface as the concrete sets. This process pushes the stones down while pulling up the sand, cement, and water to the surface. This stuff, called *paste*, fills the gaps between the gravel and makes that smooth, attractive (well, relatively—we're still talking concrete) surface.

This involves two steps: screeding and floating. You *screed*—or "strike off"—by drawing a 2-by-4 back and forth across the surface. Rest each end of the board on a form or the surrounding concrete, and hold the forward edge up slightly so that it does not dig into the soup.

The tool for floating is called, amazingly enough, a *float*, and you can make one from scrap lumber in about 10 minutes (counting time wasted looking for the wood). Instructions for making a home-made float are covered in Chapter 16 in the section "Special Tools." The process of floating is covered in step 4 in the list that follows.

Nail It Down

Don't be duped into thinking you can hammer "masonry" nails (AKA "cut nails") into old concrete—it just won't go, Joe. These nails will penetrate fresh (1- to 2-day-old) concrete, which is still pretty soft. To fasten to old concrete, however, you've got to drill or use the gunpowder-driven anchors sold at lumberyards or brickyards. See the section "Anchors," in Chapter 9, "Fast Guide to Fasteners."

If you're trying to repair an acne-infested, pockmarked section of concrete driveway or floor, your best bet is to buy a latex surface repair material from a masonry supplier. (See the section "Thin Concrete Surfacing," later in this chapter.) For medium-size jobs, you'll want to buy concrete mix in bags. For large jobs, it's cheaper to buy sand, cement, and gravel. The general recipe is 1 part of cement to 2 parts sand and 3 parts gravel. For a medium-size or larger job, do yourself a favor and rent a mixer—this stuff defines heavy!

Concrete Repair: The General Procedure

Once the preparations are completed, you can get down to the dirty work: mixing and pouring the concrete. Try to choose a day that's warm but not hot—not only is the work sweaty, but the concrete sets up too quickly in temperatures above 85° F or so. Don't work in weather colder than 40° F because it will set too slowly or freeze.

Don't Screw Up!

If you mix and pour concrete when the temperature is below 40° F, it can even freeze—a major no-no.

1. Mix the concrete according to the directions on the bag. Dry-mix the materials, and then add water and mix some more. Don't make it too soupy; that weakens the batch.

2. In hot, dry weather, dampen the old concrete around the repair to prevent overdrying of the patch. Apply a cement-water or commercial bonding agent, if needed. Then shovel fresh concrete into the repair, making sure it gets into all gaps and corners.

3. On a large job, screed the top with a 2-by-4, using a sawing motion.

4. Allow the patch to set for a while—perhaps 15 or 30 minutes. Then start floating by drawing your float around in a circle. If you start too soon, the float will dig in to the surface. If you start too late, the surface will be too hard to work on. Use light pressure, and don't expect to get too much done at once—repetition is the key. If rocks come to the surface, throw them away or push them back in. It's legitimate to add a bit of water to get the paste moving at the surface, but don't overdo it.

5. After one or two more floating operations, let the 'crete rest, and switch to a concrete-finishing trowel or a plastering trowel (both work equally well). Again, using a circular motion, pull the paste to the surface using more downward pressure.

6. It's hard to predict how many times you'll need to trowel—the best advice is to watch the concrete and make sure it sets with the finish you want. But don't overwork it, as this can weaken the surface and make it prone to "spalling," or flaking off.

7. If you want a "broom finish"—a safer surface with fine ridges for better traction—draw a garage broom across the surface as it sets. As usual, timing matters: If the mud is too soft, the ridges will be too deep; if the mud is too stiff, the ridges won't be deep enough.

Making It Stay Stuck

If a surface is fairly deep and rough, mortar and concrete will "key" (lock onto) it when you squish mortar into gaps between bricks or stones. For the best grip, the gaps should be at least $3/4$ inch deep. But what if your repair falls outside this "rough and ready" category? For example, how can you apply a surface coat to improve the appearance of a pockmarked foundation? Or, how can you make a concrete patch that actually sticks to the edge of a stoop? You do so by increasing the bond between the new mortar and the surface with a coat of cement paste or bonding agent.

Here's how:

1. Clean loose stuff from the surface with a brick chisel or a mason's hammer and a brush. Clean the surface chemically with a dilution of the muriatic acid sold at masonry suppliers or home centers. Apply the acid with a plastic brush from a plastic pail. When handling acid, observe all cautions, particularly regarding eye and hand protection.

2. When the acid has finished foaming in 2 minutes or so, wash away the remaining crud (the acid should be neutralized by now) with plenty of water. Allow the surface to dry a bit.

3. Mix up a little dry portland or mason's cement (pure cement, without sand or gravel) with water. The paste should be fairly stiff. Or, buy a bonding agent from a brickyard and follow the directions on the package.

4. Brush this goop on the surface and complete your repair before the paste or bonding agent dries.

A second solution to shallow repairs on a concrete driveway or foundation is to use vinyl cement patching, as described in the next section. This stuff claims to bond well, and it probably does. Still, clean a heavily deteriorated and flaking surface before patching, and consider using the muriatic acid treatment described previously.

Thin Concrete Surfacing

When I was in the masonry business, additives designed to help with the key masonry problem—making a thin coat adhere without cracking—were just hitting the market. Today you can buy materials that masons once only dreamed of. One material, in particular, allows you to apply a thin surface of mortar and expect it to stick—it goes by the glamorous title of vinyl cement patch, which you can buy in 20-pound bags at home supply centers.

Using this stuff is a big no-brainer: Simply clean off the surface, mix, and apply. But getting a smooth surface may be a bigger problem, as it's tough to trowel a section that's partly new patching and partly old concrete. My advice is to flatten the mud, let it cure for a while, and then make a swirling pattern with a garage broom to hide the unevenness and give a high-traction surface. You may also encounter a problem with color; the patching I used was a much lighter gray than the existing concrete. But it's flat, easy to sweep, and doesn't trap snow and ice. That's about as much as I'm prepared to ask of concrete, old or new. One final note: Be sure to cover the patch with plastic for about a week. Pull back the plastic and dampen daily.

May We Talk About Your Soggy Basement?

Some of my favorite moments in the masonry business occurred when I was called to fix a wet basement. I usually started by explaining (to my customer's relief) that most of these problems did not require expensive waterproofing, trenching, or sump pumps.

Instead, they required the low-tech solution: getting the water away from the foundation before it could sink into the ground and cause a problem. (If you don't hear this from the people who sell pumps or waterproofing, it may be because they know which side their bread is buttered on.)

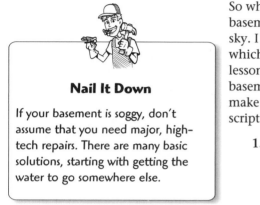

Nail It Down

If your basement is soggy, don't assume that you need major, high-tech repairs. There are many basic solutions, starting with getting the water to go somewhere else.

So when someone asked me to dry out a waterlogged basement, my first response was to roll my eyes to the sky. I wasn't being rude; I was looking for the problem, which was usually traceable to balky gutters. What is the lesson for you, dear homeowner-plagued-by-a-soggy-basement? Remove the water, and you won't have to make your basement as tight as a boat. Follow this easy script for creating a drought in your basement:

1. Standing outside the house, near where the water is entering the basement, look at the gutter. Is it leaking or plugged? Then read the section "Down in the Gutter: Repairing Eaves Troughs," in Chapter 15.

2. Next check the downspouts, which bring water from the gutters to the ground. If the spouts empty out near the problem area, direct the water elsewhere. (You can buy gutter material or flexible plastic pipe at hardware stores or lumberyards.)

3. If your house has underground piping in place to take run-off away from the house, you'll have to decide whether it's easier to clean out this piping, to install new piping, or to just bypass it entirely by running downspout piping on the surface. There's a tradeoff: Underground piping is less obtrusive but more difficult to install and maintain.

4. Finally, look at the grading (slope) of ground near the wet spot. Is the water simply doing what comes naturally—running downhill toward your house? Then you may need to add topsoil around the house and smooth it so that the water runs away. In an extreme case, you may need to build a low berm to divert water coming from elsewhere (such as running off a driveway) to a place where it won't cause harm.

This may turn into a lot of labor, but it's cheaper than a basement waterproofing job—and much more likely to work. There are no guarantees, and you can always install a sump pump or hire a waterproofer later. But do start by routing the water away from the basement.

The Least You Need to Know

➤ Put your masonry repairs on a sound footing: Clean out all rot first.

➤ There's no excuse for a homely stucco repair if you know the Jackson Pollock solution.

➤ Take the time to get a good bond between the original surface and the repair.

➤ Smoothing concrete is easy if you know *how* and *when* to do it.

➤ Water can be murder on foundations and basements. The first and cheapest solution is to keep water away from the building.

Part 4
An Inside Job

When I rented an apartment, I loved having shabby walls. Huh? That's because they screamed a silent but unmistakable "paint me!" That was just the sort of assertiveness needed to catch the landlord's attention. Now that I'm a homeowner, however, that squalor seems like injustice squared. First I've got to endure the sight of those walls, and then I've got to smear some paint on them.

Granted, the forces of entropy are not as severe inside a house as they are on the weather-beaten outside. Still, the interior is subject to considerable forces of decay—judging by the squeaky floors, rotting plaster, and peeling paint I've confronted in various houses.

But the picture is not all gloomy. The indoor home repairs described in this part of the book can be the most satisfying species of home fix-up because you can savor the fruits of your labor from the easy chair. And remember: It never rains when you're working inside. (If you swallowed that fib, I bet you haven't tried any plumbing repairs recently. But we've saved plumbing for last.)

Chapter 18

A Paneless Guide to Windows

In This Chapter

➤ How to keep your windows swinging or sliding

➤ Removing and replacing glass, step by step

➤ Screen repair and replacement

➤ What to do when your insulated windows turn traitor

If you want some air, light, or a view, a window beats a solid wall. But when it comes to staying out of trouble, I'd bet on the wall any day. Windows leak. They break. Their glass sags with age. Insulated windows, which are great for keeping cold weather out, eventually get cloudy. And some windows can't be opened without a fullback shove.

Windows come in many styles and shapes—they slide up and down, they slide side to side, and they swing from the top or side edge. The double-hung window is still one of the most common, so let's use it to get acquainted with some window lingo (see the accompanying figure, which illustrates the parts of a double-hung window). For molding advice, see Chapter 24, "A Scolding on Molding"; for weather-strip advice, see Chapter 12, "Skin-Tight: Caulking, Weather-Stripping, Insulation, and Ventilation."

Parts of a double-hung window.

A. Side jamb

B. Apron

C. Sill

D. Inside stop (parting stop)

E. Stool

F. Outer stop

G. Meeting rail

H. Sash weight or counterweight (in some windows)

I. Pocket and cover (in some windows with sash weights)

J. Counterweight spring (in some windows—replaces sash weights)

K. Head jamb

L. Muntins

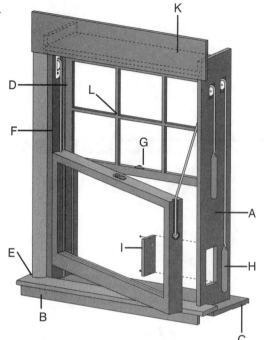
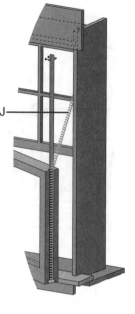

Unsticking Stuck Wood Windows

Why is a wood window like a jazz quartet? Because they both love to jam. Yuk, yuk. No more two-liners—I promise. But seriously, windows do get stuck, a problem that is most serious when caused by a shifting foundation. Although you might be able to stop this movement, repairing it is beyond idiot territory. Still, it's worth having someone do it, because foundation movement can also crack plaster or mangle doors (see the section "A Word on Foundation Repair," in Chapter 17, "Bricks and Stones: Masonry and Concrete [the Sequel]"). Here, we'll talk about windows that are jammed or painted shut, that are swollen with moisture, or that have poor counterweights or balky mechanisms.

Jammed or Painted Shut

Amazing as it may seem, people actually freeze windows shut by slobbering paint into the cracks between the moving parts (the sash) and the fixed parts (the jambs and stops). To free a stuck window, you'll need a hammer, a trowel or putty knife, and a paint scraper. You may also need a plane, a belt sander with fine sandpaper, a drill, and some nails.

1. Slip a putty knife or trowel in the cracks between the sash and the stops, and between the sash and the stool. Run the tool around the whole window, wiggling it and trying to move the sash. Be careful not to gouge the wood as you work.

2. Press up with your hand at the middle of the lower sash. If the sash moves at all, concentrate your efforts where it's still stuck.

3. If the window still refuses to move, remove one outer stop (the molding that forms the channel for the sash). Use a hammer to tap a wood chisel and/or stiff trowel under the molding to remove it. See the "Wood Sash" section later in this chapter for more paneless advice on pulling this molding without trashing it.

Don't Screw Up!

Before you apply megatons of force to any window, double-check that the lock is open and that a nail or another security device is not holding it closed. Use caution with hammers, levers, or other primitive tools on the sash (although you may need a hammer to remove the outer stop). Sometimes a 2-by-4 lever is useful for moving a stuck sash, but be careful—there's glass here!

4. Remove the sash. Prevent the counterweight ropes or straps from disappearing into their holes by attaching a locking plier to them or by tying a knot in the rope.

5. Clean out the sash channels, and lightly sandpaper or plane the edges of the sash where it binds. If there's a lot of extra paint, use a paint scraper or a very light touch of a belt sander, using medium sandpaper. Wax the channels with paraffin, candle wax, or silicon.

6. Reinstall the sash, and reconnect the counterweights. Drill new nail holes, and renail the stops slightly looser than before. (If you use the old holes, the stops will return to the position where they jammed the window.)

7. If you repaint the window, use paint sparingly, and paint the parts separately so that paint does not bridge the gap and put you back where you started.

Moisture

Damp weather swells wood, particularly if it's not protected by a sealer. If a window sticks only occasionally, you may want to live with it. Otherwise, try these suggestions:

➤ Paint the sash with water-resistant paint.

➤ Try the suggestions in the previous section "Jammed or Painted Shut." If you must trim the sash with a saw, planer, or belt sander, don't get too enthusiastic, particularly in damp weather. Otherwise, when the humidity drops, your window may rattle and admit drafts.

Poor Counterweights

Suppose the window opens, but you can't be bothered calling Arnold Schwarzenegger every time the smell of fried fish makes you yearn for fresh air. The problem may be a detached counterweight. These metal weights are suspended in hidden channels behind the jambs to balance the weight of the sash and make it easier to open. A double-hung window has two counterweights for each sash (see the previous figure detailing the parts of a double-hung window).

To remove the counterweights, follow steps 3 and 4 in the preceding procedure for opening a jammed window. Detach the ropes from the sash, and look for a removable rectangular cover (it may be painted over, but you'll see its outline if it's present). Use a wood chisel and screwdriver to remove the cover, and then rehang the weight with a new cord. Or, install spring sash kits in the pulley slots and attach to the lower sash.

If there's no cutout, you can't access the counterweights without at least tearing off the window trim. At that point, I would get rid of the ropes and go to a hardware store to buy a spring kit to support the sash.

If you're working on an aging, drafty double-hung window, consider replacing the sash, glass, and sliding channels with a kit that gives you essentially a new window, with spring supports, modern weather-stripping, and the ability to clean all the glass from the inside. These kits, which must be ordered for your window size, are a comprehensive solution to window woes, and they're much cheaper and easier than replacing the entire window.

Balky Mechanism in a Casement Window

Casement windows don't have counterweight problems, but they still know how to stick. To loosen a casement window, oil the mechanism and hinges with penetrating oil (such as WD-40 or Liquid Wrench) followed by motor oil. If that fails, carefully release the mechanism and repeat the process. You may need to use repeated applications of penetrating oil, and a few light whacks of a hammer, to loosen the mechanism. But don't break anything; you may have trouble finding a replacement mechanism.

Keeping in mind that there are many designs out there, here's how to remove and reinstall one type of casement window sash:

1. Open the sash partway, and figure out how to release the opening mechanism, which is located on the bottom of the sash. In the window shown in the top photo that follows, the bar slips down and out when it's opposite the arrow on the channel of the opening mechanism.

2. Detach the sash from the top and bottom mechanisms by sliding the catch securing the pin away from the pin, using a screwdriver (see bottom photo below).

3. Carefully slide the sash to the side so that you can pull it from the track. Disengage the bottom first, and then get a firm grip on the sash before disengaging the top.

4. Reinstall by reversing these steps.

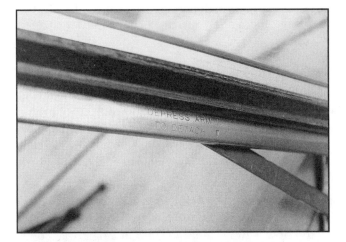

Adjust the sash until the bar is located at the arrow, and push down (you may have to hunt around to figure out how to disassemble your window if it's different from this one).

Pull out the sliding catch, and the pin will drop out of the hole. Slide the sash to the side, and remove it.

Feeling Rather Stuffy?

If your double-hung windows have the usual kind of "combination" aluminum storms, chances are that the screen covers only the bottom half. To get better ventilation (particularly on upper stories), remove the upper aluminum storm, take it to a

181

window-repair store, and have a screen made to the same size. After you install the new screen above the existing screen, you'll be able to open both sashes, allowing hot air to escape from near the ceiling.

Replacing Glass

Way back when, I hit a line-drive home run in front of hundreds of college classmates. Unfortunately, my delight was terminated by the painful, costly crash of the softball blasting through a beautiful leaded window. When it comes to breaking windows, I've found that utter stupidity works as well as softball heroics. Last winter, I attacked a housefly on the window with a magazine. The fly merrily escaped—but the pane died a sudden death. What a pain!

Wood Sash

To replace broken glass in a wooden sash, you'll need gloves, goggles, a small trowel or putty knife, a hammer, new glass, glazier's points (the tiny clamps that hold the glass in place), boiled linseed oil (or primer or diluted exterior alkyd paint), a small brush or rag, and glazing compound. If the window is accessible from the outside, you might be able to fix it in place. Clean out all the glass, and start with step 5. Start here if you must remove the sash to get access to the pane:

1. Remove one outer stop (the vertical strip of molding inside the jamb that holds the sash in the channel). Starting at one end, slip a trowel under the molding, near a nail, and pry the stop slowly away from the jamb. If a nail head comes up, pull it, protecting the wood with the trowel blade or a scrap of wood. Move along the length of the stop—don't concentrate in one place—and pry with the hammer and trowel in unison (or use two trowels) to minimize damage (see Chapter 24 for more on the correct way to pull molding).

2. Remove the lower sash, and detach the counterweight ropes or spring lifts. Don't let the ropes disappear into the jamb; grab them with locking pliers, or knot them.

3. If you're repairing the upper sash, remove the parting stop by repeating step 1 (even more delicately—this stop is tucked into a channel and is harder to remove). Once the sash is out, you're in a good position to install weather-stripping; at least clean the channel so the sash operates smoothly.

4. Wearing gloves and goggles, place the broken sash on a garbage pail. If the pane is mostly intact, lay a rag across it and beat it with a blunt object (see the photo for this step).

Be careful when removing the broken pane. Be sure to wear goggles and heavy-duty gloves.

5. Scrape the seat (where the glass meets the wood) with an old wood chisel, paint scraper, small trowel, or putty knife. If the glazier's points haven't popped out, remove them with pliers.

6. Cutting glass is no job for complete idiots, but hardware stores and glass companies have the tools and expertise to do it safely and accurately. Bring the actual dimensions of the opening, and explain that they are the dimensions of the *opening*, not the glass. Let the glass company figure out the actual size for the new pane.

7. Paint the seat with boiled linseed oil, primer, or diluted house paint so that the glazing compound will not dry too quickly, as shown in the following photo.

8. Press a small bead of glazing compound in the seat to seal the pane from behind, and then press the new pane into the bead and seat it securely.

Nail It Down

The best window-cleaner is also the cheapest. Splash some ammonia in warm water. Dip a ball of old newspaper in the solution and clean the glass. Dry the glass with a clean ball of newspaper, and then recycle the soggy paper. Use plenty of elbow grease.

9. Gently but firmly press glazier's points into place with a trowel, putty knife, or wide screwdriver. Remember, this is no time for a Hercules act!

10. Distribute glazing compound on the seat, and press it to make a smooth coat (see bottom photo below). When you're almost done, lubricate the trowel or knife with linseed oil, and glide it along the compound to leave a smooth seal.

11. Reassemble the window, and reconnect the counterweight ropes or spring lifts. Carefully renail the outer stop—it should be tight to the sash without binding it. In dry weather, the stop should be a bit loose so that when humid weather swells it, the window will not bind.

12. Let the glazing dry for about a week, and then prime and paint it.

Use linseed oil or exterior primer to seal the seat for the new pane.

Smooth the glazing compound with the trowel. For the final pass, grease the trowel with a little boiled linseed oil so that it doesn't pull out the glazing compound.

Metal Sash

If you can't access the glass from outside, you'll need to remove the sash. See the previous section "Balky Mechanism in a Casement Window," for suggestions. You may have to hunt around, starting at the operating mechanism, to figure out how to remove the sash. Then follow the previous directions for replacing a pane in wood sash, steps 4 through 8. Instead of glazing points, use the clips that held the old pane, or buy replacements at a glass company. When reinstalling the sash, lubricate the hinges and operating mechanism.

To replace a broken pane in a moving aluminum window, as in a storm window, choose between two courses of action:

➤ Remove the sash, clean out the broken glass, and take the frame to a glass company for replacement.

➤ Take the sash apart by removing the little screws at the corners. Measure the size of the glass, and have one cut for you. If the gasket holding the pane is in good shape, reuse it. Otherwise, buy a replacement.

Insulated Glass

Insulated, or double-pane, windows are a boon for people in northern climates because they eliminate the innumerable leakage and cleaning problems of older storm windows. But like most technological fixes, these windows raise problems: When the seal around the edge of the glass leaks (and it will, eventually), condensation will cloud the glass and claustrophobia will cloud the house.

The only cure is to replace the clouded glass, but you don't need to call the glass company to the house for that. Instead, you can order replacement glass (local glass companies cannot cut insulated glass; they must order it). Be sure to remove the weather-stripping so that you're measuring the actual length, width, and thickness; if you order the wrong size, you'll eat the cost. If you're not sure of these dimensions, you can remove the sash (see the information in the section "Balky Mechanism in a Casement Window," earlier in this chapter) and have a glass company measure it with calipers. Then, when your glass is ready, you can remove the sash again and install the new pane, or you can have the glass gurus install it for you.

Don't Screw Up!

For safety purposes, doors must be glazed with clear plastic such as Plexiglas, or with safety glass. Safety glass breaks into tiny, harmless fragments; it's quite heavy and expensive, and it must be ordered because glass companies cannot cut it. Although Plexiglas scratches easily, it's cheap and easy to replace.

But remember to plan ahead: Glass companies stock few sizes of double-insulated glass, and ordering from a manufacturer can take several weeks. You might be able to shorten this wait by going directly to a window manufacturer, if one is nearby.

Replacing Screens: Windows and Doors

Screens wear out, especially those feckless nylon types. Here in the mosquito capital of the world, that's an unpardonable sin. How to repair them? For ultra-small repairs, cut a patch of aluminum screen that's about 1 inch larger in each dimension than the hole. Strip away a few wires from all sides, and bend over the remaining ones at 90°. Press these wires through the damaged area, and bend them flat.

For a more extensive problem (read: total disaster) on a screen door or window, remove the door or window and place it on a flat surface, or on planks on sawhorses. Your repair technique will depend on whether you are dealing with aluminum or wood.

For an aluminum window or door, follow these steps:

1. Strip out the spline, the tube-shaped vinyl material holding the screen in place. If it's good, save it. Otherwise, buy a new one. While you're at it, buy a screen tool, a roller that you'll use to push the spline back into place.

2. Lay a new piece of screen on the opening, about 2 inches larger in each dimension.

3. Following the weave of the screen, start pressing the spline into place. Work up and around the four sides. As you press, the spline will pull the screen tight. Make sure it does not pull too tight, as the screen might break.

4. Cut off excess screen just outside the spline with a utility knife.

For a wood window or door, follow these steps:

1. Remove wood moldings that hold the screening into place. If you cannot preserve them, buy new screen bead at a lumberyard.

2. Tear off the old screen, and remove tacks and staples.

3. Lay the wooden frame on a flat surface. Raise each end with 1-by-4 lumber, and clamp at the center. This bows the screen frame, as shown in the accompanying figure on screen repair.

4. Lay the screen material over the frame, overlapping 1 inch at each edge.

5. Fasten the screen at top and bottom, using a $5/16$-inch staple every 3 inches.

6. Release the clamps, and check that the screen is tight enough.

7. Staple one side all the way down. On the other side, pull the screen tight across from each staple; then staple into place.

8. Staple the center rail, and reattach the moldings with ⁷/₈-inch brads.

9. Cut off excess screen with a utility knife.

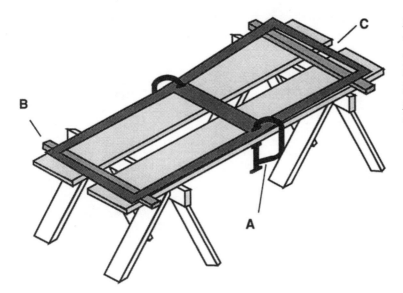

Hold the door in the center with C-clamps, supporting each end with ³/₄-inch boards. Attach the screen fairly taught, and it will be perfectly flat after the blocks are removed.

A. C-clamp

B. 1-by-4

C. Staple screen at ends first

The Least You Need to Know

➤ If humidity is jamming your windows, fight back by cleaning and carefully planing or sanding them; then seal the wood.

➤ Opening a window that's painted shut requires patience and a light touch with the tools.

➤ You can save big money—and look like a real hero—by replacing broken panes, but it's smart to have a glass company or hardware store cut the glass.

➤ When insulated glass clouds up, it needs replacement. You can take the sting out of this process by removing and replacing the sash by yourself. Remember to plan ahead—you'll need to order the glass.

Chapter 19

An Entry-Level Treatise on Doors

In This Chapter

➤ Sticks, squeaks, and sags—the enemies of a blissful entry

➤ Solving problems with storm doors

➤ Installing and replacing doors

➤ How to install a deadbolt lock

Doors! Talk about underappreciated—nobody notices them until they turn bad. But unless your house is fresh out of the box, I guess you are noticing your doors more than you'd like. Maybe they won't close without a ligament-stretching shove. Maybe they won't lock without a King Kong crank on the key. Maybe they squawk like a tyro clarinetist. Maybe all the weather-stripping in the world couldn't seal the gaps between the door and its jambs.

Doors cause so many problems that I'm surprised nobody has figured how to eliminate them. But at least designers have invented ways to make them work more smoothly—better hinges, better weather-stripping, and even better doors. So if you're getting tired of shouldering your way into your house, acting like a hybrid of Elliot Ness and The Fridge, let's get some medicine for door diseases. We'll start with a bad fit and move to hardware problems. (For weather-stripping advice, see Chapter 12, "Skin-Tight: Caulking, Weather-Stripping, Insulation, and Ventilation." For information on moldings, see Chapter 24, "A Scolding on Molding.")

Diagnosing and Curing Poor-Fitting Doors

Does your door jam in the jambs? If so, then you've got a problem with door fit. Give door hinges some credit: If you'd been slammed 10,000 times, you might be coming loose, too. When it comes to sticking, you can find plenty of causes—dry hinges, loose hinges, hinge mortises cut too deep, door cut wrong, the list goes on and on. But except for structural shifting, which can wrack a doorway out of square, every one of these problems is within idiot territory. So let's start curing your stuck doors.

The first step, as usual, is identifying the problem. The accompanying figure illustrating how to diagnose door-fit woes shows how doors usually go wrong.

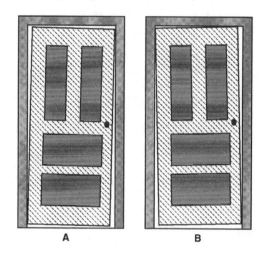

Diagnosing door-fit woes: This exaggerated diagram helps identify simple door-fit problems. Does the door seem to be the wrong size? It's likely that the real culprit is a hinge problem.

A. If the door binds at the upper latch side, tighten the upper hinge screws and/or shim the lower hinge.

B. If the door binds at the lower latch side, tighten the lower hinge screws and/or shim the upper hinge.

Solving Hinge Problems Without Coming Unhinged

Hinges that are too loose, too deep, or too shallow, can all interfere with door operation. Start by tightening all the hinge screws.

If the door is chafing against the entire latch side (that is, the side away from the hinge), tightening the hinge screws should take care of it. If you can lift the latch side a bit, chances are that the screws need tightening or replacement. Loose screws are easy to cure, and it won't hurt to check and tighten them once in a while (this is a great job for when you're feeling compulsive, or when no pressing repairs are waiting in line—as if that ever happens!). You'll need a screwdriver and perhaps a hammer, wood glue, and a dowel, golf tee, or wooden matches. Follow these steps:

1. Try to tighten the screws. Ask somebody to lift the latch side, or raise it by stepping on a flat prybar. If the screws tighten securely, you're done. If they slip in their holes, continue.

2. Find some longer flat-head screws. Traditional flat-heads should be about the same diameter as the originals and slightly longer. However, I would immediately try $2^{1}/_{2}$-inch Phillips-head deck or construction screws. On the jamb, these are sure to grab the 2-by-4 stud behind the jamb. Caution: If the screw heads are too big, they will rise above the hinge and may jam against each other when the door tries to close. If the screws grab tight and the door operates freely, you're finished. If the screws get a poor bite or jam, continue.

3. To reinforce the screw holes, pull the hinge pins as described in the later section "Oiling Dry Hinges," and remove the door. Leave the hinge plates in the jamb and door edge but remove loose screws.

4. Coat golf tees, dowels, or wooden matches with wood glue and tap them into all oversize holes.

5. After the glue has dried, position the hinges and *carefully* indent the center of each hole with a nail or awl. Drill a new hole for the screw, and then reattach the hinge, oil the hinges, and rehang the door.

Don't Screw Up!

Hollow-core doors, commonly used in interiors, are essentially two sheets of thin paneling separated by strips of cardboard glued on edge. It's easy to fasten something like a hook or a shelf to the perimeter of a hollow-core door because there's solid wood backing up the paneling. Otherwise, you'll need to use expanding-type hollow-wall anchors (see Chapter 9, "Fast Guide to Fasteners"). Stripped hinge screws can be a real problem. If longer screws don't grab, try a larger diameter. You may have to expand the countersink in the hinge with a $^{3}/_{8}$-inch drill bit so that the larger head will fit.

If tightening screws did not solve the problem, examine the hinges. The plates should be flush (level) or a hair above the jamb or door edge.

If the door binds against the entire latch side, the mortises are probably too shallow. Remove the hinges and check. If the hinge plate is too high, chisel a deeper mortise, as shown in the accompanying photo of chiseling a hinge mortise.

If the door binds on the hinge side and tends to spring open as you close it, and there is a wider gap on the latch side than the hinge side, follow these steps.

1. Pull the hinges. Remove the hinge plates. Place one on a thin piece of cardboard, perhaps from a cereal box. Using the plate as a template, cut several shims (see the accompanying photo for this step).

2. Place the shims in the mortises, punch holes for the hinge screws, and rescrew. The shim should be invisible.

3. Test the door; if the cardboard is too thick, try several sheets of copier paper.

Shimming overcut hinges. If you hold the hinge firmly in place, you can't help cutting an accurate shim. Hint: Cut on a double layer of cardboard so that the knife can cut cleanly through the top layer.

Finally, if you can rule out hinge problems, your door is likely the wrong size (just what you thought in the first place!). Read on for information about planing a sticky door.

Planing a Sticking Door

Wet wood swells, and dry wood shrinks. Swollen wood can cause doors (and drawers) to jam in their tracks. Swelling can be a nightmarish problem in areas with alternating wet and dry seasons, because if you plane a door to work perfectly in wet weather, it may turn into a real pygmy in the dry season.

To plane a sticking door, you'll need a hammer, screwdriver, pencil, and hand plane. You may also need a power planer, particularly to plane end grain. (Caution: Before starting, check whether the hinges are loose; see the previous section "Solving Hinge Problems Without Coming Unhinged.")

1. In wet weather, mark the side of the door near where it chafes against the jamb with a pencil (don't mark the door edge; you will be removing that wood). If you can't locate the bind, put a strong light behind the door, or slide a piece of paper in the gap until it sticks.

2. In dry weather, remove the door, lock, and latch (see the section "Oiling Door Latches and Locks," later in this chapter), and plane the door edge. Don't remove too much wood. To plane the end grain, rent a power planer and plane from the

edges toward the center of the door. (A hand planer is adequate for planing with the grain, but a power planer is faster and surer there, too). Concentrate your planing on the marked areas.

3. Rehang the door without installing the latch hardware, and test your work. The door should swing absolutely freely, and the gap between it and the jamb should be uniform.

4. Seal the door edges (paying special attention to end grain) with a clear sealer or water-resistant paint, to slow the absorption of moisture. Reinstall hardware, and rehang the door.

Hardware Problems

Let's say your door *would* open and close if only the hardware would let it. Let's fix those squeaky hinges and balky locks and latches.

Oiling Dry Hinges

Cars have stickers to notify you when they need a lube job (don't tell me you ignore these reminders, too!). Door hinges don't have stickers; instead, they use an annoying screech to indicate that it's time for an "oil change." Fortunately, the job is simplicity itself. You'll need an old flat-bladed screwdriver or a long nail, a hammer, penetrating oil if the pin is stuck, and an oil can and rag. Just follow these steps:

1. Examine the hinge. If there's a hole at the bottom under the pin, you've got an anti-rising hinge—go to step 4. Otherwise, continue with step 2.

2. For a *standard hinge*, pound up on the lip of the pin with screwdriver and hammer (see top photo on next page).

3. If the pin refuses to budge, spray it with penetrating oil, swing the door a few times to loosen the pin, and try again. Remember, the pin always gives way sooner or later. In extreme cases, grab the head with locking pliers and twist. Go to step 5.

4. For an *anti-rising hinge,* place a 3-inch finishing nail in the hole, and pound up with a hammer (see bottom photo on next page). After the pin rises a bit, it will pop right out.

5. Leave the pin partway out, and release the other hinge pins.

6. Remove the pins, and then remove the door, taking care not to scrunch your fingers.

7. Oil each pin with motor oil, sliding the pin through the rag until it's thoroughly coated. Oil the parts of the hinge that rub against each other; then wipe off extra oil.

8. Move the door back into place, and partly insert the top pin.

9. Insert other pins and drive them home.

Old-style hinge pins must be battered into submission with this "el crudo" removal technique. Unfortunately, the paint suffers.

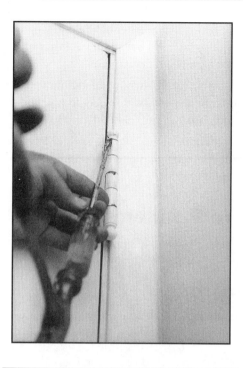

An anti-rising pin comes loose with much more sophistication; notice the hole in the bottom for the nail.

Oiling Door Latches and Locks

Molly, my neighbor, came over the other day, fuming that her husband had left her a door key that didn't work. I volunteered to try the key (which seemed safer than dragging out a ladder for some second-story work). With a bit of persuasion, the bolt turned, and Molly stepped inside with a gratified "thank you." For my part, I was pleased that nobody had thought to put any oil on that lock for years—otherwise, how could I have played neighborhood hero?

It's about as simple as this: When metal meets metal, you need lubrication, whether factory-applied or done-yourself. If you ever have trouble getting your key to turn the lock of home sweet home, or if your door latches are sticky, it's time for a lube job. You may be able to spray white lithium grease or penetrating oil into the latch and keyhole, but if your lock is quite old or extremely sticky, you'll need to take the mechanism apart and oil it. You'll need a screwdriver, some motor oil, and a rag. As you follow these steps, be sure to number or lay out the parts in order so you can reassemble the blasted thing with minimal pain:

1. The general starting point for disassembling a latch or lock mechanism is to remove the knobs or locks from both sides. When you pull the shaft connecting them, the latch or bolt mechanism should detach from the edge of the door.

   The details depend on the exact type of mechanism:

   ➤ On older doorknobs, loosen the screw on one knob; then unscrew the knob from the threaded shaft. The remaining knob and shaft will pull out in one piece.

   ➤ On newer doorknobs, push the tab coming up from inside the knob with a screwdriver while pulling the knob slightly, and pull off the knob. Then pull the other knob off with the shaft.

   ➤ For deadbolts and other locks, remove the screws holding the inner face-plate, or *escutcheon*, and then pull the lock apart.

   ➤ After the faceplate is off, on some deadbolt locks you'll need to unscrew the tumbler assembly. You may need a long hex (*Allen*) wrench to loosen a set screw inside the mechanism.

   ➤ On some doorknobs, the knob and escutcheon come off in one piece after you remove two screws from the inside.

2. At the *edge* of the door, remove the two screws (if they're present) holding the latch mechanism, and pull it out.

3. Oil all moving parts, turning them occasionally to get the oil between the metal parts (see the accompanying illustrations showing how to oil a doorknob or a door lock mechanism). Put some oil on the key, and work the lock a few times.

Put motor oil on the moving parts of the door mechanism, and rotate them so that oil gets into the dry spots.

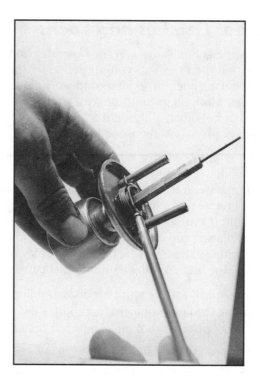

4. Wipe off extra oil, and reverse these steps to assemble. If any wood screws are loose, see suggestions in the section "Solving Hinge Problems Without Coming Unhinged," earlier in this chapter. Don't overtighten the screws. This can distort the parts and cause the lock to grind or even seize up.

So Your Door Doesn't Latch?

When a door fails to latch because the spring-powered doohickey does not slip into the striker plate (the plate on the jamb that grabs the doohickey), you may have one of these problems:

➤ The latch may be too sticky to spring into position (see the previous section "Oiling Door Latches and Locks").

➤ The striker plate may be too deep in the jamb. Unscrew the plate and stick some cardboard shims under it.

➤ The pocket under the striker plate may be too shallow, so the doohickey can't seat. Remove the plate, and drill and chisel a deeper pocket.

➤ The latch may not align with the striker plate. Look for off-center scratches on the striker plate. If the latch is slightly off-center, remove the striker plate, hold it in a vise, and file away some metal from the inside. (If you try to move the plate without changing the screw holes, it will return to the same place when you attach it.)

➤ If the latch won't grab unless you shoulder it, and if scratches on the strike plate are centered, use a file to remove metal from inside the striker plate, on the side toward the inside of the door.

Don't Screw Up!

You can buy deadbolts that can be opened only with a key—from either side. These locks are dangerous and should not be used on exterior doors. In a fire, you may not be able to find the key quickly enough.

Storm Doors

Does your wooden screen door sag? If you are as much a fan of simplicity as I am, you'll love the screen door straightener, a gadget with two rods joined by a turnbuckle. To raise the latch side and square up a sagging screen door, just screw the straightener onto the door at a 45° angle and tighten the turnbuckle. (For advice on repairing screens, see Chapter 18, "A Paneless Guide to Windows.") Here are the details:

1. With the straightener almost fully extended, hold it against the door and drill the first screw hole. The straightener should extend from about halfway up the hinge side to the bottom of the latch side. Insert a screw halfway.

2. Install the rest of the screws, and tighten.

3. Tighten the turnbuckle until the door is square and swings smoothly.

4. If the door is really rickety, screw L-shaped brackets on the corners as reinforcements.

Storm Door Operator

Storm door operators are those tubes that slowly close storm doors—at least, that's what they are supposed to do. In fact, they sometimes slam, as one did on my wife's innocent ankle last month. And sometimes—invariably during the storm of the century—they fail to close. Most people don't know you can adjust the speed of closing, but you can.

Find the speed adjustment. Look for the label: Some operators have a screw. On others, you must detach the operator at one end, turn the tube, and reconnect it. Tightening the screw or the tube should slow the closing action, and loosening should speed it up.

Unfortunately, you may need a different position in summer, when the storm door is holding only a screen, and another in winter, when the heavier storm window is in place. You could change the setting twice a year, but I set it at a compromise. Life is too short to mess with this gadget twice a year.

197

After years of abuse, the door operator can pull out of the jamb. The best way to repair this minor annoyance is to buy a new house. Just kidding. Actually, it's easy to fix, following these hints:

1. Remove the door closer, and repair splintered molding, if any, with wood glue.

2. Fill the gouged area slightly above the surrounding level with wood filler or auto-body filler.

3. Let the material harden until it's like a bar of soap in consistency, and then plane it flat with a Surform brand planer, if you have one. When the patch fully hardens, sandpaper it smooth, and then prime and paint.

4. Mark the screw holes with the bracket held $1/4$ inch from the door, and level with the closer. Drill pilot holes, and then drive in 3-inch screws, which will grab the studs behind the jamb.

5. Finally, buy a safety chain and attach it to the top, to prevent wind from mutilating your storm door next time.

Adding New Stuff

Let's face it: There are times when a door, and/or its hardware, are just going to need replacement. Warped, undersize, or ugly doors fall into this category; so does funky or worn-out hardware. In this section, we'll describe how to install a deadbolt, replace a door, and install a pre-hung door.

Installing a Deadbolt

Say you're feeling insecure at home—at least you have company. What to do? The obvious solution is to upgrade the door locks by installing deadbolts. Many doors have windows, which could allow an intruder to break the glass and reach through and open the deadbolt. That's why I place new locks more than an arm's reach from windows, if possible. Although locks mounted this low may be a bit awkward to open, they are more secure, which is the point of the whole affair, right?

To install a deadbolt, you'll need a screwdriver, hammer, chisel, electric drill (the bigger the better), $7/8$-inch bit, $1^1/2$-inch bit (you may do better to buy a hole-saw kit, with replaceable bits), the deadbolt kit, and lipstick or toothpaste (seriously!). (Some lock-installation kits include a $7/8$-inch spade bit and a $1^1/2$- or $1^1/4$-inch hole saw.)

1. Using the template supplied with the lock, drill a $1^1/2$-inch hole for the handle and latch mechanism. When the bit starts to show on the far side of the door, move the bit to finish the hole from the other side to prevent splintering (see the accompanying photo for this step).

2. Using the $7/8$-inch drill bit, bore in from the edge of the door to meet the first hole (as shown in the following photo).

3. Place the latch mechanism in the $^7/_8$-inch hole, and carefully trace its outline on the edge of the door. A utility knife gives a finer line than a pencil. (Some latches slip directly into the hole and need no chiseling.)

4. Carefully chisel along this line, deep enough to receive the latch plate. Make the mortise flat so that the latch sits evenly.

5. Using a nail or an awl, punch holes for the two screws that secure the latch. These ensure that the drill starts in the center of the hole. Drill two holes, and screw the latch into place.

Nail It Down

Metal-clad doors have advantages in terms of stability and durability, but must they look like tank armor? Sorry, I'm getting off the track. I meant to explain that it's easy to drill through the thin metal cladding to install locks and doorknobs.

6. Assemble the mechanism per instructions. As you tighten, make sure the bolt operates smoothly.

7. Now for the tricky part. Apply lipstick or toothpaste to the end of the bolt, close the door, and operate the bolt to mark the jamb.

8. Position the striker plate carefully over this mark (as in the accompanying photo), and mark the area to be removed with a utility knife. Chisel out a mortise for the plate, and then drill and chisel a deeper mortise for the bolt. Screw the plate into place with 3-inch screws, and test the bolt.

Drill from both sides for a cleaner cut. Make sure to hold the drill square to the door.

Holding the drill horizontal, carefully drill all the way into the opening made in step 1.

Take your time while positioning the strike plate—this is the only tricky part of the procedure.

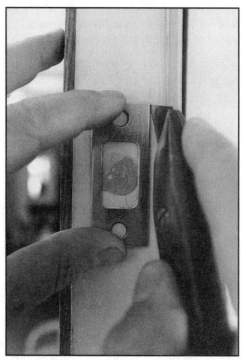

Door Replacement

If you've been reading through all these bright ideas for improving your doors, while sitting in a home whose doors are not worth saving, you've come to the right department. When doors get damaged, worn, or just plain ugly, your only recourse may be to replace them. I've put the evil eye on some homely hollow-core doors on my sons' bedrooms. For years I accepted them as part of the home landscape. Now that I have recognized their true hideousness, their days are numbered.

I haven't found the right doors yet, but when I do, I'll replace those doors with the technique described here. I'll expect to find the kind of support structure shown in the drawing of door installation, later in this chapter. If your door jambs are also beyond repair, see the section "Hanging a Pre-Hung Door," which also comes later in this chapter. If the jambs are hopelessly out of square or are not vertical, you may want to get help from a carpenter.

To replace an existing door, start by assessing exactly what's wrong with it. Is it ugly or warped but a good fit for its opening? Then use it for a template. Buy a new door, or find one at an architectural salvage yard. Remove the old door, lay it on top of the new one, and saw or plane the new one to size. Pay attention to which side is which, and mark the hinge side so you don't get confused.

If you don't have a door for a template, the job becomes harder. Here's a general procedure for marking and cutting that door. Remember to go easy on your cuts; removing more wood is simpler than adding some back!

1. Find a square angle for a starting place. Measure the diagonals of the door opening (they are equal in a rectangle), or use a square. In the illustration for hanging a door, the angle A between the floor and the hinge jamb is square because the hinge jamb is plumb (vertical) and the floor is horizontal.

2. Measure the hinge-side opening height, B. Subtract $5/8$ inch for the top and bottom clearances to get the hinge-side door height. Measuring from the door bottom, mark this height on the door.

3. Measure across the top, middle, and bottom of the door opening, D. Subtract $1/4$ inch, and use these measurements to cut the latch side (see Chapter 11, "Wood: Still Champ After All These Years," for suggestions on cutting panels). Remember, hollow-core doors are hollow. There's only solid wood around the edges, so you can't trim them much. Set your circular saw for the 3° relief shown in the accompanying figure, or plane the angle after sawing the latch side.

4. Measure the top hinge-side angle, C, and starting at the mark from step 2, transfer the angle to the door to mark the top cut.

5. Measure the latch-side height from the bottom of the opening. Subtract $5/8$ inch for clearances, and measure up from the bottom of the door on the latch side. The measurement should meet the top cut line from step 4.

6. Check your measurements again, and then saw the top and check the fit. Use a plane to smooth your cuts and remove extra wood.

7. Locate the door hinges, as shown in the illustration for positioning a door hinge. Mark the outside of the hinge with a utility knife; it's more accurate than a pencil.

201

8. Remove enough wood so the hinge can sit flush in the mortise or cutout, as shown in the photo on chiseling a hinge mortise. Take care with locating the hinges; sixteenths of an inch do count.

9. Holding the hinge in position, dent the center of each screw hole with a nail, and then drill pilot holes and fasten the hinge plates.

10. Reassemble the hinges, and shim the door in position with the top and bottom clearances listed in the drawing. Carefully mark the bottom of each hinge on the jamb. Repeat the chiseling procedure on the jamb, and attach the door.

11. Adapt the procedure detailed in the previous section "Installing a Deadbolt" to install a door latch; the steps are quite similar.

Here's how to hang a door if the hinge-side jamb is vertical and the floor is horizontal. The clearances suggested are for interior doors.

A. Angle between hinge side and floor—a true 90°, in this case.

B. Hinge-side opening height (door is ⅝ inch shorter than this)

C. Top hinge-side angle

D. Opening width (measure at three locations)

E. Latch-side height (door is ⅝ inch shorter than this)

F. ⅛-inch clearance

G. ½-inch clearance (more if the room has thick carpet)

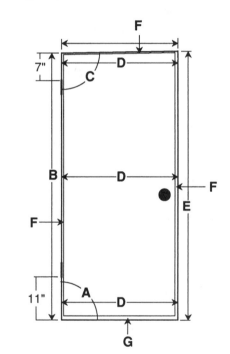

A 3° relief on the latch side, cut with a circular saw or a plane, allows the door to close.

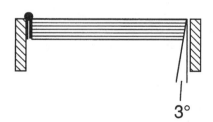

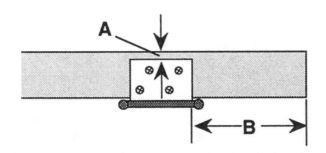

Positioning a door hinge.

A. ³/₁₆-inch clearance

B. 7 inches from bottom or 11 inches from top (typical measurements)

Take your time chiseling hinge mortises. Mark the lines with a utility knife, not a pencil. Cut the perimeter with the chisel, and then make crosshatching cuts with the chisel held vertically. Finally, hold the chisel flat and remove the wood. Don't dig too deep. The hinge should be flush with the door, or slightly above, after the mortise is chiseled out.

Hanging a Pre-Hung Door

Sometimes doors and jambs are so damaged that the best solution is to replace them together. Pre-hung doors are sold with attached hinges and jambs. Pre-hungs are relatively easy to install in a doorway whose molding and jambs have been removed, and they are far better than buying the jamb stock, hinges, and door and cutting the jambs yourself. Unfortunately, if your doorway is an odd dimension, a pre-hung probably won't fit. Interior pre-hung doors come without a threshold, but exterior pre-hung doors do have one.

The accompanying illustration of door installation shows how a standard door is secured to the framing. Just to replace a door, you're unlikely to expose that much of your house, but it can't hurt to know what's under the plaster.

If you want to replace only the jambs and reuse the door, you can buy jamb stock and fabricate your own jambs. It's a job for the perfectionist, as sixteenths of an inch matter.

Toolbox Trivia

Like people, doors are either left- or right-handed. Stand with the door swinging toward you, and look at the door knob. In a left-handed door, the knob will be on the left, and vice versa. You'll need this information to order a pre-hung door (one that's assembled with its jambs).

Before ripping out a door and jambs to install a pre-hung door assembly, measure your existing door and phone a building materials store to see what's available. Pre-hung door assemblies are sized by the rough opening, shown in the accompanying illustration. The rough opening is generally at least 2 inches wider and 1 inch taller than the finished opening (the dimensions inside the jamb), but remove the head casing to find out for sure. A pre-hung that's larger than the opening is a nightmare.

Important: Jambs are available in several widths: $4^9/_{16}$ inches works on a standard stud ($3^1/_2$ inches) plus two layers of $^1/_2$-inch drywall. A $5^1/_8$-inch is needed if there's a layer of $^1/_2$-inch insulation or old plaster in the wall. If the needed jamb width is not available, buy a wider jamb set, and then disassemble and rip the jambs with a circular saw before installing. If you rent a power planer, you can trim the jamb depth without disassembly.

To install a pre-hung door, you'll meet framing like this.

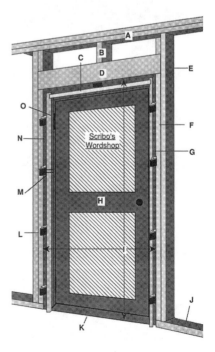

A. Plate (usually 2-by-4)

B. Cripple stud

C. Head jamb

D. Header (doubled 2-inch lumber with $^1/_2$-inch spacer)

E. King stud (continuous stud from sole plate to plate)

F. Trimmer stud (supports header)

G. Side jamb

H. Door

I. Rough opening (width × height)

J. Sole plate

K. Threshold (on exterior door only)

L. Shims (one slides past the other for adjustment)

M. 10d (10-penny) casing or finishing nails

N. Air space ($^1/_4$-inch to 1-inch)

O. Hinge

To remove and replace a door and jambs, follow these steps:

1. Pop out the hinge pins and remove the door. Unscrew the hinges from the jambs, in case the screws grab the trimmer stud.

2. Remove all casing moldings, following suggestions in Chapter 24. If you work gently, you may be able to reuse the molding, but only if the new jambs are the same size or smaller.

3. Saw through one side jamb, and remove all three jambs.

4. Stand the assembly in place. Do not remove the spacers and bands holding everything together.

5. Insert pairs of wooden shims (sold in building supply centers) between the hinge jamb and the trimmer stud. Work your way up from the bottom, holding the jamb vertical. Keep each edge of the jamb flush to the drywall or plaster.

6. Tack the jamb in place with pairs of 10d nails through the pairs of shims. Do not pound the nails home yet. This is the critical step: Check your work often with a 4-foot level, and ensure that the jamb stays plumb. It's best to be fussy: Remove nails and readjust the jamb rather than fasten it wrong.

7. Repeat steps 5 and 6 at the other side jamb, testing that the door remains properly spaced.

8. Insert a pair of shims behind the head jamb, and start two nails through the jamb. Check your work: If the door can operate and has equal clearance at all sides, finish nailing. Otherwise, back up and fix whatever's not kosher. Even experienced carpenters find this an exacting task.

9. When everything is done, finish nailing with a nail set to avoid damaging the jambs.

10. Score the shims with a utility knife, and break them off flush to the jambs.

11. Paint or stain the jambs and casing moldings.

12. Reinstall molding, again referring to Chapter 24.

Toolbox Trivia

Doors are sold in feet-and-inches dimensions. Thus, the common 32-inch-wide-by-80-inch-tall door is called 2 foot 8 inches by 6 foot 8 inches. Why? I hoped you'd ask. Simply because.

The Least You Need to Know

➤ Doors stick for a lot of reasons, few of which are serious enough to daunt an eager homeowner.

➤ Don't plane doors excessively, particularly in wet weather—you may remove too much wood.

➤ Balky door latches may call for some improvising, but you can usually revive them.

➤ Deadbolts are easy to install, although you may have to buy two jumbo drill bits to put them in.

Chapter 20

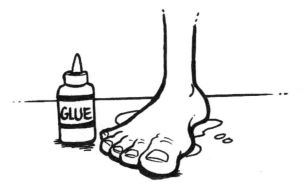

Getting a Solid Footing on Floors

Floors—if you got stomped on so much, you'd be protesting, too. Floors protest by talking back. In my house, the insubordination is worst in the kitchen, where the human equivalent of Hannibal's elephant-mounted army trudges past each day. And there's nothing I can do about it, because I stupidly had a parquet floor laid over the squeak before I got around to fixing it.

At least I learned my lesson: Don't cover up problems—fix them first. Before a new carpet was laid over old linoleum in my bedroom, I spent a couple of hours renailing the floor to the joists (support beams). I located the first joist by drilling through the floor until I hit solid wood. Then I marked out the other joists, which were parallel to the first and 16 inches away (in rare cases, joists are 12 inches apart). Finally, I pounded $2^1/_2$-inch spiral flooring nails 6 inches apart into the joists. Now, even Hannibal's elephants could not raise a squeak from that floor.

In this chapter, I discuss cures for some of the most common flooring woes, starting with suggestions for annihilating squeaks. Then I discuss some other flooring repairs that you can realistically tackle—including repairs to subfloors, carpets, and strip flooring. For information on fixing or laying tile, and for fixing vinyl floors, see Chapter 21, "Tile in Style!"

Squeakproofing

Squeaks are caused by wood rubbing against wood, or against nails, in a floor that has loosened due to structural settling, poor carpentry, or alternating wet and dry weather. Here are three ways to silence squeaks if you have access from below.

Drill holes for a series of flathead wood screws that are fully $1/4$ inch shorter than the combined thickness of the finish floor and subfloor (that's the bottom layer of wood; in new houses, it's usually plywood; in older houses, it's $3/4$-inch lumber). Ask somebody to stand on the floor while you tighten the screws to bring the finish floor (the top layer) down tight to the subfloor (see the accompanying figure). Don't overtighten; stop when the squeak does. Otherwise, you will strip the hole and have to start over.

Glue and nail or screw a cleat (an extra piece of 2-by-4) to the joist near the squeak (as shown in the top drawing on the next page). Because the cleat must hold the floor at the top of its movement, push up on it while fastening.

Tap a glue-coated shim into the gap between the joist and the floor. But take it easy— there's no point raising the board any further than it already is.

When repairing a squeaky floor from below, hold the board down and don't strip the screws. Be reasonable—the goal is silence, not punishment.

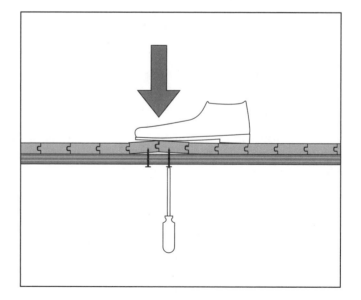

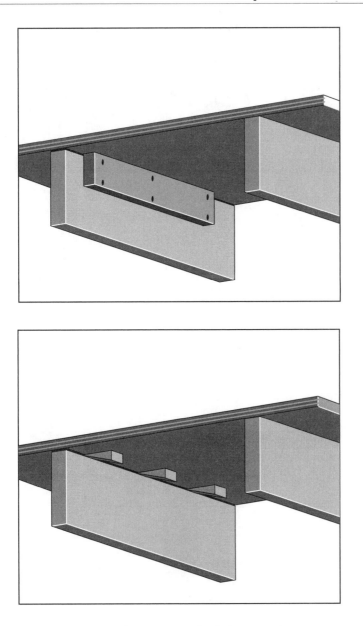

The cleat holds the floor up so the weight of people walking on it does not cause a squeak.

Shims underneath prevent the floor from moving— but use a light touch. Tap the shims into place.

If you must work from above, find the joists by:

➤ Taking up some old floor covering and looking for nails.

➤ Looking inside a floor register for joists.

➤ Probing with a coat hanger, as shown in the accompanying figure.

The other joists should be parallel to the first and multiples of 16 inches away from it.

209

Find the joist by drilling and probing with a coat hanger.

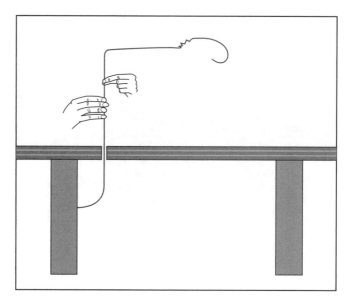

Wood screws—especially long trim screws or beefy deck screws—are much stronger than nails, but you'll need to hide a bigger head with wood filler afterward.

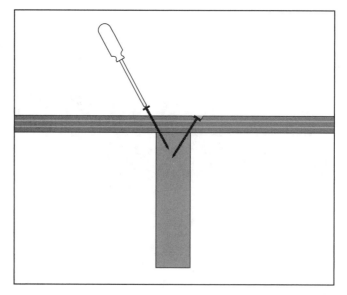

To fix a squeak from above, try these suggestions: Drill diagonal pilot holes, and hammer long casing nails into a joist. Fill the nail holes with a wood filler afterward, and sand and finish as needed.

As shown in the illustration, to tame a bad squeak, use spiral flooring nails or trim screws—as long and large as you can hide with wood filler. Before fastening, pour in a puddle of wood glue. Make sure nails and screws hit a joist; reaching the subfloor will not be strong enough. Also remember that diagonal fasteners get a much better grip than vertical ones.

Stepping Stones to Silent Stairs

My in-laws never repaired the squeakiest stairs in the world, probably because they made a perfect alarm for signaling the after-hours return of the elegant teenager I later married. If you don't need to monitor errant youths, there are several ways to silence squeaky stairs.

Let's start with a bit of lingo:

➤ Treads are the horizontal boards you walk (tread) on.

➤ Risers are the vertical boards between two treads. They're the boards you see as you walk upstairs.

➤ Stringers are the slanting framing lumber along the edges. You can access them from the underside, unless the underside of the stairway has drywall or plaster.

With the jargon under control, let's look at a few simple repairs:

➤ Drill pilot holes for long trim screws to secure the treads to risers. Or, drill diagonally into the stringers. The holes should be smaller in diameter than the screws, with a countersink, or recess, for the head.

➤ Drill pilot holes slightly smaller than long casing nails (thick versions of finishing nails). Nail at an angle for better grip.

➤ Pull out the molding between a tread and a riser (if there is one), and then insert glue-coated wedges into the gaps. When the glue is dry, cut off the visible part of the wedges with a wood chisel or utility knife, and replace the molding.

➤ From below, coat two sides of a 2-by-2 with construction adhesive, and force it against the joint between a riser and the tread. Drill pilot holes and, with somebody standing on the tread, screw it into place from below. Make sure your screws are too short to go through the tread.

Floor Framing Fixes

A weak spot in a floor can indicate a cracked or rotted floor joist. If the problem is localized, splice a pair of joists to the outside of the wounded joist. Each splice should extend at least 18 inches past the damage or should be connected to a supporting beam or wall, if one is close.

If the weakness is widespread, your floor may have undersize joists, and you're probably out of idiot territory. Caution: If electric wires or plumbing need rerouting, doubling joists can be a real bear. If you're intimidated by working with wiring or plumbing, I'd call a plumber or an electrician first.

Here's how to double a joist, as shown in the illustration on splicing a joist.

1. Temporarily shore up the center of the weak joist with a post (see the accompanying steel jack post figure).

2. Saw the doubler joists from the same material used for the original joists. Drill pilot holes in the doublers 12 inches apart along the top, middle, and bottom.

3. Apply construction adhesive to one side of the damaged joist, and clamp a doubler joist into position.

4. Drive $2^{1}/_{2}$-inch decking or construction screws through the pilot holes, and remove the clamps

5. Repeat steps 3 and 4 for the second doubler joist. After two hours, remove the brace post.

Take the sag out of a joist with this heavy-duty splice.

A. The weak joist is sandwiched between new joists.

B. The doubler joists should be the same material as the original joist.

C. The C-clamps hold everything together while you drive in the screws.

D. Space the screws 12 inches apart in three rows.

A sagging floor may indicate an undersupported beam (a *beam* is a heavy member that supports floor joists and runs perpendicular to them. Beams typically run along the center of a house). If the existing beam is in good condition, a steel jack post may remedy the problem. See the drawing of a steel jack post in position, and start at step 6 in the instructions that follow.

If you have a series of sagging joists between a beam and the foundation, you must make up your own beam. As a rule of thumb, a triple thickness of joist material that's glued and screwed together should be strong enough to support three or four sagging joists. See the previous figure on bracing a joist for advice on assembling the beam. For bigger sags, install a quadruple thickness beam, with jack posts about every 3 to 4 feet. Start at step 1.

1. Prepare the beam according to the previously detailed guidelines. Err on the side of strength.

   To install the beam safely, get two helpers and go to step 6. To install with one helper, or to do it alone, use this rope trick:

2. Screw pairs of substantial eyebolts or hooks into the joists at each end of the new beam location, as shown in the drawing.

3. Tie a length of ¹/₄-inch synthetic rope to one hook at end A. Tie a loop of rope to both hooks at end B. The loop must be large enough to hold the beam loosely—about 1 foot larger than the beam's outside dimensions.

4. Insert the beam into the loop at end B. Raise end A, and tie that rope to the hook.

5. Tighten the loop at end B. Even if the beam sags a bit, it should hold it tight enough to get the jack post in position without killing you.

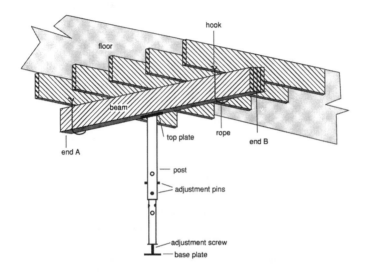

The post adjusts to many heights and is extended with a heavy steel thread. Here's the main rule: Expect no miracles. Stop raising the beam before you cause havoc upstairs. If you're installing a new beam, put a jack post about every 4 feet apart. If working alone, the ropes temporarily hold the beam in position.

To install a jack post under either an existing beam or the beam you just fastened, follow these steps:

1. Adjust a lightweight steel jack post to the proper length. Support the post on a strong concrete floor, or put a 4-inch solid concrete block under it. For supporting a very heavy load, you may need to pour a concrete footing—about 12-inch-square by 8-inch-high.

2. Use a level to ensure that the post is plumb. Screw the upper plate into the beam.

3. Snug up the post, then tighten it ¹/₈ turn every couple of days. Don't shock your house with sudden moves! Watch what happens on the floors above. The post is mainly designed to stop the decline, not to reverse the last 50 years of settling, so be judicious about how much you crank. If the plaster above starts cracking, or if windows or doors start to bind, back off.

Healing Wood Floor Surfaces

What ails thee, O wooden floor? Is it stains, gouges, or the ancient devastation of a persistent leak? Does thy varnish show gouges? Or art thou merely dull and scratched? Let's wax non-poetical and look at some repairs, small and large, for wood floors.

To make these repairs, you've got to know whether the floor has an oil finish (a blend of mineral spirits and turpentine, or the commercial equivalent), a wax finish (either paste or liquid), or a polyurethane varnish. How to tell one from the other? Oil finish gives the wood a luster but does not fill in the pores. You should know if you've been waxing the floor. Polyurethane varnish presents a clear, solid surface—you may be able to see pores in the wood but not feel them.

If you act soon, you may be able to fix problems before they get too extreme.

➤ A dull waxed floor may be restored with a rented buffer. Follow directions for the wax you'll be using.

➤ For a minor burn or defect in a waxed, oiled, or varnished floor, hand-sand the area with increasingly fine sandpaper. Scrape a deep burn with a sharp wood chisel held perpendicular to the floor. If the injury is noticeably hollow, use a wood filler. Color the repair to match the surroundings, using stain, a stain stick, or a scratch concealer. Then oil, wax, or varnish the repair area. For a waxed or oiled floor, treat the whole floor to new wax or an oil job.

Don't Screw Up!

Replacement beams are heavy, and jack posts are awkward to handle. Don't depend on the jack post to support the beam during installation. Get help from willing accomplices, or use the rope trick detailed in this chapter. Do not depend on funky toe nails to support a cumbersome beam as the post goes in.

➤ Depending on the source and the floor finish, you may be able to remove a stain by rubbing with fine steel wool and mineral spirits. Deep stains, or water damage that has separated the grain of the wood, call for either floorboard replacement or hole filling and then a complete floor sanding. Both are described later in this chapter.

Subfloor Repair

The subfloor is the layer of rough flooring resting on the joists. If it's under a wood floor, it's usually $3/4$-inch thick, either plywood or another manufactured wood product (for relatively new houses) or individual boards (for older houses). If it's under a ceramic tile floor, the subfloor may be a sheet of material bonded with portland cement. If the house is built on a concrete slab, it may have no subfloor, or it may have rigid insulation between the finish floor and the slab.

To repair a wood subfloor or patch a hole in one, you'll need a power screwdriver or a variable-speed drill, a saber saw or a keyhole saw, plywood or boards as thick as the subfloor, 2-by-4 blocking, construction adhesive or wood glue, 16d (16-penny) sinker nails, and drywall or construction screws. Once you've gathered the tools and materials, use these steps for the repair:

1. Remove any finish flooring around the damaged area.

2. If the subfloor damage or hole is not already rectangular, mark out a rectangular cutout around the damage. Drill starter holes for the saber saw blade, if needed. If you can find the joists, saw alongside them, leaving the adjacent subfloor nailed to them. Select step 3 or 4.

3. If the hole extends to the floor joists, follow these steps:

    A. Prepare enough 2-by-4 blocks to support the subfloor patch at each joist. Coat the side of each block with construction adhesive or wood glue.

    B. Nail or screw the blocks to the joists, holding them tight to the bottom of the existing subfloor. Go to step 5.

4. If the joists are away from the hole, follow these steps:

    A. Cut a pair of $^3/_4$-inch plywood or 2-by-4 blocks at least 6 inches wider than the repair. Place the blocks on top of the floor, and mark their location on the floor.

    B. Drill a few $^1/_8$-inch pilot holes through the subfloor near each end of the marked area.

    C. Smear glue on each block where it will contact the existing subfloor (see the next illustration). Clamp the block to the bottom of the subfloor with a C-clamp.

    D. Drive 2-inch drywall or construction screws through the pilot holes, as shown, and let the glue dry.

5. Cut a piece of subfloor to size. Put glue on top of the 2 blocks, and screw the subfloor to them, pulling the screw heads down flush to the subfloor.

6. If the floor will be under a carpet (as shown in the photos) or under tile or vinyl flooring, you may need to raise the surface further: Cut a second piece of plywood to size, and repeat step 5. Use pilot holes, and drive plenty of screws down flush to the surface, as in the bottom photo on the next page.

7. If you have a noticeable gap around the edges of the repaired subfloor, then carpet, asphalt tile, or linoleum may settle into it (this will not be a problem with wood finish flooring). Buy some floor filler, and squish it into the groove, following the directions on the package. But be warned: This stuff will not adhere to a floor that's loose and shifting.

The side and ends of the blocks are glued to bond to the bottom of the existing subfloor. Blocks should be wider than shown.

Make sure the block is tight to the subfloor as you start driving screws. A C-clamp would help here.

Carefully match the surface levels so that the patch is exactly flush with the floor. Take the time for accuracy here—it's now or never!

To learn how to nail strip flooring to a subfloor patch, read on.

Replacing Strip Flooring

Let's say you want to replace floorboards because they are damaged or stained. First make sure you can find replacement floorboards. Strip flooring comes in standard sizes, but if you can't find what you need at a lumberyard, find somebody who salvages old buildings. To be sure you get the right size, measure the flooring carefully and identify the wood species. The best bet is to bring a piece of flooring with you as you shop.

Wood flooring is made with square (flat) edges, or with tongue-and-groove (T&G) edges, which join to make a very strong floor. Hardwood (oak or maple) flooring is generally tongue-and-groove. T&G is "blind-nailed" through the tongue, so you won't see nails when the floor is done.

On square-edge flooring, you can usually see the nails or screws (or the plugs or fillers concealing

Don't Screw Up!

The strip flooring in new houses may actually be plywood with a hardwood veneer. You can spot this material by the unnaturally narrow and regular joints between the floorboards. You can also pull off a floor heat register and examine the edge of the flooring. If you're unsure about your flooring, I'd suggest calling a carpenter or flooring outfit. Don't try to repair these floors, because the whole floor is knitted together.

them). Square-edge is easy to repair because you can find the fasteners, and you can remove boards without disturbing adjacent ones.

T&G is difficult to repair because the boards are keyed together on the sides and ends. Ideally, your patch will emulate the staggered joints you see in your floor (this means the joints between the ends of adjacent boards do not line up). Some authorities suggest matching the staggered joints by drilling and chiseling out the old boards. You also can cut the boards with a saber saw and a fine-tooth blade (break the blade so that it reaches only as deep as the finish floor [the top layer]). But because it's very difficult to stagger joints neatly, I suggest sawing out a rectangular portion. Granted, the patch will be visible because the ends will not be staggered. But a poorly executed staggered patch may also be visible—and the work will definitely gobble up more of your Saturday.

To replace a rectangular section of strip flooring, start by letting the replacement boards dry indoors for at least 24 hours. Don't work in humid weather, either: When dry weather arrives, the boards will shrink, and gaps will appear. You'll need a circular saw, an aluminum and/or carpenter's square, a prybar, a wood chisel, a hammer, a nail set, a drill, nails, and replacement flooring. For a large repair, I strongly recommend renting a flooring nailer, as it brings the boards perfectly tight while blind nailing them. You might also want to use construction glue if the subfloor seems rickety. Then follow these steps:

1. Mark out a rectangular patch on the floor for the repair. Using a square, nail wood strips to the damaged section of floor to guide the circular saw, and *crosscut* the boards (cut across the grain—across the short dimension). Set the saw's depth just deeper than the finish flooring, and cut only two sides of the rectangle. Take your time and work patiently—this must be as close to a perfect rectangle as you can get. Don't saw the good boards around the repair. Use a chisel to finish the cuts where the blade does not reach.

2. Saw down the middle of one damaged board. It should be nailed only at the edges (through the tongue) so that you won't destroy the saw blade. Pound a prybar or big screwdriver into this saw cut, and pry out the board.

3. Remove the rest of the damaged floor, and pull all nails. If stubs of existing flooring shorter than about 1 foot remain around the edge of the patch, pull them out so you can slide new flooring into place. You may have to repeat step 2 to loosen these boards.

4. Trim one end of the new flooring square (at a right angle) using a miter box or a circular saw. When using a circular saw, cut with the bottom side up. This reduces splintering. Lay the board in place so that its groove swallows the tongue of the existing flooring. Carefully mark the other end, remove, and saw it.

5. For a stronger patch, squeeze a few lines of construction adhesive onto the subfloor. Then, matching the existing floor, blind- or face-nail the piece into

position. To blind-nail with a flooring nailer, simply follow the directions for the unit. To blind-nail by hand, drill each tongue diagonally with a drill bit that's slightly smaller than the nail. Hammer the nail most of the way into place, and complete the job with a nail set. Keep the boards tight against each other as you nail, using a rubber mallet or a hammer pounded against a block of scrap wood.

6. Cut or chisel the bottom of the groove from the last board, slip it into place, and face-nail it. Fill and stain the nail holes.

7. Sand the entire floor, as described next.

Super Sanding Techniques

Once in a while, wood floors must suffer the punishment of sanding. Floor sanding looks easy, but it's not for everyone. The key problem is gouging, caused by failing to keep the sander moving as you pit it down on the floor. You can cause a lot of damage very quickly.

Floor sanding requires renting at least two machines: a drum or belt sander for the main section, and a disk sander for the edges.

➤ A *belt* (preferable) or *drum* (more common) sander rotates a wide piece of sandpaper on the floor. This tool is your main arsenal, used everywhere except at the edges.

➤ A *disk sander*, a heavy-duty version of an orbital sander, is used for the edges.

➤ A *floor polishing machine* can clean up after the heavy artillery has left the scene. It's not essential.

➤ A *hand scraper* can be used to remove the finish in the corners, where neither sander will reach.

➤ An *orbiting pad sander,* rented from a home center or paint store, will remove old finish but not stain or wood.

Move a drum or belt sander with the grain. Start with coarse paper, and work toward finer grits. Cover the main areas with the belt or drum sander, and then trim around the edges with the disk sander. Remember: If you rent over the weekend, you'll get more machine time for the same money.

Here are some *do's and don'ts* on floor sanding.

➤ Do remove base shoe and baseboard to check the thickness of the floor. If the flooring is less than $1/2$-inch thick, or if the nail heads are starting to show through, the floor has already been sanded too many times.

➤ Do remove the rest of the trim, to avoid leaving a sharp line at the edge of the disk sander's range. See the section "Yanking Up Molding with Scarcely a Split," in Chapter 24, "A Scolding on Molding."

➤ Do protect yourself and the rest of the house from dust. See the relevant information in Chapter 6, "Health, Safety, and Common Sense."

➤ *Don't ever* put a running sander down while it's stationary—this leaves gouges. Keep the sander moving at a steady pace across the floor. At the end of the pass, ease the sander up from the floor. Remember, blemishes that are invisible while sanding become painfully obvious after the stain goes on. It's a good idea to test the surface with mineral spirits to find any remaining blemishes. Or, hold a light close to the floor—imperfectly sanded areas will reflect light differently.

➤ Do work your way down from 60- to 150-grit sandpaper (you'll need several grades for both sanders). Consider a final pass with a floor buffer to remove the lingering evidence left by the heavy floor sander.

➤ Don't work across the grain; sand with the grain. Diagonal sanding is acceptable to remove the cupping from warped boards, but only for the first pass or two. Similarly, diagonal sanding is the trick for parquet flooring, but start off with a finer abrasive—say, 80-grit or so.

➤ Don't let the abrasive get clogged; that can burn the bare wood. Change abrasive when needed.

➤ Do try scraping with a sharp chisel or using an orbital sander in the corners, where even the disk sander won't reach.

Finishing Up

Once you've finished the onerous task of sanding, you come to the more delightful staining and varnishing chores. Vacuum the room thoroughly, paying attention to window sills and other dust catchers. Rub the floor down with a tack rag—a rag dampened with mineral oil—to pick up dust.

It's best to stain and/or varnish immediately after the dust settles, before the floor can be damaged. Depending on the color, you may or may not want a stain. Stains can be mixed to get the ideal color. Find or buy a scrap of the right kind of flooring to test stains before staining the entire floor.

One option is to use penetrating oil, sometimes called Danish oil finish. These oils sink nicely into the wood and display it beautifully, but you'll need to put paste wax on top to protect the surface.

Most do-it-yourselfers use polyurethane varnish these days, which may actually be a blend of polyurethane and alkyd varnish materials. It's best applied with a wide brush or a paint pad. Never use a roller; it will leave hideous bubbles. Stir—never shake—flat and semi-gloss varnishes to get flattening agent off the bottom. Lightly hand sand the first coat of varnish with fine or extra fine paper to remove bubbles and dust. Then vacuum and tack-cloth the surface before recoating. Observe the time limitations. For good adhesion, varnishes with a high polyurethane content must be second-coated before the first coat gets too hard.

Get adequate ventilation; consider using an organic solvent respirator for closed quarters.

The fumes, combined with the nasty solvent clean-up, means I would check out waterborne varnish for my next floor project. You might need more coats, but they go on faster because the varnish dries faster, and less dust could get trapped in the drying finish. The odor also is much more tolerable, and that awful brush-cleaning-in-solvent ceremony is a miserable memory. Although a waterborne finish has less resistance to heat and chemicals than a solvent-based one, they are about equal in terms of the all-important scratch resistance.

Finally, remember that many varnishes gain strength with age. Delay restoring the full traffic on your beautiful new floor as long as possible.

If you've got only a small problem with an existing varnish floor, keep reading.

Don't Screw Up!

Thinking about renting a floor sander? My advice: Think carefully. Every time you set the sander down wrong, you'll leave an indelible mark. Unless you can tolerate the sight of these inevitable beginner's mistakes, I'd hire this job out. If you are fanatical about keeping the sander moving as you raise and lower the sanding drum, though, and if you can tolerate a mild blemish or two, go for it!

Small Problems with Polyurethane Varnish

Polyurethane varnish is great stuff—easy to apply, good-looking, and pretty durable. When it gets scratched, gouged, or worn out, though, you've got problems. It's extremely difficult to make invisible repairs on polyurethane, and a complete sanding job may be the best option.

The problem with patching polyurethane is that you've got to roughen it with sandpaper so the new stuff can adhere. But this is a lot of work if done by hand, and it's dangerous if done by machine, which is likely to gouge the wood. Sanding will lighten the bare spots, which you'll have to stain to match the surrounding floor. Then you'll have to varnish the floor and hope everything blends in (did I mention that this might sound like an advertisement for sanding the whole floor?).

Carpet Repair

Oceans of carpet—you'll see them in ads, but in my house, the carpet looks more like the Caribbean Sea. It's a beautiful expanse of color marked by—shall I call them islands? Sometimes, these stains—mementos of Maggie, the family beagle, or the house plant I watered too enthusiastically—can be cleaned. Otherwise, you can try to replace the sections of carpet. If you can't find spare carpet squirreled away in the attic or basement, steal a scrap from a closet or under a permanent piece of furniture. You'll need a utility knife with a new blade, a carpenter's square, a staple gun or tacks, double-sided carpet tape, foam padding (as thick as the original), and that replacement piece of carpet. Then follow these steps:

1. Place the replacement piece over the damaged area, matching the pattern if there is one.

2. Match the backing fibers in the replacement and the original carpet (so the grains match), and cut the patch in a rectangular shape, slightly larger than the damaged area.

3. Position the replacement piece over the area to be patched, and cut through the existing carpet along one side of the replacement piece. This makes the first side of the cutout.

4. Cut the other three sides, using the patch as a template. Make sure the patch does not shift, and try to "crowd" it so that the cutout is slightly smaller than the patch.

5. Remove the patch, and trim up the cuts.

6. Cut the foam to the same size, and staple or tack it in place (see the following photo).

7. Lay out carpet tape per instructions. I used double lines of tape, using one piece holding the old carpet in place and one holding the new carpet. Install the patch and press firmly (see the photo on the next page).

Tack the foam into place, making sure it's the same thickness and density as the original.

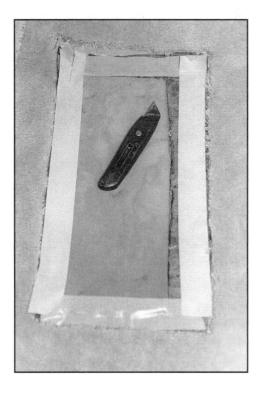

Lay out double-sided carpet tape along all four sides of the repair.

The Least You Need to Know

➤ Floor squeaks should be easy to control, if you can get under the floor. Realistically, if you must work from above, you may have to leave visible evidence of your repair.

➤ Don't be afraid of patching subfloor; it's fast and easy.

➤ For most idiots, the dream of a seamless replacement of tongue-and-groove flooring is just a dream. Still, you can make a very effective patch.

➤ You should be able to make inconspicuous repairs in carpets if extra scraps are available.

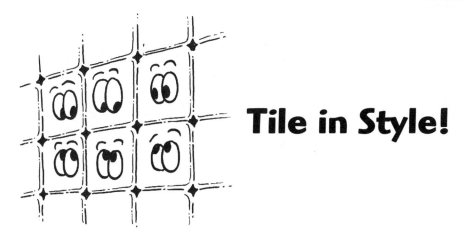

Chapter 21

Tile in Style!

In This Chapter:

➤ Cleaning ceramic tiles and replacing grout

➤ Fixing damaged vinyl tiles

➤ Laying out and installing new tiles

➤ Adhering laminated countertops to substrates

Take it from the Romans: Ceramic tiles make dynamite flooring, even if they do tend to cool your feet in a cold climate. Independent, flinty, and waterproof, tiles exemplify the durability and cleanability you want in bathrooms and kitchens.

Because ceramic tiles can break, and because the grout can get ugly or disintegrate, we'll examine some tile first aid. If you're lucky, you can find replacement tile in the basement, attic, or garage. Otherwise, shop tile stores for a reasonable match.

If you're tempted to put tile on a floor or wall, we'll tell you what's needed in terms of support, layout, and tile setting. When we're done, I hope you'll be convinced that tile setting is much easier than it seems—so long as you are not wrestling with odd shapes or uneven surfaces.

Ceramic Tile Repair

Loose or broken tile often points to a deeper problem. Ceramic tiles are inflexible, so a crack is usually caused by flimsy support, which you'll obviously need to fix first. If the underside of a floor is accessible, try to nail a second joist to each joist, or use other techniques described in Chapter 20, "Getting a Solid Footing on Floors." Otherwise, it's time to call 1-800-WOODFIX.

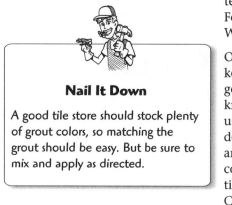

Nail It Down

A good tile store should stock plenty of grout colors, so matching the grout should be easy. But be sure to mix and apply as directed.

One of the best preventatives for ceramic tile woes is keeping it dry. If the caulking around a tub enclosure is getting long in the tooth, scrape it out with a utility knife or putty knife. Get the surface as clean as possible, using a window scraper, followed by scouring powder or denatured alcohol; then caulk with a good silicone tub-and-tile caulk. For colored tile, shop around to find a colored caulk—bright white looks hideous against gray tile. For more on caulking, see Chapter 12, "Skin-Tight: Caulking, Weather-Stripping, Insulation, and Ventilation."

If you've neglected the grout or ignored the caulking in a tub enclosure, the tiles may be sliding off the waterlogged walls. Once water loosens the tiles, your choices are to call a realtor or to remove the tiles, repair the wall, and reset the tiles.

Let's call off the real estate agents and learn to replace rotten drywall or plaster in a tub enclosure:

1. Remove all tiles that readily come off. This will probably be more than you expect, but you have to do this job right the first time.

2. Soak the tiles in water, and scrape off the adhesive so there's room for new adhesive.

3. Remove the rotten plaster, and replace it with a waterproof cement-based backing board (such as Durock or Wonderboard brand), generally following the instructions in the section "Cutting Back to the Studs and Starting Over," in Chapter 22, "Cosmetology 101: Drywall and Plaster Repair."

Then proceed to step 3 in the instructions in the next section.

Replacing Ceramic Tiles on an Existing Surface

If you're dreading a tile repair, remember that nobody looks forward to it. But if you have access to replacement tiles and work cautiously, it should not present too much of a problem. Here's the scoop on breathing new life into battle-scarred tiles.

1. Carefully chip out the broken tiles, using a hammer and a metal or stone-cutting chisel. If a damaged tile is still tightly stuck, score an "X" across it with a glass cutter, and then break the tile with a hammer and chisel.

2. Clean out adhesive and grout. Never pull up on the grout, which could loosen adjacent tiles. Don't rush.

3. When all the old grout and tile mortar are removed, place the new tiles (or the old ones, if you didn't destroy them during removal) in position. The tiles must rest a little below the surface, leaving room for adhesive.

Don't Screw Up!

When removing damaged tiles, work cautiously, or you'll loosen more tiles and curse the day you read these instructions.

4. If you need to cut tile, see the section "Cutting Ceramic Tile," later in this chapter.

5. Select a ceramic tile cement or mortar according to the instructions on the package. Use waterproof adhesive on countertops and tub enclosures. Apply the cement or mortar with the correct notched trowel (again, get guidance from the package).

6. Embed replacement tiles with a slight twist and downward push in the mortar: Use even pressure to get the surface flat.

7. Once the mortar has set, grout as described in the section "Great Grout!" later in this chapter.

Idiot-Proof New Tiling

Sick of that old linoleum floor? Eager to upgrade the kitchen counter or make a fire-proof hearth for the new wood stove? Then you're likely thinking about ceramic or stone tile, which are installed with similar techniques.

Preparation is the key to success with tile: The backing, or substrate, must be clean, dry, flat, and strong. The best substrate for ceramic or stone tile is $1/2$-inch cement board, screwed to a solid surface such as $3/4$-inch plywood. If you're serious about a good job—and because tiles can endure for centuries, you might as well be—apply a layer of latex thinset tile mortar with a notched trowel on the plywood before placing the cement board. Screw the board into the joists every 8 inches with cement board screws. These handy rust-proof screws have a wide head to hold the cement board and cut their own countersinks. Let the mortar harden for a day before walking on the floor.

Once you've got a strong, solid plane, you'll need a rectangular area to tile. That's the job of tile layout, next.

Tile Layout

To tile a counter, room, or wall, you'll need to establish square starting lines. The task is similar for ceramic, stone, and vinyl tiles.

For a *counter*: Draw a straight line across the front of the counter, and start your full tiles behind this line. Either center the tiles side to side, or start full tiles at the most prominent side.

Nail It Down

To check the accuracy of a large right angle, measure from the 90° angle 3 feet in one direction and 4 feet in the other direction. The distance between the further points (the hypotenuse of the right angle) will be 5 feet in a true right angle, as seen in the accompanying figure on laying out a tile floor. For larger areas, use a 6–8–10 triangle instead of this 3–4–5 triangle.

For a *floor*, the following procedure will make a fully symmetrical layout, with equal-sized partial tiles along each pair of opposite walls. But don't follow it slavishly: You may want the tiles to look good from a certain vantage point or to conform to the longest and straightest wall. No matter what your goal, you'll speed the layout and improve accuracy by following these hints:

➤ Use the 3–4–5 triangle technique described at left and check the right angles in steps 2–4.

➤ Place the center line in step 2 through the center of the doorway if the tiles must look right from the adjoining room.

➤ Use a chalk line (see the upcoming Toolbox Trivia sidebar) to mark the lines.

To lay out a floor symmetrically, start at step 1 in the directions for the figure on laying out a tile floor. To lay full tiles along the straightest wall, draw a line one course away from that wall. (One course equals the width of one tile plus the width of one grout joint.) Mark courses from that line.

228

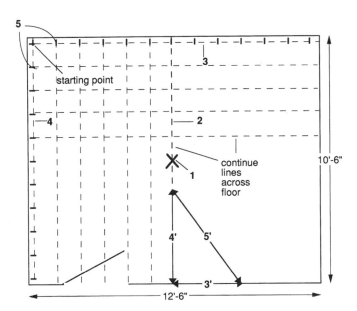

Laying out a tile floor. Numbers on the drawing correspond to the following steps.

1. Mark the center of the room.

2. Chalk a center line through this mark, perpendicular to one wall.

3. Mark the last full course along the far wall. Draw a line perpendicular to the center line through this mark. Mark off courses on this line.

4. Draw a straight line perpendicular to the line from step 3 at the last full course near the left-hand wall. Mark courses on this line.

5. The lines from steps 3 and 4 are the base lines for your layout.

Mark off all courses to complete the layout. If you have no helper, tack in a finishing nail at each course along one side, and then hook the chalk line to the nail and snap the line from the opposite side of the room.

You may want to screw a straight board to each baseline, to serve as a temporary back-up for the first courses.

Toolbox Trivia

The quickest way to draw straight lines is with a cheap tool called the "chalk line," or "chalk box." Fill the box with powdered chalk (sold at building suppliers), and extend the string. Tack a nail to the mark at one end of the line (or have a lackey hold the end). Hold the string tight across the second mark, and pull up at the center. When you snap the line, the chalk will instantly appear on the floor. Snap gently, and you can mark two or three lines without re-chalking the string. Tile pros often use hairspray to prevent chalk lines from being obliterated, particularly from floors.

Laying out a tile wall (as for a tub enclosure) is similar to laying out a floor. To make the layout fully symmetrical, find center lines on each wall so that the partial tiles at each end are equal, as shown in the accompanying figure on laying out a tile wall. It's customary to start the bottom course with a full tile in a tub enclosure. When done, rent a diamond drill bit to drill holes for the plumbing, or use a wet tile saw to nibble away from the edge of tiles.

Laying out a tile wall. Numbers on the drawing correspond to these steps:

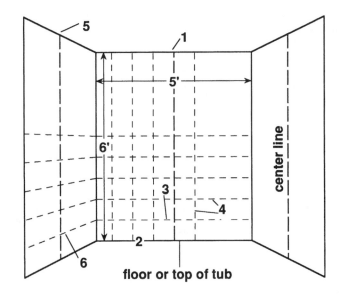

1. Draw a plumb (vertical) line at the center of the wall.

2. Find the highest point on the bottom. If the bottom is straight and horizontal and go to step 4.

3. If the bottom is not straight and horizontal, draw a horizontal line one tile plus two joint widths above the high point. This is the bottom of the second course of tile, which you will lay first. Screw a straight board below this line to support the course. Lay the bottom course after tiles are set and it's safe to remove the guide board.

4. Mark the horizontal and vertical joints with a long level and a pencil; use tile spacers to support the first course.

   See the procedure for ceramic tile-setting, later in this chapter.

To tile a tub enclosure:

5. Draw center lines on all three walls.

6. Make the first horizontal line one course above the highest point on any of the three walls. Mark this line on all three walls and use it as a starting point.

Cutting Ceramic Tile

You bought ceramic or stone tiles because they are so indestructible. But as soon as you lugged them home, you realized that they are also impossible to cut. How are you going to trim them to size? You can cut the occasional tile with a glass cutter: Score repeatedly along the cut line, place the cut line directly above a pencil, and press down on both sides.

Far better, however, is a tile cutter, which comes in two varieties. One scores the tiles and breaks them across a raised line. This tool is helpful, but buy extra tile to allow for breakage as you learn the process.

Far more effective (and expensive) is the diamond wet saw, which I'd recommend renting for a big or complicated tile job. This saw has a circular diamond-studded blade and will cut tile or stone.

It will also spray tile soup into the air, so it's best operated outdoors. Place the tile on the saw's sliding tray, and slowly move it into the stationary saw blade. A wet saw can trim $^1/_8$ inch from a tile, a trick you can't accomplish with a hand cutter. A wet saw will also make crude curves. Make a bunch of parallel cuts through the area to be removed, and then break off the scrap, as shown in the figure on a curved cut in tile.

> **Nail It Down**
>
> Tile spacers, available in various widths, are X-shaped pieces of plastic that establish a specific grout width. Make sure to place these with the correct side out; otherwise they can get jammed in the mortar. Spacers are useful for floors and are priceless for walls. Cut off one leg to make a T spacer for a bottom course on a wall or next to a wall on a floor.

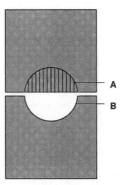

Curved cut in tile.

A. Parallel cuts in tile

B. Cuts removed to give a round cutout

To pass a pipe through a tile surface, make parallel cuts with a wet tile saw, and then break off the fragment with a long-nose pliers or tile nippers. A tile nipper—a kind of plier that grabs at the end—may be able to make this cut, if you're careful—and lucky. Score a checkerboard pattern in the area to be removed with a glass cutter, and nip out the fragment one at a time.

231

A Quick Trick for Fitting Irregular Tiles, Moldings, and So On

I cut my teeth in home repair on a farmhouse built in 1854, a place whose peculiar geometry became painfully obvious if I dared to use a level or a square in my fixes. Among the many tricks I wish I'd known is this superb method of working with irregular surfaces. This trick is handy for marking the edge of vinyl tiles so they will match an unsquare wall, for fitting baseboard along a sagging floor, and for countless other finishing touches in houses where straight lines and right angles are conspicuous by their absence. Called scribing, it can also substitute for measuring, when you want something to match up to an obstruction.

In this example, assume you are cutting a floor tile to fit against a wall that is not parallel to the last line of tiles (this is something you'd find in an unsquare room). You'll need a compass (AKA divider, which you last used to draw circles in high school), and whatever tool cuts the material in question.

1. Push the tile as far against the wall as it can go. Keep the tile square to the other tiles.

2. Set the divider to equal the overlap of the new tile on the tile beneath it. This is how much you must remove to place the new tile.

3. Without moving the tile or changing the divider setting, scribe the line. Hold the point of the compass against the baseboard, and keep the compass perpendicular to the wall.

4. Cut along this line, and place the tile.

Alex fitting an irregular tile.

A. Divider setting equals the amount of tile overlap here.

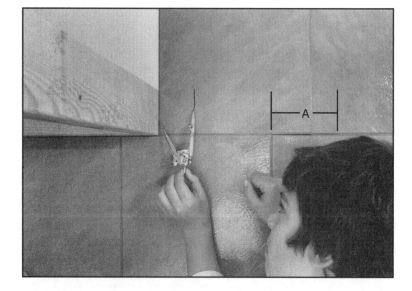

Setting Ceramic Tile

Once the surface is prepared and the layout is complete, it's time to set tile. Your layout should tell you how many tiles need cutting. Cut tile as described previously, and do any necessary masking; tile mortar can be fiendishly sticky stuff.

1. Select your mortar by reading the bags. For application to cementboard, the preferred substrate, a latex-modified thinset mortar, is the usual choice in dry locations. In tub enclosures and other wet locations, use special setting compounds suitable for moisture. Mix the mortar according to directions. Select a notched tile trowel according to the size of the tiles (larger tiles require larger notches).

2. Mortar one course at a time, to avoid obscuring your guide marks. Apply the mortar with the solid edge of the trowel, and then scrape the area with the notched edge. Take the time to get a good mortar bed; if you botch this, the entire job will be a loser.

3. Slide the tiles into place, keeping an eye on the gaps between courses. Some small ceramic tiles have little bosses on the edges that establish the gap. Otherwise, use the cross-shaped plastic spacers that are sold at tile stores.

4. After each course is placed, use a straight edge or a level to align the tiles. Eyeball the course to check for out-of-place tiles. Work quickly so you can shift tiles into position before the mortar hardens.

5. As the mortar starts to set, smooth any mortar that has squeezed out of the joints with the corner of a moist sponge. Get the mortar down low enough that the grout can cover it.

6. Apply grout 24 hours later. Read on for the goods on grout.

Great Grout!

Grout is great goo that fills gaps between tiles, but it's also the most vulnerable part of a tile job. If the grout between ceramic tiles gets discolored, try to brighten it with products sold for that purpose. Otherwise, you'll have to remove the ugly grout and regrout.

Grout must be watertight, particularly in shower or tub enclosures. To repair loose or eroded grout, remove as much loose material as possible, without loosening the tiles. Use a chisel, grout saw, utility knife, small trowel, or hooked tool. Vacuum or brush out all debris, and then regrout according to the following instructions (which apply to new grouting and regrouting alike).

Don't Screw Up!

Be sure to mix colored grout for as long as the label says, or it may harden to the wrong color.

Absorbent tiles or stones may need protection before grouting, but slick, glazed tiles will not absorb grout. To prevent absorption, protect small areas with masking tape or apply a protective chemical, sold at tile stores.

Once the tiles are prepared, the area is masked, and the grout is mixed, follow these steps:

1. Wipe the grout into the joints with a rubber grout squeegee or a rubber float (a damp sponge may work for a small area). Smear diagonally, filling all the joints equally. Quickly fill the whole job.

2. A few minutes after you started, clean the tiles by wiping diagonally across the tiles with a damp grout sponge. Pay attention to uniformity; don't gouge grout from the joints.

3. Clean the sponge often in water, and wipe periodically until the tiles are clean and the joints are uniform.

4. If necessary, use a grout remover to clean any haze left on tiles.

After a suitable interval, apply a silicon grout treatment to protect against staining. Repeat periodically.

The Other Stuff: Vinyl Tile, Roll Flooring, and Laminates

From all this attention to repairing ceramic tiles, you'd probably think that vinyl floors don't get sick. Not so. Start by diagnosing the cause of the problem. If you see regular ridges, they're probably caused by uneven subfloor. If your tiles are coming unglued, the problem is probably moisture—from a plumbing leak, groundwater, spillage around a bath, or condensation. Remember the rule: Don't bury your problems. Fix them.

For most repairs, you'll need a source of replacement flooring, either something stashed in the basement or new material that's similar enough. Perhaps you can salvage some material from under the refrigerator or a massive sofa.

Repairing Curling Vinyl Tile

Loosen the glue holding the problem tile in place with a propane torch (use a flame-spreading attachment), a heat gun, or a warm iron. Don't get the tile too hot to touch. Then remove the tile, scrape out the old adhesive, and apply new paste to the area using a notched trowel to get an even coat. (Consult the package for exact directions on applying the sticky stuff.) Clean up extra glue with the solvent specified. Then weight the patch securely until the glue is dry. Finally, apply a seam sealer, available at flooring suppliers.

Fixing Roll Flooring

Sheet flooring—linoleum and its successor, vinyl—can be repaired with this "double-cutting" technique. You may be able to see the fix-up, but only with effort. Here's how: Place a scrap of new material (larger than the repair area) over the damage, and get the pattern to match. Hold the new piece firmly under a carpenter's square, and cut through both layers. When you've cut through all four sides, remove the new piece, and scrape or use heat to remove the damaged flooring. Clean out all excess adhesive, and glue the new piece into place, following the directions on the can. Weight the patch until it's dry, and then apply a seam sealer.

Repairing Laminates

Let's say you bought into some laminated counters that are peeling. What to do?

1. Pull back the loose piece until the glue starts to put up some resistance.

2. If the area is even slightly wet, prop up the laminate with pencils (sideways) and/ or toothpicks (on end). Set up a fan to dry the area.

3. Mask surrounding areas, and then apply contact cement to the substrate and the bottom of the laminate, getting it as far into the crack as possible. Use plenty of ventilation with contact cement.

Nail It Down

A paint-stirring stick is great for applying contact cement because you can throw it out instead of cleaning it.

4. Dry the cement as indicated on the can, propping the surfaces apart. Generally, the surfaces cannot be joined until contact cement is dry to the touch.

5. Remove the props and press the laminate down, starting from the inside. Work carefully; once contact cement grabs, it won't let go. Use a rolling pin or a small block of 2-by-4 to press the laminate down.

So there it is—fabulous flooring fixes almost anyone can do. With access, spare parts, and a little ingenuity, you should be able to get those floors into a fine fettle.

The Least You Need to Know

➤ A successful tiling job depends on good surface preparation.

➤ Tile is pretty easy to lay on a flat, rectangular surface if you use the proper tools and materials.

➤ Vinyl flooring can be repaired if you can find material.

➤ When regluing laminated counters, you've got to position the laminate right the first time. You don't get a second chance.

Chapter 22

Cosmetology 101: Drywall and Plaster Repair

In This Chapter

➤ Knowing your materials is half the battle for an invisible wall repair

➤ Fixing damaged drywall and plaster

➤ Hanging and finishing drywall

➤ Finding a stud—that elusive framing in your walls—can be easy if you know the techniques

---

I am a recovering plasterer, and it's been a long time since I felt the overwhelming urge to grab a plastering trowel and start smearing a heavy, abrasive glop on the walls—in fact, the very thought twinges my shoulder. No wonder they invented drywall: It's faster, easier, and cheaper, and if it isn't as hard or durable as plaster, nobody seems to mind—except the plasterers who have gone out of business. And I'll bet a lot of them don't mind, either ....

But it seems that walls attract illnesses, drywall diseases, and plaster pathology. In the course of making innumerable plaster and drywall repairs, I learned many tricks of the trade. I'm eager to pass them along to you, if only so you won't even think about calling *me* to repair your walls! The good news is that almost any flaw in plaster or drywall is fixable. The bad news is that you'll get dirty and will need a bit of practice.

Meet Your Walls: Plaster, Lath, and Drywall

Plaster and drywall, the two common interior wall materials, are made of ground-up gypsum rock with various additives. Plaster is applied as a stiff liquid that sets into a rather hard material. Drywall is a relative of plaster sandwiched between heavy paper and sold in sheets that can be cut to size and fastened into place. Drywall is much softer than plaster, so it dents and scratches easily.

Plaster is rarely used in new construction because it asks for so much skill and effort. Most drywall is $1/2$-inch thick; the $5/8$-inch sheets used in high-class construction are stronger and better at deadening noise. The sheets are 4 feet wide by 8 feet, 9 feet, 10 feet, or 12 feet long.

Lath is a backing material nailed to the studs to hold wet plaster as it hardens. Originally, lath was made of wood strips; nowadays, it is a $3/8$-inch version of drywall.

A Note on Sand Finish and Textures

The surface on most old plaster is *sand finish*, a finishing plaster that—amazing, but true—contains fine sand. You can recognize sand finish by its gritty texture. If you're repairing this stuff, scrape off as much sand as possible around the injury with a trowel or paint scraper. Your trowel or drywall knife will ride up on this sand and leave a disgusting corrugated effect. Remember these tips:

➤ Smooth corrugations with a float or damp rag before the mud sets.

➤ Apply the final layer of patching material with the floating technique, described later in this chapter.

➤ If you're intimidated by floating, roll texture paint onto the wall after making the repair. This is a second-best solution, but it's relatively idiot-proof.

➤ Buy sand finish additive (which is sometimes sold as a traction-increasing additive for paint) from a paint store, and add it to the patching plaster or primer. If the surface is still not sandy enough, add more sand to the paint.

Texture paint and watered-down drywall compound can both hide considerable wall damage. Play around at first to get a texture you can live with for a long while. Applying texture paint with a thick-napped roller leaves a nubbly texture that resembles sand finish. If you apply drywall compound with a trowel or drywall knife, you can: a) create a stucco effect by pulling the material away from the wall with a plastering trowel, letting it set a while, and then lightly pressing the peaks down; or b) create parallel streaks with a coarse-bristled 6-inch brush.

Meet the Fixer-Upper Materials

To appreciate how many blights, blues, and blisters can afflict plaster and drywall, just glance at the shelf holding wall-repair materials at a building supplier. The following table explains how to make sense of what you'll see.

The Wall Fix-It Materials

Name	Description	Advantages	Disadvantages
Patching plaster (plaster of Paris)	A gypsum-based material for filling cracks and holes; sets by a chemical reaction, not drying.	Sets quickly and very hard.	May set before you finish tooling it; very tough to sand; leaves a smooth surface that does not match sand-finish plaster.
Drywall compound	Glue-based patching compound; sets by drying.	Cheap, easy to find, easy to work, easy to sand.	Soft, does not match sand-finish plaster.
Durabond	Portland cement-patching compound; sold to set in 5 to 90 minutes. Caution: Keep the mixing pail clean—old mud accelerates the new mud.	Easy to control, excellent for starting large, deep cracks and holes.	Very hard, tough to sand (unless you get the easy-sand variety).
Sand	A fine-grained, uniform sand sold at paint stores that may be mixed with finish material, primer, or even paint.	It's the only way to match sand finish.	None.
Crack repair tape (drywall tape)	Fiberglass or paper tape applied over cracks, then covered by patching material.	Fiberglass sticks to the wall during the repair and won't bubble. Paper is thinner, and easier to hide.	Fiberglass is thicker than and harder to hide than paper, under subsequent coats of patching. Paper must be applied over a thin coat of patching compound, and may bubble.

continues

The Wall Fix-It Materials (continued)

Name	Description	Advantages	Disadvantages
"Popcorn" texture	Sold as "cottage cheese" variety (for acoustical ceilings), or simple spray texture (for "splatter" type ceilings)	Only way to match a popcorn ceiling.	Hard to use (practice on an upside-down piece of plywood first). May be too white for an old ceiling.
"Spakfast" repair compound	We don't normally tout brand names, but this stuff, from 3M Corp., is just too good to resist. Made of tiny reflective beads, it's a non-shrinking, water-based, interior or exterior patching compound.	Easy to apply, use almost anywhere, does not shrink; primer not needed; shallow repairs can be painted immediately.	None that I've found.

Fiberglass or paper tape? Fiberglass is much easier to start because it sticks to the wall without needing mud underneath. But paper's easier to hide at the end because it's thinner. It's your choice. I've had problems with both. Maybe someone should invent paper tape with stickum on it .... Just remember to coat the tape with drywall mud before sanding.

Quick-set or regular drywall compound? Both have advantages, so it's smart to use them both. Quick-set fills deep holes and, believe this or not, sets quickly. That can subtract a full day from a drywall project. But it's awkward to use because you'll have to mix it for each job. Also, it's *very important* to keep the mud box and mixing pail clean—old mud will accelerate the set of the next batch. Drywall compound is easy to use but dries slowly, particularly in deep places. Use a fan to speed drying.

The Tools

Most tools for repairing plaster and drywall are pretty basic, and you may be able to substitute mason's tools, if you have them. See the illustration of plaster and drywall tools in this chapter.

A. A mud tray (mud box) holds the patching material; it's ideal for loading a drywall knife without spillage.

B. A corner knife is essential for mudding corners; it's more useful in new work than repairs.

C. A drywall knife (available up to 10 inches wide; buy a 6- or 8-inch model to start) is used to patch walls and apply drywall compound.

D. A plaster trowel is used to cover large areas (it's also handy for plastering and for finishing concrete).

E. A float applies finish coats, creates a sand-finish texture, and can put a smooth texture on mortar.

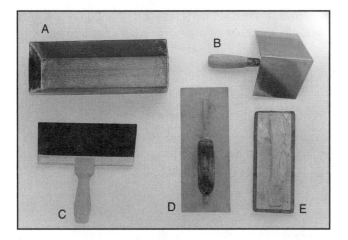

Plaster and drywall tools.

A. Mud tray

B. Corner knife

C. Drywall knife

D. Plaster trowel

E. Float

The Ten Commandments of Plaster and Drywall Repair

We've met the materials and tools. Before we plunge into the gritty task of repairing walls, let's meet the 10 commandments of wall repair.

1. Thou shalt not allow thy patching material to build up above the surrounding surface.

2. Don't bother "undercutting" the edges while cleaning out a damaged area. According to this piece of moronic conventional "wisdom" (a mainstay of home-repair books), the wound must be wider at the back so the patch can key into the crack and hold tight. Let's undercut this nonsense about undercutting. Problem 1: If you can figure out how to undercut brittle plaster without pulling off half the wall, you should be *writing* books about home repair, not reading them. Problem 2: It's not necessary. Properly applied patching bonds chemically to plaster and drywall, and bonds mechanically to hard, rough surfaces.

3. Remove all crumbling or rotted junk, without wrecking the solid material around the repair.

4. Scrape or sandpaper any ridges or burrs that rise above the surface (otherwise, the patching material will build up, and you'll have jumped from the frying pan of broken plaster to the fire of a globby, messy patch).

5. If you're matching sand finish, don't pretend that perfectly smooth patching of plaster or drywall mud will match it. See the section "A Note on Sand Finish and Textures," earlier in this chapter.

6. Moisten the edges of the damaged area before applying water-based patching materials that harden by setting (generally called "setting" type compounds). This prevents the patching from drying before it sets, which would weaken it. Don't moisten before drywall compound or other materials that harden by drying.

7. Fill deep holes with several layers of fast-setting material.

8. Thick consistency is good for deep holes; soupier stuff is better for finish coatings.

9. Always use compatible materials (if in doubt, make a small test first).

10. Stir the patching thoroughly, and keep crumbs and grit out of it. This crud inevitably rises to the surface and remains to remind you of your sinful propensity to disobey the 10 commandments of wall repair.

Fabulous Floating

The real pro secret to repairing plaster or drywall with either a sand finish or a lightly swirled finish is a homely tool called the float. (A float is not suitable for a smooth surface.) A plastering float is made of rubber that's maybe a little harder than a kitchen sponge. You can buy one for under $10. Even if you have to visit a plastering supplier or a specialty tool shop, a float is worth tracking down because no other tool patches rough drywall, plaster, and smooth mortar so quickly and effectively.

Floats are made for granular materials, so you'll need to add sand to drywall compound. For a large repair, buy silica sand at plastering suppliers; for a small area, use the sand sold as a paint additive.

Here's how to float a surface to finish a drywall or plaster repair:

1. Bring the patch up to $^1/_8$ inch below the final surface level with fast-setting mud. Let the mud set hard, but not necessarily dry.

2. Add enough sand to your drywall mud (either conventional or setting-type mud will work) to make it somewhat granular.

Nail It Down

Floating—the secret of wall repair—must occur after the mud has set for a while. Floating does two things: It moves the surface but not the body of the patching material, so the surface can conform to the surroundings. And it avoids those hideous jagged lines that result whenever a trowel rides across something hard, such as a rough surface on adjacent plaster.

3. Trowel this sand-bearing mud onto the patch, and allow it to dry or set for a few minutes. Don't fuss with the surface—leave it slightly above the surroundings.

4. When the mud has stiffened, wet the float and dampen the patch by flicking a little bit of water at it from a paint brush. Now work the float over the patch in a circular motion to flatten the surface. If the mud won't move, splash on a bit more water. If it moves too much, it's too soft. Wait a few minutes before floating.

5. When you're done, the patch should closely match the texture and level of the surface. Clean the float well with water so it won't get stiff.

Repairing Nicks and Gouges

Let's check out a few ways to easily, effectively, and invisibly patch plaster and drywall. If your wall suffers from a series of little defects, repair is simple. You'll need patching compound, sandpaper, and a drywall knife, a trowel, and (for rougher textures) a float. Follow these steps to fill in the holes:

1. Clean out anything loose or raised above the surface. If the drywall paper is sticking above the surface, cut it away with a utility knife.

2. For small repairs, I greatly prefer Spakfast, described in the previous table. Use no water with this miraculous stuff. If you're using patching plaster or another setting-type material, dampen (don't flood) the repair area, emphasizing the shallow spots. This helps prevent bubbling and loss of adhesion. Allow the water to sink in for a few minutes while you mix your mud.

3. Apply the patching material with a trowel or drywall knife.

4. Clean off the surrounding areas with the trowel, and let the patching cure a bit. For a smooth patch, scrape the area with a trowel held at about 60° to the surface. For a rough (sand-finish) patch, see the previous section "Fabulous Floating."

Don't Screw Up!

Anytime a trowel or drywall knife rides up on burns or anything rough, you will get a corrugated surface. Clean off all such imperfections first—or rely on a float to smooth repair compound.

5. A few minutes later, wipe the surroundings (not the patch) with a damp rag. The more smeared patching material you remove now, the less you'll have to sand off later—a tedious and damaging job.

6. Sand if necessary. Then prime and paint.

Covering with Drywall Tape

You can cover a small hole with several layers of drywall tape and joint compound. (This tape is also used to cover joints in drywall, where it supposedly protects against a bit of movement.) The technique is fast and easy, and will reduce the need to build up layers underneath the patch, but it may leave a mound visible on the surface.

You'll need a drywall knife, joint compound, and drywall tape. (Fiberglass tape is easier to apply than paper tape because it sticks by itself and does not trap air bubbles beneath it. But it's thicker, which means you'll have a larger mound to hide.) Use these steps to repair a hole with drywall tape:

1. Clean off all loose and ragged material.

2. Cut several strips of drywall tape, and stick them across the wound, extending about 4 to 6 inches in each direction. Fiberglass tape has adhesive, so you needn't put mud under it. You'll need to put mud under paper tape and between each layer, but the mud needn't dry between coats.

3. Cover the strips with the thinnest possible layer of joint compound (see the accompanying photo).

4. When dry, add a second coat of drywall compound, and feather the edges. You may need a third coat as well. You'll probably end up covering an area much larger than the damage because each coat must extend beyond the previous one.

5. When the last coat is dry, sand it thoroughly to blend with the surroundings.

Patching a small wound with fiberglass tape. Keep the tape thin and smooth as you cover the gap. The first coat of mud covers the tape and starts to taper the sides.

Patching with Paper and Quick-Setting Compound

The technique shown in the accompanying photo on patching with paper and quick-setting compound makes a good, inconspicuous patch for holes up to about 5 inches in diameter. You'll need a trowel or drywall knife, heavy paper (such as a grocery bag), and quick-setting compound, such as Durabond.

1. Remove loose material and anything above the wall surface.

2. Smear quick-setting compound around the back of the hole. A margin trowel is great for sneaking the mud inside the hole.

3. Fold up a piece of stiff paper, and stuff it into the hole, pushing back any insulation. Press it into the mud and let the mud set.

4. Build up the patch with quick-setting material, to about $1/8$ inch below the surface.

5. Make the final coat with joint compound, spackling compound, or finish coat plaster. Trowel or float as needed.

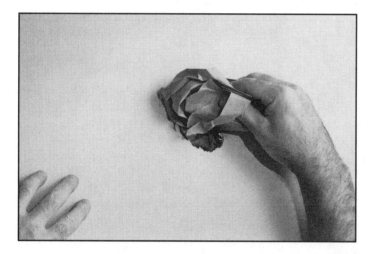

Patching with paper and quick-setting compound. Stuff the paper into the hole so that it's solid enough to support the mud. Keep the paper below the final surface level.

To make the same repair with the $1/4$-inch wire screen sold by the foot at hardware stores, continue here after step 2.

3. Cut the screen with tin snips or wire cutters so that it's about 2 inches larger than the hole in each direction.

4. Feed a wire or string through the screen to hold it. Place the screen inside the hole, and then pull it toward you to embed it in the wet compound.

5. Tie the wire or string to a dowel or rod on the surface, and let set.

6. Cut the wire or string, and remove the dowel. Press the wire below the wall surface, and smear mud onto the screen.

7. Let set again. Add more quick-set if needed, and then finish as described in step 5 in the previous list.

Cutting Back to the Studs and Starting Over

Let's say the damage is more like a disaster—the plaster is rotten, the drywall is crumbling, or the wall was once used for artillery practice. What to do? Cut the whole thing out, that's what. You'll need something to cut drywall or plaster (see step 2 of the following procedure), replacement drywall, shims (possibly), a power screwdriver and drywall screws (or a hammer and drywall nails), drywall compound, and drywall tape. These steps will help you make an invisible repair:

1. Mark the damaged area back to the center line of the nearby studs (see the section "Seven Ways to Find a Stud," later in this chapter). Use a level to mark a rectangle (as illustrated here).

Use a level to mark out a perfectly rectangular cutout—your patch will be much easier to cut.

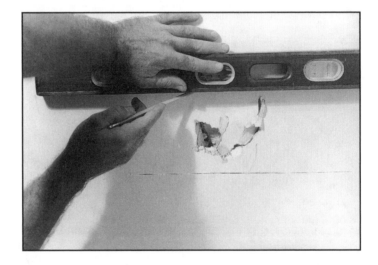

2. Nail or screw the intact wall around the sides of your cutout. Take special care to prevent cracking with plaster. Drill a pilot hole that cuts a countersink for the screw head, and don't overtighten the screw. Place duct tape along the margins of the cut to reduce cracking.

3. Cut the drywall with a drywall saw, keyhole saw, saber saw, or utility knife. Plaster is difficult to cut without wrecking the nearby plaster. If you use a saber saw, press hard against the wall to minimize vibration. With a keyhole saw, put all the pressure on the forward stroke. In old plaster, you can expect some cracking unless you use a circular saw. Sadly, this destroys the saw blade and creates a dust storm reminiscent of the 1930s Dust Bowl.

4. If you cut the wall next to a stud, screw a nailer to it using the technique shown the section "All Hands on Deck—Prepare to Be Boarded! (Replacing Rotten Deck Boards)," in Chapter 13, "In the Yard: No Rest for the Weary."

5. Cut a piece of drywall about $1/4$ inch smaller than the repair in each dimension. If necessary, shim under the drywall with strips of wood or asphalt shingles so the patch sits flush with the surface.

6. Nail or screw the drywall into place. I prefer screws—hammering can loosen the existing wall.

7. Cut off all burrs so the area is flat.

8. Stick drywall tape to the edges, and cover it with mud.

9. When the compound is dry, scrape ridges and high spots off with the drywall knife.

10. Apply another coat of compound, and feather it to meet the wall surface. Sand, apply a third coat if needed, and sand again. Prime and paint when dry.

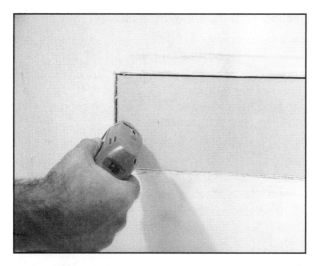

Screws cause much less damage than nails, but nails will work if you're a traditionalist.

Seven Ways to Find a Stud

In fixing walls, hanging stuff on walls, or making electrical repairs, you'll run up against the homeowner's nightmare: Where's the stud? (Studs, you'll recall, are the 2-by-4 or 2-by-6 framing lumber that supports walls.) You have plenty of alternatives for finding these elusive characters, and sometimes you'll want to use more than one technique. The worst situations are in old walls, where several layers of material really obscure the studs.

Finding the Electrical Boxes

Most electrical boxes are mounted on studs. It's a dead give-away if there's a box in the region you're searching. Generally you can just tap with a hammer (see the next hint) to figure out which side the stud is on; if you're extremely baffled, shut off the circuit, open up the box, and look inside for the fastening.

Tapping with a Hammer

This was my father's favorite technique. If you tap carefully, and if your ear is good, you'll hear the noise change from a hollow sound between studs to a tighter sound on top of the stud. This trick is not much good with thick plaster walls.

Drilling

You can find a stud by drilling (use a $1/16$-inch bit) through the wall; the resistance increases greatly when you enter a stud. Alternatively, drill a $1/8$-inch hole at an angle toward the side and probe with a cut-off coat-hanger. Because these techniques require holes, I use them only when needed: to check the accuracy of a less-intrusive method, or when I'm absolutely baffled about the location of the studs.

Measuring

Studs are usually located 16 inches (or, rarely, 24 inches) apart. Once you've found one stud (perhaps by noticing that an electric receptacle was secured to it) you should be able to measure to find the others—if the carpenter wasn't drinking too much brandy, and if you haven't found an oddly located stud, and if ….

Baseboard

The baseboard—the trim along the floor—should be nailed to the studs. Look closely for nails (they should be visible, even if the holes were filled), and use a level to follow the stud up the wall.

Magnetic Studfinder

These gizmos contain a magnet that moves (theoretically, at least) when it is attracted by the nails that fasten baseboard to studs. These studfinders may also work in drywall, where the nails are near the surface. In plaster, the nails are deeper and generally can't be detected.

Electronic Studfinder

The electronic solution, sadly, is not a surefire answer to the stud-seeking snafu. Success takes a bit of a knack and depends on the wall construction. In my limited experience, I've found this electronic "wonder" no panacea.

Installing Drywall

Let's say you don't want to find studs. Let's say you want to hang a whole wall-ful (or even roomful) of drywall. Perhaps your spouse has butchered the existing drywall while removing wallpaper (this can happen!). Perhaps you need to replace some hideous paneling. Here's a basic procedure for tackling this "edge-idiot" job. (I say "edge-idiot" because many readers will think this is completely out of their territory. In fact, it's not the simplest task in this book, but it's easier than plumbing.)

Tools: Aside from the tools listed earlier in this chapter, you will need a 4-foot aluminum drywall square and a Surform plane. Drywall sanding screens are much better than sandpaper because they don't clog. Assuming you're smart enough to want to screw the rock, you'll want a variable-speed drill with a screwdriver bit (but first see the section "A Fascination with Fastening," later in this chapter). Make sure to stock some dust masks for the sanding phase.

Materials: Most drywalling is done with $1/2$-inch drywall, sold in 8- to 12-foot sheets. Long sheets are harder to handle and may not pass through stairwells, but they do reduce the number of joint to tape, a major benefit. Water-resistant drywall is good for bathrooms and kitchens. Use cement board in shower and bath stalls. Order a little extra rock, and get a large amount delivered. You'll also need joint tape and joint compound, as described previously.

Drywall installation takes two steps. First you "hang rock," as drywall is usually called. Second, you tape the joints to finish the job. We'll take them in order.

An Invitation to a Hanging

Before you actually hang the rock, scan the room. Are there enough electrical receptacles and phone jacks? If not, this is your last chance to add them. Be religious about screwing in "nailers," or "blocking," the 2-by-4 blocks that support drywall from behind. Remember: If the rock wanders, it'll move when you try to mud it, which is a guaranteed disaster. The tops and bottoms of wall sheets of drywall should be screwed to the plate and the sole plate, respectively, as shown in the drywall installation drawing. Exterior walls must also have a vapor barrier. If you've insulated with waterproof foam panels, simply tape the joints with vapor barrier tape. Otherwise, staple 4-mil poly sheeting to the studs, using a minimum of staples.

Don't Screw Up!

Think about the next step—always. With drywall, today's errors *will* come back to haunt you. Don't hang rock until you have secure support at the end of every piece. Make sure flush surfaces are actually flush. Get all fasteners below the surface level. In short, get anal-compulsive, and don't rush things.

Once you're sure the preparation is finished, start screwing sheets to the ceiling. Plan your work to minimize joints. It's usually best to run the length of the sheets perpendicular to the joists, so all end joints meet at the center of a joist. The tapered edges along the sides of sheets should always meet other tapered edges (this simplifies taping, which is your ultimate objective at this stage). To cut drywall, see the sidebar on cutting drywall. Allow ¼ inch leeway on cuts so you don't have to go back and endlessly recut pieces.

Mark the fastener lines with a pencil and drywall square while the piece is leaning against the wall. To lift sheets, get a friend who owes you a favor. Use the crutch shown in the drawing of a homemade drywall crutch to hold the rock in place while fastening.

Walls are a little more complicated. Start at the top, where full sheets will reduce the number of joints in this highly visible location. Despite the temptation, don't make horizontal or vertical joints around windows or doors. As seen in the figure on drywall installation, sheets should reach beyond these openings.

Make the cutout in sheets 1, 2, and 3 by sawing the vertical cuts first with a large drywall saw (a rip saw will work fine). Then cut the horizontal cut with a utility knife, and break the piece backward. Mark the fastener lines, and slide the upper sheets up the wall tight to the ceiling.

Nail It Down

Cutting drywall? It's a real no-brainer. Using a square, cut through the paper on one side of the dry-wall. Bend the piece backward to break the gypsum center. Then cut the remaining paper from behind. This technique makes only straight cuts. To cut a curve or complicated shapes, use a small drywall saw, sold for under $10.

The lower pieces need cutouts for electrical boxes. Measure carefully from the upper sheet, not the floor, because you'll want a ¼-inch gap between the floor and the lower sheet. Cuts should be within ⅛ inch so the box cover will cover the opening. Cut with a saber saw or hand drywall saw (this saw is shaped like a dagger).

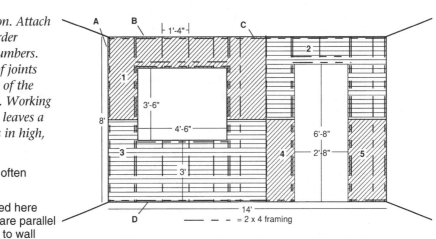

Drywall installation. Attach the sheets in the order indicated by the numbers. Note the absence of joints around the corners of the window and doors. Working from the top down leaves a minimum of joints in high, obvious locations.

A. Extra nailers often needed here

B. Nailers needed here unless joists are parallel and adjacent to wall

C. Plate

D. Sole plate

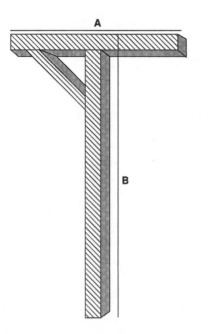

Homemade drywall crutch. Make one or two crutches like this from scrap 2-by-4s. Nudge the crutch into place before fastening the rock. Don't let it fall and break your neck.

A. Width is about 42 inches.

B. Total height is $1/2$-inch longer than the finished room height.

A Fascination with Fastening

Now that you've accurately cut the rock, it's time to fasten it. In the olden days, rockers used nails. Today, the game is all screwed up—I mean, drywall is all screwed, not nailed. Screws are stronger, easier to work with, and less damaging to the framing and rock. Because screws should penetrate the wood $3/4$ inches (longer screws are likely to pop out), buy $1^1/4$-inch screws for $1/2$-inch drywall. And while we're talking screws, consider the square-drive type, which require much less force than Phillips screws.

Don't Screw Up!

If you fail to support the rock from behind, it will wander as you start taping it, and you'll never get a decent joint. Before hanging rock, faithfully support all corners with nailers.

The key problem is setting screws just deep enough. Screws should depress the paper surface without butchering the gypsum core. By far the best tool for this is a rented screw gun. These gizmos have an adjustment that shuts off when they reach exactly the right depth. If you set a screw too deep (it's easy to do with an electric drill), drive another screw 1 inch away, and then remove the first one. At ends of sheets, only $3/4$ inch of wood is available for screwing. Drive screws at a slight angle so they do not break the gypsum and weaken the sheet.

Always press hard with your other hand while screwing drywall; you need to get the sheets tight, and screws cannot do all the pulling. Place screws 8 inches apart along the edges, and 12 inches apart on the inside framing. Near windows, doors, and

251

baseboards, place screws where they'll be covered by molding. When you're finished fastening, run a drywall knife over every fastener. Every time you hear a "zing" sound, you'll have to screw the screw a bit deeper.

Taping Joints

If you've religiously hung and fastened the rock, taping should be a breeze—almost—if you follow these taping and finishing suggestions. (The relative merits of various kinds of tape and joint compound are discussed at the previous section "Meet the Fixer-Upper Materials.") If you haven't created a monster mess by now, plan on a major dust storm during taping. See Chapter 6, "Health, Safety, and Common Sense," for suggestions on protecting your home and your body from drywall dust.

Here's the procedure for taping drywall:

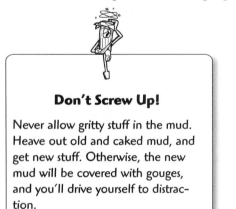

Don't Screw Up!

Never allow gritty stuff in the mud. Heave out old and caked mud, and get new stuff. Otherwise, the new mud will be covered with gouges, and you'll drive yourself to distraction.

1. Fill all deep spots, holes, and corners with quick-setting compound. Keep it below the surface. Quickly slap some mud in the nail holes, using a narrow putty knife or trowel.

2. Tape the corners; simply stick Fiberglass tape into the corner, then mud the corner as described for paper tape. Lay some mud under paper tape with a 6-inch knife, as shown in the accompanying photo. Mud a corner, and pull the mud up the corner to spread it. Fold the tape at the score on the center, and press it into the mud with the corner trowel. Don't let the mud get dry before sticking the tape to it.

3. Using similar procedures, apply tape to the rest of the walls. Smooth off all mud at the edges, but keep the overall "mudprint" less than 6 inches wide. Make sure all tape is covered by mud.

4. When dry, sand the edges to remove ridges. Don't oversand: Just get rid of the ridges. The best sanding combination—drywall screens on a drywall sanding frame—takes some of the sting out of this nasty job.

5. Switch to regular drywall compound for the last coat or two. Use a broader knife and smear mud over the previous application, working wider and concentrating on low areas, as shown in the accompanying figure on mudding a taped joint.

6. Hold a light bulb near the wall to identify low spots, and continue sanding and mudding until the wall is perfect enough. Be especially careful near ceiling lights, which produce a low-angle illumination that really shows off any flaw.

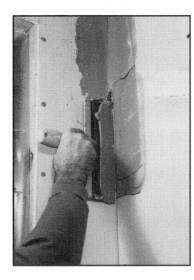 

Use an 8-inch knife to place mud on both sides of a corner, and then use the corner trowel to smooth the mud into the corner.

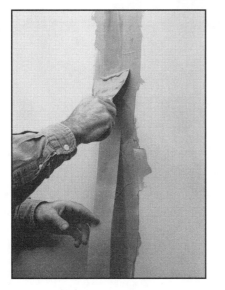

Push paper tape into the wet compound. After the taping mud sets, use wider drywall knives to smear mud over the joint. Quick-setting compound will save a day's worth of drying time.

The Least You Need to Know

➤ When you make wall repairs, never allow the patching material to build up on the surrounding surface.

➤ Floating is the best way to repair plaster with a rough finish.

➤ There's no need to undercut plaster or drywall before a repair; this only causes more damage. But do ensure that the patching adheres to the wall.

➤ The technique for repairing drywall or plaster depends on the construction and the scale of the damage.

➤ Plaster cracks easily, so use extreme caution when cutting it, particularly if it's supported by wood lath.

➤ Drywall replacement is not for the faint-hearted idiot, but it's not too complicated for the ambitious homeowner.

The Will to Wallpaper

Wallpaper may be high-class stuff, but that doesn't insulate it from the slings and arrows (and stains and peeling) of outrageous fortune. Maybe the wallpaper is intact, but the stairwalls, which your 4-year-old once used for balance before hurling herself down the stairs, shows a hundred grimy handprints.

Fortunately, wallpaper—a category that includes cloth, plastic, vinyl, and even silk—can be repaired rather easily, if you understand your material, know a few tricks of the trade, and can find some spare material.

In this chapter, I'll show you how to repair curling edges, fix holes and tears, and cover your tracks. And if you can't stand the taste of the people who once lived in your place (or if you've outgrown your own passion for black-and-silver, '70s disco wallpaper), I'll discuss how to rip it all off and start over.

Tools and Supplies You Will Need

For occasional wallpaper repair, you can do as I do and get by with an extremely limited tool kit (see the accompanying photo). Here are the basic tools you'll need:

Paperhanging tools and supplies.

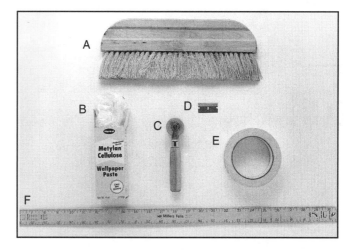

A. Brush: You may need two: one for applying paste to large areas, and another for smoothing paper after pasting. Substitute a 3- to 4-inch paintbrush for pasting small areas.

B. Paste: Must be compatible with your wallcovering (vinyl requires special paste).

C. Seam roller: Squeezes paste from seams so they will stick.

D. Razor blade: For all cutting jobs (it's got to be sharp). Hint: Save your fingers and use a sharp utility knife or single-edge razor blade. Knives with snap-off blades are particularly handy because you can get a new edge almost instantly. Otherwise, plan on using a new blade for every cut.

E. Masking tape: Holds patches in position for double-cut repairs.

F. Straight edge: For a cutting guide (or, substitute a clean carpenter's square or a T-square).

Making Invisible Repairs

Wallcovering can be damaged by improper application, dirt, or physical injury. If the plaster or drywall is damaged, repair it first, following the suggestions in Chapter 22, "Cosmetology 101: Drywall and Plaster Repair."

Patching tears, rips, and curling seams should be relatively easy, if you follow these instructions. (To replace stained and damaged areas, you'll obviously need wallcovering material—if you're lucky, the paperhangers stashed scraps in your house.)

To fix a *blister*, make one or more cuts on an inconspicuous part of the pattern with a razor blade. Usually, a bit of water on the surface will soften the paper and allow it to stick back to the wall—but test first, as water can damage some coverings. Apply white cement (good ol' Elmers Glue or its equivalent) behind the paper with an artist's brush or a toothpick, and then press the covering into place. With a damp rag, wipe away extra cement.

Repair small tears by applying white cement to the wall and pressing the covering into place. Wipe away any cement from the surface.

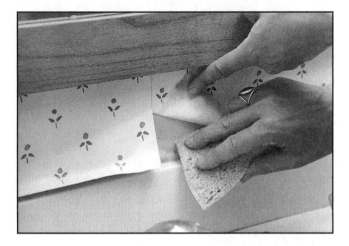

Dampen the repair area. Let it dry a bit, then apply glue across the entire loosened section.

Sticking Curling Wallpaper So It Stays Stuck

One of the most common wallpaper problems—curled edges at seams—can be tough to fix because the paper stiffens with age. Dampen the paper to increase its flexibility, but don't slobber on so much water that the paper will loosen or be damaged (it's a good idea to test the water on an inconspicuous area). You'll need a sponge, wallpaper paste or white cement, and a seam roller. Follow these steps to quell the curl:

1. Soften the curling edges by sponging them several times every few minutes. Don't stop until they flatten out easily.

2. Mix the wallpaper paste, and let it rest for a few minutes.

3. Dry the repair area as well as possible, and then get the paste between the wallpaper and the wall (as shown in the photo).

4. Press or roll the wallpaper to the wall. Clean any paste from the surface with a damp sponge.

Don't Screw Up!

Dry paste goes a lot further than novices expect. Although paste is cheap, there's no point wasting it, so mix small amounts at first. Mix in a plastic bucket or mud box, which should be the right size for a pasting brush.

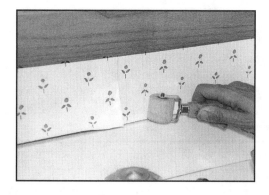

Don't roll hard enough to squeeze out all the paste. Meg eventually declared war on this cutesy pattern.

5. If you can figure a way to press something against the patch to hold it flat for a few minutes, so much the better. (Try leaning a bookcase against a piece of wood, for example.) Otherwise, return occasionally and flatten the patch.

Patching Holes and Battle Zones

To patch small areas of wallcovering, you can choose the rip-and-cover or the double-cutting method. The first method can leave edges that are almost invisible, but double-cutting is easier and still pretty subtle.

A *rip-and-cover* patch is most suitable for paper; vinyl and cloth wallcoverings won't tear the right way. You'll need sandpaper, a scrap of new wallpaper, paste, and a brush. Use these steps:

1. Feather jagged parts of the damaged area lightly with fine or extrafine sandpaper.

2. Tear out a piece of wallpaper that contains the correct pattern and that is big enough to cover the damage. Tear so that only the surface (not the backing) is visible.

3. Apply paste to the rear of the patch with a small artist's brush, and place it over the wound. The patch must exactly match the existing pattern.

4. Carefully smooth the patch with another brush, and sponge away excess adhesive.

To patch with the *double-cutting method*, you'll need a new razor blade, a sponge, a brush, spare wallpaper, paste, masking tape, and possibly a straight edge. Before starting, unroll the new paper and flatten it for an hour or so. If it's really stiff, flatten it by rolling it backward (called "counter-rolling") or pulling it backward across a sharp corner.

1. Tape a piece of wallpaper slightly larger than the injury over the repair area, matching the pattern (see top photo on next page).

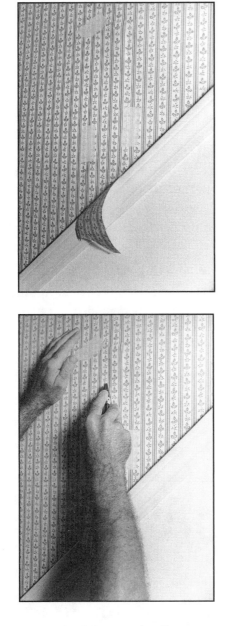

Position the patch perfectly against the surrounding pattern, and tape it into place with masking tape.

Cut deep enough to get through both layers in one slash; use a sharp knife, but don't push like a gorilla.

2. Cut through both layers of wallpaper around the damaged area with the razor blade (see the accompanying photo). Use a straight edge if your hand is not steady. (It may be better to cut curves rather than straight lines so that you can cut through the background instead of the pattern.) Try not to cut deep into the drywall, and make sure the patch does not wander while you cut.

259

3. Mark the top of the patch (if it's not obvious), and then take the piece down.

4. As shown in the photo, remove damaged wallpaper within the cuts by a combination of:

   ➤ Cutting it into strips with a knife or razor blade (don't cut the drywall)

   ➤ Dampening to soften the paste

   ➤ Scraping

   ➤ Using wallpaper remover

5. Allow the wall to dry, if needed.

6. Paste the back of the patch, and slide it into place.

7. Roll the edges lightly, and sponge off excess adhesive. Wipe with a damp rag. Return in a few minutes and press the patch down again.

The Rip-Off Remedy: How to Repaper a Room

Sometimes, what you need is not repair but repapering. Say the damage is too great, or you can't find matching paper, or you've done some remodeling, or you simply can't stand the zebras and elephants that a former owner found so stylish. In these cases, the solution is to rip down the wallpaper and replace it. It can be a fair hunk of work, but if the room is not too big or too irregular, and if you're not too much of a perfectionist, it's a reasonable homeowner job. (To paper an unpapered wall, see the upcoming section "Preparing for Papering.")

Remove the old paper by soaking, scraping, and/or pulling.

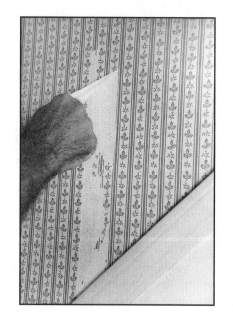

If your existing paper is well-hung—er, that is, perfectly stuck and in good condition—you can take a chance by pasting new paper over it. But it's best to pull off all the old paper and start anew. If you're extremely lucky, the old paper is a tough, strippable material that pulls down in large sheets. It's probably smart to pull off some paper before committing yourself to a complete repapering job.

If the paper does not come down easily, you'll have to soften it with wallpaper stripper or a rented wallpaper steamer and then scrape it off. This may not be a pretty process, but when you're done, you'll have clean walls. At least, that's what Meg thought when she finally decided to eradicate the tiny flowers on our bathroom. From that disaster, we learned some rules for stripping:

➤ Be scientific. Try your techniques in order, and don't commit to a whole room until you find one that works. This is a reasonable sequence of tactics:

    A. Pulling off: If you're lucky, it's strippable paper that will come down with a minimum of effort.

    B. Using wallpaper remover: This no-odor chemical may attack glue on paper that can't be pulled.

    C. Renting a steamer: Considered the ultimate in drudge work, this device is certainly effective, and far better than hacking with a putty knife.

➤ You can help the stripper and water reach the glue on waterproof paper with a wallpaper gouger. But before using one on a whole wall, check that it really helps. In our case, the lack of wall preparation prevented the gouger from doing anything more than damaging the drywall. We ended up using a steamer.

A wall that has been hacked and gouged may be too difficult to repair with drywall compound. Paper needs a solid, flat surface. Consider using one of the texture techniques described in Chapter 22 rather than papering.

Don't Screw Up!

Use care when removing wallpaper. I've seen the results of some "handy" gouging devices that seriously gouged the drywall. Drywall knives or trowels can also wreak havoc; especially on drywall that's wet from use of wallpaper removal. Sadly, a steamer is a good choice if you are interested in preserving your wall surface.

Preparing for Papering

Bring the room dimensions when you shop for new paper, and ask the store clerk to estimate how much you'll need (this can be more complicated than it seems). Buy a little extra to allow for mistakes and to ensure that you have enough to finish the job without making another trip to the store.

When choosing patterns, remember that a pattern with vertical stripes will show every error or irregularity. Broad pattern elements, or tiny ones, are more likely to hide your little flaws. If you're new at wallpapering, make sure to buy paper that's easy to handle. Avoid foil and other fragile papers—these are for pros. In the following instructions, I assume you've been sensible and bought pre-pasted paper, which saves time, equipment, and hassle. (Self-stick paper has dry glue on the back. To activate the glue, you soak the paper before application.) If you don't use pre-pasted paper, be sure to get the right paste.

Once the surface is flat and solid, clean the walls with trisodium phosphate (sold at paint stores) or the equivalent. Then examine the walls for dents, gouges, or holes, and patch according to the instructions in the section "Repairing Nicks and Gouges," in Chapter 22. If the wall has sand-finish plaster, you'll have to scrape off all the sand—an ugly prospect.

Apply something to regulate the absorption of the new wallpaper paste. The manufacturer of the new paper may specify either sizing or a primer-sealer. Apply this stuff and let it dry. Don't skip this step—at least, for the benefit of future owners, who may not share your taste in wallpaper and will appreciate the way it controls the absorption of glue.

Hung-Up on Wallpaper

Now comes the moment of truth: time for paper-hanging. No, I'm not talking about selling bonds on Wall Street, which goes by the same name, but about sticking up a new layer of wallpaper. Here, in brief, is what you need to know to hang paper. For complicated situations, I'd encourage you to consult a more thorough treatment.

In the interests of keeping things simple, these instructions assume that you are using pre-pasted paper. You will need a stepladder or some low scaffolding, a pan long enough to soak the paper, a brush to smooth the paper once it's on the wall, a level (a 4-foot model is best), a pencil, a seam roller, and several dozen single-edge razor blades with a blade holder made for cutting wallcovering. If you need to paste the paper (pros even put paste on pre-pasted paper, to increase adhesion), you'll need a paste bucket, a paste brush, and a table to work on.

You'll most likely also need an accomplice to hold paper while you paste or adjust it.

1. Start your first strip in the most prominent part of the room, as shown in the accompanying drawings: The seam is centered and the strip is centered. Work in both directions from here, following the general guidelines shown in the figure.

Because the patterns will not match at the end, your last strips should meet in the most inconspicuous part of the room, such as behind a piece of furniture. The top corners of doors are a great meeting point. A full-height fireplace or another complete break in the walls also offers an ideal ending place, or kill point.

2. Lightly mark a vertical line in the center of the room. Use a level or chalk line (these make a handy plumb line if you support the string and let the tool hang). This will be your guideline for one side of the first strip.

3. Fill your pan with water. Cut some strips a few inches longer than you need (if you are using a big pattern, lay the strips on the floor to figure out exactly how long they must be to match). Reroll the strips backward to take out the curvature. Roll over a new roll to get the counter-rolling started.

4. Following the manufacturer's directions, dunk the strips in water, and then remove and fold back each end to meet at the center ("book them"). The pasted sides will be together when the strip is properly "booked."

5. Leave the strip booked for a few minutes while it expands slightly. Otherwise, it will wrinkle on the wall.

6. Bring the booked paper to the wall, and open only the top fold. Now hang the top of the paper to the line, with a couple of inches extending onto the ceiling. Try to place it correctly to start with—lots of adjustment can cause wrinkles and tears—but do adjust it accurately by peeling it off if necessary until it's perfect.

7. Brush the strip, starting at the center, to remove air bubbles and improve adhesion. Gently press up into the ceiling angle with a taping trowel or corner trowel.

8. When the top is affixed, unbook the bottom and repeat. Trim the top and bottom by sliding a razor blade along a broad drywall knife. Use a new blade for every trim.

9. Continue hanging paper around the room. After each seam is in place, roll it with the roller to press some paste out and improve adhesion. (But don't press too hard; that squeezes out too much paste.) Check the plumbness every couple of strips.

Starting point: The seam is centered.

If this wall is the focus of the room, and if the end seams will be more than 6 inches from the corner, use the hanging sequence indicated by the numbers.

  A. Centerline

  B. At least 6 inches

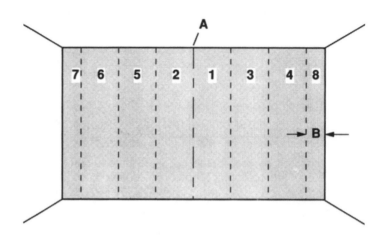

Starting point: The strip is centered.

If the centered seam approach places seams too close to the corners, hang paper on the focal wall in this sequence.

  A. Centerline

  B. At least 6 inches

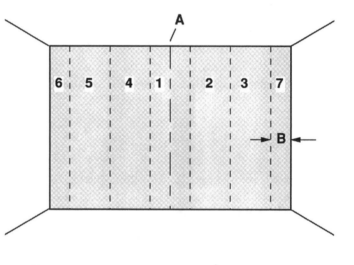

Hanging pattern: If the fireplace is the focus of the room, start hanging strips there.

  A. Starting point

  B. Alternative starting point

  C. Kill point (for either starting point)

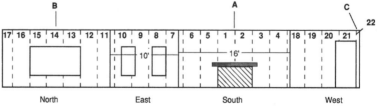

Hints for the hung-up:

➤ Don't depend on your eye to get things straight or plumb; use a ruler, a straight edge, and a level.

➤ Use sharp razor blades. Wet paper is weak, and there's no point in ripping a strip after you've gone to all the trouble of hanging it.

➤ If your paper shrinks excessively, a seam made by butting adjacent strips may open up as the paper dries. You can hang two strips, wait a half-hour, and look for shrinkage at the seam. If the seam becomes visible, make a "wired seam," using a $1/16$-inch overlap, which should be enough to help the seam stay closed after any shrinkage.

➤ Wrap corners: Extend the first strip 1 inch around the corner, and place the next strip slightly over the edge of the first strip. This allows you to return the pattern to vertical (patterns can go out of plumb due to irregularities in the building).

➤ Similarly, if your strips ever get out of vertical, simply hang a new plumb strip overlapping an existing strip. A perfectionist can double-cut the seam to get back to vertical: (1) Hang the second strip overlapping the first. Make the overlap wide enough to allow a vertical cut through both strips. (2) Hold a level vertically on top of the seam, and use it as a straightedge to cut through both layers of paper. (3) Remove the narrow cutoffs, and roll the seam.

➤ To hang around windows, tack the strip in place, and make 45° cuts in the paper toward the corner of the casing. Then push the broad knife into the corners of the casing, and cut off the paper in the normal fashion.

➤ Wipe up extra paste with a damp cloth. Don't get the seams so wet that they come apart, but don't allow any wet paste to remain on the surface.

The Least You Need to Know

➤ Curling wallpaper has an attitude problem, which you can generally solve by dampening the paper before repasting it.

➤ With a deft hand, you can rip wallpaper and make a very subtle repair.

➤ Double-cutting is a foolproof and almost invisible trick for patching wallpaper.

➤ When attempting your first wallpapering job, stick to materials that are designed for homeowners and that are inherently easy to apply.

Chapter 24

A Scolding on Molding

In This Chapter

➤ The confusing language of molding

➤ Top tricks for installing molding around windows, doors, and floors

➤ Painless molding removal

➤ Cutting molding to fit irregular surfaces

Molding is trim used to join windows, doors, and floors to walls. Ranging from painfully plain to elaborately ornate, molding is something that gives rooms and houses character, style, and elegance. It's also something that keeps out drafts.

There are a lot of reasons to learn to install molding. Perhaps yours is bent, spindled, or mutilated. Perhaps you're interested in a simple restyling. Perhaps you've got the passion to install a new door or window. Maybe you're determined to sand your floor, and you want to do it right. As described in Chapter 20, "Getting a Solid Footing on Floors," that involves removing the base shoe and baseboard.

Molding Basics

Because the function of molding is to seal gaps and look great, installation is mainly a matter of looks. Indeed, one way to dress up a room is to replace the hum-drum or overly painted molding with fresh, stained hardwood. Work one room at a time, and after a reasonable period, the old home place may deserve coverage in a home magazine.

Molding Lingo

To work with molding, you've got to know how to talk about it. (For more on window molding, see Chapter 18, "A Paneless Guide to Windows"; for door molding, see Chapter 19, "An Entry-Level Treatise on Doors.")

Base shoe: A rounded molding used between a baseboard and a floor.

Baseboard: The taller molding around the edge of a floor.

Butt end: A square end. (A butt joint is a meeting of two square ends.)

Casing: Molding flat on the wall, around a door or window.

Cope: To cut a profile on the end of molding; used for joints at inside corners.

Crown: Molding used at the joint between a wall and a ceiling.

Head: A piece that goes across the top, as a head jamb or head casing.

Jamb: The wood that encases a window or door; it's perpendicular to the wall.

Miter: To angle an end cut, usually at 45° (a compound miter joint has a miter on two axes).

Reveal (setback): A small shoulder on a jamb, left showing after a casing is nailed.

Stop: A molding nailed to a jamb to prevent a door from swinging too far. Stop molding also holds double-hung windows in their jambs.

Do's and Don'ts

➤ Do mark your cuts with a utility knife; pencils are not accurate enough.

➤ Do predrill your nail holes in hardwood.

➤ Do stain, prime, and paint molding before installation.

➤ Do use the best and most continuous pieces in the most obvious places.

➤ Do clean up the revealed edges of old jambs before reattaching casing. Use sandpaper or a plane to remove roughness, and paint, stain, or varnish to match the molding.

➤ Don't use butt joints on base molding; they will eventually come apart. Mate two miter cuts instead.

➤ Don't finish the nailing of the molding until you're sure it fits right.

➤ Don't overfasten molding. Place nails about every 2 feet or so. Use 4d nails to nail casing to jambs; use 6d or 8d to nail casing through drywall or plaster into the studs supporting windows and doors.

Yanking Up Molding with Scarcely a Split

Let's say a repair requires you to remove the baseboard and base shoe. You might want to do this before sanding a floor, or when the old molding is ugly, damaged, or painted beyond recognition. Let's give you credit for being sensible, meaning you hate the idea of buying, cutting, and staining new molding. How can you pull the darned molding off without injuring it? By slowly and carefully prying off the top piece, working with two slender, low-impact tools.

The correct way to pull molding. The trick is to work gradually, with two prying tools, and to pry directly under the nails.

Always remove one piece at a time—there's no future in trying to pull base shoe and baseboard in one operation. You'll need a wood chisel, a flat prybar, a hammer, locking pliers, and wood scraps (optional: big flat screwdriver, and margin or pointing trowel). Don't feel terrible if you break a piece; this may be inevitable with brittle wood, or wood with a crooked grain. If you're careful, you can glue them back together. To remove the molding, follow these steps:

Don't Screw Up!

You'll have to pull finishing nails in molding you remove. Don't be tempted to hammer them from behind—the usual nail-pulling technique. It's much better to grab the nail from behind with a locking pliers and swing the pliers down, pulling the head through the wood. You'll need to drill new holes to renail the molding, but the overall damage will be much milder.

1. Starting at the end of a molding, insert the wood chisel under the molding to loosen it. As soon as possible, insert the flat blade of the prybar under the molding, protecting the floor with a trowel or wood scraps. Gradually pull the piece up. When there's room for another prying tool—a hammer, prybar, chisel, or trowel—insert it and pry with two tools at once.

2. If a nail head comes up, pull it, protecting the molding from the hammer head with a scrap of wood.

3. Work your way slowly along the molding.

4. If, after you've gotten the molding off, it still contains some finishing nails, do not pull them the usual way (by hammering from behind so they come out the front). This will split the wood. See the tip at left instead.

Cutting and Installing Molding

It's vastly preferable to cut molding with a power miter box (described in Chapter 8, "The Bare Essentials with Oomph! Power Tools"), but a hand model will work acceptably, as long as you fasten it to a workbench before sawing (see the figure on sawing with a hand miter box). If the miter box floats around, you're doomed.

To attach new molding, such as after drywalling or sanding floors, or when you're sprucing up the home place, do the windows and doors first, and then move to the base moldings. (For advice on removing molding, see the previous section.)

If you've got highly irregular floors and walls, refer to the section "A Quick Trick for Fitting Irregular Tiles, Moldings, and So On," in Chapter 21, "Tile in Style!" for a message on making moldings match miserably misshapen walls. The same technique can be used to match molding to irregular surfaces.

Sawing with a hand miter box.

Clamp the miter box to a workbench, or fasten it with drywall screws to something secure, like a workbench or a hunk of 2 × 10. Otherwise, the miter box is going to wander and cause more problems than it solves.

Door and Window Molding

Nailing new moldings to windows and doors is tricky work because every flaw is obvious, and the miter joints have a nasty tendency to pull apart. Work slowly and exactly, and make sure you can find replacement molding at the building supplier before breaking anything crucial! If your molding is more complicated than what's shown, disassemble it slowly and examine its construction as you go.

Here's a general procedure for applying molding to doors. Numbers in the illustrations on installing door casing correspond to the steps here. A similar technique will work for casing windows. Remember to predrill all nail holes in hardwood trim, and *do not pound the nails home* until the whole procedure is finished!

1. Mark reveal lines $3/16$ inch or $1/4$ inch from the inner edges of the jambs.
2. Make a new butt cut at the bottom of the left side casing, and hold it in place.
3. Mark where the reveal lines intersect, and miter up at 45° from the mark.
4. Predrill four nail holes along the inner edge and four more along the outer edge opposite the inner holes. Drill one hole for a lock nail, seen in step 2 of the illustration. Tack the left-side casing into place.
5. Miter the left end of the head casing, and hold it into place. If the 45° miters do not make a tight joint, adjust either or both miters until the joint is tight.
6. Miter the right end of the head casing. Predrill both lock-nail holes, and then tack the casing in place.
7. Make a butt cut on the bottom of the right casing, and stand it in position.
8. Mark the inside and outside of head casing miter on the right casing. If the new miter cut will not be at 45°, compensate as in step 5.

Don't Screw Up!

Molding can make or break a repair job. Take your time. Try to beg, borrow, or rent a power miter box, and check that it's cutting accurately before starting. If the head jamb is level and the side jamb vertical, 45° miters will work fine. If not, test your angles on scrap wood for each miter joint. It's sad but true—with molding, half a degree really matters.

9. When you're satisfied that all joints are tight, gently nail the casings into place. (This and following steps are not numbered in the illustration.) Caution: If pressing on the outside of the casing opens the joint, insert some shims (use cedar shingles or cardboard) behind the casing, near the joint. Leave a tab hanging out so you can remove the shim if it's too thick. Otherwise, cut it off when finished.

10. Use a nail set to set the nails below the surface. It may be best to nail the larger (6d or 8d), outside nails first, and then finish with 4d nails into the jambs—this tends to close the miter joints.

11. Nail the two 4d lock nails to hold the head and side casings together.

Installing door casing. The numbers correspond to numbers in the procedure. The detail shows reveal lines set back ¹/₄ inch from the edges of the side and top jambs. The inside of the casing is nailed to the jambs. The outside is nailed to the studs around the door opening (not shown).

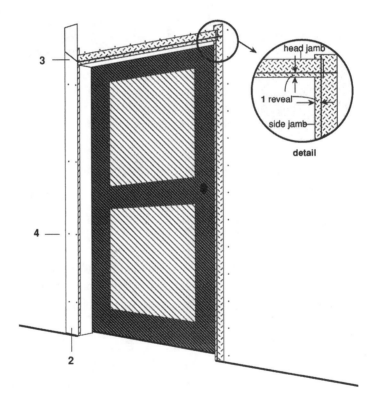

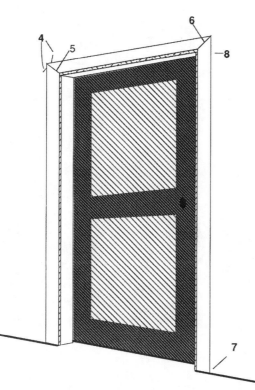

Use the head casing miter to locate the miter on the side casing. If a 45° miter is not tight, you'll have to compensate on the head and side casings. The lock nails secure the head casing to the side casings. The numbers correspond to numbers in the procedure.

Basic Base Moldings

Now it's time to cut and fasten the baseboard and base shoe. Using the longest pieces on the longest stretches, lay out the baseboard. Always predrill the nails, and don't nail anything home until you've tacked everything into place!

1. Start from an inside corner. To cut molding at an inside corner—where two baseboards meet in a corner of the room—don't cut each piece at 45°, even if that seems the obvious solution. Instead, leave piece A with a 90° end, and tack it into place.

2. Now make a miter cut on piece B. Then, using a coping saw—a kind of hand jigsaw—cut along the edge of the cut you just made (see the photo of coping an inside corner). (Fortunately this is easier than it sounds.)

3. Lightly sand the rough edge on piece B. Now, when you nail it into place, it won't pull away and leave an ugly gap where you wanted a tight joint.

4. Tack the molding into place, and work away from inside corners. Do not nail the butt-end piece too securely.

5. To cut an *outside corner,* make sure the corner is 90°. Cut two scraps at 45°, and use them to test the corner, as shown in the photo. You may not want 45° cuts, but rather whatever angle will make a tighter joint.

6. Once the baseboard is nailed, repeat the process to install the base shoe. Nail horizontally into the baseboard, not diagonally into the floor. A piece of sheet metal or a scrap of thin plywood protects the floor while you nail.

Coping an inside corner.

A. Make a 45° miter cut on the baseboard you're going to cope and mount it in a vise or clamp.

B. Carefully saw down the edge of the new cut with a coping saw to make a coped end that exactly fits the profile of the other molding.

C. A complete coped joint.

Testing an outside corner.

These gauge blocks each have 45° miters. If they do not fit exactly, alter your cuts a degree or two to match. When done, the miter angles should be equal, and the gap between the moldings should be tight.

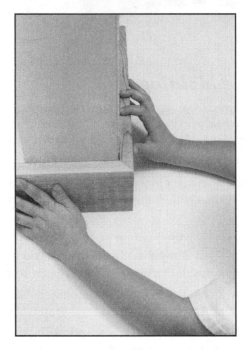

Caulking Trick

Whether you installed the molding or someone else did, you may have gaps where the molding is supposed to meet the wall. You tried to pound the molding back into place, but naturally that failed—in home repair, anything so obvious and simple is almost certainly doomed. But in this case, an even simpler solution actually works: filling the gap with a paintable caulking compound (or white caulking, if the walls are white). Cut a small hole in the cartridge tip. Apply sparingly, in one smooth motion. Smooth the stuff into place with a moistened finger or solvent-soaked rag. Paint when dry, if you want. Done.

Nail It Down

Cutting molding for a 45° miter (the kind you see at the corners of door trim) is tricky—just take it from somebody who repeatedly cuts moldings backward. Now I stand in the room where the molding will be nailed and lightly mark the location of the cut, and its angle, on the molding. Only then do I make the cut.

The Least You Need to Know

➤ By working carefully, you can remove molding intact, without damaging it or the surroundings.

➤ Molding repair depends on slow, methodical work. Always predrill nail holes, and avoid attaching the molding too securely.

➤ A power miter box will vastly help in molding installation chores.

Chapter 25

Putting a Good Face on: Choosing Paint and Painting Tools

In This Chapter

➤ Paint for practically anything from Australian arbors to antique xylophones

➤ Why new wood loves paintable, water–repellent preservative

➤ Reading problems in the existing paint to avoid similar woes next time around

---

Boy, has paint changed since I first dunked a brush into a can of evil-smelling, lead-based oil paint. By the time the paint finally dried, it was slathered with a coating of insects that had mistaken my house for an oversize sheet of bright blue flypaper. And who can forget the brush-cleaning ceremony, with those buckets of nauseating, flammable turpentine? Or hands tattooed for weeks afterward with paint spatters?

All told, it was a nerve-wracking one-two punch. And I mean this literally: Both the solvent and the lead pigment in that paint were toxic to the nervous system.

Today, lead is gone from paint (but see the section "Nervous About Leaded Paint?" in Chapter 6, "Health, Safety, and Common Sense"), and water is rapidly replacing volatile organic solvents. Furthermore, you can buy a range of specialty coatings for outdoor wood, ceilings, masonry, and wrought iron, which have solved many of the traditional pitfalls of home painting.

Although almost any paint will look good at first, I'd suggest paying extra for paint with a high solids content (because solids are what remains on the wall) and lower "vehicle," or solvent, content. Even if you're not interested in Sistine Chapel longevity, high-quality paint will repay the effort of good surface preparation and paint application.

Meet the Coating Family

The bucketsful of coatings fall into three major categories:

➤ *Surface preparers* (primers, sealers, and fillers) get the surface ready for that coating that follows.

➤ *Film formers* (paint and varnish) sit on the surface and protect from above. They last only as long as the film lasts.

➤ *Penetrating coatings* (stain, water repellent, and preservative) seep into the surface and protect from within. (The best wood preservative is factory-applied in pressurized tanks; see the section of "The Enemies of Wood," in Chapter 11, "Wood: Still Champ After All These Years.")

These coatings are often combined, and you may end up using penetrating coatings and film formers, particularly to protect the exterior skin of your house from sun, rain, and fungus.

Our trip through the paint department will start with the surface preparers, move to the film formers, and conclude with penetrating finishes. Table 25.1 explains what kinds of primers and finish coats you should choose when painting particular surfaces.

Primers and Finish Coats for Almost Any Purpose

Surface	Primer	Finish Coat
Interior		
Drywall	Latex, acrylic latex, or vinyl latex primer	Latex or alkyd wall paint, or texture paint
Plaster	Alkyd or latex primer	(2) Latex or alkyd wall paint or enamel, or texture paint
Masonry: concrete, concrete block, unglazed brick, cement board	Latex wall primer, epoxy primer	(2) Alkyd enamel, (2) latex wall paint or enamel, (2) epoxy

Surface	Primer	Finish Coat
Aluminum	Zinc chromate	(2) Latex or alkyd wall paint or enamel, or (2) aluminum paint
Galvanized steel	Acrylic metal primer or as specified by manufacturer	(2) Latex or alkyd wall paint or enamel
Structural steel and ornamental iron	Lead-free alkyd metal primer with rust inhibitors	(2) Latex or alkyd wall paint or enamel
Wood walls, ceilings, trim, cabinet work, hardboard, etc.	Alkyd primer	(2) Latex or alkyd wall paint or enamel
Painted wood floors	Industrial enamel or epoxy	Same as primer
Wood floors	Stain (optional)	Polyurethane varnish, oil finish, or wax
Exterior		
Masonry, asbestos siding, shingles, stucco, common brick, concrete walls	Fill rough surfaces first, then use self-priming latex house paint	Latex house paint
Aluminum	Self-priming house and trim (acrylic or latex)	Self-priming house and trim (acrylic or latex)
Galvanized steel	Alkyd metal primer	(2) Alkyd enamel or alkyd house and trim paint
Ornamental and structural steel	Rust-inhibiting alkyd primer	(2) Aluminum paint or alkyd
Prefinished metal siding and panels	Latex or alkyd house paint	Latex or alkyd house paint
Wood floors	Self-priming industrial enamel	Self-priming and platforms industrial enamel
Plywood	Semi-transparent preservative stain, or opaque exterior stain	Semi-transparent preservative stain, or opaque exterior stain
"	Pigmented acrylic emulsion	(2) Latex exterior solid color stain; or (2) latex house and trim
Shingles, shakes, rough-sawn lumber	Alkyd exterior primer	(2) Latex or alkyd house paint

continues

279

Primers and Finish Coats for Almost Any Purpose (continued)

Surface	Primer	Finish Coat
"	Semi-transparent preservative stain, or opaque stain	Semi-transparent preservative stain, or opaque stain
Siding, trim, doors, hardboard (bare or primed)	Alkyd exterior primer	(2) Alkyd or latex house and trim, or alkyd house paint; or (2) latex exterior solid-color stain
"	Semi-transparent preservative stain, or opaque stain	Semi-transparent preservative stain, or opaque stain
"	Exterior varnish	(2) Exterior varnish

Note: (2) indicates 2 coats needed. Due to changes in formulation and terminology, always read the label and follow manufacturer's instructions when choosing and using paint.

Surface Preparers

Surface preparers—primer, filler, and sealer—make a surface chemically and physically ready for later coats. Preparers look inward, toward the substrate (the coated material), while topcoats (the final coats) look outward, toward your admiring eyes and the sun, rain, dirt, and ultraviolet light waiting to destroy coating and substrate.

Primer is designed to penetrate the substrate and create a paint-friendly surface on top. It may also be intended to kill mildew or prevent rust. A primed surface allows some paint to penetrate and get a foothold, but it forces most of the paint to stay on the surface. Primer should not be left to weather for long, as it can be harmed by rain and ultraviolet light.

You'll need primer on unpainted drywall, plaster, wood, and metal. You don't need primer over a sound coat of paint, unless it's necessary for the specific new paint you've chosen. If you are priming a few areas in a repair job, you will spot-prime them. If the repairs are extensive, though, you're better off priming the whole surface. In any event, if more than 50 percent of the surface needs primer, prime the whole thing.

The ultimate authority on primer is the label of the new paint you're going to use. Read it and follow it.

Filler is used on materials such as rough masonry, concrete, and some open-pored woods to fill pores and make a good surface for the paint. You may be able to find a primer-filler to do two steps at once.

Sealer is used to cover nasty stains—including crayons, oily crud, and pitchy knots—that would otherwise bleed through the topcoat. Cedar and redwood, which contain water-soluble stains, both need sealing before painting.

Rust-inhibitive primer is needed before painting iron and steel. Talk about self-sacrificing! This stuff is designed to decay before the metal starts to rust; when the primer eventually gives out, it must be replaced.

Toolbox Trivia

Exterior wood primer is similar to diluted, solvent-based exterior paint (commonly called oil paint, you'll find it labeled alkyd paint in the store). So if you're short of primer (or if you just need a bit), thin some alkyd exterior paint with mineral spirits.

Film Formers

People who claim to have expertise in this field say good paint is no thicker than a sheet of newspaper. Nevertheless, this thin film faces many demands: Paint may be designed to be washable, breathable, or water-repellent; to shed water and dirt, to resist air pollution, to stay where you put it, and to look smooth and suave in whatever color you have chosen.

Let's take a tour of the paint aisle and see how the various materials stack up. As we do this, remember that paint comes in various grades. Generally, the more you pay, the higher proportion of pigment (solids) the paint will contain, and the better coverage it will give. Pigment proportions are found on the side of the can. Good quality is especially important if you want long-lasting coverage or you are counting on covering with one coat.

Alkyd paint: Alkyd has replaced oil paint as the heavy-duty option for house trim and exteriors. Although alkyd produces a more washable, durable surface than latex, you'll need to thin it with mineral spirits (the modern version of turpentine). Contrary to what you may have heard, you may paint latex over alkyd, and vice versa; as long as the old surface is rough, you'll get good adhesion.

Latex paint: Latex paints are the water-thinned workhorses of interior painting, and they work increasingly well for exterior painting. They produce hardly any fumes,

Don't Screw Up!

Don't dump old paint into the gutter, toilet, or backyard. Leave a can of latex paint open until it's dry, and then put it in the trash. Give solvent-based paint to someone who has a need for it, or save it for a clean sweep hazardous-waste collection.

and you can even use them on damp surfaces. Latexes are permeable to moisture, making them ideal for use on masonry, where moisture causes other paints to peel. These paints are not easy to wash, however.

Acrylic paint: Acrylic paints are generally water-soluble. They are a step up from latex in terms of coverage, color retention, and glossiness. Just for the sake of maximum confusion, you may see acrylic latex, which is an improved version of plain latex paint.

Don't Screw Up!

Unless you like getting loopy on solvents, use good ventilation and wear a respirator when using solvent-based paint.

Enamel paint: Enamels, made of various formulations, are glossy, durable paints used for high-stress areas such as kitchens, bathrooms, and outdoor metal. Industrial enamel is best for tough jobs, such as repainting cabinets for a bargain-basement kitchen remodeling.

Epoxy paint: Epoxy is two-part paint for heavy-duty uses such as floors, appliances, and counters. I've used this evil-smelling stuff where nothing else would work. Use a respirator, keep the windows open, and work fast—epoxy paint dries quickly into a very hard surface.

A Clear Finish on Outdoor Wood? (The Vanishing of Varnish)

When it comes to showing off the grain of wood, nothing comes close to the clear finishes of varnish and lacquer. For interior wood floors, polyurethane varnish is the finish of choice because it is hard, clear, non-yellowing, and easy to apply. This varnish is sold in matte, semigloss, and gloss finishes. Like everything else, polyurethane can suffer from time, tide, and foot traffic. For more information, see the section "Healing Wooden Floors," in Chapter 20, "Getting a Solid Footing on Floors."

Outside, however, the best reason for varnishing wood is to demonstrate your prowess with a paint scraper. Huh? Because clear varnish contains no pigment, there's nothing to stop ultraviolet light from wrecking it (and the wood it is supposedly protecting). So the decline and fall of outdoor varnish is inevitable; a year after you brush it on, the stuff will be flaking, and you will be (or should be) scraping.

If you're possessed by an urge to show off your glorious wood front door, give it some shade by planting a tree or building an overhang. Better yet, use a semi-transparent stain, which will show some of the wood grain while blocking ultraviolet light. As a bonus, semi-transparent stain is a penetrating finish, which means you won't have to perform scraping duty next time around.

Penetrating Finishes

So much for the stuff that sits on top. Let's talk about penetrating finishes, those invisible helpers that protect from below. Although stains and water-repellents are thin and splattery to apply, their many advantages over paint have gained them increasing popularity:

➤ They can't peel because they become part of the top layer of wood.

➤ They're durable because they don't crack when a change in humidity causes swelling or shrinkage.

➤ You can skip the primer.

➤ Best of all, you won't need to scrape next time around—just wash and restain.

To get these advantages, you'll need to observe the cardinal principle of penetrating finishes: They've got to penetrate. Translated, that means that the surface must be porous enough. To test for porosity, just throw a few drops of water on the surface. If it sinks in, the wood is ready for a penetrating finish. If not, the wood is either too new for sealing and must weather for a while, or a previous coat of penetrating finish is still working. Don't renew a penetrating finish until water can sink into the surface.

Nail It Down

Paint is almost never waterproof—at best, it resists water for a while. That's why experts recommend slathering on a paintable, water-repellent preservative before priming or staining new wood.

Stain

Stain—either opaque or semi-transparent—has been competing with paint as an exterior coating on wood for years. Opaque stain will even cover many kinds of paint, although a light-colored stain may not cover dark paint. For rough-textured wood, stain is the clear choice because the wood absorbs enough stain to obtain an excellent level of protection. On the other hand, smooth plywood absorbs little stain and gets little protection.

Interior stain is sold in many hues, supposedly to simulate various species of wood. When choosing these stains, remember that the wood you are working on may not resemble the sample in the store. It's best to bring an actual sample to the store; use the back of some molding, if you can't find anything else.

When applying stain, observe label directions. You may need to apply the second coat within a certain time period. Otherwise, the first coat may harden too much for the second to penetrate.

Water Repellent

Water repellent is dissolved wax that sinks into wood and dries to make the wood shed water. Some water repellents contain preservative, to make life miserable for the fungi waiting to eat your house. Paintable, water-repellent preservative, as noted previously, is your ace in the hole for preparing new, exterior wood for finishing.

How Much Paint Do You Need?

Have you ever been bamboozled by those authoritative estimates on paint cans, promising that the paint covers 400 square feet per gallon? I certainly have—usually to find myself running short of paint when I'm just about done. You can make better estimates if you consider these factors when calculating your paint needs:

➤ Surface roughness and coat thickness both influence how far a coating will go. A rough surface can easily require twice as much paint as a smooth one.

➤ If you're buying an untinted paint (or a standard color), you may be able to return extra cans. If this is true, buy more than you expect to need.

➤ Second coats go further than first coats because less sinks in.

➤ If you need three quarts, buy a gallon—it's cheaper.

➤ End grain is extremely thirsty; if you have much of it, you'll need more penetrating finish or primer.

➤ In general, thin coats are better than thick ones, but don't try to stretch the paint too far; it just won't work.

Doing the Coroner's Job: A Post-Mortem on Paint Problems

Does your house look like the showplaces in paint advertisements? Mine doesn't, either. Between the fungus among us, the smudges, and the peeling, my house—like most—is a virtual encyclopedia of paint problems. That's the bad news. The good news is that these problems offer guidance for painting tactics that will prevent their recurrence (see the following table).

A Rogue's Gallery of Paint Problems

Example	Problem Description	Likely Causes	Solution
	Checking (hairline cracks)	Swelling and contraction caused by moisture changes are loosening the paint—most common on plywood.	Scrape loose paint. Ventilate the wall. Clean thoroughly, prime the surface, and paint. Consider switching to penetrating stain.

Example	Problem Description	Likely Causes	Solution
	Chalking (whitish film on the surface)	May be natural aging of self-cleaning paint, excess moisture coming through the wall, or, on masonry, wrong paint choice.	Ventilate wall if necessary. Remove all loose paint, then scrub with stiff brush and detergent. Prime severe cases with oil- or alkyd-base material. For severe chalking on masonry, prime with a masonry conditioner.
	Alligatoring, a crazed surface that drives home-owners berserk	Second coat was applied before first coat dried; surface was too glossy; or paint was too thick.	Scrape or sand paint, clean surface, dull any glossy surface, prime, and paint.
	Chipped paint on gutters, downspouts and other metal	Poor adhesion between metal and primer.	Scrape or wire brush loose paint and feather-sand edges. Rinse metal with solvent to remove grease, then prime with the correct metal primer. Topcoat with enamel.

Painter's Tools

Just because painter's tools are basic doesn't mean you should buy them in the bargain bin. When I finally sprang for a super-expensive professional paintbrush, I was surprised to notice that it held more paint, laid the paint down more quickly, spattered less, and gave me a better job. On top of that, it'll outlast the cheapies I used to buy.

Here are the basic painting tools you need (we'll describe the tools and materials you'll need for preparation in the next chapter):

Roller tray: Holds paint for the roller.

9-inch roller: The basic tool for covering walls. Use a smooth nap for a smooth surface and a heavier nap for a rougher surface.

Roller extension: An adjustable pole, useful for painting ceilings without ladders and walls without bending. Also easier on the wrists.

1-inch trim brush: For fine trim. Use natural bristle for oil-based materials and synthetic bristle for water-based materials.

2¹/₂-inch brush: For cutting in before rolling. The angled bristles help you get into tight spots.

Drop cloth: For protecting walls, floors, windows, and so on. Note: A canvas drop cloth is less slippery than plastic, but it's more expensive. An old bed sheet on top of plastic is a cheaper alternative that gives much better traction and contains drips and small spills better than plastic alone.

Stirring stick: Do you insist on an explanation?

Painter's tool: It scrapes, loosens brushes, and, best of all, cleans rollers like no other tool.

You may also need scrapers, ladders, a hammer and nail, masking tape, newspaper, a fan for ventilation, and a screwdriver for removing and replacing electrical cover plates.

Brushes and rollers are the painter's best friend.

A. Drop cloth

B. Roller tray

C. Roller extension

D. 9-inch roller

E. 2¹/₂-inch brush

F. Painter's tool

G. Paint can opener

H. Stirring stick

I. 1-inch trim brush

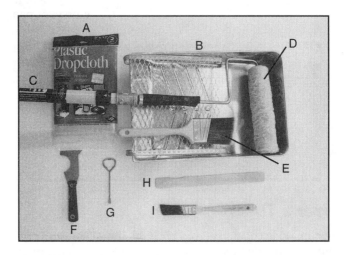

The Least You Need to Know

➤ Painting has become a lot more painless over the years with the advent of fast-drying, water-based products for many purposes.

➤ Primer looks inward; paint looks outward. That means you'll usually need both. Fortunately, some self-priming products (such as stain) serve double duty. (If you're painting over a sound coat of paint, skip the primer.)

➤ Heard the old saw about learning from your mistakes? That's advice that can save a lot of aggravation in the painting department. Understanding why things went wrong last time can prevent screw-ups this time.

Chapter 26

Lay It on—but Not Too Thick

In This Chapter

➤ The whys and wherefores of paint preparation

➤ The ins and outs of paint can etiquette

➤ The do's and don'ts of rolling, brushing, and spraying—the best ways to move paint from a can to a wall

I don't care if you're painting a single closet or a whole house—painting requires obsessive preparation. The bad news is that good prep takes time. But the good news is that it makes the painting itself a breeze, and even a delight. In fact, slipshod prep wastes so much painting time that you might as well prep it right. Not only will the paint job look infinitely better, but repainting, when that gruesome necessity finally arrives, will be far less labor-intensive.

Painting is much more straightforward than, say, plumbing or even rocketry. Still, some of the tricks of the trade revealed in this chapter can make painting a smoother, briefer, and more satisfying experience.

Preparation: The Key to Success

Paint prep involves protecting things from the paint, removing crud from the surface, fixing flaws, and putting on primer or sealer (see "Primers and Finish Coats" table in Chapter 25). The first step in prep work is to solve any problems in the substrate or previous coating. Depending on the condition of the room or exterior surface, you may have to do one of these:

➤ Scrape peeling paint.

➤ Sand alligatored paint.

➤ Attack rust with a wire brush or steel wool.

➤ Sand glossy surfaces. (Most paint adheres poorly to slick surfaces; you'll need to dull them first with sandpaper or a chemical dulling agent. See Chapter 9, "Fast Guide to Fasteners," for information on choosing sandpaper.)

➤ Kill fungus with diluted household bleach.

➤ Wash the surface.

➤ Repair trim, gutters, windows, and so on.

➤ Patch plaster or drywall.

➤ Repair and refasten siding.

➤ Prime nail heads.

➤ Mask and otherwise protect the surroundings.

These are the common tools and supplies for paint prep:

Paint scraper: The No. 1 enemy of peeling paint.

Steel wool: Removes rust from metal and smoothes interior surfaces between coats.

Window scraper: Holds a razor for cleaning paint from windows; saves endless masking.

Sandpaper: Removes or roughens old paint, smoothes wood or filler, and smoothes between coats.

Sanding belt: For quick smoothing of wood in a belt sander.

Hand wire brush: For removing peeling paint and rust.

Drill-mounted wire brush: For faster removal of paint and rust.

Masking tape: Keeps paint off light switches, outlets, and baseboard; attaches other masking, such as newspaper and plastic.

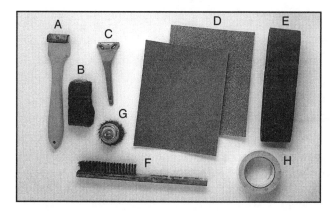

Paint prep stuff.

A. Paint scraper

B. Steel wool

C. Window scraper

D. Sandpaper

E. Sanding belt

F. Hand wire brush

G. Wire brush for an electric drill

H. Masking tape

Preparing for an Inside Job

Prep often takes more time than the actual painting because the goal is to get the room so paint-proof that you can do an aerobic paint job without hassle or stumbling over tools. In general, when you paint inside, you should start with the ceiling, then move to the walls, trim, baseboard, and floor. Here are several suggestions for interior preparation:

➤ Remove everything portable. Pile heavy furniture in the center, and cover it with a plastic dropcloth—then with a cloth or a second plastic dropcloth. (I don't trust plastic enough to use just one layer.)

➤ Assemble your ladders, tools, lights, and paint.

➤ Scan the surfaces for defects by holding a light bulb close to the wall. Then repair them, using suggestions in the section "Filling Holes in Wood," in Chapter 11, "Wood: Still Champ After All These Years"; also see the section "Repairing Nicks and Gouges," in Chapter 22, "Cosmetology 101: Drywall and Plaster Repair." Prime all patches unless you used "no-prime" patching.

➤ Clean all surfaces with trisodium phosphate or similar material (sold at paint stores), and then rinse and dry. Keep the solution out of electrical boxes.

➤ Remove outlet covers, switch plates, and light fixtures. Put masking tape across outlets and switches, and anything else you don't want to paint.

➤ Cover the floor with plastic and/or cloth dropcloths. If you're painting the ceiling, cover the entire floor. For walls only, cover out at least 3 to 4 feet from each wall. For a floor you really care about, put down plastic first, then a cloth dropcloth. The cloth absorbs the drips so that paint won't be tracked around the house, and the plastic is a barrier of last resort.

➤ Rip newspaper into 6- to 8-inch strips, and tape them on top of the baseboard so that the newspaper extends above the floor masking. If you're painting the ceiling, mask door frames and windows (but leave a slit for ventilation).

➤ If you can't be bothered masking every pane on a window (I certainly can't), return soon after the paint dries and scrape the glass with a single-edge razor blade or window scraper.

➤ Set up lights and open some windows.

Preparing for an Outside Job

Preparing for exterior painting and staining can be complicated, and I can offer only suggestions here. Again, the general sequence is stripping, patching, cleaning, masking, and painting. But outside, you've got to deal with more variables—and probably more scraping. If you need suggestions on repairing siding, consult Chapter 14, "Beauty's Only Skin Deep: Care and Healing for Your Siding."

After you examine an exterior paint project, you may decide it's not for you (see the section "Are You Ready for This Job?" later on in this chapter). If you decide to go ahead, plot your strategy. Will you scrape and prep one side at a time so you don't have to schlep so many ladders? Will you scrape the whole house and then return for the repairs so that you won't need to keep so many tools in action at once?

Power Washing

The best way to prepare a house for painting is to rent a power washer. With a gasoline engine producing water pressure in excess of 2,000 pounds per square inch, this device can cause serious bodily injury. Power washing will remove grime and chalking without detergent. If you have mildew (black blotches that come off with a solution of one part bleach to nine parts water), use the bleach solution and then the power washer.

Be sure to rent extension nozzles to let you reach the top of the house without climbing a ladder. Wear goggles and clothes that can get wet—they will. Hold the washer with two hands and start from the top, spraying in a downward direction when you can. Gradually move the nozzle closer to the wall until you get enough cleaning action. Don't gouge wood, as most amateurs tend to do. Avoid the 0° nozzles, which produce way too much pressure for house-washing purposes.

Finally, let your house dry for a week in good drying weather before painting.

Observe these don'ts of power washing:

➤ Don't use the washer as a paint scraper. Although it will remove some paint, the high-pressure washer will inevitably gouge the wood. Best bet: After washing, return and scrape by hand.

➤ Don't spray near lights and other electrical devices. Keep the spray at least 6 feet from the service (entrance) cables.

➤ Don't spray from a ladder; the recoil could knock you off balance.

➤ Don't spray into open windows, soffit vents, or other cracks and openings.

➤ Don't power-wash a house with leaded paint (this nasty stuff was banned in 1978).

➤ Don't spray hardboard siding; it's extremely sensitive to moisture and easy to gouge.

A Word on Scraping and Stripping

I hope power washing is enough to prepare your house and that you don't need to do a lot of scraping and stripping before the new coat goes on. If you've got heavily alligatored, peeling, or flaking paint, you may need one or both techniques.

The first step is to try a hand scraper. It's a little-known fact that a sharp scraper will remove more paint (and gouge more wood if you're not careful), so remove the blade and sharpen it with a metal file, holding the blade tightly in a vise. Then check out the improved action.

If scraping fails, you can up the ante to a wire brush (if the one on your drill is not powerful enough, put a wire brush in a rented, portable grinder). Use eye protection with any wire brush.

Don't Screw Up!

Scraping or stripping paint that was made before 1978 can bring you face to face with lead, a nerve poison that's particularly dangerous to children. Unless a good laboratory or a reliable test kit tells you otherwise, assume that old paint contains lead. Some municipalities restrict the washing or scraping of leaded paint; consult a building inspector for details.

From here on, the options get even nastier: a chemical stripper, a heat gun, or a propane torch. Each of these methods has disadvantages: The chemical stripper is toxic and expensive, the heat gun is slow, and the propane torch is dangerous. As we used to say as kids, "It's a free country." (Translated: I'm not making this choice for you.)

Application the Easy Way

Now that you've taken care of painting's dirty business—prep—it's time for the fun stuff: buying some paint and splashing it on. (If you need advice on using ladders, see the section "Basic Steps to Ladder Safety," in Chapter 6, "Health, Safety, and Common Sense.") With those final parts of preparation out of the way, it's time to start painting like a pro.

Some Colorful Advice

Light-colored interior paint gets dirty with age, so the same tint fresh from the can will not match. To patch a small area without repainting the entire room, take some chips of the old paint to a paint store for a match. Or, use this quick and dirty solution: Darken some of the original paint by decanting some into a yogurt container (you *have* been saving them, haven't you?). Then blend in a few drops of a dark paint made with a compatible base (that is, alkyd with alkyd, or latex with latex). Even if you don't get a perfect match, the color will be much closer.

For an entire re-painting job, examine paint samples in the light of the actual area you're going to paint. When you find a good combination, apply a quart of all colors to see how they really work. If you don't like the choice, it will be much cheaper to change your mind now—before you buy 10 custom-tinted gallons.

Paint Can Etiquette

Opening, using, and closing paint cans seems the most trivial part of painting. But if you want to do it cleanly and efficiently, follow these hints:

➤ When you first open a can, punch holes in the rim with a finishing nail. This allows the paint to drain from the rim (see the following photo).

The neatest paint can in history.

Using a sharp nail, hammer half a dozen holes in the paint can rim—before it's full of paint. This will keep the rim clean so you can actually close the can with an airtight seal.

➤ When pouring paint into a container or roller tray, immediately swipe up the drip with your brush. Clean the brush on the can rim.

➤ Before closing a can, wipe out the rim with a brush. Then hammer the lid closed. Don't pull a Neanderthal act: If the rim is clean, tapping is plenty of force to get the lid closed. How do you know it's closed? The lid will be flush with the can top.

➤ If you have more than one can of paint, mix ("box") them together so they all have the same color.

➤ For solvent-thinned paint: If the can is damaged, the rim contains dry paint, or the can has been open for a while, dump the mineral spirits you used in the brush-cleaning ceremony into the can, and then stir and close the can. When some solvent evaporates in storage, enough should remain in the paint to prevent a skin from forming.

Brushing

If you think I'm going to waste precious pages telling you how to brush paint, you're wrong. But I will paint a word picture of what I've learned in the course of painting dozens of houses.

➤ Tap the brush against the inside of the can to remove extra paint. Drawing it against the lid removes too much paint and harms the bristles.

➤ Use a paint bucket or another smaller container so you don't have to drag an entire gallon around with you. This greatly reduces the consequences of dropping a can, too.

➤ To get paint into corners, press a loaded brush into the corner, give it a bit of a shimmy to coat both adjacent surfaces, as shown in the photo on feeling cornered, and pull it off toward a flat area as the brush starts to dry out.

Nail It Down

To get a smooth surface with high-gloss paint, wait until the first coat is dry, and lightly polish it with extra-fine sandpaper or steel wool to remove bubbles and dust.

➤ On complex shapes and vertical sections, return for a quick brushing after a couple minutes. Brush in broad strokes to remove extra paint and prevent drips.

➤ Move the brush rapidly; don't start to smooth the paint until you have delivered enough to cover a relatively large area.

➤ Solvent-based paint thickens quickly in the can. If you don't thin it, the paint layer will get extremely thick. Besides, who wants to paint with molasses?

➤ On wood, stroke with the grain. Put plenty of paint on end grain, which soaks up paint and stain very quickly.

➤ To brush a broad area, quickly paint a pattern of stripes across the grain with a full brush, as shown in the photo of brushing a broad area. Then, without dipping the brush back into the can, stroke with the grain to merge the stripes and cover a large area.

➤ To hold a paint can on a ladder, cut notches in both ends of a 4-foot broom handle. Slip the handle through the rungs, and slip the bail into a notch.

➤ Lightly sand with fine or extrafine sandpaper between coats to eliminate bubbles and roughness.

Feeling cornered by corners? With a fairly heavy load of paint, place the brush in the corner and, with the bristle ends stationary, flick your wrist to one side so the bristles paint both sides of the corner. It's even easier than it sounds.

Gob the brush full of paint, and apply a series of parallel stripes across the grain (on wood). Without getting more paint, quickly brush in the perpendicular direction. A relatively small brush can cover large areas quickly with this trick.

Rolling

Rollers are the king of the interior painting hustle—it's hard to imagine painting walls with anything else. Even decks, siding, and floors can all be covered quickly with a roller. Nevertheless, rollers do have a few limitations:

➤ They spatter.

➤ They leave a stippled pattern (although you can smooth the wall with a light brushing afterwards).

➤ They stir up bubbles in some coatings, such as polyurethane varnish.

➤ They are a real bear to clean.

For basic rolling, you'll need a roller, a pan, a trim brush, and a stepladder; I would strongly suggest a roller handle extension, which reduces wrist fatigue and eliminates stooping.

Nuts and Bolts

Cutting in is not about lines or queues but about painting corners, where a roller can't reach. Cut in with a $1^1/_2$- to $2^1/_2$-inch brush, and then immediately roll the area. Or, roll and then cut in, which seems to work better for me.

1. With a $1^1/_2$- to $2^1/_2$-inch brush, cut in the edges and corners of the section you will roll first.

2. Evenly load the roller in the pan. (If you leave the roller drenched in the pan, one side will be all gooped up and the other side will be dry. When you are not working, always rest the roller in the shallow end of the roller pan, not the deep end.

3. With your first strokes, make a long "W," gradually increasing the pressure. Distribute the paint across a wide area—don't concentrate on one spot. Roll perpendicular to the "W" pattern, widening the area. Use lighter strokes so the edge of the roller does not leave ridges.

4. Roll horizontally near the baseboard to safely get within a couple of inches of the trim.

Spraying

Even if you're not a gang-tagger or graffiti artist, spray paint in a can can be handy stuff, particularly for small jobs, intricate surfaces, and metal, where brush strokes always show up. You don't need a Ph.D. to spray paint, but here are some suggestions:

➤ Shake the can thoroughly before starting, and occasionally while painting.

➤ Start the spray before the can starts to pass over the surface, and do not let up the spray until it has passed beyond the surface.

➤ Move your hand parallel to the surface; don't swing in an arc, which causes unevenness and sags.

➤ Keep the can moving, spraying light, sag-proof coats. Cover the whole surface, and give each part a few seconds to dry.

➤ When done, hold the can upside-down and spray until the stream is clear. Then wipe the spray nozzle with a rag, and cap the can. Then the nozzle will actually work when you next use it.

Test Your Mettle Painting Metal

As the old advertisement said, rust never sleeps, and while prep is important for any painting, it's crucial for painting iron and steel. The better you scrape and wire-brush iron and steel, the longer you can defer the next paint job. Unfortunately, with iron and steel, it's usually not a matter of *if* the rust is going to reappear—it's a matter of *when*.

I'm sure chemists have another way to explain it, but iron atoms in wrought iron and steel have a sick fascination with oxygen—a fascination that winds up in the unhappy atomic marriage we call rust. The surface of aluminum also oxidizes, but the oxide sticks around to do something useful: Protect the metal from further oxidation. Thus, aluminum needs less protection than iron and steel.

To paint iron and steel, you need to get the surface as clean and dry as possible, and then put on a rust-inhibiting primer. You'll need a scraper, an electric drill with a wire brush, goggles, primer and paint (liquid or spray), and dropcloths or masking. If you're really obsessed, rent a high-speed grinder with a wire brush, but use this brawny tool gingerly until you get the hang of it. For a superior job, warm the metal with a hair dryer, propane torch, or heat gun before painting. This drives out moisture (water retained in metal is the major cause of paint failure in iron and steel). Don't paint on a windy, rainy, or cold day.

Here's how to clean up the rust and apply the paint:

1. Scrape big globs of rust, and then put on your goggles and wire-brush all loose rust. If your drill has variable speed, run it flat out (as shown in the accompanying photo). A wire brush mounted on a drill is great for removing rust. Wear goggles.

2. Use sandpaper if you want to smooth paint at the margins of the repair.

3. Mask the surroundings as needed.

4. Warm the metal, particularly in damp conditions, to remove trapped moisture. If you use a propane torch, move it rapidly across the surface so you don't damage the existing paint. Get the metal warm but not too hot to touch.

5. Spray metal primer onto the warm, bare metal, overlapping onto painted areas. Keep the can a steady distance from the work, and move it parallel to the surface (not in an arc). Lay on a thin coat, and then repeat (see the accompanying photo).

6. When the primer is dry, paint the whole thing with finish paint.

Wearing gloves and goggles, wire-brush with your drill at high speed to clean up rust. Note the two-handed grip needed because the drill tends to wander.

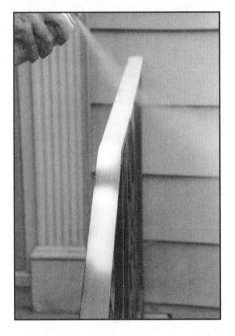

Spray metal primer with quick strokes to avoid build-up. Return several times to each area—even a few seconds of drying reduces sags.

More suggestions for painting outdoor metal:

➤ For small amounts of rust, use a rust-removing compound called naval jelly.

➤ After all this work, don't scrimp on the quality of the primer and paint. Always use a rust-inhibitive primer.

➤ Many metal enamels take a few weeks to harden, so give your new paint job a chance to mature before you abuse it.

Cleaning Brushes and Rollers

I hope cleaning brushes is not your favorite part of painting—I'm not crazy about giving advice to cleanliness freaks. I hate cleaning brushes, too, particularly after a sweaty day on the ladder. But there's one thing worse than cleaning brushes, and that's wasting money to buy new ones because I forgot to clean them the last time around. Here are some hints for keeping brushes and rollers clean:

➤ Don't let the tools get caked and dry—clean or soak them immediately after painting (if they do get caked, use brush cleaner).

➤ Add a bit of dish soap to water when you clean latex paint from brushes and rollers.

➤ Flick the brush against a log or board to remove the last bit of paint. (Or, buy a brush spinner, which does about the same thing, but with considerably more style and expense.)

➤ If you're planning to paint again tomorrow, freeze the brushes, or add some water or thinner and wrap them securely in plastic bags. Likewise, you can seal a roller and pan in a couple of plastic bags to prevent a lot of cleaning (a roller cover will disintegrate after a few days of immersion, but you can just heave it at that point).

➤ Use a painter's tool to clean a roller—the tool can pay for itself in one paint job.

➤ Prevent a skin from forming in the can by adding a couple of tablespoons of water to latex paint. For solvent-based paint, add some of the solvent used for cleaning the brush.

➤ When brushes are dry, wrap them in folded newspaper to straighten their bristles. Use a finishing nail, painter's tool, or trowel to loosen up the deep part of brushes, where paint solidifies. Store brushes flat, or hang them from a nail.

➤ Cut stray bristles from a brush with a scissors before using.

Are You Ready for This Job?

Painting can be an enjoyable diversion for a weekend or two, or it can be a miserable waste of a summer, an endless drudge that drags you away from the inner essence of summer—novels, biking, and canoeing. By the time you buy the paint and prep materials, rent the ladders, and devote several weekends to a project, you may find you've spent more in time and money than a pro would have cost you. These pointers may help you decide whether you really want to tackle a painting project:

➤ Preparation is the wild card. Badly deteriorated surfaces are a pain to prepare; if you can't face that chore, pay somebody to do it.

➤ How much heavy-duty repair (rotten soffits or window frames, moth-eaten trim) is required? Do you have the tools, skills, and time to handle this phase of the job?

➤ Renting a power washer can save a lot of time and aggravation, but be sure to allow time for drying.

➤ A big paint job may call for a lot of ladders, which you'll have to buy, beg, borrow, or rent. Warning: Scrimping on ladders can be dangerous if it causes you to overreach or to use ladders that are in poor condition.

➤ Exterior painting is mostly a spring and fall sport. Except in the warmest climates, winter is out; except in the coolest climates, midsummer is out. And you can't work on rainy or muggy days, either. Plan your schedule carefully.

The Least You Need to Know

➤ Just as possession is nine-tenths of the law, preparation is nine-tenths of painting. Don't open the paint can until you have everything clean, exposed, patched, primed, or covered.

➤ Although brushing and rolling look like real idiot work, it's goal-oriented stuff. A few basic techniques can save significant time and make the new paint job last many years longer.

➤ Iron and steel are the biggest challenge in home painting. Although rust may win in the end, the cleaner the surface, the slower its victory will be.

Part 5

Mechanicals for Non-Mechanics

At one time houses were built of lumber, nails, and hardware—and not much else. Nowadays, though, that simple list has been joined by the "mechanical" components. Think of these as your home's nervous and circulatory systems: The wiring, plumbing, and heating equipment.

I'm not going to pretend that reading a few chapters will make you into a mechanical repair whiz; mechanical problems can be a lot more subtle and confusing than a leaking roof. But there's still room for savings in the mechanical department, as you'll learn in this last part of the book. Electrical repairs, for example, are much simpler than their reputation. And even in plumbing and heating, you can save big money with small repairs and avoid the humiliation that comes from paying that miserable "job charge" for a technician to inform you, after a 30-second inspection, that your problem is a blown breaker or a closed valve.

Chapter 27

Breaker, Breaker on the Wall: Electric Fundamentals

In This Chapter

➤ Electrical jargon you must know (all meat, no fat!)

➤ Working safely with your electric system

➤ Understanding your grounding system

As with masonry and plumbing, electric repair has a sinister reputation. First of all, it's confusing because everything happens behind the scenes (or the walls, at any rate). And electricity is generally invisible until it's put to use (or, it *should* be invisible—seeing electricity in action usually means sparks at best, and fires or shocks at worst).

But a little understanding goes a long way in an electric repair. If you follow the instructions in this chapter and don't do things that confuse you (see the section "When Do You Need Electrical Help?" in Chapter 28, "Getting Wired Without Getting Zapped"), you should be able to handle most basic repairs. Fact is, wiring repairs are much simpler than most people think; in many cases, the major challenge is distinguishing black and white (wires, that is). Granted, things get confusing if you dig up buried mistakes, but that's one reason you bought this book, right?

Basic Stuff You Must Know

A book for complete idiots shouldn't be freighted with irrelevant theory—after all, who wants to read about Michael Faraday's dazzling insights into electricity when the light over the stove is flickering? Still you've got to know a few things when you want to work with whizzing electrons.

Don't Screw Up!

Your local electric code may require that a licensed and certified electrician make repairs or install new work in your dwelling, particularly in a rental unit. Ask the building inspector who handles electrical work about your situation.

First of all, the control panel for your electrical system is the fuse box, or the circuit-breaker box. These boxes use slightly different means to serve the same functions:

➤ Shut off all electricity to the house

➤ Route incoming electricity to the various circuits in your home

➤ Allow you to shut off individual circuits

➤ Control how much current (how many amps) can flow on each circuit

Fuses are one-time protectors that must be replaced when they "blow" after carrying excess current. Circuit breakers are handier because they can be switched back on after they trip. A fuse box or breaker box is rated by the maximum number of amperes (amps) it can handle; 100 amps is the minimum in new construction. Some states require that the service be upgraded to 100 amps when a house is sold.

Going Around in Circles with Circuits

Electricity can travel only in a circuit. This is a loop of conductor (mostly wire) that connects a source of electricity (in other words, the electric generator) to a load (say, a lamp, toaster, or motor) and then back to the source. Although circuits get hideously complicated in computers and space-shuttle control rooms, in houses they are essentially a loop from the hot side of the breaker box to a load, and back to the ground side of the breaker box. This loop is shown in the first illustration in this chapter. (This figure does not show the grounding conductor, which allows electricity to return to the source if metal components, such as electrical boxes, come in contact with the hot side.)

Nuts and Bolts

A **load** is anything that uses electricity in a curcuit. A circuit must have a load if current is flowing—otherwise, you've got a short circuit.

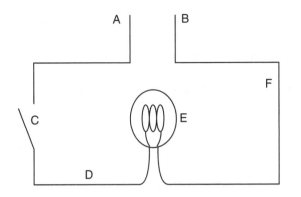

Parts of a circuit. A circuit must connect a source to a load and back to a source.

A. Source (hot side)

B. Source (grounded side)

C. Switch (shown open)

D. Hot wire (black)

E. Load (a light is shown, but it can be a motor, heater, or something similar)

F. Grounded wire (white)

Two principles govern the behavior of electricity in circuits:

➤ Electricity must return to its source. That's why you need a circuit—you can't just connect a hot wire to a light and figure that you've satisfied the National Electric Code. Not only won't the light light, but the electricity will try to improvise a way back to the source. Danger!

➤ Each circuit needs a load, such as a motor, light, or heating element. Otherwise, you have a short circuit—a connection between hot and ground without the resistance of a load. That's another recipe for disaster.

And Now for Some Lingo

You can't talk about electricity without some jargon. Fortunately, electrician's jargon is less fearsome than the average scientific mumbo-jumbo. You need to know only a few basic terms, and most are already familiar (even if you can't rattle off their definitions on command).

Alternating current (AC) is used throughout your home wiring. This current changes polarity 60 times per second (60 hertz). *Direct current (DC)* is used only in cars and battery-operated stuff, and we won't worry about it. Phew!

Amps, or amperes, are a measure of how much current is flowing. Technically, 1 amp is a number of electrons flowing per second that would vastly outnumber the pennies in the national debt. (If you need to know the exact number, you're way beyond idiot territory.) Seriously, amps are important because they tell you how much current (how much "ampacity") a wire can carry. Try to squeeze too many amps through a wire, and the circuit breaker will open, the fuse will blow, or the building will burn down. Which would you prefer?

Cable talk. The average electrical cable you'll see in your house has three conductors, or wires. The black-insulated conductor is the "ungrounded," or "hot," wire. The white-insulated wire is called the "grounded conductor" (it's often called, incorrectly, the "neutral" wire). The bare wire, called the "equipment grounding conductor," is often simply called the "ground." Confusing? You bet. We'll generally use the colors, which are much simpler. See the section "On What Grounds Is It Grounded?" later in this chapter, for guidance on grounding. See the section "Cable and Conduit," also later in this chapter, for more on cable varieties.

Volts are units of pressure, of how hard the electrons are trying to get around the circuit. Most home circuits carry 120 volts. Because the same wire can carry more power at higher voltage, heavy-duty heating appliances such as stoves, dryers, and water heaters use 240 volts.

Watts are units of power used to rate things that consume electricity, such as lamps, appliances, and tools. The basic formula is volts × amps = watts. That means a 120-volt circuit carrying 5 amps supplies 600 watts (120 × 5 = 600).

➤ *Wattage ratings*, carried on electrical appliances, tell you if a particular circuit has enough capacity for the job. If watts ÷ volts = amps, how many amps does a 1,500-watt saw draw? 1,500 watts ÷ 120 volts = 12.5 amps (which is near the 15-amp capacity of the typical home circuit). To find how many watts a circuit is supplying, simply add the number of watts drawn by each appliance plugged into that circuit. Then divide by 120 (for a 120-volt circuit) to get amps. Note that electrical devices only draw current when they're on.

➤ Incidentally, a *kilowatt hour*, the unit by which your electric utility enriches itself, is the flow of 1000 watts (1 kilowatt) for one hour, or the equivalent. A 100-watt bulb burning for 10 hours consumes 1 kilowatt hour.

Electricians also use some other lingo that's so handy we might as well define it here. A *breaker* is slang for a circuit breaker. To *reset* a breaker means to return it to operating position after it has *tripped* (disconnected after excess current flowed in the circuit). *Receptacle* is electrician-speak for what the rest of us call an *outlet*, a place to plug in an electrical cord. To electricians, an *outlet* is a receptacle *or* a switch.

Wire Size (Gauge) (Now Life Gets Confusing ...)

Wire is sized by an ancient and bass-ackwards system called *gauge*. Gauge tells you ampacity—how much current, as measured in amps—a wire can carry (a wire can carry the same number of amps at either 120 or 240 volts). Most home wiring is 12- or 14-gauge, although heavy-duty, 240-volt circuits usually use 10-gauge wire. (Why are lower-gauge wires bigger than wires with higher gauges? Because I promised this would be backwards ....)

Why should you care about wire size? It determines how much juice a circuit can carry, and also what size breaker or fuse you need to protect that circuit. Overloaded wires can get hot enough to burn. Note: Most receptacles and switches are made for 15-amp circuits; you'll need to buy special devices for 20-amp circuits. The following table lists the capacity and uses of common wire gauges. If cables are installed under insulation in conditions hotter than 86° F, or if more than three current-carrying conductors are together, the ampacity will be less than these guidelines.

Copper Wire Gauges, Capacities, and Uses

Gauge of Wire	Capacity in Amps (Equals Breaker or Fuse Rating)	Typical Uses
Copper		
10	30	240-volt circuits: Clothes dryer, range, central air conditioning, and water heater
12	20	120-volt circuits: Kitchens, workshops, and other heavy loads
14	15	120-volt general household circuits
Aluminum	Capacity in Amps	
12	15	
10	20	

Cable and Conduit

A *cable* is a group of several conductor wires inside one sheath. Modern cable, called *romex*, has a plastic sheath that usually contains one black wire, one white wire, and one bare copper wire.

Each wire is a separate electrical component. The grounded conductor (white wire) and the equipment grounding conductor (bare wire) are connected to the same place on the fuse or breaker box, but they have different jobs. The white is the normal return path on a circuit. The bare wire gives electricity a return path if insulation fails in a tool or appliance and the hot wire contacts something conductive, such as an appliance's frame.

An older form of cable is a coiled steel sheath that's called armored cable, or BX. BX made after about 1942 contains a special, uninsulated bonding wire to carry the ground. You may see this bond conductor poking through the clamp securing the cable to the box, and it's a good thing to see because it combines with the cable sheath to provide the ground. If this conductor is absent, it's *not safe* to use the steel sheath as a ground; this circuit is technically not grounded. A circuit tester may light when connected between the hot wire and the sheath, but this does not prove that enough ampacity exists to carry a current if an electrical box or appliance housing gets hot for whatever reason.

Cable is designated by two numbers. The first is the gauge, and the second is the number of insulated wires (conductors) in the cable (the ground wire is not counted). Thus, 12–2 cable has two 12-gauge conductors, and 14–2 has two 14-gauge conductors. 14–3 cable, with black, white, and red 14-gauge conductors, is used for three-way switches.

If you're wiring outdoors or underground, buy the special, ultraviolet resistant cable made for outdoor use.

Conduit is a light steel pipe that protects insulated wires. It is usually seen in basements and garages. Conduit needs no equipment grounding wire because the steel itself supplies the ground connection. Although you would need special skills and tools to work on conduit, you can easily connect romex cable to boxes wired with conduit.

Some older houses have an outdated, ungrounded "knob and tube" wiring scheme. The insulated but unsheathed wires are attached to insulated knobs mounted on the framing. The wires pass through ceramic tubes drilled into the framing. Knob and tube is legal, according to the National Electrical Code, if it's in good condition and *not covered by insulation*. Still, if I saw this stuff in my house (and trust me, I have), I'd seriously consider replacing it immediately to avoid the possibility of it shorting out. Replacing this stuff is a pro job, and an expensive one. But if you've got knob and tube, the ol' place probably needs rewiring anyway. We'll give some advice on bringing wiring up to date in Chapter 28.

Safety

I had a physics teacher in high school who warned us to work on electricity with one hand behind our backs. This was a memorable way of stressing that the most dangerous kind of shock is one that passes through your heart, as happens when a current passes in one arm and out the other.

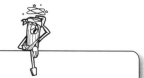

Don't Screw Up!

What's the big fuss about electrical fires? If you want to see how much heat an electric circuit can carry, remember those brighter-than-the-sun, burn-your-eyeballs sparks produced by an arc welder. That's the power of electricity. Then you'll pay more attention to good wiring and to selecting the right circuit breaker or fuse.

Let's honor the memory of Mr. Singer by avoiding shocks altogether, whether we're working on an electrical system or living with it. To do this, we must understand electricity's desires.

The nature of electricity is to always want to move from hot (or supply) to ground along the shortest, easiest path. This is why we use circuits—because electricity needs a path back home on the ground wire.

To get a shock, you must be touching a source of current—usually a defective tool, appliance, or device. You must also be grounded, either by touching something conductive that's connected to the ground, such as a pipe or electric box, or by standing on damp soil. That's why electricians sometimes wear rubber shoes—to keep themselves from being grounded and shocked.

The Golden Rule of Electric Repair

Now it's time for the golden rule of electric repair: Do unto a cold circuit, or a hot circuit may do something shocking unto you. *In other words, shut off the power, feverbrain, before you go poking around with the juice.*

Got that?

Now for the subtle rules. Make sure you switched off the right circuit breaker or fuse before you go poking into an electric circuit (see the sections "Testing a Receptacle," "Testing a Built-In Light," and "Testing a Switch," later in this chapter).

And a few more guidelines:

➤ Use tools (screwdrivers, pliers, and strippers) with insulated plastic handles just in case something goes wrong. To be extra safe, wrap electrical tape around the shaft of your screwdriver. Test your tester before *and* after using it.

➤ Avoid being grounded (unruly teenagers will love this rule!). Keep your hands dry, and don't wade around in water when messing with electricity. Remember, you are grounded every time you touch a grounded electrical box or a metal pipe. Avoid damp floors, or insulate yourself with rubber boots if you must work on them.

➤ Don't do stuff you're not confident of.

➤ Get help when you need it.

Living with Electricity

A good electric system is pretty hardy, but there's no point in trying to see how far you can push it. Here are some ways to reduce your family's electrical worries:

➤ Locate your main disconnect, the switch or fuse that controls all power to your house. It's your last line of defense in an electrical emergency, when you can't stop to figure out which circuit is causing the difficulty.

➤ Don't overload circuits (see the previous section "Wire Size [Gauge]").

➤ Never, ever solve your blown fuse or tripped breaker problems by installing a fuse or breaker with a higher rating than the circuit can handle.

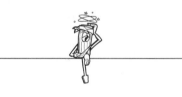

Don't Screw Up!

Don't use acid flux or acid-core solder in electrical work. These materials, used in plumbing, will cause corrosion and eventual destruction of an electrical joint. Instead, use resin flux and/or resin-core solder. Save soldering for repairing knob and tube wiring; electrical connectors are safer and easier for all other purposes.

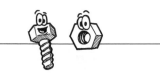

Nuts and Bolts

The **main disconnect** is the switch or fuse controlling all electricity entering your home. In a circuit-breaker box, it's marked "Main," or "100," or "200" (or however many amperes your system supplies). In a fuse box, it's the big black fuse-holder marked "Main." To shut off power, flip the switch or pull out the fuse holder.

➤ Don't hide junction boxes.

➤ Don't run extension cords under carpet, across doorways, or in damp areas. Also keep a close eye on cheapo extension cords; they cause lots of fires.

➤ Make sure your extension cord has enough capacity for the load. Cords are rated in amps (amps = watts ÷ volts). For the same load, a longer cord needs larger wire.

➤ Receptacles, switches, plugs, and electric cords should not get hot in use. If they do, investigate and fix or replace them. (However, some dimmer switches do warm up after operating for a while.)

➤ Ungrounded receptacles (two-prong) are hazardous, particularly in damp locations. In bathrooms, in kitchens, and outdoors, install a ground-fault circuit interrupter (GFCI) receptacle which prevents shock by immediately shutting off if current leaks. See "Updating an Ungrounded Receptacle" in Chapter 28.

➤ If you have young kids, install plastic protectors in any receptacles they can reach. Keep an eye out for kids who think it's fun to stick keys in a receptacle (they'll do this, actually).

Toolbox Trivia

The prongs of modern electrical plugs and outlets are not created equal. The small rectangular prong or hole carries the hot current, the large rectangular prong or hole carries the grounded leg, and the round prong or hole carries the equipment ground. Electronic devices care which wire is which, so be sure to religiously connect black (hot) to the brass screws on a receptacle, and white (grounded) to the silver-colored screws. Even if you don't use any electronics, safety requires keeping this polarity straight.

310

Testing a Receptacle

When it comes to electrical repairs, testing is the essence of safety. Thus, we'll offer tests for receptacles, lights, and switches, in that order. The tests will tell: a) whether a receptacle is wired correctly, and b) whether it is cold and safe to work on. The tests sound harder than they actually are, but if you do them right, you'll be breathing easier (ditto for your life insurance agent).

Growing up, one of my daddy's-helper tasks was helping shut off the current before Dad started tearing apart the electrical boxes. More precisely, my role was to bellow downstairs when the light or receptacle went off, meaning that he had cut off the right breaker. When my first son, Alex, was too young for this kind of hollering (it was the only form of shouting he disdained!) and I worked alone, I plugged a portable radio going full blast into the receptacle. Then I'd go downstairs and flip circuit breakers until a silence indicated the right circuit. This trick can even help shut down circuits for built-in lights. Just plug the radio into a receptacle near the light, and when it goes silent, the light circuit is probably dead, because nearby outlets are often on the same circuit. Before doing any work, though, test the receptacle or light circuit anyway, as described below—always.

The following procedure uses a $3 circuit tester, but you can save time with an EMF tester or an outlet tester (they're described in the section "Electrical Tools and Materials," in Chapter 28). You'll also need a working grounded receptacle, a screwdriver, and a grounded (three-wire) extension cord. Read the accompanying Toolbox Trivia to identify the hot, grounded, and equipment grounding slots, and then start here:

1. Go to a working receptacle, and plug in your extension cord, as shown in the accompanying photo on testing a receptacle. Stick one prong of your circuit tester in each rectangular slot of the extension cord. You may have to move the tester prongs around to get good contact. If the tester lights, the tester works. (Always keep your fingers away from the bare metal on the tester leads. And remember to always test your tester after this procedure.)

Don't Screw Up!

An electrical tester detects voltage differences between two points. If both the hot and ground slot of a receptacle are cold for some reason, the detector will not light up—an accurate reading. But if both are *hot*, it still will won't light up—a misleading reading. That's one reason to use the elaborate testing procedure we described.

Nail It Down

Test your circuit tester by inserting the leads into a receptacle you know is working. The light should light between the hot and the grounded legs. If not, clean any crud or corrosion from the leads, and retest. If it's junk, trash it. Test again after use so that you know it's *still* working.

2. Test between the hot (short slot) and the round, equipment grounding opening of the cord. If the light comes on, the receptacle is wired correctly and grounded, and the extension cord is working.

3. Leave the extension cord plugged in. Go to the suspect receptacle. If it's controlled by a switch, turn it on.

Continue here to test that a *receptacle is wired correctly*:

4. Check for power between the hot leg of the cord (the shorter slot) and the cover mounting screw and the ground slot. If there's no light, the receptacle's grounding system is faulty.

5. Check for power between the grounded (long) slot of the cord and both hot (short) slots of the receptacle. If there's no power, the receptacle is not powered, or the ground and hot are wired backwards. To correct this reversed polarity, cut the power and exchange the wires feeding the receptacle. Black (hot) should connect to the brass screws, and white (grounded) to the silver-colored screws.

6. Test between the hot leg of the cord and the grounded (long) slot on the receptacle. If there's no power, the ground is interrupted, which is a major violation. The cause could be a bad device, a bad splice, or a poorly wired device. Find and fix the problem immediately; it may reside in this box or in a nearby box.

Don't Screw Up!

Test your tester *before and after* using it to check if a circuit is cold. Otherwise, a negative reading (no light) could simply mean that the tester is shot. Also, during all electrical work, make sure nobody absentmindedly turns a circuit back on while you're working on it.

To check that a *receptacle is cold* (the circuit is switched off at the breaker box or fuse box), continue from step 3 above:

4. Switch off the breaker, or unscrew the fuse that you think controls the receptacle.

5. Test between the grounding leg of the extension cord and all six slots of the receptacle you plan to work on. If the light comes on at any point, the receptacle is hot; disconnect another breaker or fuse, and try again. If the tester lights up at a grounded or equipment grounding opening, you have reversed polarity. Shut off the circuit, open the box, and correct the polarity.

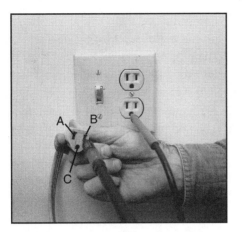

Use a grounded extension cord and a working receptacle to test another receptacle. On the receptacle and the extension cord, the long slot (A) is the grounded (return) leg, the short slot (B) is the hot (ungrounded) leg, and the round slot (C) is the equipment grounding leg.

Testing a Built-In Light

These tests can tell: a) whether a built-in light (one wired to a wall switch) is wired correctly, and b) whether it is cold and safe to work on. We'll use the same tools as in the previous section "Testing a Receptacle." Remember: Always test your tester afterwards!

1. Go to a working receptacle and plug in your extension cord, as shown in the photo on testing a receptacle. Stick one prong of your circuit tester in each rectangular slot of the extension cord. If the tester lights, the tester works. (Keep your fingers away from the uninsulated metal on the tester leads. You may have to move the tester prongs to get contact.)

2. Test between the hot (short slot) and the equipment grounding (round hole) of the cord. If the light comes on again, the receptacle is wired correctly and grounded, and the extension cord is working. Leave the extension cord plugged in.

3. With the circuit breaker or fuse on, turn the wall switch on and remove the light bulb. Test for power between the ground slot of the extension cord and metal on the body of the light. If the tester lights, the hot wire is touching the lamp body—danger! Find the problem and fix it, or pitch the light!

To check that a *built-in light is wired correctly,* continue with these steps:

4. Test between the ground slot of the extension cord and the center terminal of the lamp holder. *Don't touch* the metal screw-shell holding the lamp! If the tester lights and the wall switch turns the test light off, the switch correctly controls the receptacle (if it passes the next test as well).

5. Test between the hot leg of the extension cord and the screw-shell holding the lamp. If the tester lights, the lamp has a ground. Move the wall switch and repeat. If the test light goes off, the ground leg is switched—danger! Cut off the circuit, open the switch box, rewire the hot and grounded wires (see the section "Switches," in Chapter 28), and retest.

6. Test between the hot leg of the cord and the rest of the lamp body. Ideally, it will be grounded and the light will come on (although older lamps are seldom grounded).

Don't Screw Up!

Some electrical boxes contain wires unrelated to the fixture in the box. These wires don't connect to the fixture, and you should not touch them. If they are controlled by a different circuit breaker, *they will be hot* even after you shut off power to the fixture in the box. This occurs mainly in conduit and particularly in basements, where lots of circuits tend to originate.

To check that a *built-in light is cold*, continue here from step 3, above:

4. Turn the wall switch on. Put one tester lead in the grounded leg of the extension cord, and touch the other lead to the terminal at the base of the bulb holder. If the tester lights with the switch in either position, the light is connected to the supply wires; go to step 5. If the tester does not light, call an electrician; there is no safe way to know whether the circuit is off.

5. Turn whichever circuit breaker or fuse you think feeds the circuit off, and repeat step 4. If the tester lights, try disconnecting another circuit. If it does not light, operate the switch and retest. Once the breaker or fuse can switch the test light on and off, you have located the correct circuit. Shut the circuit off with the breaker or fuse.

Testing a Switch

These procedures will tell you whether a single-pole switch a) is wired correctly or b) is safe to work on. (One single-pole switch controls a light or appliance by itself; two three-way switches control one light. Three-way switches are generally found at each end of a stairway or hallway.) Read on to see how to test that three-way switch is cold.

1. Go to a working receptacle and plug in your extension cord, as shown in the photo on testing a receptacle. Stick one prong of your circuit tester in each slot of the extension cord (avoid the round, ground hole). If the tester lights, the tester works. (Always keep your fingers away from the uninsulated metal on the tester leads.)

2. Test between the hot (short slot) and the ground openings of the cord. If the light comes on again, the receptacle is wired correctly and grounded, and the extension cord is working. Leave the extension cord plugged in.

To test whether a *single-pole switch is wired correctly*, continue with these steps.

3. Shut off the circuit you think controls the light. Remove the switch plate, and pull the switch out slightly.

4. Test between the hot leg of the extension cord and the grounded (white) wires. If the tester lights with the switch in both positions, the ground is okay. (Only switches wired before the light—as described in the section "Switches," in Chapter 28—have white wires. Switches wired after the light have one cable, with one black wire and one white wire. Because this white serves as a hot, or black, wire it should be painted or taped black.)

5. Test for power between the hot leg of the extension cord and a) a bare wire (if present), b) the body of the switch, c) and the box—if it's metal. If the tester lights up every time, the switch is properly grounded. If no ground wire is present but the light still comes on, the box is probably grounded by BX or conduit. Switch boxes in old systems lack any ground, which is okay. If you are making major improvements, get an electrician to ground them.

6. Test from the grounding leg of the extension cord to either black wire of the switch. If the tester lights, the switch has power. To test that the *circuit is cold*, shut off circuits until the tester does not light in this situation.

To test that a *three-way switch is cold*, proceed here after step 2. (Three-way switches are easy to recognize because they have no on or off markings; two switches control one light.)

Don't Screw Up!

Old wiring was not designed for operation above 60° C (140° F). Newer light fixtures may require wire with a higher heat rating, either 75° C or 90° C. If the wire in your ceiling fixture is not labeled, it's probably 60° wiring. Do not install a fixture requiring higher heat tolerance without replacing the wire, which will mean bringing a new supply to the light from the switch.

Nail It Down

So you've religiously checked your electrical tester in a working outlet before starting your tests? Great. One final note: After you confirm that a circuit is cold, and before you take your life in your hands, check the tester one last time on the working outlet. It never hurts to be safe: The life you lose could be your own!

3. Shut the circuit off.

4. Test between the equipment grounding (round) hole of the extension cord and all three switch terminals. Flip the switch and retest all terminals. If the tester never lights, the switch is cold and safe to work on—as long as the tester is still working.

Toolbox Trivia

Your entire electrical system should be grounded—connected to the earth with two separate metal conductors. Systems are commonly grounded by connection to the water pipes, as close as possible to the pipe's entry into the house. Beware of any fittings: They may have plastic components that insulate rather than conduct. There should be a jumper cable bypassing the water meter. The second ground often goes to a long metal stake, or a piece of buried reinforcing rod. If either ground is missing, call an electrician.

On What Grounds Is It Grounded?

The ground system allows electricity to safely leave your house if a hot wire contacts a metal object, such as an electrical box or appliance case. The ground system requires a good connection to—believe it or not, Ripley—the ground! Typically this is a water pipe and a grounding stake, a long metal rod driven into the ground near your foundation. This is really a redundant safety; the major ground is supplied by one of the three conductors that supply your house from the utility.

A ground is a safety measure that comes into play only if something screws up. If, for example, the insulation on an electric tool fails while you're running it, or if water gets inside a toaster you are touching, you want the electricity to drain away through the ground wire rather than your body.

In modern systems, every electric circuit has a ground, which connects to every receptacle and metal electrical box. (Plastic boxes are not grounded, and many switches are grounded only through contact to a metal box. We'll cover more about boxes in the next chapter.) The ground conductor in a cable is easy to recognize because it's bare copper. In steel conduit, the conduit itself provides the ground. In newer BX (armored cable), a bare wire inside the sheath is the ground conductor.

The ground system should take nothing for granted. In general, the bare equipment grounding wire entering a box goes to a wire connector that connects to a) a wire grounding the box, b) a wire to the greenish hex-head screw on the body of the receptacle or switch, and c) a bare wire going to other fixtures on the circuit. (Older switches seldom have grounds.) (For information on modernizing receptacles, see the section "Updating an Ungrounded Receptacle," in Chapter 28.)

Got Aluminum Wire?

Most homes are wired with solid copper wire, a soft, light-brown metal that's an excellent conductor. But in the 1960s and early 1970s, some houses were wired with pure aluminum wire, a silver-colored metal that's cheaper than copper. This cable is usually marked "aluminum" every few feet on the outside. Aluminum wire caused a lot of house fires and is discontinued for interior use (it's still legit for service entrance cable, the stuff that connects your system to the utility).

Although aluminum wire conducts well, problems arose from its incompatibility with fixtures designed for copper. If your house has all-aluminum wire, be sure to use fixtures marked CO/ALR. (If they're hard to find, try an electrical wholesaler.) Copper-coated aluminum wire—AKA "copper-clad"—requires CU/AL type fixtures, the same ones sold for pure copper wire.

A good tactic for dealing with aluminum wires is to buy special twist-on connectors sold for connecting aluminum to copper wires. These connectors allow you to use fixtures designed for copper. The aluminum wire enters the box and is joined by the connector to a short piece of copper wire, which then connects to the switch or receptacle.

Don't Screw Up!

Never switch the white, grounded wire. It's an essential safety that allows current to drain back to the utility instead of trying to drain back through your body. Switch only hot wires, which should be black or red. White wires should be grounded, but in light circuits white may serve as a hot wire; if so, it should be tagged with black tape or paint. In wiring, don't count on nuttin'. Always test.

Diagnosing Problems

If the problem refuses to locate itself, use this troubleshooting table as guidance. Otherwise, see the section "Problems at the Circuit Breaker or Fuse Box," which follows.

Troubleshooting Table

Symptom	Cause and Cure
No power anywhere.	Power out from utility. Phone the utility.
	Main fuse blown or breaker tripped. Replace or reset.
	Main disconnect switch thrown. Check and reconnect.
Some power is out.	Blown fuse or tripped breaker. Find and replace (fuse) or reset (breaker).
Some power out, but no breaker looks tripped.	Breaker is tripped, but handle has not moved much. Flip breakers off and on until power is restored.
Some power is out, but breakers and fuses seem fine.	A switch, breaker, or fuse at a "sub-panel" has cut off the electricity. (A sub-panel is a second panel fed by the main panel.) Find the sub-panel, and turn the switch, reset the breaker, or replace the fuse.
Breaker or fuse blows repeatedly.	Disconnect everything from that circuit. If problem persists, call electrician. Otherwise, connect appliances one by one until the problem recurs; get that appliance fixed.
Fuse is melted (examine with flashlight).	Overcurrent may be due to high current needed to start a motor (such as in the refrigerator, etc.) on the circuit. If the circuit supplies a motor, replace fuse with a "time-delay" fuse designed for motors.
Fuse is blackened.	Caused by a short circuit. Find problem and repair before replacing fuse.

Problems at the Circuit-Breaker or Fuse Box

The heart of your electrical system, and its main safety feature, is the fuse box or circuit-breaker box. These boxes (you'll have one or the other, but seldom both) control the maximum amount of current flowing in the circuits, and also allow you to shut off circuits. Some common problems are described in the preceding table.

Although you want to know where the fuse or breaker box is, you don't want to be intimately familiar with it because that's a sure sign of problems. Still, it's best that problems show up at the fuse box because the alternatives are rather grim. So as you, gentle reader, stumble down the stairs with a new fuse in one hand, a flashlight in the other, and an oath on your lips, remember that the fuse that just blew may have prevented a fire. Overloaded circuits get hot fast (you could say lightning fast).

The rating of each circuit breaker or fuse depends on the size of the wires and fixtures on the circuit. Because 12-gauge copper wires can carry 20 amps, a circuit wired with 12-gauge wire and 20-amp devices should be controlled by a 20-amp fuse or circuit breaker. Similarly, because 14-gauge wire can carry 15 amps, the breaker or fuse would be rated at 15 amps. (Aluminum has less ampacity, as discussed previously.)

Breakers or fuses blow when the circuit is asked to carry too much current—due to a malfunction, or simply because too many things are drawing current. So before you screw in another fuse or switch the circuit breaker back on (reset it), try to figure out why it blew. Did you just plug in a vacuum cleaner to a circuit that was already carrying a heavy load? Plug the vacuum into a different circuit, and then restore the circuit.

Don't Screw Up!

If you feel compelled to remove the inside cover from your breaker or fuse box, get out your rubber gloves and rubber boots, and then, before you actually do anything, go to the phone and call your electrician. Unless you're in the middle of a city-wide blackout, some parts of the box may still be hot even after you throw the main disconnect.

If breakers or fuses blow once in a great while and you can figure out why, it's not something to get too excited about—that's their job. But if it happens repeatedly, or if you don't understand the reason, sniff around. Really: You may sniff the putrid burned-plastic stench of hot electrical insulation, a sure-fire sign of trouble. If this bloodhound imitation fails, try to isolate the problem by unplugging stuff from the circuit, and slowly add things back until you trip the breaker or blow the fuse. Breakers can get tired and fail to carry their rated current; these breakers need replacement. If you're confused or intimidated, there's no shame in calling 1-800-BLU-FUSE and asking for an electrician.

Toolbox Trivia

Motors draw a lot of current when starting up—enough to blow some normal fuses. If the startup of a motor in a refrigerator or other appliances is blowing fuses, try using a delay (AKA "slow blow") fuse. If that fails, move some loads to another circuit. If the fuse still blows, have a technician check out the appliance causing the problem.

Making a Circuit Map

If you're regularly blowing fuses or breakers, chances are that at least one circuit is undersized. If there's a motor on the circuit, see the previous Toolbox Trivia sidebar. Pay special attention to electrical heating devices—heaters, toasters, and coffee pots. These gadgets can slurp more juice than a dozen light bulbs.

If these hints don't help, it's time to make a circuit map, a floor plan listing the receptacles, built-in appliances, and lights on each circuit. Circuit maps are also handy for future electrical repairs because they show you which circuit to shut down (although you will *test* the circuit anyway before you dig in, won't you?).

Don't Screw Up!

A receptacle supplied by two hot wires is a "multi-wire branch circuit." In these hook-ups, most common in kitchens, the top and bottom half of the receptacle are fed by separate circuits. One half may function after a breaker has blown. However, they should be wired by a double-pole breaker, so both circuits will go off at once. Caution: *Do not* join white (grounded) wires at the receptacle in these circuits. Join the whites only with screw-on connectors; then connect a short white wire to the receptacle. If you're upgrading such a receptacle that's fed by separate breakers, consult an electrician.

To make a circuit map, you'll need a circuit tester, a clipboard, and a pen. Turn off one breaker or unscrew one fuse, and walk through the house and list which receptacles, lights, and appliances don't work. Repeat for the other circuits. Don't be surprised if circuits meander through the house; electricians often run cables so that a room has several circuits and so that a blown breaker or fuse will not darken everything in the room. Post the map near the breaker panel or fuse box.

Now add up the wattage of devices on the problem circuit, and divide by 120 (for a 120-volt circuit). The sum should be less than the amperage rating of the circuit (which is marked on the fuse or circuit-breaker handle). If it's higher than this rating, move some appliances to other circuits, put in another circuit to share the load, or call an electrician.

Be aware that most of the loads on a circuit are unlikely to be operating at once, so the circuit can feed more loads than it may seem. The big thing to watch for when making a circuit map are the heating loads from electric space heaters, toasters, and room air conditioners. These heavy, continuous loads should be served by a separate circuit.

The Least You Need to Know

➤ Electricity likes to go around in circles, or circuits. Interrupting a circuit is dangerous if it's not done correctly.

➤ The golden rule of electrical repairs is to shut off the circuit—and then test that it's really off—before opening up anything.

➤ Some elementary troubleshooting can help pin down the source of electrical problems.

➤ A circuit map can help you isolate overloaded circuits and simplify future wiring work.

Chapter 28

Getting Wired Without Getting Zapped

What does wiring have in common with politics and espionage? Like politics, it's all about connections, about working the network and finding the source of power. Like espionage, it involves deception because the electrical system should blend in with the local landscape.

But while the occasional political shock keeps people reading the papers, shocks have an entirely different meaning in electrical work. If you use your circuit tester and common sense, follow the testing guidelines in Chapter 27, "Breaker, Breaker on the Wall: Electric Fundamentals," and if you don't do things you don't understand, you'll stay out of the headlines while keeping your electrical system in top shape.

Electrical Tools and Materials

Electrical repair doesn't call for much in the way of tools, and the main ones are cheap. But don't try to skimp—get a circuit tester and a wire stripper at the absolute minimum.

A *circuit tester*, AKA electrical tester or circuit probe, is your safety net (see the accompanying photo of electrical tools). It tells you when a circuit is dead and thus safe to work on. It tells you if the ground is working. And it tells you when you've wired something correctly—all without requiring a Ph.D. on your part. The cheapest testers have short wires, or "leads"; I use one that's about 4 feet long. Occasionally that's very handy; usually it's just extra wire to get tangled. A great alternative, not shown in the photo, is an EMF tester, which can detect voltage without even touching a conductor (about $10). You can quickly check the wiring of a receptacle with a receptacle tester (under $10). Simply plug it in—the lights will tell you if the receptacle is kosher. One final point: Always test your tester, as described in Chapter 27.

Use a *soldering iron*, *resin flux*, and *electrical solder* to solder wires. Soldering guns are handy because they heat up immediately, but a 40-watt soldering iron is cheaper and plenty adequate for occasional use. Although electrical connectors are usually faster and safer, you may need soldering to repair knob and tube wiring or to connect phone cables. I'll describe how to make a solder joint later in this chapter.

You can cut romex cable with a cable shear, a pair of *tin snips*, or a big diagonal-cutting pliers. I would not buy a tool specifically for cutting cable unless I planned on doing a lot of wiring. For occasional use, the blade of big wire strippers or long-nose pliers will work just fine.

I once knew a penny-pincher who tried to do electrical work without a *wire stripper*, and he stripped insulation with a pair of cutting pliers. Half the time, after I'd worked myself into a lather fumbling with a Medusa's headful of wire, the wires broke where the pliers had nicked them. When I finally came to my senses, I was flabbergasted at the efficacy of strippers. One flick of the wrist, and you've got a shiny, stripped, intact wire. Fancier strippers have shears for cutting electrical screws, which can be handy on occasion.

A *utility knife* is useful for stripping the outer sheath from cable (not the insulation on the conductors). Cut straight down the middle of the cable so that you don't injure the insulation on the wires. You can also remove the sheath with a vegetable peeler or a romex stripper, a tool made for the purpose. Never try to remove the outer and inner insulation in one step.

You may need $1/2$- to $3/4$-inch *drill bits* to route romex cable through studs or joists. Spade bits are cheap and fast (until they hit a nail and get dulled, at any rate).

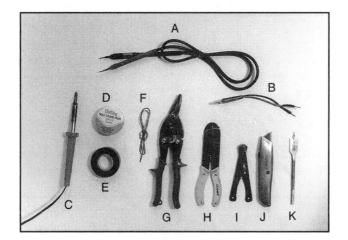

Electrical tools you may need.

A. Circuit tester, with long leads

B. Circuit tester, with short leads

C. Soldering iron

D. Resin flux

E. Electrical tape

F. Solder

G. Tin snips

H. Stripper, with wire cutter and electrical bolt cutter

I. Stripper, with wire cutter

J. Utility knife

K. $1/2$- to $3/4$-inch spade drill bit

Electrical Boxes and Paraphernalia

Electrical boxes, AKA junction boxes, are the skeleton of your wiring system, the bones that protect the cables, connectors, and devices that actually supply Mr. Sparky's services. In repair work, you're generally stuck with whatever boxes you find, but you should be able to recognize the basic types for the occasional replacement of a corroded or undersize box, or for adding receptacles and switches. Boxes come in various depths; unless the wall cavity is unusually shallow, choose the $2^{1}/_2$-inch depth, which allows more room for wires and devices. Boxes with angled corners are much easier to place into a hole in an existing wall because the cables won't snag on the wall.

The National Electrical Code regulates how many cables can enter a box of a given size. This is partly because it's tough to put too many wires in a box. And it's partly because wires can get too hot if too many are stuffed in together. The size in cubic inches is stamped on the inside of a plastic box, and is possibly listed on the label of a metal one. Here's how to figure whether a box is acceptable for a certain use, if all conductors are the same size:

Calculation	Example: One Receptacle with 2 14-2 Cables
Each hot and grounded conductors (black and white, usually) = 1	4
All equipment grounding (bare) wires = 1	1
A receptacle or switch = 2	2
All cable clamps = 1	1
Add	8
Multiply by 2 for 14-gauge wire (2.25 for 12-gauge)	16 cubic inches minimum size required

The next illustration shows the typical electrical boxes listed here:

Plastic box: Easy to use because it needs neither grounding nor cable clamps (but remember, the *devices* in this box must be grounded). Plastic boxes are weaker than metal ones.

Shallow switch box: Used for switches and receptacles in tight quarters.

4-inch square box: Can be used for two receptacles—called double-duplex receptacles; it's usually nailed to a surface in a basement or garage and is covered with a steel plate.

Round box: Used for a ceiling light fixture (or use an octagonal box). In some areas, local electrical codes require a box used in a ceiling to be listed for ceiling-suspended (paddle) fan support, in case anybody decides to put a fan in the ceiling.

Handy box: Screw several handy boxes side by side for multiple switches and receptacles.

Box with tapered corners: Simplifies installation in an old wall because the cables won't snag on the drywall.

Electrical boxes. Each style may come with a variety of mounting and cable-clamping devices.

A. Plastic box

B. Shallow switch box, with two romex connectors in place

C. 4-inch square box

D. Round box

E. Handy box

F. Box with tapered corners

You'll also be needing some stuff to go inside those boxes, such as receptacles (commonly called "outlets") and switches. Many of these things are cheap enough to keep around for an emergency repair (shown in next photo).

Mounting straps: Used for attaching boxes to drywall or plaster. With the box in the wall, hold the strap by the two short ears, and slip the long leg and then the short leg behind the drywall. Hold the box at the proper depth in the wall, bend the ears over the edge of the box, and fold them tight into the box, bent 180°. These straps, called Madison Holdzits, were invented in my hometown, Madison, Wisconsin.

Receptacle with ground-fault circuit interrupter (GFCI): Used for receptacles in kitchens, bathrooms, and garages. You may connect extra receptacles to the back of the GFCI to protect them as well.

Grounded duplex receptacle: The standard 15-amp plug-in. Also available in a 20-amp version.

Single-pole switch: One single-pole switch controls one or more lights. (Note: Two three-way switches, not shown, are used to control a single light fixture from two locations.)

Porcelain light fixture: The cheapest and handiest fixture for places where appearance is your lowest priority. Don't use it in closets or wherever it could touch flammable material.

Protector plate: Shields romex cable running near the outside of a stud or joist from nails. Use this if the cable runs through a hole that's less than $1^1/4$ inches from the edge of the wood.

Electrical staples: Use to attach cable in accessible locations.

Screw-on wire connectors: Use to connect wires with a simple twist; easy to remove.

Romex clamps: Use to secure romex cable as it enters a metal box.

Cover plates: Use to cover receptacles and switches after the wiring is done.

Electrical paraphernalia.

A. Mounting straps

B. Receptacle with ground-fault circuit interrupter (GFCI)

C. Grounded duplex receptacle

D. Single-pole switch

E. Porcelain light fixture

F. Protector plate

G. Electrical staples

H. Screw-on wire connectors

I. Romex connectors

J. Cover plates

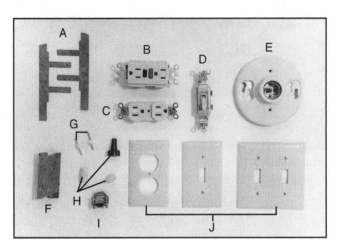

Got Connections? You'll Need Them

Connections are the glue that holds an electrical system together, so you'll need to learn the simple but crucial tricks for making connections with screw-on wire connectors, and the slip-in and screw terminals on switches and receptacles. If all else fails, you'll need to learn to solder.

Connecting with Screw-On Wire Connectors

The easiest way to connect un-stranded (solid, single-conductor) wire (the kind you'll find in your walls) is with fast, cheap, and virtually idiot-proof screw-on wire connectors. You can also use these little plastic gizmos to connect stranded wire, though it's a bit more difficult. Often called by the trade name, Wire Nuts, these connectors make a good joint that still can be taken apart.

Each size screw-on connector works on the combination of wire sizes and numbers that is listed on the package. I keep three sizes around—plenty for any wiring problem I'll face.

Screw-on wire connectors are a real no-brainer to use. You'll need a wire stripper, the connectors, and possibly a pair of pliers. Use these steps to join wires with these handy connectors:

1. Strip all wires about ⁵/₈ inch (see the package for the exact length).

2. Hold the wires with the ends aligned and flush, and slip the nut over the top (see the accompanying photo).

3. Twist the nut clockwise, as seen from the top. If you have a weak grip, tighten gently with pliers.

4. Tug to check that all wires are tight. You should not be able to see exposed bare wire (unless you're joining ground wires).

Don't Screw Up!

According to the National Electric Code, the only place where it's safe to join wires is in junction boxes, and all junction boxes must be accessible without taking walls apart. So don't join wires outside a box, and don't hide a box behind a wall. If you really need to make a connection where there's no box, install a box in a wall or ceiling. You can put in a receptacle or cover the box with a blank cover plate that is accessible from the room.

That's all there is to it—no goop, no heat, no solder.

You can also use screw-on wire connectors on multi-strand wire, but it's more difficult. Twist the wires together, screw on the nut, and then tug securely to make sure all wires are joined. Multi-strand wire, which is more flexible than single-strand wire, is used in extension and appliance cords as well as dimmer switches. But don't put screw-on connectors on extension cords—it's not safe.

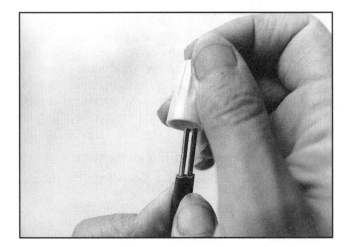

To connect wires with a screw-on wire connector, just slip the connector on top of the stripped ends of the wires, and twist it clockwise.

329

Connecting to Switches and Receptacles

Electrical outlets—properly called receptacles—often serve to connect cables and generally have four slip-in connectors and four screw terminals. Switches always have screw terminals and sometimes slip-in connectors as well.

Don't Screw Up!

Extension cords remain the single biggest cause of house fires. If the insulation fails and the current jumps to the grounded side, the resulting arcing may not pull enough current to trip a circuit breaker, but can still heat up and cause a fire. The moral of the story: Buy good cords, and keep an eye on old ones. When you see the first sign of heat or wear (let alone exposed wires), pitch the cord.

Nail It Down

Having trouble reinstalling a fixture in a box with a snarl of wires? Make a U-shaped bend in the wires about $1/2$ inch away from the screw-on connector, and then grab the connector with pliers and stuff the wires into the back of the box. This tactic avoids stress to the joint and damage to the insulation.

Don't go overboard in connecting to receptacles: You can connect only two pairs of conductors (two black and two white) to any receptacle. If you need to connect more than that, first attach the wires to screw-on connectors, and then bring short wires out to connect to the switch or receptacle. (Before filling a box with an astronomical number of cables, see previous discussion of box size. There are limits to how many wires you can safely stuff into a box.) To supply a light from a receptacle's box, connect the light cable to screw-on connectors, not the built-in connectors on the receptacle. The National Electric Code prohibits connecting lights directly to receptacles.

Slip-in connectors, which are identified by small holes in the back of the receptacle, are used for No. 14 solid copper wire only. A strip gauge on the back of the receptacle shows how much insulation to remove—about $5/8$ inch. Then just stick the bare end of the wire into a round hole on the back of the receptacle (white goes near the silver-colored screws, and black near the brass screws). The connector will grip the wire; just give a tug to make sure the connection is solid. To release the wire, stick a finishing nail (the circuit is off, isn't it?) into the slot near the wire, and then yank the wire out.

Long-nose pliers are the best tool for connecting a wire to a screw terminal, as shown in the photo. Even before you tighten the screw, the hook should grab the terminal. Don't make the loop backward, or the loop will open as you tighten the screw. Connect only one wire to each terminal! With a wire stripper, screwdriver, and long-nose pliers, use these steps to connect a wire to a screw terminal:

1. Strip about $3/4$ inch from the wire.
2. Make a hook—not a loop—with the pliers.

3. Slip the hook over the screw in the direction shown.

4. Squeeze the hook (ape-man force not needed) with long-nose pliers.

5. Tighten the screw, making sure the wire stays under the screw head without overlapping itself.

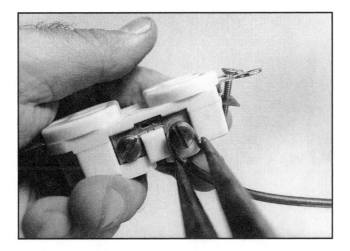

Long-nose pliers are perfect for closing a hook over a screw. Then simply tighten the screw for a secure connection.

Soldering? Nothing to It!

Soldering is a technique for joining pieces of metal by melting another metal—called solder—on them. Clean copper wires are easy to solder; dirty or corroded wires are impossible. To do it right, you'll need a wire stripper, a soldering iron or gun, non-acidic flux, solder, sandpaper, and electrical tape.

As we've said before, you should need to solder only when working on knob and tube wiring or telephone wiring. If that's what you're doing, don your safety goggles (to protect your eyes from molten solder) and follow these steps:

1. Plug in your soldering iron and set it aside to warm, with the tip safely in the air.

2. Strip about $3/4$ inch of insulation from each end of the wires you're joining.

3. With fine sandpaper, lightly sand the bare ends to remove corrosion.

4. Twist the wires tightly together so that the joint will not move during soldering. The electrical and mechanical connections should not depend on the solder.

5. Apply some soldering flux to the joint.

6. Touch the iron's tip to the solder to pick up a small puddle of molten solder, which conducts heat better than a dry iron.

7. Hold the iron to the joint until the flux begins to boil. A clean, well-fluxed joint will pull in the solder when the joint is hot enough. Then touch solder to the joint (*not* the iron) and let it run into the joint (see the following photo).

8. Heat for another few seconds, and then remove the iron. Don't blow on the joint; it will be weak if it cools too quickly. Flick the extra solder off the iron.

9. When the joint has cooled, clean the joint with rubbing alcohol and bind it with electrical tape. Finito!

When you solder a joint, hold the iron on the joint for a few seconds after the solder starts to melt so that it really penetrates.

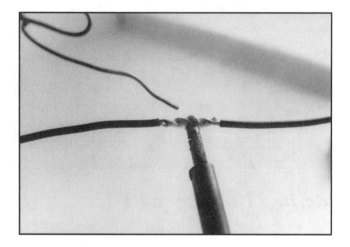

Don't Screw Up!

Important: The grounded (or white) wire is never switched. The grounded wire must always be continuous so that current can return to the circuit breaker or fuse box. Switches always control the supply of current *to* the light, never the current *from* it. If a white wire is used as a hot wire, however, it is switched and flagged with black tape.

Switches

Switches usually control built-in lights, but they also can control receptacles, motors, fans, and other conveniences. To make sure a switch is wired correctly, or is cold, see "Testing a Switch" in Chapter 27. Let's get acquainted.

One single-pole switch controls one or more lights. The switch has two terminals, and its toggle is marked "on" and "off." A single-pole switch can be located either before or after the light it controls. Both configurations control current to the light; the wiring pattern is chosen for convenience at the time of wiring.

In a switch *before the light*, the power comes through the switch. Because a white (grounded) wire is present in the switch box, you can wire a receptacle to this switch box. See the wiring illustration for a switch before the light.

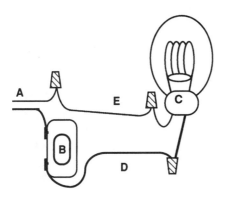

Switch before the light. The power reaches the switch, and the wire is switched before it reaches the light (ground not shown).

A. Supply

B. Switch

C. Light

D. Black (hot)

E. White (grounded)

In a switch *at the end of the run*, or *after the light*, power comes through the light box. The white wire supplying the switch will be hot, so it should be painted black or flagged with black electrician's tape. Because there's no grounded wire at the switch box, you can't add a receptacle to the switch. See the drawing of the switch after the light.

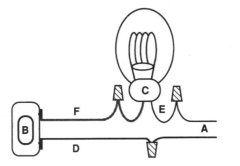

Switch after the light. Supply is through the light box.

A. Supply

B. Switch

C. Light

D. White serving as hot (flagged with black tape)

E. White serving as grounded conductor

F. Black (hot)

Two three-way switches are used to control one or more lights (they're commonly found at both ends of stairs or hallways). A three-way switch has three terminals, and the toggle is *not* marked on and off because you cannot tell from the toggle position whether the light is "on" or "off." Three-way switches require a cable with three conductors (red, black, and white), plus a bare equipment grounding wire. The wiring of a three-way switch depends on the configuration; you can generally replace a broken one simply by reconnecting the wires as you find them.

Three four-way switches can be used to control a light. They have four terminals, but they're rare and are beyond idiot territory.

Need More Receptacles?

The need for receptacles—AKA plug-ins or outlets—has mushroomed along with the invention of a million uses for electricity: dehumidifiers, heat guns, hair dryers, curling irons, bacon-fryers, seal-a-meals, electric can openers—the creation of these electrical "necessities" has been a triumph of the twentieth century and a boon for the wiring industry. If you've lived in a house that was last wired 50 years ago, you know that nobody foresaw how much juice a home would eventually need. When you try to plug in all this junk—whether in a home office, a kitchen, or a basement—you're going to suffer outlet envy.

If a grounded receptacle is nearby, a simple solution to the shortage of receptacles is to screw a six-receptacle expander to the face of the receptacle. Or, you can double up an existing receptacle by installing a pair of duplex receptacles in a new, double-size box at the same location. You'll have to remove the receptacle and the box, and cut the drywall or plaster to hold a 4-inch box. (If the existing box is a handy box, you can screw a second to it, possibly without removing any wiring.) Cut short leads of black, white, and bare wire to connect the two receptacles, side by side, and you'll have four receptacles.

Don't Screw Up!

Treat old wires with respect. They're likely to be brittle (as is their insulation), and if one breaks, you may end up with a lead that's too short.

But if you don't have electricity where you need it, or if you can't abide the sight of a snarl of wires hanging from one box on the wall, you'll need to install a receptacle. Remember, as you think about putting in more plug-ins, that each circuit has a capacity, in amps, that should never be exceeded. To figure out how many amps are already on a circuit, see the section "Making a Circuit Map," in Chapter 27. A final note: The devices on a circuit can draw more total amps than the rating, but not all at once.

Installing a Receptacle: The Basics

When deciding where to place a receptacle, the first step is figuring out where you want it. Then you'll have to figure out whether you can get power to it; running cable to a new receptacle is the hardest part of installing receptacles. You may need an electrical permit to extend a circuit for a new receptacle. The following places should be relatively easy:

➤ Near an existing receptacle (see the section "Running Cable in the House: Your Options," later in this chapter).

➤ On the opposite side of a wall with an existing receptacle.

➤ Near an accessible basement, attic, or attached garage (see the section "Using the Basement or Attic," later).

➤ Anywhere you can tolerate the sight of surface cable carriers on the wall or baseboard (see the section "Surface Wiring," later).

➤ Beneath a switch box that contains a grounded (white) wire (see the section "Adding a Receptacle to a Single-Pole Light Switch," later).

If you're within one stud of the existing receptacle, there's no need to do heavy construction to connect the cable from the old receptacle to the new one—a big time-saver. The receptacles can also be on the opposite sides of a wall, as shown in the following drawing.

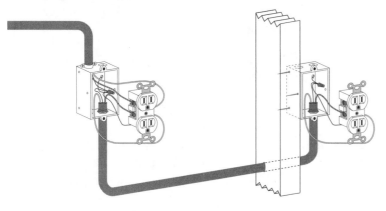

One easy way to double a receptacle is to install another receptacle nearby, or on the opposite side of the wall.

To install a new receptacle, you will need a drill, a level, a saber saw or keyhole saw, a screwdriver, a circuit tester, a wire stripper, a new receptacle, an electrical box, screw-on wire connectors, and a cover plate. Use these steps to install the receptacle and connect it to an old receptacle:

1. Plan how you will get power to the new receptacle. You may be able to feed cable through one stud by drilling with a long drill through the hole that the box left in the drywall. You can also run cable along the baseboard, or through a ceiling or basement. If you can't get power to the receptacle, stop and find a better location.

2. Measure the height of other receptacles in the room. Locate the studs in the area (see the section "Seven Ways to Find a Stud," in Chapter 22, "Cosmetology 101: Drywall and Plaster Repair"). It's easiest to screw the new electrical receptacle box

Nuts and Bolts

A **cover plate** is what you see covering a receptacle or a switch on the wall. Blank cover plates close boxes that contain wires but no switches or receptacles. Steel cover plates are sturdy enough for use in basements or garages.

to a stud. It's less desirable, but you also can screw it to wood lath or secure it to drywall with those sheet-metal thingamajiggies shown in the photo of electrical paraphernalia earlier in this chapter. Now mark a horizontal line at the receptacle location with a level.

To place a receptacle accurately, mark the first line with a level. A torpedo level is quite handy for this job.

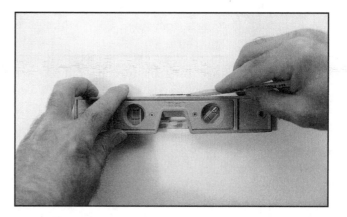

3. Shut off the circuit (see the section "Testing a Receptacle," in Chapter 27), and pull the faceplate off the existing receptacle. Pull out the receptacle and make sure you have enough room in the box for a new cable. (See the previous information on calculating allowable box sizes. You may have to install a larger box.)

4. Trace the new box to mark the cutout on the wall, as shown in the accompanying photo.

A box serves as its own template.

5. Using a ³/₈-inch bit, drill holes to start the saw, and allow room for the screws.

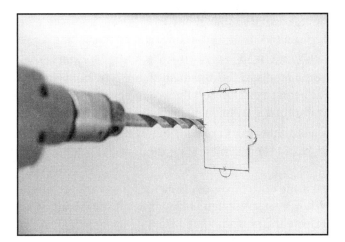

Holes allow room for the saw blade to start. For the box shown, drill at the X marks to allow room for mounting screws and brackets, and then saw from the drill holes.

6. Cut the opening with a saber saw, keyhole saw, or drywall saw. Press the saber saw against the wall to reduce vibration. Make the hole slightly larger than the box but smaller than the cover plate.

7. Disassemble the box that will supply power to the new box. If the wiring seems complicated, mark the wires to simplify reassembly. In general, though, everything should be black to black, white to white, and bare to bare. If the box lacks built-in cable clamps for the new cable, loosen the box, remove a knock-out, insert a romex clamp, and screw it tight.

8. Feed cable from the new box location to the existing box, through the connector. With about 10 inches sticking out of the old box, tighten the connector and remount the old box.

9. Strip the outer insulation from about 8 inches of the new cable. Don't cut the inner insulation.

10. Strip wire ends, and observe the cardinal rule of wiring: black to black, and white to white. Using a screw-on wire connector, connect the old ground wire supplying the old box to:

    A lead connected to the old box (unless it's a plastic box, which needs no grounding)

    A bare lead connected to the old receptacle

    The bare wire of the new cable

11. Reinstall the receptacle, but not the cover plate.

12. At the new box, cut the new cable so that about 10 inches will protrude from the box. Draw the cable into the new box, and tighten the cable clamp.

13. Fasten the new box to the stud, using two or three 1¼-inch drywall screws. If no stud is available: Slip some Madison Holdzits behind the box, hold the box-front flush with the wall, and bend the strips into the box; screw the box to wood lath; or use a box with self-mounting strips.

14. Wire up the new receptacle, referring to step 10. Screw the receptacle to the box, and turn on the circuit to test the receptacle (see the section "Testing a Receptacle," in Chapter 27).

15. If there's a problem, examine both boxes to check for loose wires or failure to keep colors separate. When everything tests okay, shut off the circuit, screw on the cover plates, and restore the power.

Adding a Receptacle to a Single-Pole Light Switch

Switches offer an easy place to connect receptacles—if both hot (black) and grounded (white) wires are present. How can you tell? Shut off the circuit, remove the switch plate, remove the mounting screws holding the switch, and gently pull the switch from the wall.

If only one cable enters the box, the switch is "after the light." The box has only hot wires (the white wire in the cable should be painted black or flagged with electrician's tape), and you can't wire a receptacle (see the figures illustrating single-pole switch wiring earlier in this chapter). However, if two cables are coming into the box, and one black wire from each cable connects to the switch, the switch is "before the light." The two white wires should each be joined with a wire connector; ditto for the two bare wires. You're in luck—you can wire a receptacle to this box.

To attach a receptacle to a single-pole switch before the light, you'll need a circuit tester, a stripper, a box, a receptacle, screw-on wire connectors, and a cover plate. Then follow these steps:

1. Turn off the circuit (see the section "Testing a Switch," in Chapter 27). To figure out which black wire supplies the box, turn the switch to "off," turn the circuit back on, and carefully hold one lead of the tester to ground, and the other to each switch terminal. The supply hot wire is connected to the terminal that is now hot. Flag that wire with tape.

2. Shut off the circuit again. Insert your new cable into the box, remove the outer insulation, and strip the ends about ¾ inch.

3. If you are afraid of getting confused, mark the wires with tape. Remove the black wire you flagged from the screw terminal.

4. Strip both ends of an 8-inch piece of black wire. Join this lead with a screw-on connector to the old black supply wire and the black wire feeding your new receptacle. Push these wires into the back of the box.

5. Loosen the connector holding the white wires, insert the white wire from the new cable, and retighten. Repeat for the ground wire. (You may need larger connectors to hold the extra wires.)

6. Attach the 8-inch black lead to the screw terminal you loosened in step 3. This supplies the light switch.

   You should now have these connections at the switch box:

   > **Black:** One screw-on wire connector joins the old supply wire, the wire to the new receptacle, and the 8-inch lead supplying the switch. The other switch terminal remains connected to the black wire to the light.

   > **White:** One connector joins all three wires.

   > **Bare:** One screw-on wire connector joins the incoming equipment grounding wire to a lead to the box, a lead to the switch (if it has a ground screw), and the ground going to the new receptacle. (Many switches are grounded by contacting a grounded box rather than a ground wire.) Reassemble the switch.

7. Make the following connection in the new (receptacle) box:

   > **White and black:** Connect to their respective terminals on the receptacle (black always goes to the brass-colored screw).

   > **Bare:** A wire connector joins wires from the old box, the new box, and the receptacle.

8. Restore power and test the new receptacle as described in the section "Testing a Receptacle," in Chapter 27. Replace cover plates.

Don't Install a Receptacle If ...

Although you can add an extra receptacle or two to most circuits, some circuits—such as those feeding a refrigerator or a furnace—should be left alone. Why? So a problem with another device on the circuit, say a video game or a bacon-fryer, does not trip the breaker and shut down your furnace on a January night, while you are slurping margaritas and watching the sunset in Acapulco.

Likewise, all 240-volt circuits, used for water pumps, stoves, dryers, and water heaters, should feed only one appliance. These circuits are easy to recognize because the circuit breaker is twice as big as normal and the receptacle is a three-prong monstrosity.

Finally, a receptacle should not be connected if it will overload the capacity—in cubic inches—of the box that would supply it. See the previous information on box capacity.

Updating an Ungrounded Receptacle

Relatively new wiring systems should have floor-to-ceiling grounding. Older systems are another story, however. They may contain ungrounded receptacles (which have two slots and no round grounding hole).

Grounded receptacles are safer for you and the electrical equipment, but that doesn't stop people from cutting the grounding prong off the plug on a new computer or answering machine so they can stick it into an ungrounded receptacle. The next time you do this, heed the voice of your conscience—or your soon-to-be orphaned children—and do something slightly more intelligent, such as installing a grounded receptacle or a GFCI (ground fault circuit interrupter) receptacle.

It's easy to install grounded (three-hole) receptacles *if the box is grounded.* But it's hard to know if the box is effectively grounded. Even if a tester lights between hot and the electrical box, that does not prove that the ground can carry enough current to be safe (see the section "Cable and Conduit" in the previous chapter for more on grounding systems). The best course is to replace an ungrounded receptacle with a GFCI receptacle. The GFCI can also protect receptacles wired to the back, as described later in this chapter. Using a circuit tester, a screwdriver, and a GFCI receptacle, here's how to install the GFCI:

1. Shut off the circuit and pull the box apart.

2. Attach black and white wires to the appropriate terminals of the GFCI (see the previous section "Installing a Receptacle: The Basics"). The wires that bring electricity to the box go to the terminals marked "supply." If you're attaching other receptacles to the GCFI, their wires connect to the "load" terminals. It's vital to get this part straight.

3. Check that the GFCI is working, following the self-test procedure on the package. Label the receptacle "No equipment ground" so that users know that the ground is absent, and test it monthly to make sure the GFCI is still working.

Replacing a Weak Box

Electrical boxes are best fastened to studs, but some are connected—more or less securely—to plaster or drywall. For a switch this may not matter, but the constant tugging on plugs can dislodge a receptacle. To replace such a box, select the right box from the discussion of electrical boxes and paraphernalia earlier in this chapter. Then follow these instructions:

1. Shut off the power and open the old box. Label the cables, if needed, to prevent confusion. (Usually, the wires are simply connected black to black and white to white, so labels are optional.)

2. If the drywall is badly damaged, fasten a 1-by-3 or a scrap of drywall next to the opening by screwing through the front of the drywall. The board should just allow room for the new box and behind the drywall.

3. Pull the cables through the clamps and into the new box. Slip the new box into place, and tighten the clamps.

4. Using one or two coats of quick-setting patching compound, repair the damage around the box. The 1-by-3 gives a backing for the patching compound

5. Reconnect the cables as described in the previous section "Installing a Receptacle: The Basics."

If an electrical box is feeling shy and has receded into the wall, here are a couple of solutions. Cut off the power, remove the screws mounting the receptacle or switch, and place some washers between the screw hole on the box and the device. Short of washers? Bend off those ears on the corners of a switch or receptacle, or coil some 14-gauge electrical wire to make whatever size spacer you need. After some fiddling around, you'll eventually get the device flush to the wall. However, see the tip here before trying either tactic.

Don't Screw Up!

An electrical box in a combustible wall (wood, for example) must be flush with the outer surface of the wall. In a non-combustible wall, such as plaster or drywall, a box must be within $1/4$ inch of the surface. If your box is farther back than is permitted, slip an add-a-depth or a similar box extender into the box to fill the gap.

Running Cable in the House: Your Options

Electricity can't take the plane, and it can't take the train from point A to point B. If you want to give electricity a ride from an old receptacle or switch to a new one, you've got to run some cable. Make no mistake: This can be the most unpleasant part of updating an electric system because it could require you to rip out drywall (which *would* be fun, if you didn't have to repair it!). Let's look at some relatively painless routes for new cable.

Baseboard

A baseboard molding that is at least 3 inches high offers a decent location to run cable. You will need a utility knife, a hammer, a small drywall saw, drywall screws, scrap drywall, a drill with a $1/2$-inch or larger wood-metal bit, and a carpenter's square or straight length of 1-by-3. After you've gathered your tools, use these steps to put the new cable in place:

1. Pull off the baseboard at least as far as the first stud past the new cable run (see the section "Yanking Up Molding with Scarcely a Split," in Chapter 24, "A Scolding on Molding").

2. Cut the drywall horizontally, $1/2$ inch below the top of the baseboard (measure the baseboard if it's not obvious where it was on the wall). Cut the drywall

vertically down the middle of each stud past the cable run. Remove the drywall strip.

3. Drill a $1/2$-inch hole through the bottom of each stud for the cable path. Drill as high as you can reach (to avoid nails) and close to the center of the stud. To prevent injury from nails or screws, the cable cannot be closer than $1^1/4$ inch from the edge of the stud. If the holes are too close to the front edge, use the protective plates shown in the previous photo of electrical paraphernalia.

4. Put the cable into place, and feed it into the old and new boxes. Let 12 inches protrude from the box to allow enough wire for connections.

5. Finish your electrical hookups and test, as described in the previous section "Installing a Receptacle: The Basics."

6. Cut a new piece of drywall to fit, screw it in place, and replace the baseboard. Don't bother taping the drywall; it will be hidden by the baseboard. Its only job is to let the baseboard lie flat.

7. Renail the baseboard, taking care not to nail through the cable. Fill the holes with wood filler and stain or paint.

Using the Basement or Attic

If you need a new receptacle near the floor on the ground floor, you may be able to wire it through a basement or crawl space. Eighteen-inch drill bits are useful for this kind of work because they can go all the way from the new box into the basement. (Do some reconnoitering first so you don't drill into something awkward, such as wiring, ducts, or pipes.) You can also wire through the attic, using the same jumbo drill bit.

Surface Wiring

If this discussion of sawing drywall or drilling floors is making you queasy (who said this would be a bucket of laughs?), check out the homely but sometimes acceptable solution called surface-mounted wiring. You've seen this stuff, usually as an earth-tone blemish running along baseboards and walls. Surface wiring is adaptable and easy to use, although the receptacles look suspiciously like rectangular blobs stuck to the wall. You may be able to hide surface wiring behind furniture. If you can't abide this and can't get a wire to the new receptacle any other way, hire an electrician to put in new receptacles or circuits. They can work miracles by fishing wires through inaccessible places.

When Do You Need Electrical Help?

The easy answer is after you get confused, but before the sparks start flying. Wiring, like particle physics, has a way of sounding simpler when someone else describes it, and there's no way two chapters can cover every circumstance you might encounter. For example, say you find an ugly knot of wires inside a box, many of them not connected to the fixture in the box. Although this may be normal—electricians route wires wherever it's most convenient—these wires could be fed by several breakers or fuses. In this case, how can you be sure every wire is cold? You could open up screw-on wire connectors and test the wires, but they may be hot. A determined do-it-yourselfer could pull the main disconnect to work on the circuit under a flickering flashlight. But this might be a good time to call the wire wizards.

Three- and four-way switches are another potential problem area because there are so many ways to wire them. (If you're just replacing a switch, you can probably get by wiring the new one exactly as the old one was wired, using masking tape to identify wires. But if you can't tell which switch is causing the problem, either replace them all or pick up the phone instead of the circuit tester.)

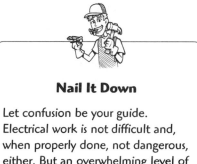

Nail It Down

Let confusion be your guide. Electrical work is not difficult and, when properly done, not dangerous, either. But an overwhelming level of confusion on your part is a sign worth heeding. Get advice, get help, or get both.

You also may run into wiring done by a blew-it-yourselfer, somebody who ignored the fundamentals of wiring: grounding, matching wire colors, and observing circuit capacity. It may be hard—bordering on impossible—to correct that kind of work, and I wouldn't suggest it. When my friend Paula had such a problem, she wisely called an electrician. He almost didn't charge her—he got such a kick out of trying to straighten out the bungled wiring!

Plugged In: The Telephone Story

Now that telephone companies are charging astronomical rates to install and repair phone wiring, homeowners have an incentive to understand this wiring. Fortunately, standardization and a modular, plug-and-play mentality have prevailed in phone wiring for many years, and phone wiring is extremely simple.

And because the voltage in a phone system is low, you don't even need to worry about shutting off circuits (however, the 90-volt dc ringing current can still give you a pretty decent jolt if the phone happens to ring when you're monkeying with the wiring). Thus, if there's a quick-disconnect at the telephone company interface (where the house wiring meets the phone company's wiring), it's smart to open it before working on the lines.

If you want to add jacks (phone outlets), just observe these pointers:

➤ Phone cable has three or four conductors. Four-conductor cable (black, red, green, and yellow) can carry two separate lines. The three-wire cable can carry one line.

➤ Modular jacks are used to attach the lines from telephones to the phone cables running through a house. They are marked B, R, G, and Y, to indicate wire color.

➤ Modular plugs come in two sizes. The larger ones link phones to the wall wiring; the smaller ones link handsets to phones. The plugs are not interchangeable.

343

➤ Electronics supply stores stock a good range of gizmos for linking phone systems: wire, connectors, staples, and jacks. For example, they sell a splitter, which allows a modular jack carrying two phone lines to feed two separate phones. They also sell a device that converts the old four-prong phone jacks to the modular style; simply slip one into the old jack, and then plug the modular plug into it.

➤ When you're running phone cable in the house, an 18-inch drill bit ($^3/_8$-inch diameter) can be handy for reaching between floors.

➤ To connect a new jack: Attach wires to the terminals on the metal block where the phone wire enters the house; solder into a phone cable; or attach to an existing phone jack.

The Least You Need to Know

➤ Before doing any electrical repair, shut off the circuit, and then test that it's really off. Then test your tester.

➤ Grounded circuits are used in all modern construction. You can easily update an ungrounded receptacle by installing a receptacle with a ground–fault circuit interrupter.

➤ Choosing the right electrical box can simplify repairs.

➤ Electrical devices are made for easy connections; screw-on wire connectors can handle most other connections.

➤ Replacing switches is usually just a matter of copying the existing connections.

➤ Adding receptacles can be easy, difficult, or impossible; the limiting factor is how easily you can run cable to the new receptacle.

➤ Baseboards, attics, basements, crawl spaces, and receptacles on the other side of the wall are all good sources of power for a new receptacle.

➤ Phone wiring is as simple as matching wire colors.

Chapter 29

A Welcome Blast of Hot Air: Heating System Tips

In This Chapter

➤ Troubleshooting and maintaining your heating system

➤ Simple tune-ups and repairs you can make

Heating systems can be temperamental. When my first son, Alex, was trying to get himself born, I pleaded with my heating repair guy, "I'm in the delivery room, and my wife is about to give birth, and my neighbor tells me it's 44° F in my house, and it's *winter* here in Wisconsin, and could you *pulleeze* get over to my house before the pipes turn to icicles?"

This story is true. It's also true that you could prevent this kind of humiliation (and countless other kinds) by not having children. That's giving the furnace more power than it deserves. The lesson I took away is to pay more attention to sob stories from the furnace in the first place. You see, I already knew the clanky old thing had a cracked heat exchanger, and that's the one part that can't be replaced in most furnaces.

At least I earned a good story from the experience, as did the repairman, who's probably still chuckling about that moron who thought the only way he could get immediate service was to lie about his wife being in labor!

Heating systems do two things: They create heat, and they distribute it. Heat usually comes from burning natural gas, propane, or fuel oil; it's usually distributed as hot air, hot water, or steam. With so many fuels and designs in service, there's no way this chapter can cover them all.

And while I had intended to talk about air conditioning as well, there is nothing user-serviceable in the average cooling system. Even though I've written a book on industrial and commercial air conditioning, I still hire an expert to work on my system, so you shouldn't feel bad if you do likewise. The same precaution applies to heat pumps, which use air conditioning technology to heat and cool the house. However, the thermostat, filter, and duct information that follows does apply to air conditioning and heat-pump systems.

Instead of discussing things that are best left to experts, in this chapter I'll concentrate on user-serviceable parts of the heating system and then conclude with some trouble-shooting suggestions.

Understand Your Thermostat

A thermostat is a thermally operated switch that signals the furnace to start or stop burning. The thermostat calls for heat by sending an electrical signal to open the gas valve (in a gas furnace) or to start the burner motor (in an oil furnace). When the house warms up enough, the thermostat shuts off the flame. Thermostats don't directly control the heat distribution system—that's the job of the fan-and-limit control (see the accompanying figure illustrating the roles of the thermostat and fan-and-limit control).

Roles of the thermostat and fan-and-limit control in heating mode.

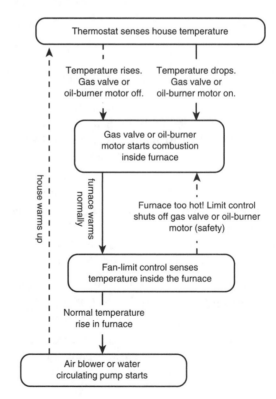

When the house temperature drops below the set point, the thermostat sends an electric current to open the gas valve or start the oil-burner motor. When the furnace warms up, the fan control closes a switch, sending current to the air-circulating fan or the water-circulating pump. If the furnace gets too hot, the limit control closes the gas valve or stops the oil-burner motor, shutting down the furnace for safety. In cooling mode, the thermostat starts the cooling system when the set point is exceeded.

To reduce energy consumption, set-back thermostats can be set to a cooler temperature at night (and sometimes during the day, when the house may be unoccupied). The idea is that you can stay warm when you're up and about, but you sleep in cooler, more economical conditions. The thermostat package may give some indication of how much money a set-back thermostat should save over a conventional one.

Some thermostats (usually older ones) have an adjustable anticipator mechanism to prevent rapid on-off cycling of the furnace. The anticipator allows the room to cool a couple of degrees before the furnace restarts; otherwise, the furnace would

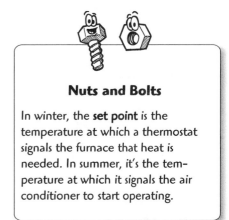

Nuts and Bolts

In winter, the **set point** is the temperature at which a thermostat signals the furnace that heat is needed. In summer, it's the temperature at which it signals the air conditioner to start operating.

continually cycle on and off, which is not just annoying but also harmful to the system. If your furnace is cycling too rapidly, increase the anticipator setting (consult the instructions for your thermostat). On the other hand, if the furnace is cycling too slowly and the room cools too much before the furnace kicks in, reduce the anticipator setting.

Fan-and-Limit Control

The fan-and-limit control is a thermally operated switch that regulates the blower (in hot-air systems) or circulating pump (in hot-water systems). (See the figure earlier in this chapter.) This switch can wear out with age.

The fan portion of the switch signals the heat-circulating apparatus to start operating after the furnace has warmed up sufficiently; otherwise, the system would circulate cold water or air. (The lag between the burner start-up and the start of the circulating fan is called the system delay.)

The blower or water pump keeps running after the burner shuts off. When the furnace temperature falls below a second cooler set point, the fan or pump stops circulating and the whole system idles until the thermostat calls for more heat. If the furnace gets too hot for any reason, the limit control shuts off the burner to prevent fire.

Pilot Lights, Thermocouples, and Gas Flames

A *pilot light* is a small flame that burns constantly in older gas furnaces and water heaters. Its job is to light the gas so the furnace can start operating. Just above the pilot light is a *thermocouple*, a thermally operated safety device. If the thermocouple does not sense heat, it thinks the pilot light is off and shuts down gas flow.

You won't see a pilot light on modern furnaces and water heaters, which use electric (spark) ignition instead. Electric ignitions are highly reliable and economical because they don't burn gas unless heat is needed, but they are not owner-maintainable.

To light a pilot, follow these steps:

1. Turn off the main gas valve.

2. Find a long match while you wait 5 minutes for any gas to dissipate.

3. Turn the gas valve to "pilot."

4. Now press the red button on the pilot valve and light the pilot. The button overrides the thermocouple, allowing gas to flow even though the pilot is off.

5. Hold the red button down for a minute, while the pilot warms the thermocouple. The pilot should stay lit when you release the button. If it doesn't, wait 5 minutes for gas to dissipate and repeat the process.

6. Turn the main gas valve to "on." If the thermostat is calling for heat, the furnace or water heater should ignite. In any case, the pilot should remain lit.

On a gas furnace, the main burner should make a blue flame with a few tips of yellow. This gives the highest efficiency and makes the least soot. You should be able to adjust the air intake to achieve this kind of flame, but see the section "Know When You Need Help," later in this chapter, first.

Furnace Wiring

As a safety measure, a furnace should always get a separate electrical circuit. Otherwise, a short circuit in something less important, such as a lava lamp, could blow a fuse and freeze your home in January. (How does the lava lamp know to malfunction in January, while you are out skiing the Rockies? Karma, that's why. But that's slightly beyond our scope.)

If my furnace blew its breaker even once, I would go scurrying, supplicant-fashion, to my furnace guru—a furnace should never draw anything near the 15 amps that would trip a breaker or blow a fuse.

Replacing Filters for Fun and Profit

Furnace filters—found in hot-air systems only—are generally quite easy to replace, and you can find the common sizes at anything from a supermarket to a hardware store. Your best guide to the frequency of replacement is the condition of the used filters. If only a little crud has accumulated, then you may be replacing them too often. But if the filter is a filthy gray, you've waited too long. It all depends on how dusty your house is and on how much of that dust gets into your ducts.

Allergic? Then Meet These High-Performance Filters

Because simple filters don't catch enough flying crud for people with serious allergies, companies have begun selling high-performance dust catchers. You'll have to get a furnace specialist to install these gadgets because the ductwork must be changed, but the payoff is fewer allergic reactions and possibly a cleaner house. Some of these improved filters have an accordion-shaped paper filter that you can clean with a vacuum. Even more effective are electrostatic precipitators, which put an electric charge on the dust and then pull it to a disposal plate by electrical attraction.

Adjusting Air Flow

Forced-air heating systems should have a damper (an adjustable shut-off plate) in each duct to regulate airflow. You can see the simple lever handles that operate these dampers in ducts in the basement or crawl space. These handles follow the plumber's convention for valves: When the handle is oriented across the line of flow, the valve is closed; when it's parallel to the flow, it's open.

You can use dampers to balance the air flow around the house. If a room is too hot, close the damper a bit; if it's too cold, open its damper (or close other dampers to force more hot air toward the cold room). If you have trouble figuring out which duct goes where, ask someone to bang on the various registers while you listen—or feel for the banging—on the ducts in the basement. Then label the ducts with a marker.

Bleeding Radiators

Like politicians, radiators (which distribute heat in hot-water systems) are prone to filling with hot air. Unlike politicians, however, radiators are equipped with a valve for removing ("bleeding") this hot air. The air prevents the radiator from filling with hot water, preventing the furnace from distributing enough heat. The bleeder valve is at the top of each radiator; some valves require a special, square wrench (hardware stores sell them); others turn with a screwdriver. Just open the valve until water comes out, and catch the spill in a cup. Bleed the system every fall, and then refill the system with water by opening a valve on the water inlet to the reservoir or boiler. The water level should be indicated on a clear tube on the tank.

Draining the Boiler

Hot water systems have boilers—big tanks that are usually in the basement—and boilers collect sludge. Once a month during the heating season, it's a good idea to drain a couple of quarts of water from the boiler to remove most of the sediment. Look for a valve near the bottom, but use a bit of caution. If the valve has not been operated for a long time, it may not close securely or it may need repacking (see the section "Faucet Repair [Dig It! Trouble with the Spigot?]" in Chapter 31, "Either It Leaks … [Plumbing, Part I].").

Troubleshooting

Troubleshooting the heating system can grow into a murky, complex subject that is not idiot-proof. The following troubleshooting guide can cover only the most obvious problems (see the following table).

Troubleshooting Heating Systems

Problem	Cause	Cure
General problems		
No heat, no response from furnace	Blown breaker or fuse	Reset breaker or replace fuse
	Thermostat not calling for heat	Repair or replace thermostat
	Emergency safety switch off	Turn switch on
	Furnace door open	Close door
Gas burner not functioning	Pilot out	Relight pilot (see "Pilot Lights, Thermocouples, and Gas Flames," earlier in this chapter); clean pilot opening if gas is not coming out
	Pilot valve set in "pilot" mode	Set in "heat" mode

Problem	Cause	Cure
Pilot won't stay lit	Thermocouple; see "Pilot Lights, Thermocouples, and Gas Flames," earlier in this chapter) is loose or broken, shutting the gas valve	Tighten thermocouple connection nut slightly, or replace thermocouple
	Pilot flame is not heating the thermocouple	If flame is misdirected, readjust pilot fixture or thermocouple; or turn pilot valve to enlarge pilot flame
Oil burner malfunctioning	Empty oil tank, oil filter plugged, or valve shut	Add oil, turn valve, or replace filter
	Burner motor not starting	Check the furnace switch (if your home has two, one on the burner, and another at the top of the basement stairs, both must be "on")
		Push the reset button on the safety control on the furnace stack. Push the reset button on the burner motor.
Forced-air systems		
Inadequate flow of warm air	Dirty filter	Clean or replace filter
	Registers closed	Open registers
	Air registers dirty or blocked by furniture or drapes	Clean registers or move obstructions
	Air leaks in ducts	Find leaks and cover them with duct tape
	Dampers on ducts closed or maladjusted (can also cause large temperature differences between rooms)	See "Damper Adjustment," earlier in this chapter

continues

Troubleshooting Heating Systems   (continued)

Problem	Cause	Cure
Hot water systems		
Top of radiators or baseboard heaters are cold; inadequate heat	Air in the system	See "Bleeding Radiators," earlier in this chapter
Water coming out of valve on top of the expansion tank	The tank should contain air and water; if it's hot all over, it's waterlogged	Call heating technician safely bleed the tank
Leaks at shut-off valve on radiator or baseboard heater	Valve packing is dry or worn	Try tightening nut around the valve stem. If that doesn't work, drain system until water level is below the valve, and repack (see "Faucet Repair" in Chapter 31).

Know When You Need Help

Heating work, like other repairs, is not for everyone. As usual, the key sign that you need help is confusion. Because many of the repairs involve electrical controls, you must be comfortable working with simple control systems, and possibly with various electrical gauges, which is totally out of our league. And don't forget that many people recommend an annual service call on oil and gas furnaces, just to keep them in tune. My advice: Skim off the cream of the repairs and maintenance, and leave the heavy lifting to the pros.

The Least You Need to Know

➤ Many minor sources of heating system trouble, including problems with the furnace and the heat-distribution system, should be within your grasp.

➤ A furnace should always occupy its own circuit to prevent unrelated problems from shutting off your heat.

➤ A variety of high-tech filters can ease life for allergy sufferers.

➤ If you're feeling that queasy "Can I really do this?" feeling, back off. The heating system is no place to learn which way a screw turns.

Chapter 30

Champion Chimneys

> ### In This Chapter
>
> ➤ Chimney safety and inspection
>
> ➤ Safe wood stove and fireplace operation
>
> ➤ Chimney maintenance and repair
>
> ➤ Chimney flashing explained at last

Chimneys, once made exclusively of masonry, have branched out into steel versions. Steel chimneys are lighter, safer, and more flexible; you can even install them in ceilings without bothering with a foundation. But some things have not changed. Chimneys still require a bit of thought. They still leak, and they still can threaten to burn your house down if they're not installed and maintained properly.

Chimneys of fireplaces, and particularly wood-burning stoves, can accumulate a great deal of highly flammable material called creosote, which condenses on the relatively cold walls of the chimney. If you operate such an appliance, you must be on the lookout for signs of creosote build-up. We'll deal with inspection, safety, flashing, and other chimney repairs in this chapter. See Chapter 29, "A Welcome Blast of Hot Air: Heating System Tips," for some words on the furnace. Let's start by inspecting and cleaning the chimney.

Inspecting and Cleaning

The first step in chimney inspection is to stand back and take a good look from the ground. Does the chimney need tuckpointing? If so, see Chapter 17, "Bricks and Stones: Masonry and Concrete (the Sequel)." Is it tightly caulked against the house? If not, see Chapter 12, "Skin-Tight: Caulking, Weather-Stripping, Insulation, and Ventilation." If it is pulling away from the house, or if it has major cracks, you're out of idiot territory. It's time to call a mason.

Now get up on the roof. Does the cap look sound? If not, see the section "That Caps It Off," later in this chapter. How is the flashing? If it's coming loose, or if you already know it's leaking, see the section "Chimney Flashing Loves Leaking," also later in this chapter.

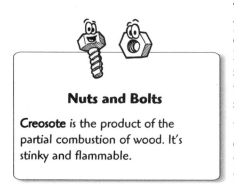

Nuts and Bolts

Creosote is the product of the partial combustion of wood. It's stinky and flammable.

To look inside the chimney, attach the brightest light you can find to a long pole and stick it down the chimney. Look for cracks, a creosote build-up (which looks like flaky dust or a gooey glaze), or anything suspicious, such as gaps between the clay flue tiles. Stick the light into the chimney from below if you can, and stare upward, looking for the same problems.

Unfortunately, this kind of inspection may not reveal every crack, as I recently learned. My inspection told me that my 50-year-old chimney was in good enough shape to begin burning wood, and I later found that the chimney was leaking smoke—out the side. Still, this inspection is likely to catch obvious flaws. For the ultimate in chimney inspection, hire a firm that uses a television camera. The process is expensive, but it will find flaws that other techniques won't.

Go inside the fireplace and look for loose firebricks, the heat-resistant bricks that line the firebox. If you find any loose bricks, see the section "Repairing Masonry and Concrete for Keeps," in Chapter 17, for advice on repairs. Use refractory cement, sold at brickyards, instead of regular mortar. If the firebricks are sound but the joints need mortar, clean out the joints and then push refractory cement into them with a margin trowel or putty knife. When the mortar is almost set, smooth it with a stiff brush.

Chimney Cleaning

A surprising number of people wouldn't think of cleaning a chimney, but if you have the right ladders, it's usually pretty simple. The time-tested approach will remove most dry creosote, the flaky, dusty kind. Put some chains in a burlap bag, and hoist the bag up and down on a rope. Make sure to wear a dust mask and close the doors of the fireplace or wood stove. If there are no doors to close, tape plastic over the opening; chimney gunk is pungent and dusty, about the worst imaginable combination. Then, while still wearing your dust mask, gently brush accumulated dust into a dustpan.

If you're of a mind to spend money, or if you have congealed creosote, buy chimney cleaning brushes (sold in 6-, 8- and 10-inch round sizes; and in rectangular sizes, including 8-by-8 and 8-by-12). Also buy some 4-foot extendable Fiberglas handles, which screw to the brush and to each other.

Santa Don't Like Your Chimney, and Other Ruminations on Chimney Fires

If you burn wood in a fireplace or stove, you owe it to yourself to keep a close eye on your chimney. The hazard is simple: An accumulation of black, stinky creosote can catch fire and burn your house down. Creosote condenses on the flue, which is relatively cool. This glop burns quite hot (above 1,500° F). Chimney fires often burn unnoticed and are a major cause of house fires.

To contain chimney fires, chimneys must be lined with a metal or ceramic flue liner, which supposedly can withstand the high temperature these fires create. Before using a chimney for burning wood, I'd ask a chimney expert or mason to inspect it. If the chimney is not lined, or if its lining is inadequate, you can get a stainless steel liner installed. Paying for a liner is probably cheaper than buying a new house after a house fire.

Don't Screw Up!

Caution on wood-burning chimneys: Current building codes prohibit having flammable material closer than 1 inch to the chimney. Obviously you won't be able to make an old chimney match this standard, but keep it in mind during renovations.

Creosote condenses on the chimney most quickly if you

➤ Burn green (uncured) wood, or pine and similar softwoods

➤ Set an airtight stove to burn slowly (with the air intakes almost closed)

➤ Have a cold chimney, with lots of exposure to the outside

➤ Have a long chimney

Removing a serious creosote accumulation is a pro job. But if the chimney is in good condition (as demonstrated by a recent inspection), you can burn out light creosote accumulations by starting fires with a lot of paper and plenty of air. A big fire will briefly enter the chimney and flare off the creosote before it gets a chance to cause problems. *Do not* try this unless you are sure the chimney is clean and in good condition, though, as it could start a chimney fire. (To repeat: If you're not sure the chimney is clean and sound, *don't operate* the stove or fireplace.)

Chimney Caps Top Chimney Tops

Chimney caps are screened hoods that keep rain, birds, and other animals out of chimneys and prevent downdrafts in fireplaces. When a raccoon got into our house through the fireplace, I was glad I'd left a window open so it could escape, as vermin can do quite a number on woodwork. Nevertheless, it was all I could do to repair the molding—the alternative was dropping a grand on a new window.

Toolbox Trivia

A chimney cap may be important even if the fireplace attached to the chimney is not in operation, as I learned the hard way. We returned from a vacation to find the glass fireplace doors lying on the living room floors, and tooth and claw marks on one window. We concluded that we were witnessing the aftermath of a gruesome battle between my house and—what? Those sooty black paw prints gave it away. A raccoon had slid down the chimney, zapped through the glass doors, and, panic-stricken, clawed its way out through the half-open window.

Far better to prevent disasters like that by installing a chimney cap. A cap might have prevented a second raccoon, whose skeleton I later found in the fireplace, from meeting an untimely death.

Chimney caps do more than keep vermin out of the house. A screened cap will prevent birds from nesting in the flue. If you operate a fireplace, a flat cap can help prevent downdrafts from smoking up your home. Any masonry chimney can benefit from protection from rain afforded by some caps.

If you have access to the chimney top, an aluminum chimney cap is simplicity itself to install. The simplest type clamps to the masonry flue. If the flue does not protrude above the masonry, you may have to fasten the cap to the brick or masonry. Use the TapCon screws or anchors described in Chapter 9, "Fast Guide to Fasteners," to secure the cap to the masonry. Anytime you drill into the cap, seal the surface with some good caulking; the worst thing you can do is create a pool where water gathers and freezes, pulling apart the fragile chimney top.

Inspecting and Repairing the Top

From years spent repairing masonry chimneys, I came to two conclusions. First, people love to ignore problems they can't see. Second, it's expensive to ignore problems on masonry chimneys. Masonry deteriorates with weather, and repairs that you could easily make today can grow to expensive pro jobs down the line.

Scan your chimney for missing mortar, and tuckpoint as described in Chapter 17. If the top is deteriorating, use several coats of vinyl cement patching, described in Chapter 13, "In the Yard: No Rest for the Weary." Make sure to bond the patching carefully to the flues, and smooth it toward the edge so water will drip away from flues. When done, it may help to caulk the joint between the cap and the flue with butyl caulking. If the cap is really deficient, see the next section.

> **Nuts and Bolts**
>
> Here's some confusing lingo. A **chimney cap** is a (usually) metal structure that prevents rain, snow, and animals from entering a chimney. A **chimney top** is a masonry or concrete structure at the top of a masonry chimney. It usually bulges out slightly to prevent water from dripping down the sides and generally strengthens the chimney. Why is this confusing? Because some people use the terms interchangeably.

Building a New Top

Chimney tops take a real beating from rain, frost, and snow. Sadly, if the top falls apart, the rest of the chimney won't be far behind because the top must keep rain from entering the chimney and destroying it from inside.

To cast a new concrete top, you'll need:

➤ A saw

➤ A power screwdriver

➤ Some $2^1/_2$-inch drywall screws

➤ Some heavy wire or reinforcing rod

➤ About 8 feet of 2-by-4 and 8 feet of 1-by-4

➤ A bag of dry concrete

Then follow these steps:

1. If the masonry is really loose at the top, remove a course or two of bricks until you reach solid material. At least 3 inches of flue must protrude above the solid material to follow this procedure.

2. Saw a pair of 2-by-4 bottom forms $1/_4$ inch longer than the longer dimension of the chimney. Saw another pair of 2-by-4s $3^1/_4$ inches longer than the chimney's shorter dimension. It's best, but not essential, to cut a 15° bevel (as shown in the detail drawing) on the top edge of each bottom form. This allows rain to drain away from the chimney.

Don't Screw Up!

When working on a chimney top, remember that you'll be handling heavy, awkward objects, such as wood and pails of concrete. If you can't do the work standing on the roof, consider making or renting a scaffold for this tricky operation.

3. Hammer four masonry nails into the mortar to support the bottom forms level with the top of the bricks, as shown in the figure of casting a chimney top, step 1. If nails won't work, use four TapCon screws.

4. Screw the bottom form together, and rest the form on the masonry nails to check its fit.

5. Remove the form from the chimney. Saw a pair of 1-by-4 side forms so that the ends are flush with the bottom forms, and saw a second pair long enough to complete the rectangle. Screw these pieces to the outside of the 2-by-4 bottom forms, overlapping onto the 2-by-4s by $1^1/_4$ inch. Screw the ends of the side forms together. This step is shown in the figure casting a chimney top, step 2.

6. Place the assembly on the chimney top. If there is a big gap between the bottom forms and the chimney, stuff fiberglass insulation or something similar into the gap.

7. Bend wire or reinforcing rod, and lay it around the flue.

8. Mix one bag of concrete thoroughly (this will be enough for most chimney caps; keep a second bag on hand in case it's needed for a larger cap). Dampen the existing masonry, and pour the concrete in place.

9. Raise the wire or reinforcing rod from the bottom while the concrete is fresh. Adapt the instructions from Chapter 17 to finish the concrete. Be sure to leave a slope so that the water drains toward the outside. Wrap with plastic to allow complete hydration.

10. Remove the forms after a couple of days. Put mortar or caulking in the holes made to support the forms.

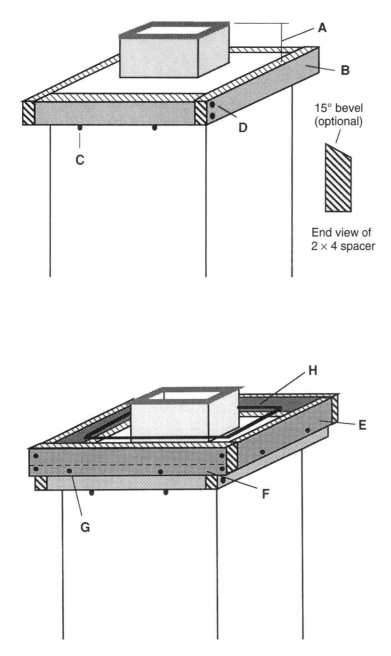

15° bevel
(optional)

End view of
2 × 4 spacer

Step 1: The 2-by-4 gives a 1¹/₂-inch overhang, which allows rain to drain to Spain (or at least away from the chimney). Screw the assembly together on the ground to minimize your air time. The 15° bevel, which allows water to drain away from the chimney, is helpful but not necessary.

A. At least 3-inch clearance

B. 2-by-4 bottom form

C. Nails or screws to support form

D. Screws fasten ends of 2-by-4s

Step 2.

E. 1-by-4 side form

F. 1¹/₄-inch overlap onto 2-by-4

G. Screws secure 1-by-4 to 2-by-4

H. Reinforcing rod or wire prevents concrete from cracking

359

Chimney Flashing Loves Leaking

When I was in the masonry business, I learned how chimney flashing loves to leak. The stuff is complicated and handmade, and it's supposed to seal a gap between a chimney and a roof that moves with temperature changes. How much effort you're willing to devote to the repair will depend on how accessible your chimney is. Gooping the flashing with tar may work for a while, but a re-flashing job is much more likely to succeed.

A huge build-up of roofing tar on the flashing is a dead give-away that somebody has failed to repair the leak. Then it's time to remove the flashing and fashion new flashing yourself, using the instructions that follow. If the bricks are loose, or if the mortar is crumbling, call 1-800-CHIMBLY or a local mason—you need a chimney rebuild. Fortunately, the decrepit masonry rarely extends much below the roof line.

Finding That Leak

The first step in fixing a chimney leak is finding it. Does the chimney leak on the bottom, side, or top?

A leak on the bottom could indicate a problem with the bottom (base) flashing, but because water runs downhill, it can also result from flawed side or top flashing. If you're sure the base flashing is guilty, remove the existing flashing and look for the leak. Fashion new flashing to match the existing flashing, and secure it into place using the methods described in the section "Base Flashing," later in this chapter.

A leak on the side may indicate a problem with step flashing or counter flashing (the leak could always be dribbling down from the top, too). Side leaks are often caused by counter flashing pulling away from the brick (see the section "Side Flashing," later in this chapter). Unlike bottom and top flashing, the counterflashing can be replaced without removing shingles.

Remove and examine a piece of counterflashing. Generally, you will see signs of water if it's leaking. If the leak is widespread, remove all the counterflashing and fabricate new pieces, or (much recommended) switch to the one-piece counterflashing described later. If the step flashing seems intact, you may get away without replacing it.

A leak on the top probably results from damaged top flashing, which is described in the section "Top Flashing," later in this chapter. Unless the problem is with the top counterflashing, you'll have to loosen some shingles to repair top flashing.

Small leaks at any part of chimney flashing may result if warm air exits the attic and condenses on the cold metal near the chimney. Stuffing fiberglass insulation into the air leak from below might help. Otherwise, these leaks are hard to cure without a new roofing job. The permanent fix is to bring a layer of ice dam material or roofing felt from below the shingles up under the flashing. (Don't do this on a chimney serving a wood-burning stove or fireplace; there must be 1-inch clearance between the chimney and flammable material. See Chapter 29 for advice on chimneys and wood-burning stoves.)

Fixing Flashing

Now that you've found the problem, let's talk solution. For minor leaks, your first step is probably an application of roofing tar and a decision to hope for the best. If a huge build-up of goop indicates that previous owners have tried that trick, you are in the market for a re-flashing job. This is something an ambitious homeowner can accomplish (on an accessible chimney) with the directions that follow, especially if only a few leaking parts need replacement.

Follow these hints as you test your flashing skills:

Nuts and Bolts

Flashing is metal that seals leaks between two building elements. **Counterflashing** is metal that goes over the flashing to complete the seal. Just to be confusing, both are sometimes called plain flashing.

➤ Make the flashing from galvanized steel, which is stronger and stiffer than aluminum. Buy a roll that's 20 inches wide.

➤ Bend flashing over a 2-by-4. Don't bend too far—the object is to make bends that end up pushing the flashing against the brick.

➤ Use heavy-duty butyl caulking to hold flashing and counterflashing in mortar joints.

➤ Existing flashing usually makes a good template.

➤ If existing flashing is the wrong size, use the detail diagrams that follow instead. Make a cardboard template for the angle between the roof and the chimney, and then use it to mark cuts and bends on various pieces.

➤ The techniques described in the section "Presto-Chango Shingle Replacement," in Chapter 15, "Gimme Shelter—and Other Advice on Repairing Roofs," will help you remove and replace shingles during flashing work.

Base Flashing

The first piece of flashing to be installed on a new flashing job is called, logically enough, the base flashing. See the figure of base and step flashing.

1. Clean out the mortar joint at the top of the flashing, without disturbing the bricks.

2. Bend this flashing from a 20-inch-wide piece of galvanized flashing metal, as shown in the base flashing illustration. Use the existing flashing as a guide, or take dimensions from the base flashing detail. Make the bottom bend so that the flashing presses tight to the chimney.

3. Bend the top at a right angle to make a $3/4$-inch tab for insertion into the mortar joint.

4. The base flashing sits mainly on top of the shingles. Slip it into the mortar joint, snug it up against the chimney, and fasten with two to four roofing nails across the bottom. Tar the nail heads.

5. Pump butyl caulking into the mortar joint, and wedge the tab tight with roofing nails. Avoid disturbing the flashing until the caulking sets; then remove the nails.

Base flashing is made of one piece of 20-inch flashing metal. To install step flashing, work your way up the side, bending back the shingles to slip the flashing into place.

A. Base flashing

B. Tab in mortar joint

C. Step flashing

D. Curl shingles to insert step flashing

The base flashing has no counterflashing, so it must be made accurately. Dimension A comes from the chimney.

A. Chimney width plus $^{1}/_{4}$ inch

B. $^{3}/_{4}$-inch tab

C. Bend so that the vertical section pushes against the chimney

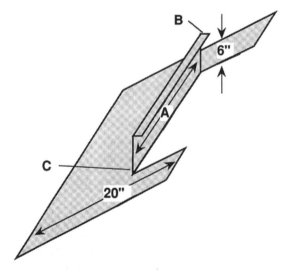

Side Flashing

Side flashing is built of step flashing and counterflashing. You can buy ready-made step flashing, or you can bend it from 12-inch squares of flashing metal. Here's how to replace side flashing, as shown in the illustration of side and top flashing.

1. Starting at the bottom, carefully lift the shingles with a trowel, and insert the pieces of step flashing beneath them, as shown in the step flashing illustration.

2. Fasten each step flashing with one roofing nail, placed at the top and away from the chimney, where it will be covered by the next piece of step flashing.

3. Side counterflashing is traditionally made in several pieces that are inserted into the brick joints that step up the chimney side. To follow that pattern, use existing pieces as a guide. It's easier and more effective to make a one-piece counterflashing, as shown in the counterflashing figure. I'll explain this superior approach here.

4. Saw a groove $3/4$-inch deep in the side of the chimney, above all the step flashings. Use a masonry blade in a circular saw. Protect your eyes, and make the cut in two or three passes.

5. Cut a piece of flashing 4 inches longer than the chimney, measured diagonally, as shown in the side counterflashing detail. Make it a total of $1/4$-inch wider than the distance from the groove to the shingles, measured square to the roof. This leaves $1/2$-inch clearance between the counterflashing and the shingles, once you've bent the $3/4$-inch tab.

6. Bend the $3/4$-inch tab along the top, and place it in the groove. Cut this tab at each end of the chimney, and bend the ends 90°. The bottom tab rests outside the base flashing; the top tab rests under the top counterflashing. Trim the ends to make $3/4$-inch tabs.

7. Slip the counterflashing into the groove. Fill the groove with butyl caulking, and wedge the tab into place with roofing nails.

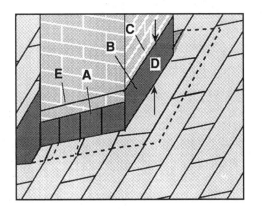

Step flashing prevents leaks by routing water out of the shingles. The top flashing shown is suitable for a relatively narrow chimney, where a cricket is not necessary.

A. Step flashing

B. Top flashing

C. Clean this joint

D. At least 6 inches

E. Groove for one-piece counterflashing

363

One-piece counterflashing is easier to make and more watertight than the older multi-piece counter-flashing. You'll have to saw a groove in the chimney, parallel to the roof line.

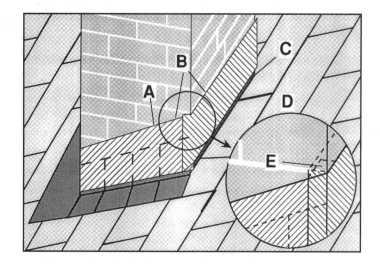

A. Side counterflashing tab goes in groove

B. Top counterflashing covers top flashing

C. 1/2-inch gap between counterflashing and shingles

D. Detail

E. Tabs folded into mortar joint

Cut a groove in the bricks and use this simple, secure side counterflashing.

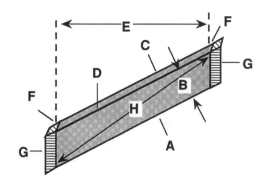

A. Roof line

B. Bend at 1/2 inch less than distance from groove to shingles, measured square to roof

C. 3/4-inch tab

D. Bend so vertical section pushes against the chimney

E. Chimney width

F. Cut tab

G. Bend

H. Cut flashing 4 inches longer than this

Top Flashing

Top flashing comes in two varieties. Standard-width chimneys use the flashing shown here; wider chimneys use the cricket flashing described in the next section.

Standard-Width Chimneys

If you're lucky enough to have a relatively narrow chimney—say about 2 feet or less—you can use this top flashing technique.

1. Clean out the mortar joint that received the old top counterflashing. If no joint was used, select the lowest joint that's above the side flashing and at least 6 inches above the shingles.

2. From a piece of 20-inch flashing material, cut a duplicate of the original top flashing, or use the dimensions suggested in the figure of top flashing. The section against the chimney should be $1/4$-inch wider than the chimney. Don't bend it too far, or the flashing will pull away from the chimney.

3. Loosen the shingles and slip the upper section of the flashing under them. The "tails" of the flashing extend down the sides, above the step flashing.

4. Restore the upper shingles in place, and lightly nail them. Tar the nail heads.

5. Cut a counterflashing for the top, as shown in the top counterflashing detail. The flashing should be 3 inches longer than the chimney width and $1/4$-inch wider than the vertical distance from the joint cleaned in step 1 to the shingles. After you bend the $3/4$-inch tab, the flashing will start $1/2$ inch above the shingles.

6. Bend the $3/4$-inch tab to a slightly acute angle. Cut the tab $1\frac{1}{4}$ inches in from each end, and bend each end 90°. The lower tabs cover the side counterflashing.

7. Insert the top tab into the mortar joint, add butyl caulking, and wedge the tab tight with roofing nails. The acute angle from step 6 holds the counterflashing tight to the top flashing.

Use these dimensions to cut and bend a top flashing.

A. Chimney width plus ¹/₄ inch

B. ¹/₂ inch below the mortar joint

C. Bend so that the vertical section pushes against the chimney

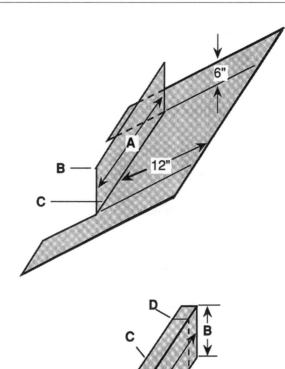

Top counterflashing detail.

A. Chimney width plus 3 inches

B. Height of mortar joint: ¹/₂ inch

C. ³/₄-inch tab

D. Cut tab 1³/₈ inches in from each end

E. Bend 90°

Wide Chimney

A leak on the top of a wide chimney may indicate the need for a "cricket," a pyramid-like device that diverts water to the side so that it cannot gather at the center. (Caution: Flashing a cricket is not simple. When you're done, it's got to be watertight!) To make and install a cricket, follow these steps:

1. Tear back some shingles above the chimney, and cut two triangular pieces of ¹/₂- or ³/₄-inch exterior plywood, as shown in the figure on making a plywood cricket.

2. Screw the lower edges of the cricket to the framing (if possible) with deck screws, or screw into the sheathing if necessary. From above, screw a galvanized steel strip over the joint between the plywood pieces.

3. Carefully measure a sheet-metal flashing to go over the cricket, and nail it into the roof at the top, as shown in the figure of flashing a cricket.

4. Install counterflashing into the brick, using the previous technique described for standard-width chimneys. Replace the shingles as described in the section "Presto-Chango Shingle Replacement," in Chapter 15.

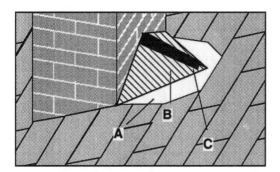

The plywood halves of the cricket are mirror images of each other. Screw them to the framing or decking. A strip of sheet metal joins the tops.

A. Remove shingles

B. Cricket

C. Sheet metal joining strip

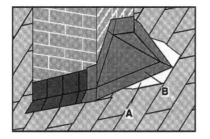

The cricket flashing, made of 20-inch flashing material, extends up the roof beyond the cricket. It is bent around the side flashing.

A. Remove shingles

B. Cricket flashing

The Least You Need to Know

➤ Chimney tops prevent deterioration of a chimney. Chimney caps keep vermin from infesting your house.

➤ Chimney fires are a leading cause of fire in northern states, but they are highly preventable.

➤ Chimney flashing takes a lot of work, but with proper guidance, an advanced idiot should be able to tackle it.

367

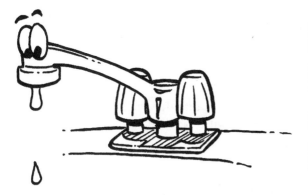

Chapter 31

Either It Leaks ... (Plumbing, Part I)

In This Chapter

➤ The principles of plumbing, with a practical bent

➤ Protecting your home from hydraulic havoc

➤ No more leaks and drips: fixing the common faucet styles

So you've been putting off that little plumbing repair? Believe me, I understand the fear of plumbing—did you notice I left it for last in this book? I remember installing a water softener, a "simple" project that consumed seven aggravating hours, three trips to the hardware store, and most of my stock of marital goodwill.

I'm not the only do-it-yourselfer who finds plumbing gnarly. A few years ago, while trying to fix my kitchen sink, I installed a repair kit—and watched as a drip grew into a steady stream. Then I put in a "universal" replacement cartridge—and uncorked a geyser to rival Old Faithful. My friend Richie Salomon called with the kind of wisdom that could come only from a Sanskrit professor who spends his spare time fiddling with a '53 Studebaker. "You bought a 'universal' repair kit," he sneered. "That means it fits everyone's but yours."

So with a grateful nod to Professor Salomon for his ancient Indian wisdom, Chapters 31 and 32 will plumb the mysterious depths of plumbing—the stuff you can't live with, but that you can't live without either.

The Basic Principles of Plumbing

Everybody knows that plumbing is devious and vindictive, a fountain of bafflement and consternation. Plumbing breakdowns cause people to grab the phone faster than anything else. But plumbing starts to make sense once you understand that it responds to simple physical laws:

> Water seeks its own level.

> The more pressure there is, the more likely a leak is.

> Drain pipes get larger as they go downstream because they must carry more water. Supply pipes get smaller as they go downstream, because they carry less water.

> Hot water is more corrosive than cold water.

> Falling water in a drain must be replaced by air from the venting system.

> Don't put anything (such as leaded solder or other contaminants) in your water supply that you don't wish to drink.

> Record the sequence of parts during disassembly by laying them out in order, facing the same way. You'll find that the most innocent-looking parts go back together in a bewildering number of sequences—all but one wrong!

> Plumbing is governed by plumbing codes (contact your city or township building inspector for information).

> Finally (and this time I mean it literally), don't get in over your head. If you're totally confused, get information or get help.

Water Quality

Because people often drink the water that comes from their pipes, it pays to pay attention to the condition of those pipes. If you're a city person, the city water system should be testing the supply, but it wouldn't hurt to check that it is doing its job. If you drink your own well water, it certainly seems logical to have the water tested occasionally; if it is contaminated, install a filter or take other corrective measures.

A major cause of home water contamination is lead pipes, which were installed until about 1929. If your house was built before then, I would suggest testing for lead in the water. At the very least, look around for lead pipes—you'll see a soft, gray metal that's shiny when scratched. Tin solder, used to join copper pipes until recently, contained some lead, but it's a much smaller source of contamination. Nevertheless, you will do future soldering of copper pipes with lead-free solder, won't you?

If you have lead pipes, you can reduce your lead consumption by running the tap until it's cold before drinking or cooking with water, particularly in the morning. Don't drink hot water, which dissolves more lead.

Hard Facts on Hard Water

Hard water contains high levels of dissolved calcium and magnesium salts, which originate in rocks the groundwater flows through. These salts are usually called lime when they build up on something. If you have hard water, you may notice a white deposit on drinking glasses and inside pipes and the toilet tank. Hard water is much less effective for cleaning clothes than soft water because you need more additives, and soil tends to redeposit in the washer.

Lime does have one benefit: It accumulates inside pipes, coating lead pipes and leaded solder, thus helping prevent water contamination. Nevertheless, lime is hard on the plumbing because it clogs small openings and builds up inside the water heater. (I think of lime as the cholesterol of a plumbing system.) Here are some suggestions for controlling lime problems:

➤ Lime can clog the holes underneath the *toilet* rim (these hard-to-see holes feed water into the bowl to cleanse it during flushing). If they're clogged, ream them out with a bent coat hanger, and then flush the toilet and clean them again.

➤ Lime can clog holes in a *shower head* (look for a blocked or dribbling stream). Remove the screws holding the face plate (you probably won't need to remove the shower head) and soak the spray nozzle in strong vinegar. (If there's no faceplate, unscrew the shower head and disassemble it.) After a couple of hours, poke a wire or nail through the holes, and then reassemble the head.

➤ Lime can cause big problems in a *water heater,* where it builds up and acts as an insulator, reducing efficiency. The best solution is to install a water softener that removes lime before it reaches the heater.

➤ If lime builds up on fixtures (around the spigot or faucets), you may be able to dissolve it with strong vinegar. If this doesn't work, try one of the commercial acids sold for this purpose—using goggles and rubber gloves, naturally.

Tools and Materials

Plumbing can call for a wretched number of special tools, but for most purposes, the few basic ones shown in the photo of plumber's tools will serve. Here are the bare minimum tools:

Plunger: You may need two: a small one for sinks and a big one for toilets.

Pipe wrench: Smaller ones are handy for tight quarters, such as under the sink; larger ones are great for rusty pipe joints. The 12-inch model shown is a compromise size.

Pipe cutter: Cuts copper pipe quickly and cleanly.

Joint compound: Lubricates, rust-proofs, and seals threads of steel pipe. Greatly simplifies disassembly later. Or, substitute the more expensive pipe-thread tape. Don't confuse joint compound with the cement that joins plastic pipe.

Seat reamer: Smoothes seats during washer replacement in compression faucets.

Smooth-jawed (monkey) wrench: Turns polished fittings without wrecking the finish (or, substitute an open-end or adjustable wrench).

Seat remover: Unscrews seats in compression faucets. One end is square, the other hexagonal.

Propane torch: Solders copper pipe and thaws frozen *metal* (not plastic!) pipes.

Lead-free solder: Makes a nontoxic joint in copper pipe.

Soldering flux: Prevents corrosion and helps solder to flow and bond to metal.

Packing (graphite variety shown): Seals the shaft in older faucets.

O-ring: Various sizes seal many newer plumbing fixtures, including faucets and toilets.

Washers: For compression faucets only.

Caution: Depending on your plumbing project, you may also need a plumber's snake (used to unclog drains), cleaner and cement for PVC (polyvinyl chloride) pipe, buckets, a hacksaw, a rag, a level, a bountiful supply of patience and ingenuity, and almost anything else in your home toolbox.

Plumber's tools.

A. Plunger
B. Pipe wrench
C. Pipe cutter
D. Joint compound
E. Seat reamer
F. Smooth-jawed wrench
G. Seat remover
H. Propane torch
I. Lead-free solder
J. Soldering flux
K. Packing
L. O-ring
M. Washers

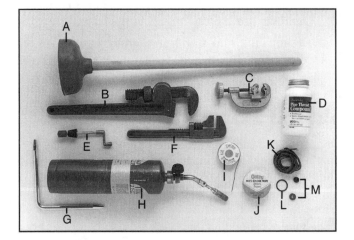

A Little Terminology Goes a Long Way

When it comes to suggestive lingo, nobody can beat plumbers, who describe the mating surfaces (you listening, Dr. Freud?) of pipes and fittings as male or female. The names of the common plumbing fittings are only slightly less self-explanatory, although they are significantly less titillating (see the following table).

Fitting Identification

Fitting	Name	Description
	90° elbow	Turns a corner. The "street elbow" variation has one male and one female end. The "long-sweep 90° elbow" connects to horizontal drain runs.
	45° elbow	Also available in a $22^1/_2°$ version.
	Reducer (bushing)	A male-to-female fitting that changes the size of piping; you can put one inside another to make a bigger change in size.
	Coupling	Joins two same or different diameter pipes. (A female thread or soldered fitting is on both ends.)
	Union	Joins two pipes that cannot be turned because both ends are fastened. Unscrew the large nut, and the union comes apart.
	Nipple (male)	A short section of pipe, available in various thread and lengths; joins two fittings, such as valves and elbows.
	Plug	Closes a female port on a fitting.
	Cap	Seals the end of a pipe.
	Tee	Makes a three-way intersection of pipes with same or different sizes.
	Wye	Used for drain and waste lines; has a better flow than standard tees. The side outlet is angled, so water enters the drain without slowing down.

Shut It Down with the Main Water Shut-Off

The main shut-off is the valve that controls all water entering the house; it's usually located in a fiendishly inaccessible location next to the water meter, on the exterior wall near the front of the house. If you need to be convinced of the importance of main shut-offs, listen to the story of a Waterloo, Wisconsin, couple who had enough sense to flee south during the brutal winter of 1979 but not enough brains to shut off the water. When a pipe froze in the basement, rising water snuffed out their furnace and formed a giant block of ice in the basement. By the time the unlucky couple returned from sunny Florida, their front steps were cloaked in a cascade of ice.

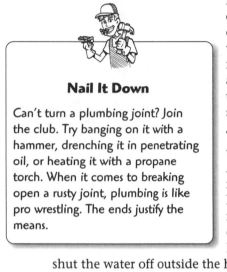

Nail It Down

Can't turn a plumbing joint? Join the club. Try banging on it with a hammer, drenching it in penetrating oil, or heating it with a propane torch. When it comes to breaking open a rusty joint, plumbing is like pro wrestling. The ends justify the means.

That flood is the best argument I know for shutting off the water when you leave town, particularly in winter. And because almost every plumbing emergency can require quick action at the main shut-off, it wouldn't hurt to test the valve before you really need it. Unfortunately, because the shut-off is seldom used, it may not close completely, or it may leak around the stem. Repairing this valve is a pro job because you've got to shut the water off outside the house; once it's in working order, though, many plumbing repairs will be much easier. In a house supplied by a well, shutting off the circuit breaker feeding the pump will eventually shut off the water—after the pressure tank empties.

If the shut-off is partly effective, you should be able to make some repairs. Close the main valve off as much as possible, and then open a faucet below the one you're fixing (or at the same level, if necessary). This relieves the water pressure so that you can complete the repair without a flood.

Emergency Repairs

If you've got a leak that needs stopping now, first close the main shut-off (see the previous section). If that doesn't work, or if you want water in the house for some other reason (such as drinking or flushing), the following techniques should slow the leak enough to be caught in a bucket while you plot a permanent repair or await the plumber.

➤ Stretch electrical tape around the leaking pipe. Dry the pipe as much as possible, and wrap the tape tightly around it.

➤ Take a section of garden hose, slice it lengthwise, and clamp it in position with pipe clamps.

➤ A locking pliers (preferably with a curved jaw) should hold a pliable patch in position for a while. If you have several pairs, use them, too.

If a threaded joint is leaking, try to disassemble it, smear some joint compound on the threads, and screw it back tighter. Unfortunately, you can do this only if one end of the pipe can move, or if the pipe has a union. If a union is present, loosen the union to detach the leaking joint. Similarly, if you need to splice in a new section of threaded pipe to repair a leak but neither end can turn, you'll have to install a union in the line. That's getting toward pro territory—although, as a determined idiot, you should know that some plumbing shops (and many hardware stores) will cut and thread steel pipe for you.

Faucet Repair (Dig It! Trouble with the Spigot?)

Faucets shut off the water supply, theoretically, without leaking, grabbing, or requiring steroid-enhanced muscular force. The old compression faucets controlled hot or cold water individually and were used in pairs. Most newer faucets use one handle to control both flows, usually with a cartridge or a ball mechanism. As we look at these faucets in your involuntary introduction to plumbing, remember that you may meet variations on the general theme—yet another reason to bring the carcass of the faucet to the store when you buy parts.

Fixing Compression Faucets

Compression faucets close the flow of water by pushing a washer against a seat. Most failures are due to a worn-out washer, but because the root cause is often a rough seat that tore up the washer, seats and washers may need to be replaced together. You'll need a screwdriver and a wrench, and possibly a seat-dressing tool or a seat-removing tool. You'll also want faucet grease or Vaseline, and pipe joint compound. Use these steps to repair the faucet:

1. Turn off the water, preferably at a shut-off valve just before the faucet, or otherwise at the main shut-off.

2. Pull off the handles by removing the handle screw (see the figure illustrating compression faucet repair). You may have to pry off a decorative cap on top of the handle first.

3. With a smooth-jawed wrench, loosen the bonnet nut. Then slip the handle back on and unscrew the stem.

4. Shine a flashlight on the seat, or poke it with your little finger. It should look and feel smooth. If the seat is rough or uneven, the new washer won't seal against it and will be damaged. If you see a square or hexagonal opening for a wrench inside the seat, your best bet is to replace the seat (step 5A). If the seat is fixed (laundry sinks, for example, often have nonreplaceable seats), smooth it with a seat-dressing tool (step 5B).

5A. *Remove the seat* with a seat-removing tool (some plumbing terms are *so* logical!). Slip the tool into the seat, tap it into place, and unscrew. Take the seat to a plumbing supply or hardware store, buy a replacement for each faucet, and install them with the same tool. Put pipe joint compound or Vaseline on the threads so that they'll come out easily next time.

5B. To *smooth a fixed seat*, buy or rent a seat-dressing tool and insert it into the faucet so that it sits squarely; then clean up the seat with the coarse cutter. Switch to the finer blade, and repeat. Be sure to hold the tool perpendicular to the seat.

6. To *replace the washers,* first decide whether you need a beveled or flat variety (flat washers are more common, but each style comes in several sizes). Don't just replace what you find—some bozo might have used the wrong type. All washers are held in position by a retaining rim. If the rim is broken, get a new stem; replacements are usually pretty easy to find if you bring the old stem to the hardware store. The washer screw should come right out (despite years of immersion in water); simply screw a new one into place. Use brass screws, *not* steel ones, which will rust and never come out.

7. For a good repair, apply faucet grease or Vaseline to the mating metal parts and inside the packing. This allows them to operate smoothly.

8. Thread the stem into the bonnet nut, and screw the nut into the faucet. Before the final tightening of the bonnet nut, back off on the stem so that it does not bottom against the seat and fight the tightening action.

9. Restore the water pressure. If the faucet leaks around the stem, keep reading.

Compression faucet repair. You'll see countless variations on this basic design for the compression faucet.

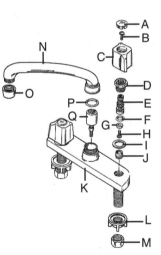

A. Decorative cap	J. Seat
B. Handle screw	K. Faucet body
C. Handle	L. Lock nut
D. Bonnet nut	M. Supply nut
E. Stem	N. Spout
F. Washer	O. Aerator
G. Seat washer	P. O-ring
H. Washer screw	Q. Diverter (diverts water to spray hose)
I. Washer	

Get Packing (or, Does Your Stem Leak?)

Many compression-faucet problems take place at the seal between the bonnet nut and the stem. This seal may come from an O-ring (a special washer) or, in older faucets, a flexible material called *packing*.

You can recognize packing leaks because they occur only when the valve is open (when the valve is closed, there's no water pressure on the packing). If the packing is really loose, the stem may slop around a bit. Often, you can seal a packing leak by tightening the bonnet (use reasonable force—if you squeeze too tight, you will seize the handle in place). If tightening fails, unscrew the bonnet nut and check the variety of packing material. If it's a glob of material pressed into place, replace the packing and retighten. If the seal is made by a solid packing washer or an O-ring (a narrow washer surrounding the stem), just replace the washer or O-ring.

Cartridge Faucets

Cartridge faucets use a replaceable, cylindrical cartridge to mix and control the flow of hot and cold water. Although you might be tempted to buy cheap, replacement seals instead of the whole cartridge, you'll do better in the long run replacing the entire thing.

The cartridge for a Moen brand of faucet is fixed in place with a retainer clip. Other types are held in place with a nut. To disassemble, turn off the water, pull off the handle, pull off the stem nut or clip, and pull out the cartridge (see the illustration of cartridge faucet repair). You may need to use a special cartridge tool to get the thing apart. To make sure you remove all the parts, compare what you remove to the contents of the replacement kit. Then simply slap the replacement cartridge back into place. If the faucet operates stiffly, try using faucet grease; cartridges can lime up.

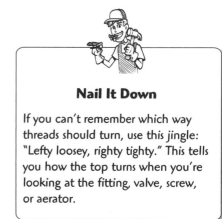

Nail It Down

If you can't remember which way threads should turn, use this jingle: "Lefty loosey, righty tighty." This tells you how the top turns when you're looking at the fitting, valve, screw, or aerator.

Cartridge faucet repair.

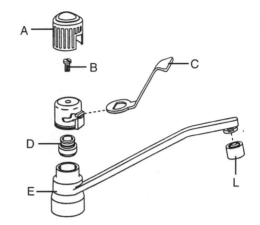

A. Handle cap

B. Handle screw

C. Lever handle

D. Retainer pivot nut

E. Spout assembly

F. Cartridge

G. Retainer clip

H. Spout O-rings

I. Escutcheon

J. Deck gasket

K. Lock nuts

L. Aerator

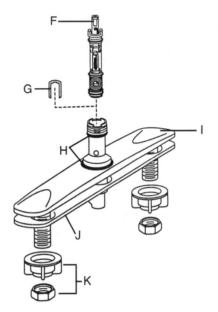

Ball Faucets

Ball faucets are an alternative to cartridges, and they're considerably cheaper to repair. You'll need a repair kit, new O-rings for the spout (optional), an allen wrench (which may come with the kit), arc-joint pliers, and plumber's luck. Here's how:

1. Shut off the water and loosen the allen-headed set screw on the bottom of the handle (see the next figure, illustrating ball faucet repair). Remove the handle.

2. The adjusting ring should be visible; tighten it slightly and test whether the faucet still drips (drips can be caused by inadequate pressure on the seals).

3. If the faucet still drips, remove the adjusting ring and pull out the cap and the ball under it.

4. The seals are the two small disks under the ball (see the figure on following page). Note their location and remove them. Don't lose the springs!

5. With the faucet apart, you might as well replace the O-rings sealing the spout (unless you'd rather face another repair in a few months). Pull up on the spout, and twist to remove it. Carefully dig the O-rings and any lime build-up from their grooves. Then put new O-rings in the grooves and twist the spout back into place.

6. Put the new seals in place, and press the ball and cam back into position, making sure the seals don't jump out as you do so.

7. Screw the adjusting ring back on, and tighten firmly. Turn the water on, and tighten some more if it's leaking. Then replace the handle.

8. While water is running, push down on the handle. If water leaks out under the handle, tighten the adjusting ring.

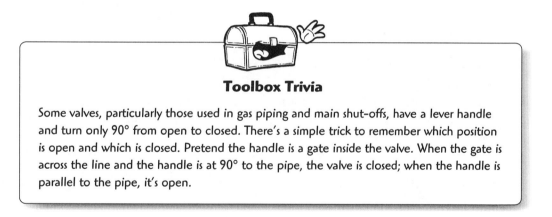

Toolbox Trivia

Some valves, particularly those used in gas piping and main shut-offs, have a lever handle and turn only 90° from open to closed. There's a simple trick to remember which position is open and which is closed. Pretend the handle is a gate inside the valve. When the gate is across the line and the handle is at 90° to the pipe, the valve is closed; when the handle is parallel to the pipe, it's open.

Ball faucet repair. The set screw releases the handle to begin the disassembly. The springs push the seats against the ball to control flow.

A. Handle

B. Set screw

C. Adjusting ring

D. Cap

E. Spout

F. Aerator

G. Spout sleeve

H. Slip ring

I. Cam and packing

J. Ball

K. Seat and spring

L. Faucet body

M. O-rings (spout seals)

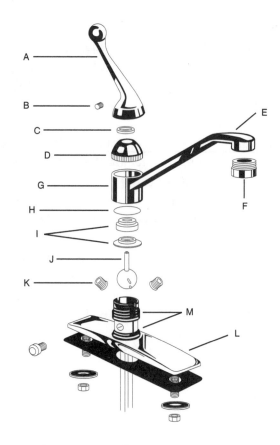

What About Low Water Pressure?

If your faucets have lost their former oomph, it's likely that the aerators are plugged (you should always be so lucky; this is the cheapest and quickest plumbing fix you'll ever make). Aerators (see the following photo) are screens mounted on the end of faucets to conserve water and create a foamy stream. Simply unscrew the aerator body from the end of the spout with pliers (protect the chrome with adhesive tape), take it apart, and clean rust and crud from the screens. You may have to do this every few months, but it's amazingly effective.

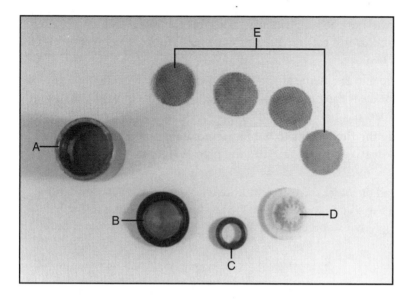

Aerators come in many variations. The main rule is to keep track of the parts as you remove them so that you don't replace them backward.

A. Body

B. Inlet screen

C. O-ring

D. Flow restrictor

E. Screens

For clogging caused by liming, see the section "Hard Facts on Hard Water," earlier in this chapter.

Note: If you have a private water system, low pressure can be due to a faulty or water-logged air tank, or a problem with the water pump. Both of these repairs are beyond idiot territory.

To conserve water in dry regions, or to conserve the energy used to heat water, hardware stores sell (and some utilities give) low-flow aerators and shower heads. In addition, some shower heads have an adjustment knob on the side to slow the flow.

Soldering Copper Pipe

I used to be so scared of soldering copper pipes that I used a baroque, overly exacting technique. Needless to say, it backfired; I botched the job by overheating the metal. Truth is, a clean, fluxed, good-fitting joint is almost impossible to solder badly, as long as you supply enough heat while avoiding overheating. That's because clean copper and hot solder have an irresistible attraction called capillary action, which pulls the solder evenly into a joint.

You'll need a propane torch, sandpaper, emery cloth or steel wool, flux, and lead-free plumbing solder. Use these steps:

1. Inspect the fittings and the pipe. They should be sound, round, and free of nicks and deformities. Check the joint: Does the pipe enter straight, giving a tight fit? Correct any problems now, while the pipe is cold.

2. Clean the mating surfaces (the outside of the pipe and the inside of the fitting) with fine sandpaper, emery cloth, or steel wool. Get them bright and clean.

3. Apply no-lead flux to both mating surfaces, assemble the joint, and twist it a bit to distribute the flux. Don't eat the flux or inhale more fumes than you must—the stuff isn't real healthy.

4. Light the torch and aim the flame at the fitting. Do not concentrate the heat; move the torch and heat the pipe as well as the fitting. Concentrate your heat at the most massive part of the fitting.

5. A few seconds after the flux begins to bubble, remove the torch and touch the solder to the crack between the fitting and the pipe. A hot joint will pull the solder in.

6. When an even bead of solder forms around the whole joint between the fitting and the pipe, pull the solder away and let the joint cool for about a minute without disturbing it. Now you can wrap a wet rag on the joint to cool it faster.

Plastic Pipe

If you're ancient enough, you may remember the immortal advice Dustin Hoffman received in the movie *The Graduate*. The future, he was told, was "plastic." In plumbing, certainly, copper and steel now face competition from a growing number of plastics. In general, these plastics are cheaper and easier to use than metal—although they require simpler tools, they are not for every situation. Some plastic, for example, can handle only a limited amount of pressure, or only cold water. To extend a metal plumbing system with plastic, buy fittings that join plastic to copper, steel, or cast iron.

Consult your local building code to see what's allowed in your area; here's a brief rundown on some of the plastic pipe on the market.

➤ PVC (polyvinyl chloride): Used for drains and vent lines

➤ ABS (acrylonitrile butadiene styrene): Used for drains and vent lines

➤ CPVC (chlorinated polyvinyl chloride): Allowed for water piping in some areas

➤ Polybutylene: Allowed for water piping in some areas

➤ Polyethylene: Used in well piping

Joining Plastic Pipe

Some types of plastic pipe can be joined with special fittings that are tightened with a wrench. Others can be joined by pushing the pipe into a fitting. Many plastic pipes are welded together using a special solvent; make sure you buy the right solvent for your pipe material. Here's the general procedure for welding plastic pipe with solvent:

1. Cut the pipe square at the end with a hacksaw (use a miter box, if you have one).

2. Using sandpaper, trim off burrs and roughen the outside to prepare it for solvent.

3. Line up the joint dry.

4. Disassemble the joint. When everything is ready, wipe solvent on the pipe end and inside the fitting.

5. Press the pipe into the joint until it bottoms, and then give it a quarter turn. Quickly make any adjustments to the position of the fitting—you won't get a second chance because plastic can bond in less than a minute. Let the joint set up.

Frozen Pipes—and How to Avoid Them

Frozen pipes sound so, er, boring. Nobody has them anymore, right? Well, according to one insurance company, 250,000 Americans have them each year. And, if you read the horror story in the section "Shut It Down with the Main Water Shut-Off," at the start of this chapter, you know frozen pipes can spell disaster.

The pipes most likely to freeze, amazingly enough, are those in cold locations such as underheated crawl spaces, basements, and along outside walls. The following sections offer suggestions for preventing the big chill.

At Hose Connections

Outside faucets (called sillcocks or hose bibbs) are a prime place for a freeze-up. Disconnect the garden hose before freezing weather. If you have a "frostproof" sillcock, removing the hose should take care of it, as long as you haven't left a fitting in place that seals the water in. Frostproof faucets shut off inside the wall and drip dry to prevent frost. You can recognize them because some water drips out after you shut them off. If the faucet is not frostproof, close the valve inside the wall (if there is one) on the pipe supplying the hose connection. Then open the faucet to let it drip dry.

Other Anti-Frost Measures

➤ Warm up the foundation by caulking cracks.

➤ Put insulation between the pipes and the cold (pipe insulation will help for a while, but eventually the pipe will reach ambient temperature unless water is flowing).

➤ During the winter, keep the thermostat up (believe it or not, heat can prevent freeze-ups). Open cabinet doors in the kitchen so that warm air can reach pipes under the sink. If you split the scene in winter, shut off the main water valve and ask a neighbor to monitor the house temperature.

➤ As a last resort, if you can't warm pipes in any other way, install pipe tape. To prevent fire, buy a UL-approved product and follow all directions.

Four Thaws for Icy Pipes

Let's say you've got some frozen pipes. What to do? First, open a faucet at the end of the pipe to give the water some place to go after it thaws. Then select among these warm-up options:

➤ Wrap the pipe with rags, and pour boiling water over them.

➤ Warm the pipes with a heat gun or heat lamp.

➤ Wrap the pipe with a heating pad.

➤ As a last resort, if you are comfortable with a propane torch, put a flame spreader in place and move the torch around on metal pipes only. Be careful, and don't work near any wood or foam insulation.

Once you've thawed the pipes, it's time to figure out how to avoid a freeze next time. See the section "Frozen Pipes—and How to Avoid Them," earlier in this chapter.

Don't Screw Up!

Natural gas is supplied at low pressure, so it's less likely to leak than water. Use joint compound on good, clean threads, and avoid Tarzan-style tightening, which is a recipe for stripping threads and cracking fittings. After you restore the gas pressure, brush on some soap suds to test the joint. Bubbles indicate a leak. Do not use matches to test for leaks!

Your Water Heater

Let's face it—life would be pretty squalid without a water heater. And while water heaters don't need much maintenance, it won't hurt to make sure the safety valve is working and to drain sludge from the bottom of the tank once in a while.

The *pressure-temperature relief valve* on top of a water heater is an essential safety feature because an overheated water heater could cause a steam explosion and send shrapnel right through the roof. The valve has a small handle and is attached to the overflow pipe running down the side of the heater. Once a year, test the valve by lifting the handle and making sure that water runs out the overflow tube and that the valve snaps shut afterward. If it doesn't, call a plumber—an inoperative valve is a hazard. (This valve will spill water into the overflow, so keep a bucket handy. Never attach a hose to the overflow, for safety reasons.)

Over time, sludge can build up inside water heaters. Remove sludge every few months by draining the tank through the valve at the bottom. Let the water run until it's clear.

To adjust the temperature in an electric water heater with two elements (which most have), set the upper thermostat about 10° warmer than the lower one. (Because warm water rises, the top of the tank will always be warmer than the bottom.) If you have small children, avoid burn hazards by limiting the temperature to about 125° F. (Note: Electric water heaters can cost more than twice as much to operate as gas heaters, so I wouldn't spend much repairing one.)

Putting the Kibosh on Water Hammer

Water hammer is the loud clanking you hear when you quickly close a faucet; it's caused by the sudden stopping of water in the pipes. Water hammer sounds obnoxious and can loosen the piping. If your house has this problem, you need to add support for the pipes, have a plumber install water hammer arrestors, or simply close the faucets more slowly.

Some houses have air chambers in the piping, dead-end fittings containing air designed to prevent water hammer. If yours has them, you may be able to restore the air in the air chambers and temporarily silence water hammer. You will need a working main shut-off and these instructions:

1. Close the main shut-off.

2. Open valves on every floor of the house, particularly the lowest valves, and wait about 15 minutes so the entire plumbing system can drain. Air will replace the water in the pipes and air chambers.

3. Shut the faucets and open the main shut-off. Your air chambers should be restored, and water hammer should be a noisome memory. If this cure works, you'll have to repeat it periodically. And don't be surprised if some of your faucet aerators get plugged by grit that gets loosened by this little fix-up.

The Least You Need to Know

➤ Water systems can benefit from a surprising amount of preventive help, most of which will increase your convenience or comfort and reduce your maintenance bills.

➤ Faucet seats—the overlooked cause of many drippy faucets—can be repaired or replaced.

➤ Believe it or not, many faucets are built to be repaired. The hardest part is often figuring out how to take them apart; the rest should be easy.

➤ Hard water can cause a damaging lime build-up in many parts of a plumbing system.

Chapter 32

... Or It Doesn't Drain (Plumbing, Part II)

In This Chapter

➤ Drains, traps, and vents—solving the mystery of where it all goes

➤ Preventive maintenance for drains—how to stay out of the sewer-cleaning business

➤ A realistic, step-by-step approach to cleaning drains

It's time to cut the crap. You didn't start this chapter from some abstract interest in the plumbing code, or a fascination with the flow of filthy water. You're reading in hopes of getting some action in the drains, right?

Right. So let's get right down to the dirty work and get that drain back in business. We'll start with the least dramatic techniques and move to increasingly invasive procedures (as the M.D.s put it) that you might need if milder techniques fail.

Feeling Trapped by Your Trap?

A trap is a U-shaped piece of drainpipe that's usually directly beneath the outlet of a plumbing fixture. Traps have two important purposes: to create a water seal so you can avoid intimate contact with the sicko world of sewer gas, and to give crud a place to hang up so you can test your new plumbing skills (just kidding).

Traps look simple, and they are. But because the water seal is so important, plumbing codes strictly limit the design and construction of traps (see the illustrations of traps). For example, multiple traps are forbidden because they create too much resistance to the flow; thus, you should not see a trap beneath a toilet, which has a built-in trap.

A good P-trap: Notice that the slip-joint connector on the discharge (sink) side is above the water seal. This three-piece trap is a common, adjustable item sold in all hardware stores; it can be swiveled and extended to fit most sinks. 1¹⁄₂ inches is more common, but there is a 1¹⁄₄-inch variety too.

A. Sink tailpiece

B. Slip-joint nuts

C. Water level in trap

D. To drain pipe

The water seal can be siphoned from this illegal S-trap, which should be replaced.

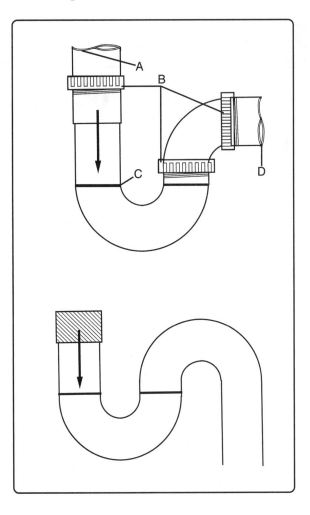

Venting

You won't see vents very often, but they are a critical part of your plumbing system because they allow air to replace water as it leaves a drain and preserve the water trap that blocks odors from entering the house. Without a vent, you'll get a vacuum and a sluggish, gurgling drain. If your vent is plugged, you may be able to ream it out by sticking a long drain auger (or "snake") into the round vent pipe sticking through the roof. Retrofitting vents in an old house is strictly a pro job, but it will vastly improve the performance of the drains.

About the only drawback of vents is that they limit the effectiveness of a plunger, which can pressurize only the section of pipe between the drain and the vent. But that's a small price to pay for vents' real benefit: preventing the funky, unhealthy stench that results when a water trap is sucked dry by the vacuum created as water goes down an unvented drain. Vented drains have a second benefit: They stay cleaner because water flows more quickly through them.

Going Down: Fixing the Drain Is ... Less Disgusting Than Ignoring It

Logically, the first step in cleaning a drain is to make sure the clog is a local problem, not a systemic one. If two or more drains suddenly plug up, I'd bet a gold-plated plunger that the cause is something affecting both drains, such as a major clog or a plugged vent. Because these problems can be harder to reach, they're a good reason to call for help. If only one drain is screaming in agony, read on.

Hair and Soap Scuzz

If you're lucky, your problem is caused by something as simple as hair, soap scuzz, and other flimsy unmentionables on the strainer or just inside the drain. You can probably remove these clogs with long-nose pliers, a bent coat hanger, or "mechanical fingers," a long, three-fingered tool for grabbing stuff in inaccessible places.

After you get the drain working again, resolve to keep wannabe cloggers such as bobby pins away from the sink, and forget about dumping cooking grease down the kitchen sink. You can prevent further accumulations of soap, grease, and hair by flushing the drain with plenty of hot water. Put 4 to 5 inches of hot water in the sink or tub, and then pull the plug so that the water can scour the drain pipe; do this weekly if you can remember.

Drain Chemicals

If your drain is still flowing, but too slowly for your taste, you may start wondering if a miracle chemical could solve (or should we say dissolve?) your woes.

Lye is a good preventive measure for occasional cleaning. But be *sure* to read and follow the label, because lye can solidify in a drain if left too long. And use protective clothing and goggles. (If you go blind, how are you going to read another *Idiot's Guide*?)

Enzymes (chemical extracts from microorganisms that have generations of experience breaking down organic matter) are good for maintenance because they're far less hazardous than acid or lye. But keep your eye on the label—you probably need to use them periodically.

Sulfuric acid and various other preparations are sold for cleaning drains. Most experts won't use them on a totally clogged drain because pressure can build up and the pipes can explode, or at least heat up and corrode. (And if the acid doesn't work, you'll have to work in pipes full of acid—a nasty prospect.) Even if a clog does get loose, it might travel to an even worse location and get stuck. Finally, acid can also damage chrome plating and possibly metal pipes.

Acid is much better for preventive maintenance on drains that are starting to slow because it eats away all sorts of organic yuck. Protect metal on the sink or tub with Vaseline. Remember: The acid cure can work, but only if you disobey the natural instinct to ignore plumbing problems until they absolutely can't be ignored any longer.

If you decide to use acid, use plenty of caution:

➤ Put on gloves and goggles.

➤ Read the label.

➤ Keep some baking soda handy to neutralize any acid that gets on your skin.

➤ Don't mix chemicals. (Did you think we were recommending a do-it-yourself Frankenstein course here? No. Drain cleaner and bleach, for example, form a toxic combination.)

Plunger (the Plumber's Friend)

Are you slightly offended by the sight of a plunger near the toilet? Not me—I take it as a sign that the homeowner knows that when something goes wrong with a drain, there's scarcely time to visit a hardware store: Immediate action is needed. Plungers exert a hydraulic force on the contents of a drain (and whatever is plugging it), but they are only effective up to the vent connection (which may be just inside the wall).

If you follow the advice of my friend Carl Lorentz, who makes plumbing his living, you'll get two plungers: a big one for toilets and a junior size for sinks. Combine forces on bathtubs: Use one plunger on the drain, and use the other to seal the overflow (without that seal, you can't put pressure on the drain). To plunge a sink, plug the overflow with a rag because the second plunger may not fit. If you're having trouble making a seal, put some Vaseline on the end of the plunger.

Here's how to plunge a drain:

1. Add a few inches of water to the fixture (if it's not full of liquid yuck to begin with!).

2. Roll the plunger into the water to minimize the amount of air trapped inside the bell.

3. Pump up and down as hard as you can while holding a good seal. Then give one final pull and break the plunger free. You may have to plunge for several minutes. With any luck, you'll hear a famished groan as the drain sucks down a load of filth.

If a couple of more plunging efforts fail, your choices are to disassemble the trap, use a pipe auger, or call a pro. Let's look at disassembly first.

Drain Disassembly and Replacement

A trap may plug up. Even if the clog is deeper in the pipes, removing the trap may gain you access to the clog. The good news is that new traps are quite easy to remove and replace; the bad news is that not all traps are new. You'll need a flashlight, a bucket, a rag, a pipe wrench, new washers for the trap (they're usually $1^1/_2$ inches in diameter), a coat hanger, and a strong stomach. You may also need a replacement trap and a pipe auger. Follow these steps:

1. Position the bucket under the trap and remove the cleanout, if there is one. From here, you might be lucky enough to see and remove the clog (just like you might be lucky enough to win the lottery every time! It's possible, but not likely). More likely, the clog will squirt out into your eye.

P-trap removal and cleanout. Remember the rule: lefty loosey, righty tighty. Reverse this rule for a nut that's facing away from you on a horizontal pipe.

2. Loosen the three large nuts on the trap (see the next photo). If you're feeling fastidious, use cloth to protect the chrome plating on metal nuts.

3. Pull the trap apart, and remove any obstruction you see.

4. If you need to, dig around in the drain with a coat hanger and pull out any blockages. (Or, see the section "The Plumber's Snake," later in this chapter.)

5. Once you've removed the clog, push the washers onto the male ends of the trap (see the following photo) and loosely assemble the trap.

6. Put the trap into position carefully; if you get it right the first time, you won't need nuclear-scale force on the nuts.

Toolbox Trivia

Most drainpipe—for tubs and kitchen sinks—is made in $1\frac{1}{2}$-inch diameter. Small sinks in bathrooms—called lavatories—use $1\frac{1}{4}$-inch piping. When buying washers—or a new trap—make sure you know which diameter you need. It's best to bring the trap to the store.

Place new washers on the pipes before reassembly. Make sure the washer is evenly seated before tightening the slip nut.

A. Washer

B. Slip nut

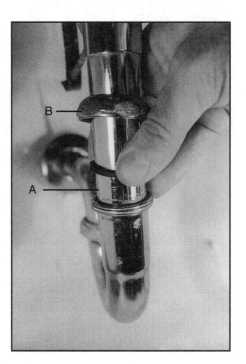

The Plumber's Snake

Pipe snakes, or *augers*, are flexible tools that supposedly can be threaded into a drain to loosen and remove whatever kind of unmentionable crud is clogging it. The continual need for drain cleaning has spawned many inventions; the best tool for you depends on your talent, your wallet, and your luck.

➤ A simple *plumber's snake* is made of flat, flexible (spring) steel.

➤ A *rotating snake* is slightly more expensive—and much more effective. The snake looks like a long spring, and it's flexible enough to get through a couple of elbows before it gets jammed. It has a handle that rotates it as you thread it into the piping.

➤ A rented electric *drain-reamer* is more effective, but make sure you're confident using it so that you don't wreck the plumbing.

➤ A special toilet-cleaning snake called a *closet auger* has a right-angle end so that it can reach inside the toilet trap. But be careful not to force the auger—you could break the inside wall of the toilet.

Some people suggest using a garden hose as an improvised snake, but I'd be hesitant because they don't seem flexible enough to get through drains.

Drain Auger Techniques

Sinks: You may be able to run an auger through the trap into the drain, but it's more likely that you'll have to work through the cleanout at the bottom of the trap. If there is no cleanout, disassemble the trap and thread the auger directly into the horizontal stub of pipe leading into the wall. You may be able to remove a cleanout plate on the big drain stack below a sink and feed the auger through the opening. Turn the handle of the auger clockwise, and if you think you've hooked something, gradually withdraw the auger as you continue turning.

Tubs: Remove the overflow plate and the stopper and stopper linkage. Snake the auger through the overflow opening, and crank, moving the auger back and forth, to pick up or dislodge the clog. If your tub has a drum trap (look for a metal plate in the floor near the tub or inside an access panel), open the cover on the drum and run the snake in both directions from the trap. You may want to try your plunger once more before taking a drum trap apart—they're tricky.

Toilets: Feed a closet auger (mentioned earlier in this section) into the trap, being careful not to chip the china bowl. Working firmly but carefully, push the snake into the trap and feel for an obstruction. When you think you've hooked one,

Don't Screw Up!

Utter plumbing purgatory occurs when you jam a snake in the pipes. This brilliantly converts a routine problem into a disaster that requires an expensive visit from the plumber or drain cleaner. It's embarrassing—and something you can avoid by taking care not to get in over your head. If you truly don't understand what you're doing, don't try it!

pull it out. If you must use a straight (sink-type) auger, be extra careful with the china—and wear rubber gloves! Because toilets are porcelain, and because porcelain is fragile, you may want to go back to the all-important plunger. Pencils, toothbrushes, dentures, diaphragms, and toys can all plug toilets. If the toilet continues plugging, it either needs repair or something is wedged in its innards. Empty the bowl, and use a flashlight and small mirror to inspect the trap. Then use a bent coat hanger to extract the object.

How Toilets Flush—and Other Modern Miracles

Ever wonder how a toilet works? Nobody does—until they go on strike. It's just like the old bluesman said, "You don't miss your water 'til your well runs dry." So if you're still reading, I assume you have what the spies call a need to know. How does a toilet do its critically important task?

1. When you pull the handle, the lift arm lifts the stopper valve, and the tankful of water rushes into the bowl, pushing the putrid cargo into the water trap and down the drain (see the accompanying photo).

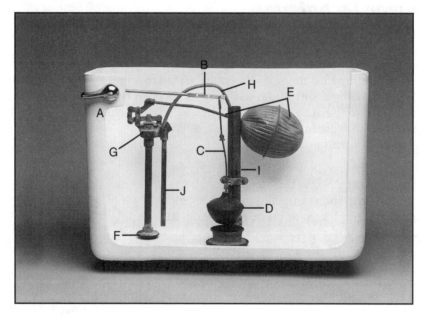

The guts of an old toilet.

A. Handle

B. Lift arm

C. Lift wire

D. Stopper valve (or flapper, in newer installations)

E. Float and arm

F. Water supply

G. Ballcock valve assembly

H. Bowl refill tube

I. Overflow tube

J. Tank refill tube

2. As the float drops, it opens the ballcock valve, and fresh water enters the tank through the tank refill tube. At the same time, fresh water flows through the bowl refill tube and overflow tube, refilling the bowl.

3. When the tank empties, the stopper valve drops back into place, sealing the tank and allowing it to fill. Meanwhile, the overflow tube continues filling the bowl.

4. When the water level is high enough, the float shuts the valve, ending the cycle.

Toilet Troubleshooting

Water should not circulate from the tank to the bowl except while flushing. If the toilet runs (periodically refills its tank), water is entering the bowl when it's not supposed to. Pour food dye in the tank. If the bowl water turns color before you flush, here's the cause:

The ballcock valve is not shutting off soon enough, and water is rising above the overflow tube and flowing into the tank. Bend the float arm down so that the valve shuts off sooner. If you have the replacement valve shown in the photo on updating your toilet's innards, loosen the clip and slide the float down the guide wire. Check that the float arm operates smoothly. Then read the next section on ballcock, "Replacing Their Guts."

The stopper valve seat is damaged or dirty, and water is leaking into the bowl through the bottom of the tank. Read the next section, "Replacing Their Guts."

Hints for Good Toilet Operation

➤ To make sure the mechanism is not snagging itself, watch a full flushing cycle with the tank uncovered.

➤ Check that the stopper and float are not waterlogged. The float should ride on top of the water, and the stopper should stay up during the whole flushing cycle.

➤ Check the holes under the rim, and ream them with a coat hanger if they're plugged (see the section "Hard Facts on Hard Water," in Chapter 31, "Either It Leaks ... [Plumbing, Part I]").

Don't Screw Up!

For the fastidious few, there's always the chance that germs can live in the toilet. To kill them, pour some bleach into the bowl before working on it. Decontaminate snakes and tools in 1 part bleach to 10 parts water.

Replacing Their Guts

Toilets have come a long way since somebody first realized the virtues of not having to march to the backyard every time nature called. Modern toilet replacement mechanisms are such a vast improvement that even semi-operable old mechanisms can reasonably be replaced. First, the new equipment is mostly plastic, so it won't rust. Second, the simplified design omits many traditional trouble spots. Third, it's cheap.

And fourth, as I learned yesterday, after the old ballcock in my toilet seized up, they're incredibly easy to install. (Call it luck, fate, or coincidence; I figure my house was reading this chapter over my shoulder.) I'll start by explaining how to replace the ballcock, and then I'll talk about replacing the flush valve.

The ballcock refills the tank and bowl when the tank level drops during flushing, and it shuts off when the tank is full. Replacing the old valve should take less than half an hour. You'll need a pair of arc-joint pliers or locking pliers, a knife, and a monkey wrench. To replace the ballcock, follow these steps:

1. Shut off the water supply below the toilet (see the photo showing how to loosen the shut-off). Close the main water shut-off if this valve is not working or is absent. Then flush the toilet to drain the tank, and sponge out the remaining water.

2. Remove the old ballcock by loosening the water supply connection and the big nut mounting the ballcock to the bottom of the tank.

3. For a good seal, clean the area around the hole in the bottom of the toilet tank with steel wool. Twist the replacement assembly to adjust its height, as shown in the photo of the replacement valve. Place the washer on the tube, and insert the tube through the hole.

4. Loosely connect the water supply and the mounting lock nut. Then tighten both nuts.

5. Attach the refill tube to the valve. Cut the tube to length, and clip it to the overflow pipe, as shown in the photo.

6. Turn on the water supply, and retighten the packing nut on the water supply valve. Flush out the valve per instructions, and adjust the tank water level with the clip on the float. If you see any leaks, tighten the appropriate fitting, and you're done.

If the shut-off valve is tight, loosen the packing nut with a wrench.

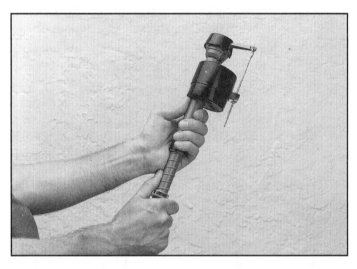

The new valve must be adjusted to the height of the toilet tank.

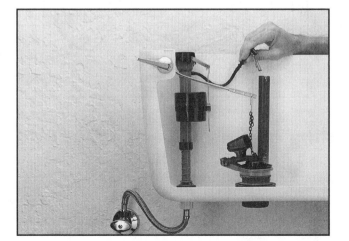

The flexible refill tube slips into an elbow that clips on the overflow pipe.

The flush valve assembly is another piece of antiquated toilet equipment that should be replaced rather than repaired. Replacement valves, called flappers, simply slip down over the overflow tube. If the seat is damaged, look for a kit with a replacement seat. You'll need a sponge, steel wool, and a working shut-off to install a flapper.

1. Shut off the water, drain the tank by flushing the toilet, and sponge the tank dry.

2. Remove the old tank ball or flapper, leaving the overflow tube in place.

3. Press a mounting adapter over the overflow tube, unless one is already present (see the drawing showing the new stopper valve in position).

4. Slip the new flapper into place on the mounting adapter, positioned so that it can move freely.

5. Adjust the chain so that it's slightly slack, and then cut off extra chain.

Don't Screw Up!

If a toilet wobbles, or if the floor around it is weak, the doughnut-shaped seal between the toilet and the floor is probably leaking and rotting the floor. To replace this seal (it should be replaced periodically, preferably in advance of a leak), either lift the toilet from the floor, clean the seat, and replace the seal; or call the plumber.

Replacing a flush valve.

A. The adapter on the overflow tube supplies the mounting points for the new flapper valve.

B. Make sure the flapper doesn't snag against anything and that it securely contacts the seat.

The Care and Feeding of Your Garbage Disposal

Garbage disposals, once a symbol of conspicuous consumption, are now standard equipment on new homes. They are pretty reliable, if not exactly trouble-free.

Do not assume that you need a garbage disposal. After I faced a second replacement, I decided to liberate myself from this obligation, and I went back to the traditional drain—with a strainer. It's worked ever since, and I don't have to put up with the hurricane roar of the disposal. I simply removed the unit, disconnected the power supplying the switch so that there was no power at the disposal (even when the switch is on), and removed the disposer itself. Then I bought a replacement fitting to connect the sink to a standard drain, and I installed standard drain piping to connect the sink to the wall drain.

If you don't want to dispose of the disposal, here's some advice for a happy garbage-eater:

➤ Keep indigestible crud such as peach pits and silverware out of the disposer.

➤ The slower you feed the disposer, the fewer plugging problems you'll have.

➤ When a disposer is overloaded, a built-in circuit breaker should trip to prevent damage to the motor. If the disposer is silent when you switch it on, give it a minute to cool down, and push the reset button—it's generally on the bottom of the unit.

➤ If the grinder is stuck (you'll hear loud humming when you hit the switch), loosen it with an allen (hexagonal) wrench. If you can't find the one that came with the unit, use a standard allen wrench. Shut off the switch, insert the wrench into the socket on the bottom of the disposer, and turn until it's free; then try the power again, with plenty of water.

➤ If the disposer quits draining or springs a serious leak, chances are that it's plugged near the wall. See the photo of P-trap removal and cleanout, earlier in this chapter, for advice on cleaning the pipes.

➤ When you operate the disposer (which should be more often than once a week), run as much water as you can to send the crud on its way.

➤ Do not dump animal fats or byproducts in garbage disposals, especially if you have a septic system.

➤ If you're the fastidious type, grind up ice cubes or cubed potatoes, followed by $1/4$ cup of white vinegar. Then rinse with clean water to detoxify the grinder.

Toolbox Trivia

At least half of U.S. sewage systems apply their treated sewage sludge to farmland in a massive—and usually beneficial—recycling project. So when you grind up the old carrot stew in your garbage disposal, you may actually be cooperating in industrial-scale composting. Can you beat that for guilt-free goulash-grinding?

The Least You Need to Know

➤ Chemical drain cleaners are most effective for cleaning drains that still are partially functional. Otherwise, you risk explosion or other problems.

➤ Plungers are surprisingly effective at opening plugged drains, if you stick with them for a while.

➤ Replacing the working parts of a toilet can be easy, fast, cheap, and effective. Don't bother repairing parts that are easier to replace.

➤ Garbage disposals can be overloaded, but between the reset button and the allen wrench, chances are that you can resuscitate them without calling for help.

Nuts and Bolts Glossary

allen wrench   A hexagonal wrench made of solid steel, which is inserted into a socket in an allen screw or bolt.

amps (amperes)   Units of current flow in an electric circuit or device.

anchor   A fitting used to secure to masonry, drywall, and other hard-to-fasten materials.

anti-rising pin   A hinge pin that cannot rise by itself out of its socket.

auger   A spring-like cleaning tool for drains and traps. Also a large drill bit with heavy screw thread.

back saw   A rectangular hand saw with a stiff back made for accurate cuts with a miter box.

baseboard   Molding around the perimeter of a room that trims the junction between the wall and the floor.

bleeder valve   A valve on top of a radiator that lets air escape so that the radiator can fill with water.

blind-nailing   Nailing so that the nail cannot be seen when the work is finished, usually done on tongue-and-groove boards.

book   To fold pasted wallpaper over on itself so the paper can relax, or expand.

boxing   Mixing two cans of paint to match the colors by pouring one into another several times.

breaker box   See *circuit-breaker box*.

calcium carbonate (lime) $CaCO_3$, a component of mortar and portland cement.

casement window   Windows whose sashes are hinged vertically.

circuit   An electrical loop connecting a source, a load, and the source; allows current to flow.

circuit breaker   A safety device that shuts off a circuit if a dangerous amount of current is flowing, or if you want to work on the circuit.

circuit-breaker box (breaker box, or circuit-breaker panel)   A central control panel containing circuit breakers; controls current to circuits in the house.

circuit tester   A device that lights up when current is flowing.

concrete   A blend of portland cement, gravel, sand, and water that hardens by setting, not drying.

countersink bit   A drill bit that removes enough wood so that the head of a screw can sit flush to the surface.

crawl space   A recess under a house that's up to 4 feet tall.

creosote   A preservative once used to protect below-grade wood, now used only in industrial applications; also a different, flammable substance that can build up in chimneys.

crosscut   To cut wood 90° to the grain.

cut in   To prepare for rolling paint by brushing edges and corners and other places the roller can't reach.

damper   An adjustable plate that regulates the flow of air in a duct, or of smoke in a chimney.

decking (roof)   The layer of wood that holds the shingles, also called *sheathing*.

DIY   Do-it-yourself.

drill chuck   The rotating clamp that holds the drill bit.

dry rot   A fungus that destroys damp wood, leaving the wood looking dry.

drywall   Wallboard made of gypsum sandwiched between heavy paper.

eave   The overhang at the bottom of a pitched (sloping) roof.

elbow   A pipe fixture that changes direction.

equipment grounding conductor   The conductor (either bare wire or steel conduit) that provides a safety return path for electricity that contacts the wrong part of an electrical system.

face-nail   To nail a board so the nail head remains visible.

fan-and-limit control   A thermally operated switch that regulates the air blower or water-pump motor in a heating system. It also shuts the furnace down if the furnace overheats.

fascia   The eave board, usually behind the gutter.

ferrous metal   Metal containing iron (such as steel). Subject to rust.

finial   An ornamental top on a post or column.

finish (concrete)   To smooth concrete as it sets.

fixture (device)   An electrical switch or receptacle.

flashing   Metal that joins various planes of a roof, or a roof to a chimney, vent, and so on.

float   A flat tool used to smooth stucco, patching plaster, and concrete.

flush   Describes surfaces that are in one plane.

framing   Two-inch thick lumber that forms the structure of a house.

fuse   A device that prevents a circuit from carrying a dangerous amount of current.

fuse box   Box that contains fuses and controls electric circuits.

galvanized steel   Steel coated with zinc to prevent rust.

gauge   A system for measuring the diameter of wires and the thickness of sheet metal. Larger numbers are thinner.

Glazier's points   Tiny metal fasteners that hold glass in window sash while glazing compound is applied.

glazing (glazing compound)   A flexible sealing material that seals a window to a sash. Also called *putty*.

grade   Ground level.

ground   A safety system that gives electricity an escape route if a hot wire contacts something it's not supposed to, such as a metal electrical box. See *grounded conductor* and *equipment grounding conductor*.

grounded conductor   The wire that returns electricity to the source (generally white).

ground-fault circuit interrupter   A device that shuts off the power if it detects a dangerous leakage of current.

hammer drill (or rotary hammer)   A drill that turns the bit and hammers it into the work at the same time; good for drilling concrete and masonry.

hollow-core door   A door with two veneer surfaces and a hollow interior.

HVAC   Heating, ventilating, and air conditioning.

ice dam   The accumulation of ice on a roof, formed by melting snow.

inner stop   The molding that separates the upper and lower sash tracks in a double-hung window.

jamb   The 1-inch wood enclosing a door or window; holds the door hinges or window tracks.

jointer   A masonry tool that shapes and compresses the mortar joint between bricks or blocks.

joist   Framing that supports a floor or ceiling.

junction box   An electrical box used to hold switches, receptacles, and so on.

lag screw   A heavy-duty wood screw with a hexagonal or square head.

latch side   The side of a door away from the hinge.

light   An individual piece of glass in a multipane sash.

load   Anything that uses electricity in a circuit.

mineral spirits   A replacement for turpentine, used as paint thinner, made from petroleum distillates.

miter   An angled cut in wood, used to form a joint.

mortar   A mixture of portland cement, lime, mason's sand, and water; makes the joints between bricks, blocks, and stones.

mortise   A shallow, rectangular cavity removed from wood to allow a hinge to sit flush.

muriatic (hydrochloric) acid   Acid that cleans up masonry by removing old mortar from the surface.

OC (on-center)   The distance between centers of repeated components, such as studs.

out of square   Meeting at an angle other than 90°.

outer stop   The vertical strip of molding inside a double-hung window jamb; holds the lower sash in place.

penny   System for identifying nail length.

plate   A cover plate used to finish off a receptacle or switch; also the pieces of framing above and below the studs.

quarter-round   A molding that's shaped like one-quarter of a circle, when seen from the end.

rafter   Lumber supporting the roof decking.

rake edge   The slanting edge of a sloping roof.

receptacle   What electricians call an electric outlet; a place to plug in an electrical device.

reducer (plumbing)   A fitting that changes the size of a pipe to connect different-size pipes and fittings.

ridge   The horizontal line across the top of a pitched roof.

riser   The board that connects two treads in a stairway; has a vertical face.

romex   Plastic-wrapped cable, commonly used in home wiring.

roof tar (roof cement)   A sticky goop used to seal holes in roofs.

sand finish   A finish plaster containing sand; makes a regular, rough surface when floated.

sash   The movable wood or metal element holding glass in a window.

seat   The ledge that holds a light in a sash; also the sealing component in a faucet.

self-priming paint   A coating that works as a primer or a finish coat.

service panel   See *circuit-breaker box.*

shakes   Wood siding or roofing material made by splitting pieces of wood.

sheathing   A thin structural layer used under siding and roofing; holds the nails for the surface layer (called *decking* on a roof).

sinker   A cement-coated nail, thinner than a common nail; used for nailing 2-inch lumber.

sizing   A primer used to regulate the adhesion of wallpaper paste.

snake (auger)   A spring-like tool for cleaning drains.

soffit   The horizontal underside of a roof overhang.

solid-core door   A door made entirely of wood, usually used on the exterior.

spall   A surface degradation of masonry.

square   At a 90° angle; a tool used to mark or saw a 90° angle.

stop   Plumber's jargon for a shut-off valve.

strike off (screed)   To remove extra wet concrete and smooth the surface by pushing and pulling a 2-by-4 across it.

stringer   The slanting piece of framing that supports a stairway.

stud   The vertical 2-by-4 or 2-by-6 framing that supports a wall.

stud gap   The void between adjacent studs.

subfloor   The rough floor, laid directly on the joists.

substrate   The level of material supporting the thing you're fastening.

sweat   To connect copper pipe by soldering.

switch, single-pole   A switch that controls a light or appliance by itself.

switch, three-way   A switch used in pairs to control a single light fixture.

tar-and-gravel (built-up) roof   A flat roof made of gravel laid on top of hot tar.

tee (plumbing)   A fitting that connects three pipes in a "T" formation.

thermocouple   A heat sensor that shuts off the flow of gas in a gas furnace when the pilot goes out.

thumb-hard   Material that has hardened or dried enough to show the imprint of a thumb.

toe-nail   To nail at an angle, as through the end of a stud.

tongue-and-groove (T&G)   Board with a tongue on one side and a channel on the other; forms an interlocking floor.

topcoat   The last coat of paint, stain, or clear finish.

traveler wires   Pair of wires connecting two three-way switches.

tread   The part of a staircase you step on.

vapor barrier   An impervious layer used to prevent humidity from migrating in a house.

VOC   Volatile organic compound, often a solvent in paint, varnish, or stain, which is usually toxic.

volt   A unit of electrical pressure.

water seal   A pool of water in a plumbing trap that prevents sewer gas from entering a dwelling.

watt   A unit of electrical power (equals amps × volts).

weather-stripping   A flexible material that seals a movable piece to a fixed piece.

Wire nut   Brand name for a plastic nut that screws onto the end of wires to join them.

Index